Studies in Modern History

General Editor: **J.C.D. Clark**, Joyce and Elizabeth Hall Distinguished
Professor of British History, University of Kansas

Titles include:

James B. Bell
THE IMPERIAL ORIGINS OF THE KING'S CHURCH IN EARLY AMERICA
1607–1783

Jonathan Clark and Howard Erskine-Hill (*editors*)
SAMUEL JOHNSON IN HISTORICAL CONTEXT

Eveline Cruickshanks and Howard Erskine-Hill
THE ATTERBURY PLOT

Diana Donald and Frank O'Gorman (*editors*)
ORDERING THE WORLD IN THE EIGHTEENTH CENTURY

Richard D. Floyd
CHURCH, CHAPEL AND PARTY
Religious Dissent and Political Modernization in Nineteenth-Century England

Richard R. Follett
EVANGELICALISM, PENAL THEORY AND THE POLITICS OF CRIMINAL LAW
REFORM IN ENGLAND, 1808–30

Andrew Godley
JEWISH IMMIGRANT ENTREPRENEURSHIP IN NEW YORK AND LONDON
1880–1914

William Anthony Hay
THE WHIG REVIVAL 1808–1830

Mark Keay
WILLIAM WORDSWORTH'S GOLDEN AGE THEORIES DURING THE
INDUSTRIAL REVOLUTION IN ENGLAND, 1750–1850

William M. Kuhn
DEMOCRATIC ROYALISM
The Transformation of the British Monarchy, 1861–1914

Kim Lawes
PATERNALISM AND POLITICS
The Revival of Paternalism in Early Nineteenth-Century Britain

Marisa Linton
THE POLITICS OF VIRTUE IN ENLIGHTENMENT FRANCE

Nancy D. LoPatin
POLITICAL UNIONS, POPULAR POLITICS AND THE GREAT REFORM ACT
OF 1832

Karin J. MacHardy
WAR, RELIGION AND COURT PATRONAGE IN HABSBURG AUSTRIA
The Social and Cultural Dimensions of Political Interaction, 1521–1622

Robert J. Mayhew
LANDSCAPE, LITERATURE AND ENGLISH RELIGIOUS CULTURE, 1660–1800
Samuel Johnson and Languages of Natural Description

Marjorie Morgan
NATIONAL IDENTITIES AND TRAVEL IN VICTORIAN BRITAIN

James Muldoon
EMPIRE AND ORDER
The Concept of Empire, 800–1800

W.D. Rubinstein and Hilary Rubinstein
PHILOSEMITISM
Admiration and Support for Jews in the English-Speaking World, 1840–1939

Julia Rudolph
WHIG POLITICAL THOUGHT AND THE GLORIOUS REVOLUTION
James Tyrrell and the Theory of Resistance

Lisa Steffen
TREASON AND NATIONAL IDENTITY
Defining a British State, 1608–1820

Lynne Taylor
BETWEEN RESISTANCE AND COLLABORATION
Popular Protest in Northern France, 1940–45

Anthony Waterman
POLITICAL ECONOMY AND CHRISTIAN THEOLOGY SINCE THE
ENLIGHTENMENT
Essays in Intellectual History

Doron Zimmerman
THE JACOBITE MOVEMENT IN SCOTLAND AND IN EXILE, 1746–1759

Studies in Modern History
Series Standing Order ISBN 978–0–333–79328–2 (Hardback)
978–0–333–80346–2 (Paperback)
(*outside North America only*)

You can receive future titles in this series as they are published by placing a standing order. Please contact your bookseller or, in case of difficulty, write to us at the address below with your name and address, the title of the series and the ISBN quoted above.

Customer Services Department, Macmillan Distribution Ltd, Houndmills, Basingstoke, Hampshire RG21 6XS, England

---

Church, Chapel and Party

Religious Dissent and Political Modernization in Nineteenth-Century England

Richard D. Floyd

Washington University in St Louis

First published 2008 by
PALGRAVE MACMILLAN
Houndmills, Basingstoke, Hampshire RG21 6XS and
175 Fifth Avenue, New York, N.Y. 10010
Companies and representatives throughout the world

PALGRAVE MACMILLAN is the global academic imprint of the Palgrave
Macmillan division of St. Martin's Press, LLC and of Palgrave Macmillan Ltd.
Macmillan® is a registered trademark in the United States, United Kingdom
and other countries. Palgrave is a registered trademark in the European
Union and other countries.

ISBN-13: 978–0–230–52540–5 hardback
ISBN-10: 0–230–52540–7 hardback

This book is printed on paper suitable for recycling and made from fully
managed and sustained forest sources. Logging, pulping and manufacturing
processes are expected to conform to the environmental regulations of the
country of origin.

A catalogue record for this book is available from the British Library.

A catalog record for this book is available from the Library of Congress.

10   9   8   7   6   5   4   3   2   1
17   16   15   14   13   12   11   10   09   08

Printed and bound in Great Britain by
CPI Antony Rowe, Chippenham and Eastbourne

For Desirée, Griffin, and Daisy

Contents

List of Map and Tables

Acknowledgements

I have incurred a great debt to many in the course of conducting this research and writing this book.

I would like first to thank my many mentors in History both from The College of William and Mary in Virginia and from Washington University in St Louis. Professor James McCord in particular provided thoughtful criticism and sound wisdom in my early days as an historian, and is indirectly responsible for many of the paths my career has taken since I was an undergraduate. Above all, I am grateful to Professor Richard Davis, an exemplary historian, a gentleman, and a friend. No one could hope for a finer advisor.

I must also acknowledge the kindness and courtesy of many libraries and research institutions, both in the United States and the United Kingdom. In St Louis, I would like to thank the staff and librarians of the Reference and Inter-Library Loan Departments of Olin Library; in London, I am grateful to the British Library Newspaper Library (Colindale), the Family Records Centre, the Guildhall Library, and especially the Institute for Historical Research; in Bedford, to the Bedfordshire Record Office; in Brighton, to the Brighton Local Studies Library; in Durham, to the Durham University Library and the Durham Record Office; in Exeter, to the Devon Record Office and the Exeter Local Studies Library; in Ipswich, to the Suffolk Record Office (Ipswich Branch); and in Nottingham, to the Nottinghamshire Archives Office and the Nottingham Public Library Local Studies Library.

Martin Cavanaugh regularly assisted me in tracking down obscure references. Dr Ted Floyd and Macon Finley helped me make the best sense of the numbers I crunched in Chapters 8 and 9, and Professor Stanley Sawyer confirmed the significance of these data. Professors Iver Bernstein, Steven Hause, William McKelvy, and Timothy Parsons all read this work in an earlier stage, and they asked good questions and offered sound criticism. Professor Derek Hirst also read an early stage of this work. Professor James Sack read a much earlier version, and gave encouragement which I have always appreciated.

As a sign of the times, I should acknowledge the online community of historians, scholars, and enthusiasts who comprise the H-Albion and Victoria-L listservs. Over the years, they have selflessly provided quick confirmation of a name or date, clarification of a circumstance, and similar assistance or insight. The arguments and discussions that list-members entertain never fail to spark an interest in some angle of studying the past I had hitherto not considered.

I must also thank the staff and editors at Palgrave Macmillan: Professor J.C.D. Clark, Michael Strang, Ruth Ireland, and Vidya Vijayan. In the past, I had wondered at the praise occasionally lavished on such individuals. I now know what it means to work with prompt, courteous, and helpful editors—and I can only imagine what it would mean to work with bad ones.

On personal levels, I would like to acknowledge the kindness, assistance, and good humour of Elisabeth Davis and Becky Ravoula from the Center for the History of Freedom (St Louis). I am grateful to Gill Greenwood of West Bridgford, Nottinghamshire, for her grace and hospitality in recklessly sharing her Victorian home, regardless of the perils of a very young family. And I would like to mention the camaraderie and insight offered by some of my fellow students in History. In no order of priority, I acknowledge Matt Brown, Mike Markus, Chris Pepus, Mick Rutz, Sam Snyder, and Jill Wooten.

Of course, I am grateful to my parents, Edwin and Mary Floyd, who have always supported and encouraged me, even when they did not exactly know what I was doing.

Most of all, I am thankful for and indebted to my wife, Desirée, for her help, great wisdom, and love. It is to her and our children, Griffin and Daisy, I dedicate this work.

St Louis, Missouri
Christmas Eve 2006

Abbreviations

County archives, record offices, and libraries:

BLNL	British Library Newspaper Library (Colindale)
BRO	Bedfordshire Record Office
DuRO, BC	Durham Record Office, Broadsides Collection
FRC	Family Records Centre (London)
NAO	Nottinghamshire Archives Office
NPLLSL, EC	Nottingham Public Library Local Studies Library, Election Collection
SufRO, GC	Suffolk Record Office (Ipswich Branch), Gibble Collection

Newspapers:

Bedford Beacon (BB)	*The Beacon* (Bedford)
Bedford Mercury (BM)	*Bedford Mercury and Huntingdon Express: General Advertiser and Reporter for the Counties of Bedford, Buckingham, Cambridge, Hertford, Huntingdon, Northampton, Oxford, and their Vicinities*
Bedford News (BN)	*The Bedford News, and Advertiser for Beds, Hunts, and the Surrounding Counties*
Bedford Times (BT)	*The Bedford Times, and General Advertiser for Beds., Hert., Hunts, Bucks., Cambs., and Northamptonshire*
Cambridge Independent Press (CIP)	*The Cambridge Independent Press and Huntingdon, Bedford, and Peterborough Gazette*
Durham Advertiser (DA)	*The Durham County Advertiser and so on*
Durham Chronicle (DC)	*Durham Chronicle, or General Northern Advertiser*
Daily Times (EADT)	
Ipswich Journal (IJ)	*The Ipswich Journal; and Suffolk, Norfolk, Essex, and Cambridgeshire Advertiser*

Suffolk Chronicle (SC)	*The Suffolk Chronicle; or Ipswich Weekly General Advertiser and County Express*
Nottingham Journal (NJ)	*The Nottingham Journal and so on*
Nottingham Review (NR)	*Nottingham Review and General Advertiser for the Midland Counties*
The Times	*The Times* (London)
Trewman's Exeter Flying Post (TEFP)	*Trewman's Exeter Flying Post, or Plymouth and Cornish Advertiser*

Poll books and electoral registers:

DPB 1835	*Proceedings and Poll, at the Durham City Election..., with the Speeches, on the Day of the Nomination, and at the Close of the Election* [1835 general election] (Sadler Street, Durham: George Walker junior, 1835)
DPB 1837	*Proceedings and Poll, at the Durham City Election..., with the Speeches, on the Day of the Nomination, and at the Close of the Election* [1837 general election] (Sadler Street, Durham: George Walker junior, 1837)
DPB Apr 1843	*The Proceedings and Poll at Durham City Election...: with the Addresses, Speeches, &c., on the Day of Nomination, and at the Close of the Election* [Apr 1843 by-election] (Sadler Street, Durham: George Walker junior, 1843)
DPB July 1843	*The Poll at the Election of One Citizen, to Serve in Parliament, for the City of Durham..., with the Addresses, &c. Previous to and After the Election* [July 1843 by-election] (Sadler Street, Durham: George Walker junior, 1843)
DPB 1847	*The Proceedings and Poll at Durham City Election...: with the Addresses, Speeches, &c., on the Day of Nomination, and at the Close of the Election* [1847 general election] (Sadler Street, Durham: George Walker junior, 1843)
IPB 1832	*The Proceedings and Poll at the Election for Two Members for the Borough of Ipswich* [1832 general election] (Old Butter Market, Ipswich: S. Piper, Albion Press, 1833)
IPB Jan 1835	*The Proceedings and Poll at the Election for Two Members for the Borough of Ipswich* [Jan 1835 by-election] (Ipswich: R. Deck, 1835)
IPB 1847	*The Poll..., Proceedings, &c.* [1847 general election] (Tavern Street, Ipswich: Hunt and Son, 1847)

NPB 1832   *An Alphabetical List of the Burgesses, Householders, and
                Freeholders who Polled... for the Election of Two Burgesses to
                Represent the Town of Nottingham in Parliament* [1832
                general election] (Bridesmith Gate, Nottingham: Richard
                Sutton, 1833)

Others:

DNB   *Oxford Dictionary of National Biography* (1st edn)
Dod's   Dod, C.R. *Electoral Facts from 1832–1853, Impartially
                Stated, Constituting a Complete Political Gazeteer* [1853]
                H.J. Hanham, ed. Brighton: Harvester Press, 1972.
Hansard   *Hansard's Parliamentary Debates*, 3rd session. London:
                C.C. Hansard, 1830–1891.
McCalmont's   McCalmont, Frederick H. *McCalmont's Parliamentary Poll
                Book: British Election Results*. 8th edn Vincent, J. and
                M. Stenton, eds. Brighton: Harvester Press. 1971.
ODNB   *Oxford Dictionary of National Biography* (2nd edn)

Part I

What has religion to do with politics? How can there be any sound politics without religion?

Address to the Christian Electors of Nottingham, November 1832, signed a Protestant Dissenter

'I know the Dissenters. They gave us the emancipation of the slave. They gave us the Reform Bill. They gave us Free Trade.'

Lord John, 1st earl Russell (1792–1878)

1
Introduction: The Politics of Dissent at the Time of the Great Reform Bill

'What has religion to do with politics?' The question was asked in a handbill posted in Nottingham in the run-up to the election of the first reformed House of Commons in December 1832. Signed only 'a Protestant Dissenter,' the handbill supplied the answer with yet another rhetorical question: 'How can there be any sound politics without religion?'[1]

The importance of the role played by religion in understanding modern British history has been accepted in various degrees for much of the last century. Indeed, it was the combined influence of Methodism and broader evangelicalism in the church and dissent that the French historian Elie Halévy identified as having *made* modern England.[2] Recent scholarship has further confirmed the far-reaching significance of religion in British history well into the nineteenth century,[3] but until the last decade, it was striking how relatively little attention historians of Britain paid to those protestants outside the Church of England.[4] Granted, these dissenters never amounted to a majority of English men and women—but as active religionists, they came by mid-century very near to equalling the Anglicans, and at the local level they often surpassed the establishment in influence and even membership.

Yet in spite of the evident importance of religion in shaping nineteenth-century politics and society, and the renewal in attention on dissent, there has never been a consensus on the role played by religious dissent—beyond an agreement that it mattered. Consequently, unsubstantiated conjectures have all too often been passed as proven fact. It has, for instance, been confidently asserted that dissenters were the backbone of the liberal party.[5] But it has also been asserted, as often and with as great confidence, that at least half of them, the Methodists, were staunch conservatives. Still other historians have embraced the 'no

politics' rule of the first half of the nineteenth century, that is, that
Wesleyan Methodists refrained from political activity altogether. And
whatever their ordinary allegiance, it has been argued that at various
times the alienation of nonconformists from their liberal allies, usually
demonstrated by abstention, exercised a powerful influence on elections. Then again there has been speculation on the effect of nonconformist alienation from one another, particularly as indicated in the
aforementioned case of Wesleyans from the older dissenting denominations, and the undoubted break between a traditional Unitarian lead-
ership and a burgeoning evangelical rank and file. This hardly leaves us
much firm ground for assessing the political significance of a body of
electors of generally accepted importance.

Some of the modern historian's confusion in discussing dissent no
doubt arises from the complications involved in knowing whom to
identify as dissenters and, consequently, what sort of numbers they
represented. Ironically, dissenters did not exist, at least not in a formal
sense, before the 1650s or 1660s, when a series of acts designed to restrict
their activities and eventually drive them out of existence gave them
legal reality for the first time. (Earlier, it had simply been assumed that
everyone who was not a Catholic was a member of the Church of
England.) By dictating that clergymen in England and Wales must use
the Anglican *Book of Common Prayer* for public worship, the 1662 act of
uniformity created dissenting or nonconformist clergymen, by ejecting
from their livings those who refused to conform. Thus a single act of
legislation made dissenters of roughly one-fifth of the clergy of the
Church of England. They dissented from the doctrines or forms of the
Church of England, and either could not accept one or more of the
Thirty-nine Articles of Faith, or disapproved of some part of the *Book
of Common Prayer*. They dissented and they refused to conform: hence
the names their followers were to bear with pride for two centuries. The
five-mile act of 1665 further restricted dissenting clergy by prohibiting
them from living or preaching within five miles of any town they had
formerly served.

The indirect impact of these two acts on the laity is hard to measure,
but others were enacted to restrict the nonconformist rank and file, as
well. The corporation act of 1661 required all members of town governments to take the Anglican communion as a qualification for office; the
conventicle act of 1664 outlawed meetings of five or more dissenters for
purposes of worship; and the test act of 1673 provided that all who held
office under the crown must, to qualify for that office, take communion
in an Anglican church. Yet how many people were affected as dissenters

remains unclear. A few years later, James II judged there to be as many dissenters as Anglicans in England. This estimate was ridiculously high, and reflected his political motives, desirous as he was to downplay the extent of the influence of the Church of England, as a means of reasserting Roman Catholicism in England. Others have put the figure as low as a mere 5 per cent of the population, which is just as certainly too low.

At any rate, dissent as a percentage of the population declined throughout much of the eighteenth century, as indeed did religiosity in England generally,[6] although the period did witness two related developments, the effects of which would be felt fully only in the next century—the birth and expansion of the movement founded by John Wesley, and a wider evangelical revival, which came to transform trinitarian dissent. Due in large measure to these phenomena, English dissent grew impressively for much of the nineteenth century, both in absolute numbers and as a percentage of the population. But even then, there remains debate over details. In the first half of the century, most contemporary estimates reckoned dissenters between a tenth and a quarter of the population,[7] and one modern historian has estimated that 30 per cent of England was nonconformist in 1820.[8] Even when we consider seemingly sound evidence, such as the census of religion, the data are still open to interpretation.[9] Nonetheless, based on the finding of the 1851 census, it seems likely that 18.9 per cent, or less than a fifth, of the population of England attended non-Anglican services at mid-century.[10] This figure, which seems unimpressive in its own right, becomes more substantial when compared against the rate of Anglican attendance, which was only 20.2 per cent, or slightly more than a fifth, of the English population. For the 1851 census of religion appears to have revealed that 60.9 per cent of the men, women and children in England, or far more than the combined number of churchgoers, did not attend any religious service on census Sunday.[11] Anglicans were therefore only slightly ahead of the protestant nonconformists and other Christians, accounting for 51.6 per cent, or slightly more than half, among those who attended a religious service on census Sunday. Their claim to be an established religion seemed more dubious than ever.

In respect to those ten millions who attended no service at all, the census's original compiler allowed that 42 per cent, or more than two-fifths, of society might, on any given Sunday, be legitimately absent from church or chapel.[12] By this reckoning, still over three millions who had no unavoidable impediment failed to attend any religious service. Contemporaries rather naïvely regarded the 1851 census, based on attendance, as accurately representing belief,[13] and therefore judged some one-third of the English population to hold no religious conviction.[14] Subsequent scholarship discredits so literal a reading of the census data,[15] and it seems likely that tiredness, sickness, overwork, and related matters—especially among the working classes—were a greater impact than hostility or indifference to religion, in influencing non-attendance in church or chapel.[16]

So it is evident that the distribution of chapel or churchgoers, as part of the whole population, means very little. Nevertheless, it is probably true that the one-third of the English population who did not attend a religious service on census Sunday were also, in most cases, without the vote or much other social or political influence. What this meant was that, even among regular churchgoers, Anglicanism could no longer lay a realistic claim to its demand for a dominant place as the established religion. Moreover, as suggested above, the full potency of an interest group, religious or otherwise, is not always accurately measured as the sum of its apparent parts, and in many cases, nonconformist missions, outreach, and other forms of organizations may well have further boosted their influence on English society, political and otherwise.

The peculiar character of England's system of parliamentary representation, for instance, particularly after the reform act of 1832, increased the electoral, and consequently the political, weight of dissent throughout much of the nineteenth century. On the eve of parliamentary reform, about 55 per cent of the electors cast votes for candidates standing for counties, but county members comprised only 16 per cent of the House of Commons.[17] Thus over one-half of the English electorate returned less than one-sixth of the members of parliament. The other 45 per cent of the electorate voted in borough constituencies, which returned the lion's share of MPs, and dissenters tended to be clustered in urban areas. Thus even before the repeal of the corporation act in 1828, before which non-Anglicans had been electorally disadvantaged by officially nurtured prejudice and close tory corporations, nonconformists benefited from this disparity. One historian has estimated dissenters' share of the electorate in 1832 (i.e. on the eve of reform) around one-fifth which, taken with the population estimates in that period, suggests that nonconformists were not under-represented in the pre-reform era.[18]

Through the repeal of the so-called test acts in 1828, dissenters in England had realized much of their object of civil equality.[19] Curiously, this may have made them more, rather than less, keen for parliamentary reform. For so long as the stigma of the test acts remained, its removal took centre-stage in any dissenting political agenda, and parliamentary and even other religious reforms took second place. But dissenters still had a number of grievances. England remained a confessional society into the mid-nineteenth century, and to be outside the established church affected one's status. In stark terms, membership in the Church of England remained a vital requisite for full participation, full benefits and, arguably, even for full citizenship.[20]

This, in part, was what inspired dissenters to support parliamentary reform. The campaign to repeal the test and corporation acts had proved what effective organization could accomplish, and with that major grievance removed, dissenters were ready to turn their efforts to lesser ones. They recognized that the removal of their other grievances would require a strong voice in parliament, and therefore they were eager for its immediate reform. This was achieved in 1832, and with that milestone behind them, dissenters turned to more personal goals: church rate abolition, admission to the universities, marriage and burial rights, and so on. To all these ends, it was natural for the dissenters of the mid-nineteenth century to remain allied with the whigs, who had, although with varying degrees of enthusiasm, championed civil and religious liberty for the better part of a century-and-a-half. And in maintaining their alignment with the whigs—or, as they were increasingly called from this point onward, liberals—nonconformists unsurprisingly adopted many tenets of liberal ideology, even when they were apparently distinct from religious concerns. Thus free trade, the abolition of slavery, and parliamentary and municipal reform—all which might be called liberal issues—were in the nineteenth century, as they had been in the eighteenth century, dissenting issues as well. They were judged as directly related to the greater cause of civil and religious liberty, which had long been a whig and dissenting slogan, and would remain a liberal and dissenting one.

Religion was clearly a hot topic, and the continuance of an established church became increasingly hard to square with a society that claimed to cherish equality before the law. Any resident of a parish, for instance—whether Anglican or not—was liable to pay a local tax for the support of the church, as well as to pay a tithe to support the clergy. Such incongruities were especially galling after 1832 and, in the view of one authority on Victorian religion, such matters 'made immediate difference to a man's practical thinking *and his vote if he had a vote.*'[21] Other historians have agreed, and noted more specifically—although not always with substantiating evidence—that dissenting electors voted to return liberal candidates as members of parliament, and Anglicans preferred conservatives.[22]

Curiously, no recent study has investigated the political activity of dissenters in what was arguably the most important period of English constitutional history in the nineteenth century—that is, the years immediately following the first reform bill of 1832. One recent work studies the somewhat later mid-Victorian period, and examines the politics of dissent from the period between the general elections of 1847 and 1867, or up until the second reform bill, which dates the author identifies as

> the period from the time when English Evangelical Nonconformists began to mobilise as a self-conscious, distinctive force within national politics—replacing a trust in the leadership of the Whigs with a desire to place their own men in Parliament—until many of those very people, by then securely in the Commons, as well as their Nonconformist supporters, began to place their trust in the leadership of Gladstone.[23]

The same historian gives priority to the role played by nonconformist principle, informed by biblical and theological convictions, which led ineluctably to justice and equality. Another work has taken the case up again, for the period after the third reform bill of 1885 and well into the twentieth century, to show that nonconformity 'was generally the most potent predictor of the vote.'[24] But no one has yet seriously pursued similar questions for the period just after the first reform bill of 1832, and certainly no one has focused specifically on the voting behaviour of Methodists and other nonconformists. This study argues that the comparative neglect of the period before the two works previously mentioned has distorted and diminished the role of dissent in the period, and that the patterns of political alignment demonstrated for the second half of the nineteenth century were equally true of the first half, at least as far back as the reform crisis of the early 1830s.[25]

Local studies have tended to support such conclusions, to varying degrees and in a necessarily limited context, but no one has yet addressed the question on a broad scale and in a systematic manner.[26] The present research, which examines five general elections and over a dozen by-elections in five English boroughs—representing unique regional economic interests and dominant local industries, as well as different prevailing varieties of dissent—greatly clarifies this picture (Map 1.1) in a framework of national significance.[27] Its focus on these 40 electoral

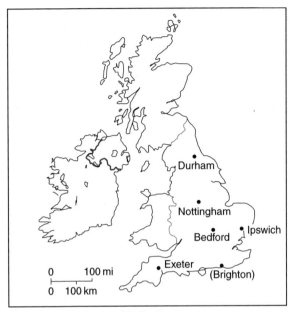

©1998 National Geographic Society

Map 1.1   Location of six English boroughs

contests and four parliaments between 1832 and 1847 is not only a significant period in English constitutional history, but also one in which all the
major issues which thereafter divided dissenters from the Anglican establishment (and the politically liberal from the politically conservative)—
church rates, for instance, education, and the disestablishment of the
Church of England—made their appearance. It is in this formative period
that fuller comprehension of the political behaviour of dissent is particularly crucial, for, as the present study argues, these same issues divided
not only dissenters from Anglicans, but also liberals from conservatives.

This research reveals, through a combination of conventional and
innovative approaches, a clear connection between dissenting religion
and liberal politics, and an only slightly weaker association between
Anglicanism and conservatism. It also demonstrates that, politically
speaking, Wesleyans and the older dissenting denominations were virtually one, and nothing suggests that any major nonconformist denomination ever acted to support conservatives.

Moreover, the weight religion carried in inspiring public opinion
regularly trumped other issues which have conventionally received

more attention in most treatments of the period: that is, controversies surrounding the new poor law, responses to economic and agricultural depression, attitudes to Chartism, schemes of national education, and so on. These matters were regularly subordinated to the concern—virtually inescapable in the nineteenth century—of the relation of church and state, and the role of dissent outside that relationship.

But the present research argues that religion did more in the early- and mid-nineteenth century than merely define the terms of political debate in England, and that dissent did more than merely lend a hefty bloc of electoral support to liberal candidates seeking seats in parliament. By adding the divide between political liberalism and conservatism to the division that already existed in society between dissenters and Anglicans, English nonconformists, in their aggressive challenge to the status quo, took a long step in the direction of creating the two-party system familiar later in the century. Whereas electors and even MPs were generally not fixed in their positions on, what seem to us, vital questions regarding domestic, colonial and foreign policy, they were for the most part resolutely fixed in their positions regarding the special roles of church and state, and the place of dissent as regarded that relationship. The argument developed in the following chapters strongly supports the conclusion that, at both the constituency and the parliamentary levels, religion was the engine that drove English politics throughout the nineteenth century.

2
'A Free Trade—a Free Vote—and a Free Religion...': The Politico-Religious Landscape of Reformed England, 1832–1847

2.1 Introduction

A satirical magazine, published in Nottingham on the eve of the April 1841 by-election, reported that 'On the way home [from political meetings] the [radicals] destroyed the windows of most of the churches, and the Tories exercised similar justice on the chapels of the Dissenters.'[1] A handbill from Ipswich, printed before the general election of 1847, likened the hostile proceedings of the borough's conservative and liberal interests to the sale of two greyhounds, named Churchman and Dissent. The advertisement noted that both had been sired by 'Bigot, out of Ignorance,' and further observed the dogs' respective diets: 'Churchman will keep in good condition on Bank Notes. Dissent will thrive on Coppers.'[2] To be sure, such items were meant to be comical, but nonetheless reveal telling patterns connecting denominational and political preference in the 1830s and 1840s.

Chapter 3–7 examine these relationships in detail, in the framework of analysing the circumstances and controversies surrounding all of the parliamentary elections in Durham, Nottingham, Ipswich, Bedford, and Exeter from 1832 to 1847. Of course, a number of questions were broached in this period, depending on national as well as local contexts. The present chapter paints in broad strokes the politico-religious landscape of these five constituencies, as a means of introducing the gripping issues of civil and religious liberty that faced candidates, members of parliament, and electors (and occasionally those without the franchise), in the years following the reform act of 1832.

11

2.2 Nominators, agents, friends and supporters: the alignment of dissent with liberalism and the church with conservatism

As we shall see in the next chapter, on all four occasions, the Hon. Arthur Trevor stood to represent the Durham conservatives, it was an official of the church—and on one occasion a canon of the cathedral—who nominated him.[3] A similar pattern of denominational preference revealing political affiliation occurred in Ipswich in the same period, in that case most clearly identifying dissenters as supporters of liberalism. The Alexanders, a prominent family of Quaker entrepreneurs,[4] had longstanding associations with liberal politics in the borough.[5] Their family-owned bank in Ipswich was the great rival of the one owned by J.C. Cobbold, a staunch churchman and conservative—the former known as the 'Yellow' bank and the latter as the 'Blue' (the respective colours of whig-liberals and conservatives in nineteenth-century Ipswich). Samuel Alexander, an alderman and leading yellow, nominated the liberal candidate, James Morrison, at several elections in the 1830s, and after his death in 1838 other Alexanders continued the family's association with liberal politics. Frederick Alexander was active in support of both liberal candidates, Rigby Wason and George Rennie, in 1841, and seconded the nomination latter in the general election that year. Another family of Ipswich Quakers, the Ransomes, who manufactured agricultural machinery and railway equipment, also engaged actively on behalf of liberal politics in the borough. James Allen Ransome stood as a councilman for the yellows in the 1840s and was later an alderman; it was probably he who nominated the liberal candidate Sir Hugh Edward Adair in the 1847 general election.[6]

Other dissenting denominations besides the Friends favoured liberal politics in Ipswich—as indicated in the general election of 1841, ostensibly fought over the fate of agricultural protection—in which Baptists and Congregationalists took active roles in promoting the two liberal candidates. On the other side, the Anglican Revd Edward Woolnough was notable as 'one of the staunch friends of the conservative cause' in 1841 and at other times.[7] It is also noteworthy that, in 1835, another Anglican clergyman, the Revd William Charles Fonnereau, led the triumphant return from prison of Messrs Clamp, Bond and Cook, three of the men who had been convicted of bribery and other electoral misconduct in the conservative interest.[8] Guns and fireworks were exploded to celebrate the clearly partisan occasion and, tellingly, church bells were rung.[9] Parish church bells were rung in Ipswich on other occasions to celebrate conservative victories, but the same courtesy was never extended to the liberal interest.[10] For their part, Ipswich liberals on at least one occasion enlivened the celebration of a political victory by burning an effigy of a bishop![11]

The Congregationalist Revds William Alliott and Samuel Hillyard and over two dozen other dissenters, both ministers and laymen, met regularly in Bedford throughout the 1830s and 1840s, to coordinate pressure on parliament to secure dissenters' interests, and in 1847 the Revd Alliott spoke as an honoured guest at the liberal dinner celebrating the return of Sir Harry Verney.[12] Alliott was also the surname of a prominent nonconformist family in Nottingham, whose members furnished at least three Congregationalist ministers, and exerted themselves on behalf of the borough's liberal and dissenting interests. The Revd Dr Richard Alliott senior had been active in anti-slavery agitation in 1832,[13] and he was most likely the same Mr Alliott whose house—'where the show of colour and ladies was exceedingly grand'—was a significant feature on the chairing procession of the liberal members Hobhouse and Larpent in 1841. The procession also visited the house of Mr Higginbottom (where the ladies and decorations were similarly fine), a prominent nonconformist and chair of the local Tee-Total organization.[14] Another Alliott, Edward, wrote with disgust to a friend in Hamburg on the occasion of John Walter's conservative victory against the liberal Quaker Joseph Sturge in a by-election in 1842, and Charles Bishop, a General Baptist, organized a political meeting on behalf of Larpent[15]

The circumstances of rival political dinners at Exeter in 1837 provide further revealing examples of the politico-religious alignment of conservatism with the church and of liberalism with dissent. If it is unsurprising that a clergyman, the Revd C.C. Bartholomew, gave the grace at a conservative dinner, it is suggestive that the event opened with the singing of *Non Nobis Domine*, to celebrate the occasion of Sir W.W. Follett's uncontested return for the borough, followed with the toast of 'Church and State...followed by 3 times 3, and one cheer more.'[16] In the course of the evening, Samuel Kingdon, the chair of the dinner, proposed a toast which he knew all present would welcome:

He...g[a]ve them their highly talented, excellent, and greatly respected Prelate the Bishop of the Diocese,...and would ask if there was an Englishman who did not know the service rendered to this country in the House of Lords, by the Bishop of Exeter.[17]

After the applause had died down, the chairman explained that the bishop, Henry Phillpotts, staunchly defended the conservative principles of the country, and proposed a toast of 'the Bishop and the Clergy of the Diocese.'[18] Three times three were drunk once more, and the Revd Bartholomew rose again to defend at length his public participation in a conservative meeting. He

> ma[d]e no apology for appearing amongst them.... [W]hen the Church itself was threatened and Religion endangered, for the clergy to remain passive would argue but little for the firmness of belief in the goodness of their cause....

Indeed, he proceeded, 'it would be a gross dereliction of duty in them to remain inactive or in a state of neutrality.'[19]

Meanwhile at the liberal dinner, to celebrate the uncontested return of Edward Divett, the honoured guest denounced the 'hitherto priest-ridden' character of Exeter, and 'regretted... see[ing] so many of the Clergy engaged in political matters....' In contrast to the Revd Bartholomew's frank advocacy of a conservative agenda, Divett 'hoped in the future that the Bishops would discourage, not as in many places promote, Political Topics.' In a similar vein, Mark Kennaway, who nominated Divett at the hustings ten years later, decried the practice whereby 'Bishops at stated periods leave their immense charge[s], and resort to London for political purposes and pursuits, the end of which is money.'[20] And Lord Rancliffe commented favourably on an archdeacon in Nottingham who, when asked for assistance before the 1832 election, stated 'that he did not intend to meddle in the affairs of the election, [and] that he thought it inconsistent with his profession and calling to mix himself up in party contests....'[21]

2.3   The legacy of the repeal of the test and corporation acts and Catholic emancipation

Besides the clergy, and also in contrast to most liberals, a large part of Follett's supporters were military men. In Exeter alone, Captains Shortt and Brutton supported Follett's return in 1844; Gen. Samuel Mortimer delivered the requisition to Lord Lovaine to stand in 1841; and at the dinner in 1837, Gen. Molesworth 'was proud to say the Army were all true blue [i.e. conservative]: a radical officer was a perfect anomaly; a radical parson might be a little worse.'[22]

General Molesworth's observation reflected an outstanding fact of English history from the mid-seventeenth to mid-nineteenth centuries. It went beyond the association, commonplace in old regime Europe and other societies, linking the command corps of the military and naval forces with social and political leaders of society, and consequently, with principles of conservatism: the explicit connexion between commanding military positions and the Church of England ran deeper. For in England, from the time of its first implementation in 1673 until its repeal in 1828, the test act had provided that all who held office under the crown must take communion in an Anglican church as a qualification for office. The corporation act of 1661 made the same requirement of all members of municipal governments. (These test acts were not touched by the so-called toleration act of 1689.) A series of indemnity acts, from 1727 on, relieved dissenters of the penal consequences of the corporation act, and the law, sometimes enforced, barred a dissenter from taking part in town government until 1828.[23] In the military, this amounted to an Anglican monopoly over access to rank, and even after repeal of the test act, it was widely recognized that the church and military were birds of a conservative feather.[24] Campaigns to end the test and corporation acts had been major political goals for dissent in the eighteenth and early nineteenth centuries, and it was in whig and liberal ranks that the nonconformists found their champions.

A related issue, which mainly affected Ireland, was Roman Catholic emancipation. In 1828, the year the test and corporation acts were repealed and a year before Catholic emancipation was secured, an open letter addressed 'To the inhabitants of Newark,' some 20 miles from Nottingham, made clear that, in the view of many conservatives—and certainly of its patron, the ultra-tory duke of Newcastle (1811–1864)—the tory party had been primarily dedicated for the previous 20 years to defending the Church of England from the threat of popery.[25] The emphasis on 20 years most likely was an allusion to conservative opposition to the short-lived mainly whig government, the so-called ministry of all the talents, of 1806–1807, which had, during its brief tenure, managed to abolish the British slave trade before it was driven from office over its efforts to remove the disabilities of both Catholics and dissenters in the military. The latter proposal went too much against the conservative tenor of the time (especially for King George III), and control of the government returned to tory hands.

Of course, the association of liberals and their predecessors defending the rights of those outside the establishment, and conservatives protecting the privileges of the Church of England, in reality extended well before the first decade of the nineteenth century. Conservatives and Anglicans, as well as liberals and nonconformists, were keenly aware of this long history of politico-religious association, as the many allusions to the struggles for and against Anglican dominance in the seventeenth and eighteenth centuries attest.[26] But both camps preferred to rally round struggles of a more recent date. Conservatives in the late 1820s and beyond, conveniently forgetting that he had been the first prime minister to propose Catholic emancipation, repeatedly drew attention to Pitt, who had defended existing institutions of state (including the Church of England), and liberals raised the memory of Fox, who had championed the rights of dissenters.[27]

But the repeal of discriminatory legislation against dissenters and Catholics gave liberals and dissenters something new to talk about, and the next generation of reformers repeatedly hearkened back to the triumphs of 1828 and 1829.[28] Even candidates with no real claim to association with the test and corporation acts repeal or Catholic relief played up the events, as Edward Divett did in Exeter in his 1835 eulogy of Lord John Russell:

> Gentlemen, he was the champion of civil and religious liberty, the man who was the constant supporter of the Catholic claims in the unreformed House of Commons too—and ... the man who procured for the Dissenters that act of justice the repeal of the Test and Corporations act.[29]

2.4   Parliamentary reform

Agitation for the repeal of the test and corporation acts and Catholic emancipation gave way to the reform crises of 1830–1832. These debates were generally not fought on grounds of denominational rivalry, but there can be no doubt the reform bill of 1832, with its extension of the urban franchise, was a particular boon to nonconformists. As 'a Dissenter of forty years' standing pointed out in a letter to the editor of *The Standard*, 'the vast advantages of the Reform Bill [were] to us even more than to Churchmen.'[30]

The liberal *Nottingham Review* also took the view that the reforms of 1828–1832 were interrelated steps leading inevitably to the great goal of British freedom. In the first issue for the year 1833, its editors reflected that the events of 1832 had seen England finally 'rescued from the tutelage and thraldom [sic] of her old oppressors. ...' The paper had been founded 24 years earlier—probably not coincidentally, shortly after the

Grenville-Fox government was frustrated in it efforts to push through relief for Catholics and dissenters—to promote three great objectives: repeal of the test and corporation acts, Catholic emancipation, and the reform of parliament.[31] And with these measures secured, the editors of the *Review* looked forward to days of great change. The securing that year of legislation to emancipate West Indian slaves suggested those hopes would not be disappointed, but the pace of reform legislation slackened thereafter, and by the spring of 1841 the *Nottingham Review* put forward a new agenda, which included agitating the causes of dissenters, and specifically, immediate and absolute abolition of the church rate.[32]

Meanwhile the editors of rival *Nottingham Journal*, which liberal critics decried as the 'authorised organ of Sir Robert Peel,'[33] described their position as

> convinced that the welfare and happiness of the Nation at large depended, under Providence, on the efficiency and stability of those institutions in Church and State, which have guaranteed this country a greater share of intellectual greatness, moral power, and rational freedom, than has ever fallen to the lot of any other empire.[34]

Such priorities, especially as regarding the role of the Church of England, stood in stark contrast to those advanced by the *Review*.

2.5 The campaigns to abolish colonial slavery and terminate West Indian apprenticeship

With the debates of 1828, 1829, and 1832 resolved satisfactorily, the next big issue to arouse political dissent, as suggested above, was the abolition of slavery in Britain's colonial possessions. Subsequent chapters show that candidates for parliament in 1832 could hardly remain silent on the subject of colonial slavery, and liberals came down most heavily in favour of those proposals calculated to appeal to dissent: immediate abolition without compensation for former slave-holders. Nor was this attention to the issue wasted, for it certainly attracted voters. A requisition to stand for the borough of Bedford, signed by over 130 liberal electors, gave especial notice to Samuel Crawley's championing of abolition, and the printed address by the Bedford Union Society also gave particular attention to abolition as a liberal issue in 1832.[35] (Tellingly, liberals regarded Crawley's anti-clericalism as another credential in his favour.)

Certainly, the abolitionist movement enjoyed a wider base of support than dissent alone.[36] But contemporary observers who, for strategic purposes declared that emancipation was no mere sectarian cause, were well aware, especially on the hustings, that it was particularly a concern of dissent. Two handbills posted in Bedford late in November 1832 claimed that 'men of the highest moral and religious character both in the Church and among the Dissenters. . . .' engaged actively in pursuit of the emancipation of British slaves;[37] and the same point was made two weeks later, in the report of a meeting of the Nottingham Anti-Slavery Association.[38] Such repeated and decided emphasis, especially as it was not questioned, seems to give the lie to the contention that there were no grounds for putting one group—that is, dissent—before others in its ardour for abolition. Moreover, at least four of the speakers at the meeting in Nottingham were nonconformists: the Revds Richard Alliott, Philip Gell, James Edwards, as well as Mr George Gell.

Almost certainly referring to the nonconformist electors of Exeter, Edward Divett called the abolition of slavery 'a subject [about] which he knew many excellent persons in this city, of the most pure and philanthropic views, felt very deeply.'[39] In another appeal to the Foxite legacy of championing the causes of dissent, Gen. R.C. Ferguson took the opportunity of his nomination for Nottingham to recall his own involvement in curtailing the trans-Atlantic slave trade in 1807.[40]

Of course, if dissent in England distinguished itself disproportionately in its fervour for colonial abolition, it need not follow that Anglicans held any peculiar regard for the institution of slavery. Nevertheless, certain foes of slavery and the Church of England alike tried to make the case. References to 'the thralldom of the Test Act' were probably intended to elicit comparison with the plight of English dissenters before 1828 and the slaves of the West Indies.[41] Criticism of 'every slave-holding Gladstone and pro-slavery advocate in Parliament' was mostly likely designed to draw attention to the late proclivities of certain Anglican families, since, in the early 1840s, the most prominent scion of the Gladstone family, William, MP for Newark, had distinguished himself chiefly as a defender of the Church of England.[42] And at least some conservative Anglicans unflinchingly accepted the association with slavery. In a reckless burst of candour, in 1835, the *Nottingham Journal* allied its sympathies plainly with former slave-owners by quoting with approval from *Westmacott's Exposé of four years of Whig government*, which criticized the late liberal ministry for having 'freed slaves (who live better than our own peasantry, and repaid us for freedom with revolt) merely to satisfy dissenters. . . .' This, and other instances of liberal impolicy, the exposé continued, had cost taxpayers £30 million.[43] In view of their evident hostility to abolition, it must be inferred that 20 millions of these, or fully two-thirds of the expenditures these conservatives begrudged, derived from the compensation paid out to former slave-owners—all, in their view, *'merely to satisfy dissenters.* . . .'[44]

Obviously abolition was more of a central concern in 1832–1833 than it would be thereafter, since parliament passed legislation to end slavery on 23 August 1833, and slaves throughout the empire became legally free on 1 August the following year. But the fire of abolitionism was kept stoked thereafter, mostly by liberal candidates and MPs, and most likely in attempts to appeal to nonconformist electors. Typically this was in the form of litanies of praiseworthy reforms liberal governments had accomplished;[45] although the plight of West Indian blacks received renewed attention with the debates leading up to their early release from apprenticeship on 1 August 1838.[46] In 1837, T.C. Granger, liberal candidate for Durham, described the continuation of colonial apprenticeship as one of the most important issues facing the next parliament. Until the practice was ended, Granger said, the enslavement of blacks continued in all but name, and a £20 million fraud was committed against the nation.[47] And, as we shall see in Chapters 5 and 7 in the instances of Ipswich and Exeter, the free trade debate was easily turned from the merits of protective duties on sugar to competing schemes for encouraging abolition in Cuba, Brazil, and elsewhere. The same argument was used in Nottingham in 1841, and as late as July 1847, *Trewman's Exeter Flying Post* reported on an anti-slavery meeting held in Exeter.[48]

2.6   Irish appropriation and Peel's first ministry

A few exceptions aside, however, no big movement was afoot to oppose the abolition of colonial slavery, and 'the next two years [after the reform act] were a time of political quiescence.'[49] The period of relative calm broke, in the fall of 1834, when the liberal ministry announced its plans to reform the tithe system of Ireland and apply the expected surplus to education schemes. The king dismissed the ministry, and a general election became imminent. Of course this crisis was only one among several high water marks in the nineteenth-century struggles to settle relations of church and state,[50] and despite the 'political quiescence' of 1833 and 1834, it had been religious division that fueled what controversy did exist. Conservatives in Ipswich, for instance, continued to harp on old subjects: 'they attacked Roman Catholics, especially O'Connell, and Dissenters who wished, they claimed, to destroy the Church Establishment.'[51] The liberal government became particularly unpopular in Ipswich, and its support by the borough's MPs, Morrison and Wason, blemished their reputation among their constituents. Familiar patterns of clerical intolerance for liberal legislation were evident, and the first critics to petition against the government's new poor law were church and parish officials.[52]

The Melbourne ministry's proposals for the Irish church in the fall of 1834 were part of a broader plan of reform for the establishment of church and state in the United Kingdom, in a sense, dating to the seventeenth century. One liberal in Exeter went so far as to place the reform act of 1832 in a longer tradition of liberal reforms, the most important of which had been the repeal of the test and corporation acts in 1828 and Catholic emancipation in 1829.[53] Likewise in Ipswich, another liberal called 'Church Reform...as necessary as Parliamentary Reform.'[54] And as detailed in a subsequent chapter, the liberal candidate for Exeter based his initial hostility to his conservative opponent chiefly on the latter's opposition to the reform bill. That issue being put to rest, however, what continued to divide the liberal and conservative candidates were all matters of church and state.[55]

The fate of the church in Ireland was a particular concern for dissenters in England (as well as Roman Catholics and Presbyterians in Ireland) because it was viewed as a bellwether for the fate of the church in England. Its establishment was far more vulnerable in the smaller island—and any dampening of its prestige or position was regarded as a hopeful sign of reform, just as any successful defense of it was taken as strengthening the bulwarks against reform at home. From a liberal perspective, Catholics in Ireland were merely 'asserting their rights,' in a manner perfectly consistent with the goals sought by dissenters in England.[56] Conservatives and Anglicans therefore redoubled their efforts to defend the established church, in Ireland as well as in England.

Anglican alarmists in Ipswich took up the cry of *Church in danger* in the weeks leading up to the general election of 1832, drawing attention particularly to the Church of Ireland.[57] The Anglican laity of Durham brought before both houses of parliament a petition 'against the IRISH CHURCH REFORM BILL,' on grounds the government's proposed alienation of church property threatened to reduce the hitherto independent and dignified character of church officials to mere servants to volatile public opinion.[58] Other conservatives complained that liberal policies in general intended to 'overthrow the Altars of the Protestant Faith,' and encouraged Anglicans to rescue 'the Altars of God from desecration' by voting only for staunch churchmen.[59] One conservative journal dismissed all ecclesiastical reform as an elaborate sham designed to win popularity from nonconformists and other allegedly unprincipled voters, by raising up false hopes of the money stripped from the church,[60] and the petitioners in Durham concluded by stating firmly that no government had the right to alienate ecclesiastical property, suppress bishoprics, or otherwise interfere with the governing of the established church.[61]

In keeping with their negative opinion of those inside or outside the establishment who sought to weaken the bonds connecting church and state, conservatives were suspicious of the Irish MPs on whom the governments of Grey and especially Melbourne relied so heavily.[62] A poem printed in Ipswich alleged that the supporters of the liberal candidate Rigby Wason consisted in the main of Roman Catholics and other 'Infidels,' and another handbill condemned the Melbourne ministry for having 'promoted and fostered Popery,' and having 'aimed a "heavy blow and great discouragement at Protestantism in Ireland...."'[63] A ditty that circulated in Bedford claimed that, if returned to office, a Melbourne ministry would simply 'submit to O'Connell's dictation,' and the conservative *Nottingham Journal* likewise deplored the influence of Daniel O'Connell on English liberals.[64] Liberals in Nottingham, in contrast, regarded Viscount Duncannon's endorsement by O'Connell as very much in the candidate's favour.[65]

2.7 Early demands for disestablishment in Ireland and England

Whereas it was occasionally difficult to distinguish whether conservatives' hostility to dissenters was rooted primarily in politics or doctrine, liberals in most cases tried to make clear that their objection was to the position the Anglican church enjoyed as the established Church of England, and not to the church itself.[66] Nevertheless, there can be no doubt that criticism of the church as a state establishment was occasionally supplanted by overt attacks on the church or its doctrines. Evidently inspired by the demands of the liberal candidate Rigby Wason, to settle the church rate question in a fashion acceptable to dissenters, one member of his Ipswich audience broadened the demand for restructuring and cried out 'Pull down the Church.'[67]

Nor was there any doubt, in the judgment of the whig *Bedford Beacon*,[68] that one natural consequence of continuing to accord undue privilege and power to the established church in Ireland was to encourage Orange extremism. In reporting on the murder of two young Irishmen, aged ten and 19 years, by members of the Orange Order, the *Beacon* allowed that '[t]he records of Indian warfare might furnish some faint similitude to this...,'

> if it were not, that the Indians had to plead on their side that they were turning their fury against a race whom they had known, almost exclusively, as their implacable enemies—the 'pale faces,' by whom they were slaughtered and driven from their hunting territories, and the graves of their fathers.[69]

Thus the *Beacon* considered Orange activists as savage as the Indians of North America, but lacking justifiable rancour. And the bloodthirsty lawlessness of Orangeism, the *Beacon* made clear, was a hardly exaggerated manifestation of the culture conservatives sought:

> It is vain for the Tory party to gloss over the simple truth:—This murder is a perfect representation, an embodiment of the principles and spirit of old Church and State Toryism, or, to use the more correct word, Orangeism in Ireland. ... In this may be seen the fruits of the Irish system under the Tory rulers—the natural results of that policy, which, under the pretext of favouring true religion, was leveled at the foundation of all religion, and directed against the native humanities of the majority of the Irish people.
>
> That the same party would again act on the same principles, if they had the power, who can doubt?[70]

Other concerns regarding Ireland would draw attention away from religious issues for much of the next decade or so, but they never disappeared completely. The liberal Henry Spearman made the fair treatment of the Irish a centrepiece of his campaign for Durham in 1847.[71] But by and large, significant reform of the Church of Ireland would have to wait, and the promise of the aborted liberal legislation of the mid-1830s was only partially realized, to the chagrin of dissenters.

Granted, two of the six major grievances identified in 1833 by the United Committee (comprising representatives of the Dissenting Deputies, Protestant Society, and the General Body of Dissenting Ministers in London)[72] were removed in the summer of 1836, with passage of the marriage and registration bills.[73] And dissenters were further compensated in their gains from the reform act of 1832, and even more from the municipal reform act of 1835, which a modern authority has judged '[t]he most important political advance achieved by Dissenters in the 1830s, indeed in the whole of the nineteenth century....'[74] But the greatest goal of dissent remained unachieved in this period: the abolition of the church rate.[75]

2.8 The church rate controversy

Although in practice the burden imposed by the church rate was not very onerous—indeed, in one notable case, the charge complained of was half a shilling[76]—the 'most sustained campaign for the removal of a grievance during this period [i.e. until its repeal in 1868] was the one for the abolition of church rates...,'[77] and this pursuit inspired dissenters like nothing else had since 1828 and 1829. Liberals in Ipswich were denouncing the church rate as early as the general election of 1832: they complained it was obnoxious to dissenters, but as yet merely aspired to adjust the manner of its collection, in a manner favourable to dissent, rather than to abolish it altogether.[78] During the next decade, Nottingham experienced at least three major waves of enthusiasm for church rate abolition. All three peaks of agitation corresponded to a parliamentary election—the by-election of July 1834, the general election of July 1837, and the by-election of April 1841—and in all three elections, candidates' positions on proposed church rate legislation proved to be powerful determinants in the outcome of the contests. If this is to be expected in the case of the 1837 general election, which, in large part, was waged nationally on the question of the church rate, it is a striking example of the prevalence of denominational rivalry in political discourse in the 1841 election, especially since the conservative candidate, John Walter senior, pegged the entire appeal of his campaign on the borough's spirited hostility to the new poor law—nonetheless, electors and the other candidate successfully made the church rate a pivotal concern of the contest.

Early in July 1834, over 50 nonconformists from different denominations assembled at the Baptist Chapel in Park Street, Nottingham, 'for the purpose of appointing a Committee to watch over the interests of the Dissenters.'[79] They rejected the limited scope of the government's proposal regarding the church rate, which simply transferred payment of the church rates to the consolidated fund, leaving dissenting taxpayers still supporting them: what they demanded now was complete abolition. To this end, they planned the immediate coordination of regular correspondence with dissenters from across the kingdom, with a unified deputation constantly in London.[80] Yet abolition seemed no closer to realization two years later, and a meeting of nonconformists in Ipswich passed a resolution

> [t]hat his Majesty's Ministers, by suffering the present session of parliament to pass away without any attempt to settle the church-rate question, have disappointed the hopes and betrayed the confidence of their best friends; and violated the pledges repeatedly given to the Dissenters of this empire.[81]

From this point on, especially, nonconformists in England became increasingly dissatisfied with the liberal government, which hitherto they had regarded as their patrons.

Further resolutions of the meeting in Ipswich objected to proposals for commutation rather than abolition of the church rate, called a meeting of nonconformists from across the country to confer with the government on nonconformist grievances, and finally, moved

> [t]hat in case of a dissolution of parliament, preference be given (other qualifications as Reformers being equal) to candidates who will distinctly pledge themselves to vote for the extinction of church rates.[82]

The next spring, an anti-church rate assembly in Bedford, which included members of the Church Rate Abolition Society, formed a deputation to consult with the liberal member for the borough, Samuel Crawley, to secure a pledge for satisfactory votes in parliamentary divisions on the church rate and other dissenting concerns.[83] Liberal electors in the borough gathered together ten years later, in the summer of 1847, to hear a harangue by the Quaker orator Henry Vincent, and chief of the complaints he railed against in near apocalyptic language was the failure of any government to act decisively on the matter of the church rate.[84] Later that same year, the Dissenting Deputies drew up a fresh list of grievances, at the top of which was the church rate.

The editors of the liberal *Nottingham Review* expressed confidence that G.G. de H. Larpent would win in April 1841, mainly on the grounds that he favoured church rate abolition and that the conservative candidate, John Walter senior, dared ask for

> the suffrages of the numerous body of the electors of Nottingham, who are dissenters, and who without doubt, form a majority of the electors. . . . The [contest] must be decided upon the church rate question.[85]

In fact, the *Review* was wrong, and Walter won a comfortable majority—albeit one that was stained with (probably just) accusations of corruption. Nonetheless, the point is well taken that dissenters had an incentive to vote for Larpent over Walter, and most likely they did so.[86] But liberals more generally, not only dissenters, wanted to be rid of the church rate. As we shall see in a subsequent chapter, its immediate abolition was one of the four goals of the *Review* in 1841,[87] and liberals in Nottingham, who opposed the conservative Horace Twiss in 1837, gave as the principal cause his unwillingness to commit to church rate abolition or other reforms.[88] It is further suggestive that neither the requisition to the mayor of Ipswich, to

> convene a Meeting of the Inhabitants of the Town on as early a day as possible, to take into consideration the propriety of Petitioning the Legislature in favor of the measure of His Majesty's Ministers for the Abolition of Church Rates.

nor the consequent petition to the government (signed by 36 and 83 inhabitant householders, respectively) once mentioned the peculiar plight of dissent.[89] Obviously opponents of the church rate in Ipswich viewed the matter a general concern of the liberal interest. Nor was it likely to have been mere happenstance that the excitement among liberal circles in Nottingham was noted to be somewhat diminished, on the occasion of one of the borough's liberal members, Viscount Duncannon, being appointed home secretary (with rumours of his elevation to the peerage)—since the news coincided with a public sale of property, seized for non-payment of the church rate.[90] The assessment for the church rate, it is worth repeating, was in most cases trivial, and thus instances of seizure of property were nearly always deliberately courted by the defaulters—or 'recusants,' as sympathizers frequently identified them[91]—calculated to draw attention to the unjust nature of the measure. In this respect, the campaign had something of a *cause célèbre* in the case of John Thorogood, a dissenter who added contempt of court to his failure to pay a rate of sixpence, and was imprisoned for nearly two years[92] The *Nottingham Review* was still raising the spectre of this injustice in 1841.[93]

On the other side, the Revd C.C. Bartholomew, in eulogizing the conservative member for Exeter in 1837, especially applauded Sir W.W. Follett's vigorous exertion on behalf of preserving the church rate as the best index of his unfaltering allegiance to conservative principle.[94] Sir William had himself, three days earlier, stated to the

Exeter Central Conservative Association his belief that 'It is an essential ingredient in the principles of Conservatism, to resist any attack on the Church....'[95] And the most effective attacks conservatives made on liberals, in Bedford and Exeter in 1837 and in Nottingham in 1841, were on the grounds of liberals' advocacy of church rate abolition.[96] Thus it is evident a vigorous stance in favour of the church rate was part of a broadly conservative, rather than narrowly Anglican, agenda—although to be sure, the two nearly always went hand in hand.

Conservatives argued that the church rate was no practical grievance: witness the paltry sixpence for which some church rate martyrs had been imprisoned. Follett in Exeter claimed that attacks on the rate were designed as 'not so much a relief of the Dissenters, as a measure for stripping the Dignitaries of the Church of the possessions of that Church....'[97] Others insisted that cries for abolition were merely the thin edge of the wedge leading to disestablishment, and no doubt such fears had substance. At a meeting in Nottingham in July 1837, a further aim on the agenda was to be rid of 'the evils of a national establishment' by the complete 'separation of Church and State....'[98] These dissenters, of different denominations, denied any political objective; they made clear that their goals were

> 1st. The abolition of all political laws compelling the payment of money for the support of any one system of doctrine and discipline:— 2d. The abolition of all laws which make the canons of the establishment and the proceedings of ecclesiastical courts binding on the public at large:— 3d. The abolition of all laws which give peculiar dignities and privileges under state authority to individuals belonging to any particular sect:— And 4thly, to the abolition of all those laws which impose silence on persons in office, respecting the alliance between church and state.[99]

The liberal-radical *Bedford News* pledged in one of its inaugural numbers that

> [r]eligious controversy shall never find any place in these columns, except in those political questions of Church and State where it is impossible altogether to shut out all reference to the peculiarities of the dominant and would-be dominant sects.... Civil and Religious Liberty can never be perfectly attained in any country where there is a State Church establishment.[100]

In a similar vein, a witness to the first marriage in a dissenting place of worship in Nottingham commented,

> GREAT IS THE TRIUMPH OF PRINCIPLE achieved this morning; a blow is struck (not, Sir, at the religion of the Established Church—not at the efficiency of the Episcopal Church to promote real godliness in the land; these, I firmly believe, in common with the best friends of the Establishment, will be greatly promoted, by removing every just ground of complaint from Dissenters)—a blow is struck at the dominancy of one section of Christians over other sections of Christians—a blow is struck, under which, though bigotry may writhe and struggle, yet bigotry cannot long survive. The march of principle is rapid—*vires acquirit eundo.* He who resists, stems a flowing tide, and all he reaps is to be overwhelmed by the mighty waters.[101]

2.9 Opposition to agricultural protection

The next big issue to face the nation and the electorate was the fate of the Corn Law, one of the major focal points in the general election of 1841. Although this did not, strictly speaking, in any way touch on questions of church and state or of dissent, it could never, as evidence from subsequent chapters makes plain, be fully separated from that wider debate. This was as much the case for mainstream Anti-Corn Law League candidates such as Maj. Gen. John Briggs, a churchman, in Exeter as it was for the rabid free trader and Quaker gadfly to agricultural protection, John Bright, in Durham. Others besides Anti-Corn Law League activists recognized the strong link between preserving the Corn Law and the financial well-being of the church. A few weeks before the 1841 election, the *Bedford Mercury* asked of three typical Englishmen—Messrs Baker, Grocer, and John Rawbone, the epitome of a labouring man—'Pray, ... what think you of the Bread tax?' They all opposed it. But Messrs Clergyman, Landlord, and Farmer responded strongly in its favour. The *Mercury* concluded that 'The Landlord—the Clergy—the Farmer, are the only three really benefited; and so all the nation is [burdened with] a heavy Bread tax to pamper these three classes. Citizens, will you allow this *monopoly?*'[102] Elsewhere in the same number, the *Mercury* intimated the church's strong interest in maintaining a high price for corn, and warned labourers not to believe clergymen who preached that cheap bread would lead to low wages.[103] It is not too much to say that total free trade had become as much a nonconformist as a liberal aim by the early 1840s, and the old slogan of 'civil and religious liberty' was gradually giving way to a broader statement of liberal principle: 'A Free Trade—a Free Vote—and a Free Religion....'[104]

2.10 The Maynooth grant

The final major religious controversy to enliven English political debate between 1832 and 1847 was the passage of the Maynooth College act, which increased the government's endowment of the largest Roman Catholic seminary in Ireland, and provided additional funds for rebuilding. The matter got an explicit nod in Bedford in the summer of 1845, when the newly launched *Bedford News*, a self-proclaimed radical weekly, judged as 'the leading question of our age—the question of STATE-ENDOWMENTS OF RELIGION.'[105] Nationally, most of the electorate had to wait nearly two years to formally register their opinion on the Maynooth grant, until the general election of 1847. But the electors of Exeter got a head-start, with the borough's by-election in July 1845, whose contest was coloured entirely by the electors' and the candidates' positions on the recently secured revision of the Maynooth grant. Liberal electors stood united behind the Anti-Corn Law League candidate, Gen. Briggs, but the conservative ranks were initially '[f]rittered away into small sections....'[106] Sir John Thomas Buller Duckworth, who presented himself on behalf of the conservative interest of the borough, had not, in the estimation of many conservatives, expressed his hostility to the recently passed Maynooth legislation in sufficiently plain terms. In an open letter dated 30 June, an elector who identified himself as Civis urged 'Fellow Protestants and Citizens' to exercise their votes

> well, and [only] support that Candidate for your Suffrages who pledges himself to uphold the PROTESTANT FAITH of your country, for which your forefathers have bled and died....England expects every Man to do his duty, and calls upon you, at this momentous crisis, to prove to the world that the glorious Reformation was not achieved in vain.[107]

Trewman's Exeter Flying Post reported that mostly conservatives attended an open political meeting called in defence of protestantism, where it was resolved to accept as an MP only one who 'would oppose every measure in Parliament of a character and tendency similar to the Maynooth College Bill' and, if he had sat in parliament previously, clearly prove that he always voted against Maynooth. To this end, they found they could with a better conscience vote for Gen. Briggs who, although avowedly bent on dismantling agricultural protection of any kind—regarded by most modern historians as a hallmark of the conservative party—had spoken decisively against Maynooth, and pledged always to oppose any extension of state endowments for religious purposes.[108] Sir John Duckworth had condemned the Maynooth grant just as soundly, was outspoken in the vehemence of his anti-Catholicism, and defined his principles of conservatism as rooted in defence of the Church of England—but, having refused to make any pledge regarding future conduct, could not convince Civis and other conservative Anglicans of the sincerity of his protestantism.[109]

During the course of the next week, Duckworth succeeded in satisfying conservative consciences, and the *Flying Post* predicted his easy return for the borough.[110] However, a body of Anglicans, led by the Revd William Hockin, John Bacon, and John Palk, remained steadfast in withholding their support. They corresponded with Duckworth 'on the subject of those Principles upon which [they] consider[ed] the Polity of a Protestant Government should be conducted,' and were not satisfied with his response. No matter what direction the conservative van was heading, in the reins of Sir Robert Peel and likeminded apostates, the true blue Anglicans, whom Hockin et al. judged to form the heart and soul of the party, would remain steadfast to 'True Protestantism.'[111]

Subsequently Bacon conferred with Duckworth on the same matters and, 'though entertaining…adverse Sentiments…in reference to Concessions to Popery,' withdrew his opposition. Thereupon, Hockin and Palk reaffirmed their doubts regarding Duckworth, and urged their

[f]ellow Protestants, not to give [their] votes to Sir J. Duckworth, unless he will give you a distinct answer to one of the two following Questions, viz:—If he had been in Parliament during the discussion of the Maynooth Bill, which way would he have voted?—Or, in case of any similar measure being hereafter proposed, say for instance the Endowment of the Roman Catholic Priesthood, which way will he vote?

'Protestants be firm,' they concluded, 'and insist upon an answer to one of these Questions.'[112] Evidently Duckworth's responses satisfied most of the borough's conservatives, and he sat for Exeter until his retirement in 1857.

The Maynooth controversy continued to burn brightly in Exeter and other boroughs two years later. A letter to the editors of the *Bedford*

Times on the eve of the general election for the most part railed against Catholicism and the Maynooth grant, and concluded by directing undecided electors to a tract entitled 'The Christian's part in the General Election.'[113] T.C. Granger, sitting liberal member for Durham, accounted for and apologized to his dissenting friends for having voted contrary to their desires.[114] And, as we shall see in a Chapter 5, a single apostasy in regard to Maynooth was enough for the conservative electors of Ipswich to cast off J.N. Gladstone, otherwise a dependable conservative and staunch Anglican.

2.11   English politics and dissent, 1832–1847: summary and conclusion

Thus it seems obvious that, other weighty matters notwithstanding— for example, parliamentary reform, controversy over the new poor law, foreign and colonial policy, matters of free trade, and so on—a mainstay of English politics in the decade-and-a-half following the reform act of 1832 was the question of the proper position of church and state, and the role played by dissent outside that relationship. Such matters were not new to the period after 1832, and nor would they by any means be settled finally in the next 15 years. These questions polarized electors and members of parliament alike, and were the clearest indicator of what separated the developing liberal and conservative parties of the nineteenth century.

3
Religion and Politics in a Northeastern Cathedral Town: The Case of Durham

3.1 Durham: Introduction*

In the English and Welsh boroughs, the election for the first reformed House of Commons was held on 11–12 December 1832. In many constituencies, however, interest in the contest was so intense that electioneering and related activities had been underway since the previous spring. The reform bill had survived its third reading in the House of Lords on 4 June and received royal assent on the 7th, but in Durham, one contender had already announced his candidacy as early as April, and all the candidates were in the field by the second week of May.

3.2 The 1832 general election in Durham

'Though a young man' in 1832, William Charles Harland (1803/04–1863) was described favourably by the *Durham Chronicle* as 'one of the old School of Reformers'[1] and, for his own part, Harland declared his 'unqualified attachment' to the reform bill. In the removal of abuses and the restoration of national welfare and security, Harland was a proponent of what he called 'rational liberty,' which included the

---

*The borough of Durham was an inland county-town in the northeast of England, located on a steep hill inside a bend on the River Wear. It was the site of an ancient cathedral and, since 1832, home to the University of Durham. Its population increased from 10,125 to 13,188 between 1832 and 1851, and its registered electorate increased from 806 to 1157 between 1832 and 1852. Chief economic interests were in coalmining, the woolen industry, and carpet-, paper- and rope-making. According to *Dod's*, the marquis of Londonderry and the earl of Durham retained some electoral influence after 1832, but neither of a commanding nature.

encouragement of all branches of civil liberty, and especially the promotion of religious liberty, as well as the prospect, equally dear to dissenters, of the immediate abolition of colonial slavery.[2]

The programme of the other liberal candidate, William Richard Carter Chaytor (1805–1871), remains more obscure, in large part because of the quality of surviving sources.[3] Nevertheless, Chaytor made it clear that he stood on the same principles as his fellow liberal, Harland, and therefore presumably appealed to dissenters, as well. He explicitly stated as much toward the close of his preliminary canvass, calculating that the same constituency would vote for both him and Harland.[4]

The *Durham Chronicle* concurred: it regarded Harland and Chaytor interchangeably, and reported with favour that both candidates were pledged to a series of reforms which included, significantly, the commutation of tithes and other adjustments to the revenues of the Church of England, as well as the reduction of its temporal authority. Any man who shrank from such measures, in the estimation of the *Chronicle*, was 'not of a calibre suited to the temper and necessities of the times.... "Let no such man be trusted!" '[5]

No doubt whom the *Chronicle* had in mind was the lone conservative candidate, the Hon. Arthur Trevor (1798–1862), member for the borough since the previous year.[6] Liberals in Durham criticized Trevor for his patronage from the borough's closed and aristocratic conservative influence and, perhaps equally, for his identification with the Church of England. Indeed, the two influences were often seen as virtually one.

> Mr. Trevor [the *Chronicle* reported] comes forward as the nominee of the Marquis of Londonderry, and the champion of the Church—as the minion of corruption in its worst form—destitute both of the power and of the inclination to serve the people.... He will serve his master rather than the people, and block all wise and beneficial legislation.[7]

Such class tensions were unusually advanced in Durham during the first half of the nineteenth century, and the massive bulk and splendor of the cathedral—memorialized by Sir Walter Scott (1771–1832) as 'Half Church of God, Half castle 'gainst the Scot'[8]—no doubt reinforced the sense of inequality. The cathedral's latter role having become superfluous by the nineteenth century, contemporaries of Scott who were less sympathetic to the establishment reapportioned these qualities somewhat—rather less church of God, and rather more bastion of the privilege enjoyed by the Anglican hierarchy in association with the conservative establishment in the town.[9] Unquestionably the Church of England 'possessed its greatest concentration of resources' in Durham.[10] The archdeaconry was in a position to take advantage of new industries, and the bishop and resident clergy both were enriched by coal and lead production.[11] Moreover, Durham's clerical establishment possessed nearly half of the county's advowsons. Not surprisingly, those who felt they did not share in the advantages of the establishment resented such privileged sinecures and egregious abuses, and it was common rhetoric in the early nineteenth century, when addressing the populace in Durham, 'to point to that "big building,"' meaning the cathedral, 'and wish it was pulled down.'[12]

Denounced by Daniel O'Connel as 'the meek and modest representative of the clergy of Durham'[13]—and considered by many to be 'the vassal of the peer, and [of] the trained bands of the holy brotherhood of the church'[14]—it was alleged Arthur Trevor could hardly be expected to champion the interests of the weak or the poor, or those who dissented from the Church of England, and the *Durham Chronicle* summed up the conservative candidate as

> The creature of an unprincipled, reckless, and despicable oligarchy—the enemy of all improvement—the sworn foe of all change, and especially of such as may appear likely to close the national purse-string against the paupers, or we may say truly, the pick-pockets of the state....[15]

Strikingly, the passage did not make clear which influence—aristocratic or ecclesiastical—was the greater evil, suggesting, perhaps, that the two could hardly be distinguished.

As the *Durham Chronicle* had predicted in June, '[t]he people, even in cathedral cities,' refused to return a conservative member to the first reformed House of Commons,

> —even though [he] be supported by the countenance of the great underlings of the church,—the men who,—for 'admonition' or 'example' we marvel?—graced his progress by their mighty presence; nor will they be scarified from the performance of their duty, notwithstanding the paid servants of the state are suffered to leave their regiments to squander their time and their 'eloquence' in propping up the filthy admonitions of corruption.[16]

Harland and Chaytor were returned for Durham with 440 and 404 votes, respectively, and Trevor was defeated with 383 votes cast in his favour. Although it remains difficult to assess Chaytor's canvass, it is clear that much of Harland's appeal was in his positions regarding issues about which dissenters felt strongly. It is equally plain that those who were hostile to Trevor portrayed him as the champion of a bigoted church, and no friend to dissent.[17]

3.3   The 1835 and 1837 general elections in Durham

Certain continuities in the circumstances of the next two electoral contests in Durham make it convenient to consider them together. For one thing, the same three candidates stood for the borough in these elections, and the same two men were returned as members. More importantly, controversies over the position of the Anglican church as an establishment of the state were powerful factors influencing the candidates' electoral appeal, as well as the decisions of the electorate.

The first of these contests, the general election of 1835, was made necessary by the decision of William IV to dissolve parliament, following a liberal ministry's plan to appropriate funds from the Irish church for a scheme of education. Consequently, no serious candidate for parliament could avoid questions of religion, at least insofar as they touched matters of ecclesiastical reform.[18] This crisis, which marked the last time a British monarch dismissed a government that enjoyed the support of a majority of the House of Commons, remained at the fore of political rhetoric and electoral concerns in the general election of 1837, to which was added the controversy over the fate of the church rate.

The elector who introduced W.C. Harland on the hustings in 1835 drew particular attention to the constitutional crisis posed by the actions of the king, evidently in defence of the established church. Harland's nominator in 1837 invoked the spirit of the repeal of the test and corporation acts, Catholic emancipation, and parliamentary reform—which together, he claimed, had heralded a new era in Britain; he warned of a restoration of the corruption prevalent in the eighteenth century, when 'exclusion on account of religion' was the norm, if electors returned a conservative House of Commons.[19]

Speaking for himself, W.C. Harland gave even greater priority to religion in January 1835 than he had done two years earlier. He nailed his colours firmly to the mast in his nomination speech, stating unequivocally 'that there is no question at the present moment in which the public feel more interest than that of a reform in the English and Irish

Churches.' In regard to the Church of England, Harland pledged to support any measure which aimed to redistribute her revenues more equitably, in the belief that such general reform would in turn effect the redress of two specific evils: pluralities and non-residence. By redistributing ecclesiastical revenue, Harland desired to relieve poor clergymen, who filled multiple livings out of necessity, and to reduce the number of those with abundant resources but few obligations. He acknowledged that reform of the Irish church was a delicate concern, not the least because some even questioned parliament's right to legislate in regard to its funds. Nevertheless, he maintained that it was within the right of the parliament of Great Britain to enact legislation appropriating ecclesiastical funds for secular purposes and, in view of the fact that seven-eighths of the inhabitants of Ireland were not Anglican, these funds ought to be appropriated, and diverted to a general system of national education. The other great question of the day, according to Harland, consisted of 'the claims of the Protestant Dissenters,' and he promised to seek for them 'the fullest civil privileges,' stopping only short of disestablishment.[20]

In the next contest, Harland made more explicit the connexions between liberalism and religious inclusion, on the one side, and conservatism and religious exclusion, on the other. '[T]hose measures [of the present ministry] which tended to do away with civil and religious distinctions,' he stated from the hustings, 'have been opposed by the other [i.e. conservative] party. . . .'[21] He further alleged that conservatives had unjustly misrepresented certain proposals for ecclesiastical reform in attempts to blemish the reputation of the liberal government:

> Now, gentlemen, an attack has been made against the present government that they have been hostile to the Established Church, and their wish to relieve the Dissenters from the burthen of Church-rates has been quoted in proof of the truth of this accusation.[22]

Harland denied the allegation. Neither the government, nor Harland, nor any liberal, based on those convictions, could be accused of 'wishing to destroy the establishment and [foment] revolution. . . .'[23] As he emphasized in 1835, Harland remained 'a Churchman, and . . . always oppose[d to] any separation of church and state,' and he continued to 'believe that a church establishment, on the right footing, [wa]s most important to national well-bring.'[24] Nevertheless, he advocated freedom of conscience, favoured church rate repeal, and supported certain reform proposals for Ireland, especially the tithe and corporation bills.

In addition to these pledges in regard to future conduct—and as he had done in the previous election—Harland reminded his listeners of the reforms liberal governments had already achieved, including the municipal corporations act, which had benefited so many nonconformists living in the boroughs, and the abolition of slavery.[25]

Perhaps in rebuttal to the allegations in 1832, when he was accused of subservience to the church and boroughmongers, Arthur Trevor commenced his speech from the hustings in 1835 with the proclamation that he was no man's nominee, but stood, for the third time since 1831, at the request of many of the electors of the Durham.[26] As they had been in the previous election, his positions on reform generally, and settling the relation between church and dissent specifically, were the opposite of Harland's; although in addressing his constituents, Trevor seemed reticent to broach such potentially volatile issues directly. Instead he preferred vague and general advocacy of cautious reform, if and when necessary, and, in marked contrast to W.C. Harland, he failed once to mention religion directly in his words from the hustings.

In 1835, Trevor declared himself 'bound... to uphold all local interests [and] to have a jealous eye on those institutions, charitable or otherwise, connected with' Durham, and in 1837 he promised to defend the different privileges of every class in his constituency.[27] In spite of such repeated expressions of respect for the interests and concerns of the entire Durham constituency—'local, collective, and individual'[28]—such language is equivocal. Understood in one fashion, it must have implied sensitivity to the religious concerns of those dissenters who comprised probably around a third of the borough's electors, and most likely a greater share of its inhabitants. On the other hand, no such commitment was stated explicitly, and could be denied if desired.

Indeed, it was only after the conclusion of a poll—when no harm could be done, so to speak—that Trevor's reticence subsided and he spoke openly on those controversies which separated Anglicans and dissenters. After the poll had been declared in 1835, Trevor directly addressed religion for the first time, and acknowledged himself to respect those opinions, 'as well political as religious,' that differed from his own. Only after he was chaired did he promise fair treatment for 'churchmen and dissenters,' or pledge to investigate proven ecclesiastical abuses.[29] In 1837, it was only in his address after the poll that Trevor first revealed his position on the question of the Church Leasehold, and even that amounted to nothing more than a promise to ascertain first 'what the feelings of the great bulk of [his] constituents were on the subject.'[30] And it was on these occasions, after the poll was concluded and he was safely returned, that Arthur Trevor could safely state, without ambiguity, his admiration for the established church, and his defence of it in the face of any inroads from the dissenting interests. It was at the close of the 1837 general election, for instance, that he first stated in public his conviction that so-called reformers were, in reality, plunderers of the church.[31]

Aside from the substance of his addresses, and his less formal comments afterwards, the nature as well as the words of his principal, supporters reiterated the connexion between Trevor (and the conservative party) and Anglicanism. Officials of the church nominated the conservative candidate in 1835 and 1837, and although their statements, like those of their nominee, were cautious and designed not to offend, their presence on the hustings stands in striking contrast to Harland's liberal nominator, who abhorred the bad old days of the previous century and a confessional society. It was the layman F.D. Johnson, however, who seconded Trevor's nomination in 1835 and 1837, who evinced some of the more extreme ill feeling between Anglicans and dissenters and, by extension, conservatives and liberals. In 1835, he seconded Trevor as 'the advocate of those principles, in Church and State,' which, he trusted, were held dear by everyone in Durham, and in 1837, he endorsed Trevor as 'the warm and disinterested advocate and defender of the established religion, and the unflinching opponent of bigotry and fanaticism.'[32] These were Johnson's respective appraisals of the church and of dissent in belief, and of conservatism and liberalism in politics, and were doubtless shared by many.

The third candidate who stood for Durham in the general elections of 1835 and 1837 was Thomas Coalpitts Granger (d.1852) of the Inner Temple. Although clearly to the left of centre, he consistently denied any coalition with Harland, and declared himself to be 'a shade more liberal' than the sitting member.[33] Indeed, on the basis of some of his positions—to say nothing of his temperament—it seems most appropriate to label Granger a radical. He appeared frequently unrestrained, on the hustings and elsewhere, and, on some accounts had launched a vigorous and highly personal attack on Trevor in the run-up to the 1835 contest. Certainly in both 1835 and 1837 he challenged the qualifications of a candidate whom he claimed represented the aristocracy, rather than the electors, of Durham.

In response to conservative allegations that he was a 'Destructive,' Granger admitted he was 'proud of the name. He was a Destructive of every abuse existing in our institutions.... Wherever he could find one, he would pursue it with an unsparing hand....' Moreover,

Granger challenged the right of '[t]hose who accuse Reformers of being Destructive [to] assume ... to themselves the honourable appellation of Conservatives,' accusing them either of hypocrisy, 'or the most profound political aposta[sy].' For those men, the Hon. Arthur Trevor included, had spent their political careers prior to 1832 as opponents to parliamentary reform, but now, in their so-called conservatism, proclaimed themselves the preservers of the reform act. Granger was not satisfied with the explanation given, that the change was due to the fact that the reform bill had become the law of the land.

> Why [he exclaimed], it was the law of the land, at no distant period, to burn old women for witchcraft; and until seven or eight years ago, a peer of the realm might commit highway robbery, rob a church, or steal horses, and this without any punishment for the first offense. [It was ridiculous that t]he laws of the land were to be obeyed while they continued....[34]

In 1837, T.C. Granger laid out a more detailed programme of broad and thoroughgoing reforms, which included voting by secret ballot and the adoption of triennial parliaments.[35] But in the campaigns of 1835 and 1837, he never once engaged those issues which, this study argues, were crucial in the years following the reform act of 1832—he left unmentioned ecclesiastical reform, and failed to state his positions on Catholicism in Ireland or dissent in England.

Nor was he returned in either contest. In both 1835 and 1837, the electors of Durham returned a split representation, with the conservative Arthur Trevor comfortably at the top of the poll, and the incumbent liberal W.C. Harland in second place.[36] In the three contests after the passage of the reform bill, Harland had made it clear that a vote cast for him was a vote cast in favour of dissent and, in Ireland, of Roman Catholics—at the expense of the income and prestige of the establishment. The Hon. Arthur Trevor clearly represented the opposite party, and it followed that, under a ministry which he supported, dissenters and Catholics would be the losers, or at least no very substantial winners. And in a borough noted for its nonconformist chapels as well as its Anglican cathedral, both men evidently had electoral appeal. But it is worthwhile to consider the unsuccessful T.C. Granger more closely. For, as a subsequent chapter elaborates,[37] and in spite of his absolute silence on what are conventionally regarded as dissenters' grievances, the dissenting electorate of Durham unquestionably threw its support behind Granger in 1835, and in 1837 supported him even more strongly than it did Harland. This is most likely due to the strong position Granger took on apprenticeship in the West Indies—the only matter he addressed in detail in 1837, and one with which dissenters identified passionately.[38]

Granger had, he said, repeatedly applauded the abolition of slavery, passed in 1833 and implemented in 1834, but regretted to learn that the plight of West Indian blacks had not improved markedly, and in some cases had deteriorated since emancipation. Colonial slavery had been abolished only in name, Granger argued, and he accused West Indian planters of having committed a £20 million fraud against the nation's taxpayers. He pledged himself to work ceaselessly until the so-called system of 'apprenticeship' was terminated. The fact that Granger's position in this respect, as well as on other liberal or even semi-radical causes, could win over the dissenting electorate so convincingly argues strongly that the nonconformist political interest was as committed to an advanced liberal agenda, as it was merely to narrow and selfish aims of ameliorating the conditions of dissent.[39]

3.4 The 1841 general election in Durham

The Hon. Arthur Trevor, recently elevated to the Irish peerage on the death of his father, declined to stand for the borough in the general election of 1841 and, since Harland had also retired from politics and the conservatives initially put up two candidates, there briefly appeared the possibility that conservatives could claim both seats. In the event, however, a breach between one of the conservative candidates, William Sheppard, and Durham's chief conservative patron, Lord Londonderry (1778–1854), resulted in Sheppard's withdrawal from the race.[40] The other conservative, Capt. Robert FitzRoy (1805–1865),[41] RN, was returned uncontested with the advanced liberal T.C. Granger, and the borough continued its split representation in the House of Commons.

3.5 The April 1843 by-election in Durham

Twenty-one months later, Peel's government appointed FitzRoy governor general of New Zealand, and a by-election was necessary.[42] The next day, on 25 March 1843, Arthur Trevor, now Lord Dungannon, announced his re-entry into politics, declaring himself 'unchanged in principle, [and] unchanged in an anxious desire to serve you....'[43] Liberals in the borough cried foul at the closed dealings of the local conservative interest, and requisitioned Thomas Gisborne to contest the election. Gisborne was already engaged as candidate for Nottingham;[44] however, and for a while it seemed Dungannon's only opposition would be an obscure candidate, James Williams,[45] who presented himself to the borough as a Chartist in all but name, and tellingly included in the list of abuses he opposed '[t]he CORRUPTION OF RELIGION, and the violation of the rights of conscience, by a STATE CHURCH.'[46] At the eleventh hour, however, the day before the poll and only two-and-a-half hours before the nomination, the Anti-Corn Law League agitator John Bright (1811–1889), identified by one authority as 'the most important figure in the history of mid-Victorian radicalism,'[47] arrived in Durham to contest the election.[48] His chief programme was free trade and 'especially [opposition] to the Monopoly in the Nation's Food, created by the Corn-Laws,' but he couched the argument in broader terms of 'battling for the rights of the People [against] the unjust usurpations of the Aristocracy.'[49] Nevertheless, as the contest pitted the Quaker radical Bright against a staunch churchman, its terms of debate could hardly avoid the questions of church and state relations. As John Bright declared a few years later:

> Let it be remembered that I am avowedly a member of a Noncon-formist body. My forefathers languished in prison by the acts of that [i.e. anglican] Church. . . . Within two years places of worship of that body to which I belong have been despoiled of their furniture to pay the salary of a minister of the Established Church; and when I look back and see how that Church has been uniformly hostile to the progress of public liberty, it is impossible for me to refrain from protesting against the outrages committed by the Government on the Nonconformist body for the sake of aggrandizements of a political institution, with which, I hope and believe, the time is not far off when this country will dispense.[50]

As had been the case on the occasions of his two previous nomina-tions, Dungannon was introduced by a clergyman, and the Revd George Townsend (1788–1857), a canon of the cathedral, described an MP's obligations as twofold: first he served his constituency, and second he served 'the general interests of the monarchy, the church, and the public.'[51] In these matters, the Revd Townsend judged, and especially in his service to the Church of England, Dungannon was a particu-larly suitable candidate.[52] A layman seconded the nomination, drawing favourable contrasts between Dungannon's experience as an MP and

Bright's qualifications which, in his judgement, were 'more suited to the meridian of Rochdale or Manchester than to the latitude of the city of Durham.' John Bright was nominated and seconded on the hustings by men who mostly drew attention to the region's economic distress and played upon the anti-aristocratic class antagonisms that often were part of their candidate's rhetoric.

For his part, Dungannon relied on his constituency's past familiarity with him, and gallantly stepped aside, to permit his unknown rival to introduce himself. He merely observed that both he and Bright 'wished to see plenty everywhere—to see our arts, manufactures, and agriculture progressing in improvement....'[53] But Dungannon did not believe in free trade as a magical panacea for all ills and distress.

Bright began his address by discussing the Corn Law, but quickly widened the argument. For agricultural protection, he maintained, was designed wholly and unjustly to favour one class over another. It is easy to see how such an argument could apply to questions of the justness of a privileged state church, and Bright made the connexion explicit, stating 'I am in favour of no monopoly; whether it be a monopoly of legislation, or a monopoly of religion, or a monopoly of commerce.'[54] He closed with a tirade against

> the giant evil...spread through the length and breadth of the island and the empire,...of monopoly, of oppression, of disregard [of] rights..., and of total subserviency to an oligarchy which has brought this mischief on the country....[55]

Bright's expression, it should be noted, applied specifically to the claimed monopoly of the Church of England.

The poll was held the next day amid torrents of April rain and, by the afternoon, it was clear that Dungannon had carried the day with 507 votes. Nevertheless, and especially in view of the brevity of his canvass, Bright managed a respectable showing with 405 votes polled in his favour. Perhaps optimistically, he expressed confidence that, had his canvass been three days rather than two-and-a-half hours, he would have been duly elected for the borough. In his closing address, John Bright again identified the church as an illiberal force in Durham, attributing his defeat to the combined 'weight of Cathedral and Aristocratic influence against' what he judged to be the borough's natural tendency to liberalism.[56]

He fell back on familiar ground, addressing the merits of free trade generally and the repeal of the Corn Law specifically, and reiterated his opposition to all monopolies, whether commercial, legislative or, significantly, religious.[57] Next Bright hurled sharper barbs at the church, asserting that 'no class of people in this country [was] more interested in the maintenance of the Corn-laws than the Clergy of the Church of England.' In this he referred to the terms of the tithe commutation act, which calculated the clergy's revenue based on the yield of the land—or, as Bright provocatively and rather disingenuously put it, on the price of bread. Consequently, he said, the 'enormous influence' of the clergy was most reprehensibly, 'in almost all the parishes of England, ... bound up in the conservation of [the Corn Law—]the most unjust, the most oppressive, and the most destructive enactment which ever was recorded upon the statute book of this or any county.'[58] He continued:

> It is a most unhappy circumstance that any body of men holding their position in society, assuming sacred functions, professing themselves the ministers of the purest system of morality and religion ever known upon earth, men who call upon you to leave the grovelling things of earth, and all the miserable dross and tinsel by which you are surrounded; to direct your thoughts to higher and holier objects; to carry your aspirations towards heaven rather than stoop to the things of earth,—I say it is a misfortune that by a law made by the Parliament of the country, this body of men, especially appointed to take charge of the flock, should, instead of being the shepherds, appear to all men's eyes as the shearers of the flock; and that their enormous influence should, in almost all the parishes in England, be bound up in the conservation of the most odious, the most unjust, the most oppressive, and the most destructive enactment which was ever recorded upon the statute-book of this or any other country.[59]

On this searing note, having connected the controversy over Corn Law repeal inextricably to the broader issue of the place of an established and privileged church in a society whose law claimed to enshrine the principle of civil and religious liberty, John Bright left Durham immediately, in order to arrive in London in time for an Anti-Corn Law League meeting the next night.[60]

Dungannon's victory address defended the landed classes, and emphasized 'a connecting link between all classes of society [i]n this country...If one falls, the other will fall in turns....'[61] He acknowledged the severity of the depression, but again rejected the impolicy of turning to naïve theories of trade which threatened to drain bullion into foreign coffers. Dungannon said little specifically in regard to religion, besides drawing attention to the Christian duty which inspired all his actions, but Mr Johnson, who nominated the conservative candidate in 1835 and 1837 and had on both occasions intemperately abused dissenters, was not above poking fun at the defeated Quaker candidate, whom he repeatedly and sarcastically labelled as 'Friend Bright,' gleefully jibing that 'everything that is *bright* and glittering is not always to be relied upon.'[62]

3.6   The July 1843 by-election in Durham

But the conservative triumph was short-lived, for the result of the poll was petitioned against, the election voided, and Dungannon unseated three months later. He retired from the House of Commons,[63] and John Bright stood as the Anti-Corn Law League candidate in the consequent by-election that summer.

Bright was in London when the vacancy was announced, but commenced his canvass immediately, with the circulation of a handbill which, in general terms, praised free trade and criticized the pervasive and destructive influence of the aristocracy in Durham.[64] Two days later, he addressed what one contemporary described as perhaps the largest assemblage ever in Durham, and began his speech by raving against the monarchy, aristocracy and House of Lords. He condemned legislation proposed by conservatives which made education available to working-class children only through the lens of Anglican religious instruction, and alleged that—in this respect and others—the present conservative government catered only to certain interests, such as West Indian planters, the wealthy, those betrothed to English princesses and, significantly, the clergy.[65] John Bright proceeded to elaborate in detail each of these interests—including, apparently, those with designs on an English princess![66]—but unfortunately the handbill's state of preservation has rendered the rest of the text illegible. What remains clear, however, is that Bright recognized certain interests which he claimed were inherently inimical to those of the people, and that one of these was the established Church of England.[67]

John Bright began his speech following the nomination with an expected attack on protectionist policies, but quickly shifted gears, to condemn the present ministry's positions on education and Ireland.[68] In the former respect, he rejected any government-funded scheme of education encumbered with doctrinal instruction, and in the latter, he commiserated with Irish opposition to the Irish arms bill and other grievances:[69]

They complain of the Established Church of Ireland as a grievance; and so it must be admitted to be, when only one in ten of the population belong to the Church. It is just as unfair to have a Protestant establishment sweeping up the ecclesiastical revenues there, as it would be for a Romish establishment in England to sweep up all the ecclesiastical revenues of this island.[70]

John Bright returned briefly to Corn Law repeal and his credentials as a free trader, and then advanced a blatantly incendiary proposition regarding the inevitability, and even desirability, of revolutionary action. He asserted that history had never known a revolution that had hurt the general people. He acknowledged with satisfaction that revolutions had toppled kings, ministers, governments, and even churches—but Bright regarded all these as expendable institutions in comparison to the welfare of the people.[71]

Bright's opponent was Thomas Purvis, a barrister, who 'stood on the independent (i.e. anti-Londonderry) Conservative interest.'[72] So far as we can tell, Purvis never elaborated his political agenda much beyond a bland inclination 'to support the Conservative principles which have placed the present Administration in power'[73] and Bright's personal appraisal of the man was

'All we know of hi[m] is, that nothing can be known.'[74]

Bright won the by-election on 26 July, with 488 votes polled and a majority of 78 over Purvis's 410, and the conservative *Durham Advertiser* waxed indignant that '[t]he hitherto-considered Conservative City of Durham has now to submit to the galling imputation of having been the first in the empire to return a Chartist to the House of Commons—for, although he successfully managed to conceal this fact, there is no doubt that Mr Bright's political principles are founded on Chartism.'[75]

It was alleged that a number of 'dignitaries of the Cathedral Church in Durham' had voted for Bright and,[76] as an exponent of the Anglican establishment and adamant in its belief that only its true advocates were conservative, the *Advertiser* fumed against those '[c]ertain dignitaries' who had

given their support to a man who scoffs at Church principles—who would pull down the Church as willingly as abolish the Corn-Laws—who [opposes educating the factory poor] because such a measure would tend to strengthen the establishment; and whose principal supporters, both in point of station and in numbers, received every mention of the word Church... with peals of laughter or yells of derision and scorn.

The *Advertiser* continued:

We reverence the office of a minister of religion, and we would not cast reflections upon the Clergy, even where we think their conduct reprehensible were not that conduct such as to involve a most weighty, a most important principle. But, when we see ministers of the Church voting for a Quaker, in opposition to a Churchman— when we see those who should be most anxious to uphold, to strengthen, and to extend the Church—oppose a gentleman, whose most earnest desire is to do that which their position renders it a duty incumbent upon them to do, and support one who would abolish the Church—the question becomes a most grave one, and renders it impossible for a public journalist, who has the interests of the Church at heart, to refrain from animated version, however painful that duty may be. Had the candidate been a friend of the Church and a Whig, we should not have thought it necessary to allude to the matter—we never conceived that Whiggery, in the abstract, was incompatible with any disciple of its being a good Churchman; but when the candidate was a rabid dissenter—a man notorious in his own neighbourhood for the most vexatious attempts to annoy and injure the Church—one, moreover, in favour of the levelling principles [of universal suffrage]....[77]

Unfortunately, the state of preservation of this number of the *Durham Advertiser* obliterated the close of this colourful passage, but the gist is obvious, and the implication is equally clear. There existed an inextricable relationship between conservative principles and the established institutions of the state and of society—the keystone of which was the Church of England. The relationship was, or ought to have been, the *Advertiser* believed, inviolate: the interests of conservatism and of Anglicanism were fundamentally the same. Conservative government bolstered the church and defended its interests, and it was therefore incumbent—if nothing else, out of self-interest—on its ministers and officials to take an active role in promoting such a state of affairs. And if the fortunes of the church were linked to conservative political interests, they must by association be tied to the interests of privilege and aristocracy—indeed, John Bright seemed to regard the several interests as virtually one.

3.7   The 1847 general election in Durham

Once again, three candidates contested the representation of Durham in the general election of 1847. T.C. Granger, incumbent since his uncontested return in 1841, stood for the liberal interest, along with a local JP and president of the North Durham Reform Association, Henry John Spearman (1794–1866), and Capt. Sir David Edward Wood (1812–1894), who had been invited by his uncle to stand for the borough, stood for the conservative interest.

Granger's nominator praised his nominee for his connexion and sympathies with Durham and his exemplary attention to parliamentary duties, and summed up his character as 'a friend of civil and religious liberty, [and] an enemy to all abuses, let them exist as they will.' The other candidates' credentials were rather more vague: Spearman's nomination consisted mostly of a eulogium on John Bright, and Capt. Wood's principal recommendations were, first, that he was a soldier and, second, that he was not Thomas Granger! As his nominator said, the borough had had Granger for six years: 'I say, try Capt. Wood....'[78]

Granger's address from the hustings confirmed his liberal sympathies, and especially his intention to 'do all in [his] power to promote the cause of civil and religious liberty....' He deemed it necessary, however, to account for certain parliamentary votes which he believed might have offended some of his most strenuous supporters. In one instance, he referred to an educational grant proposed by Russell's liberal government, and in this respect he admitted having voted, reluctantly, for the government's measure. His reluctance was based chiefly on 'a very great defect in [the bill]: [that] a large body of our fellow-citizens were excluded from its benefits.' Granger referred to Roman Catholics, and in an argument which he hoped would appeal to dissenters, deemed it gross injustice that any denomination should be compelled to contribute to the state, without the full benefits derived from that taxation. Granger was 'not prepared to make concessions to one [religious] party in preference of another...,' and, in spite of his high regard for the principle of voluntary education in theory, had found that, in practice, voluntary exertions in this respect were simply inadequate.[79] Granger also admitted, on similar grounds of pragmatism, having voted in favour of the Maynooth grant. 'But though [he] concurred in that grant, [Granger was] not prepared to agree to any grant, of money or privileges to any sect even including the established church itself.' The grant to Maynooth, by comparison, was educational, not religious, and it assisted a state-supported school of longstanding.[80]

Granger's supporters whom he feared having disappointed with these votes unquestionably were the nonconformist component of the Durham electorate who, as an extension of their animosity to a connexion between church and state, tended to oppose government intervention in education. Nonetheless, Granger had stood by his conscience and, in spite of these votes, remained confident that dissenters supported his liberal agenda.[81]

Captain Wood addressed the constituents next. He acknowledged himself a political novice, with no parliamentary career either to recommend him or to justify, and offered no pledge beyond his desire to 'uphold the Constitution in Church and State....' He maintained that Anglicanism must be preserved as an establishment of the state, to prevent the decay and loss of every vestige of religiosity. 'The same power that separates the Church from the State,' he warned, 'could turn the noble edifices that adorn your city into theatres for debating on the equilibrium of arches, or the expansion or contraction of metals....' This was the direction in which the government of Lord John Russell was leading the country, Capt. Wood insisted, and liberal legislation was designed not to secure civil and religious liberty, but rather to stamp out all religion.[82]

Wood's words regarding dissent are harder to grasp. He acknowledged that there was a great want of religious instruction, particularly in the northeast, and that times were hard, especially for those engaged in mining or mechanical pursuits. He further conceded that it was the ministers of the dissenting sects who carried out the lion's share of consoling the populace, and bringing the gospel to the region. But Capt. Wood contended that if he and likeminded men were returned to parliament, much might be done to relieve the poor of their present burdens.[83] Thus he implied a conservative government would do a better job than a liberal one of easing the poverty suffered in the northeast and elsewhere, and once that was accomplished, the Church of England would assume its proper role and take care of the rest! Regardless of the illogic of Capt. Wood's proposals, and despite what he probably intended as a palliative acknowledgement of the efforts of dissenting ministers, what remains clear is his high regard for the church, and his scarcely concealed contempt for dissent.

The rest of his address was equally bizarre. In what reads almost like a parody of incoherence and cant, he spoke of Napoleon and Hindus,

Oregon and Jamaica, Afghanistan and India. He praised the innovators of Durham for their efforts to extract nitrogen from the atmosphere, to improve dyeing techniques, and to apply the principles of lightning to assist in communication. He expressed interest in emigration and colonization, boasted of having read government reports, and prided himself on discerning the differences between North America, Cape Colony, Berbice, and Van Dieman's Land! He claimed to have read widely on agriculture and commerce, and implied it was difficult to know whether a liberal or a conservative government was better suited to handle the intricacies of such diverse and weighty matters![84] Captain Wood concluded: 'As a plain soldier, I have spoken my mind, and resign my lot into your hands, with many thanks for favours already conferred.'[85] If it is impossible to gauge precisely what agenda Capt. Wood proposed to advance, it is telling that he declared himself a conservative and, in his few instances of lucidity, made plain his championing of the church, and his unfriendliness to those outside it.

The sense of the political programme advanced by the third candidate, H.J. Spearman, was easier to follow: he had opposed the late conservative ministry and advocated reform. Spearman did not address religion directly, but from his lengthy assessment of the just grievances of the Irish, it is obvious he championed the rights of those outside the establishment, and his words would have carried appeal for nonconformist electors.[86] He was returned with his fellow liberal, T.C. Granger, and Capt. Wood returned to life 'as a plain soldier,' serving with distinction both in the Crimean War and the aftermath of the Indian Mutiny.[87]

3.8   Durham: conclusion

In short, religion was a lively topic in every election for Durham City in the decade-and-a-half following the reform act, and most candidates made clear their preference either for preserving the rights of the establishment or extending privileges outside the Church of England. Candidates evidently recognized the number and electoral significance of nonconformists, and even those who defended the church tried to avoid unnecessarily alienating dissenters.

4
Religion and Politics in an Industrial Midland City: The Case of Nottingham

4.1 Nottingham: Introduction*

It is not so easy to summarize the course of parliamentary elections in Nottingham, which experienced 11 elections during the years 1832 to 1847.[1] If more complex than the Durham elections of the same period, the proceedings in Nottingham also tended to be less edifying, and outright bribery and riot were as likely influences on electors as issues of policy. In the 1841 general election, in which fewer than 700 electors polled, the liberal candidates lavished £12,000 on the borough, and the conservatives £5000—or nearly £25 per voter. The same election was marred by violence ranging from fists and occasional spencerings[2] at one end, to stones, brickbats, and knives at the other. Many people were injured, and several were stabbed. In the confusion, one candidate was pick-pocketed on the hustings, and another feared himself constantly 'in danger almost of [his] life.'[3] The *Nottingham Review* reported that

> A thick bludgeon, with a spike three inches long was handed to the Mayor, said to have been taken from some person on the hustings; the confusion was so great, that we could not ascertain from whom the deadly weapon was taken.[4]

---

* Located on the River Trent, the borough of Nottingham was a county-town and chief seat of the hose and lace manufactures. Its population increased from 50,680 to 57,407 between 1832 and 1851, and its registered electorate increased from 5220 to 5260 between 1832 and 1852. In addition to cotton and silk hose and lace, its economic interests included shoe-making and accessory operations such as dyeing, frame- and engine-making, and so on. *Dod's* reports little or no personal electoral influence in the borough, although the conservative duke of Newcastle owned much property in the neighbourhood.

49

Police proved insufficient to maintain order, and a company of the 3rd Dragoons was called out to patrol the streets at night. As the biographer of one MP for the borough observed, 'A Nottingham candidate led a hazardous and expensive life at voting time.'[5]

Although liberals in Nottingham managed to maintain both seats in the House of Commons throughout the 1830s (as indeed they had since the first decade of the century), strong dissatisfaction among the working classes with the new poor law, passed by the liberal Melbourne ministry in 1834, prompted an 'unholy alliance'[6] of the town's Tories and radical working classes to oust a liberal candidate. The rest of the period was tainted with further allegations of bribery on both sides, leading to a flurry of petitions, parliamentary commissions and inquiries, voided elections and by-elections—as well as some back-room negotiations between the parties, to reach compromise and avoid scandal. Yet through all these murky machinations, as we shall see, the beacons lighted by burning questions of church and dissent still shone through.

4.2   The 1832 general election in Nottingham

In a handbill dated 28 November 1832, two weeks before the election of the first reformed House of Commons, the conservative Lt James Edward Gordon (1789–1864) announced his candidacy and laid out his policy.[7] Lieutenant Gordon emphasized first his 'INDEPENDENCE, in the fullest and most unrestrained sense of the term,' and then described a political creed based on tried and true protestantism.

> The ground-work of my political, as well as my religious profes-sion of faith [he stated], is PROTESTANTISM—the Protestantism of the Bible and the British Constitution—the Protestantism, in other words, which combines the religious principles of the Reformation, with the political principles of the Revolution of 1688. Within the limits of that creed are to be found the true standards of religious and moral obligation, and the only safe principles of legislation in a Protestant State.[8]

Earlier associations with broader-based evangelicalism having given away to an uncompromising Anglicanism and, most especially, vehe-ment anti-Catholicism, Lt Gordon had gone so far as to attempt a second protestant reformation in Ireland![9] Clearly his domestic policy would be defined by rigorous attention to protestant religion.

Similarly, in matters of foreign and colonial affairs, Lt Gordon claimed guidance by Christian principles. He was determined to end slavery immediately (though he insisted on adequate compensation for the owners), advocated a foreign policy of non-intervention, and sought for all colonists the same civil and religious rights found in Britain.[10] The precise sense of such a position, of course, is ambiguous, for it must imply limits and restrictions as well as extensions or openness.

Lieutenant Gordon reiterated much the same positions from the hustings, repeating that

The great cardinal principles on which [he built his] creed are the protestant religion and the principles of the reformation....Those constitutional principles gave birth to our present religious and political liberty, and if separated they would be but a disjointed skeleton.— There must of necessity be a connexion between the constitution and the principles of the reformation; if you wish to see the example of political principle separated from religious feeling, look across the ocean, where——[11]

Here Gordon was cut off by groans, hisses and roars, and cries of 'Let religion alone.' Only partial order was restored, although Lt Gordon was able to restate his conviction that 'the genius of christianity' was linked both to abolitionism and 'the spirit of the British constitution.' Earlier in the week, Gordon had condemned slavery as against the laws of god and man.[12] His address concluded with some comment on the church but, a contemporary account observes, no one listened or heard.[13]

Avowed coalitions were not regarded as anathema in Nottingham as they were in other districts,[14] and the two other candidates, Gen. Sir Ronald Crawford Ferguson (1773–1841),[15] KCB, and John William Ponsonby (1781–1847), Viscount Duncannon, made no effort to conceal their alignment with one another in standing for the borough's liberal interest. They conducted their canvass together, and printed a single handbill to announce their candidacies.[16] Though the message of the handbill was not so permeated with the language of religion as was Lt Gordon's, its more succinct reference on the matter was more specific than anything Gordon produced. Ferguson and Duncannon affirmed themselves friendly to the extinction of tithes, whose system, they claimed, created enmity between ministers and their flock; and they were committed to all reform within the establishment which tended to make the church of England more conducive to its original purpose, namely 'the spread of true Religion.'[17]

On the hustings, Thomas Wakefield[18] summed up his nomination for the incumbent liberal by invoking those who supported the repeal of monopolies, the removal of taxes on knowledge, emancipation of the Negro, as well as church reform, to vote for Gen. Ferguson. Mr Alderman Oldknow seconded the motion on the recommendation of Ferguson's 26 years of consistent behaviour in championing the liberties of the people, most of that time in the face of tory ministries and when such advanced positions were unpopular in the House of Commons. Oldknow drew particular attention to Ferguson's support, while representing the Kirkcaldy burghs, for Catholic emancipation and the repeal of the test and corporation acts.[19] General Ferguson opened his address in a similar vein: he said that he had come to Nottingham in 1830 'a steady supporter of civil and religious liberty, [and] an advocate of reform in every branch of the state. . . . '[20] He recalled the bad old days—when only six or seven MPs had championed liberal causes—when Wilberforce annually introduced his motion to end the slave trade, and Pitt made a flowery defence of it. But, Ferguson emphasized, the determination of Charles James Fox, after only six months in office, had been enough to end the trade forthright.[21] General Ferguson's invocation of the memory of Fox is suggestive, for another great cause associated with him and his short-lived ministry of all the talents—the only whig ministry in 50 years—had been unflinching support for Roman Catholic emancipation, for which position George III promptly threw the government out. Ferguson pronounced the tenor of the country suitably altered since the beginning of the century: it was more in step with his continued advocacy of religious liberty which, he allowed, extended to a greater degree than was found in most people. He believed 'that every man who worships God conscientiously, and obeys the laws, [wa]s entitled to the right of a citizen.'[22] Ferguson advocated church reform, on the principle that pay ought to be commensurate with service, but he 'would take away all great salaries for doing nothing.'[23]

Viscount Duncannon stood for Nottingham with both the endorsement of Lord Althorp (1782–1845), his patron and relative, and Daniel O'Connell, Irish MP, leader of the Catholics in parliament, and chief agitator for the previous decade for ameliorating conditions in Ireland. George Augustus Henry Anne Parkyns, 2nd Baron Lord Rancliffe,[24] nominated Duncannon, and slipped into a characteristic diatribe. He had always regarded it as a *sine qua non* that 'overgrown churchmen [should not receive between £35,000 and £40,000 p.a.] to appear in the House of Lords in fancy dresses, to oppose the rights of the people. . . . '[25] Instead they ought, as ministers of god, to tend to the needs of the people. Francis Hart esquire seconded the nomination, asserting that Duncannon's previous conduct spoke for itself: as MP for various constituencies,[26] he had fought side by side with Gen. Ferguson for civil and religious liberty. Hart declared finances to be in a parlous state, and affirmed that a ministry with the support of Ferguson and Duncannon would 'apply *both* to *church* and *state*' the principle 'that every useless office should be reduced....'[27] Viscount Duncannon offered himself to the electors of Nottingham on a platform similar to, if more detailed than, that of his colleague, Ferguson. He stood for a litany of reforms, '[f]irst, and most important' of which was to reform the Church of England. As an Anglican, Duncannon did not seek to destroy the establishment, 'but,' he stated, 'I cannot shut my eyes to its abuses, and I shall therefore support the abolition of sinecures, pluralities, and a complete revision of the system of tithes.'[28]

Nottingham was as swept up in the tide of the reform crisis of 1830–1832 as any other district of England, and the polls on 11 and 12 December confirmed this: Gen. Ferguson and Viscount Duncannon led with a convincing margin—2386 and 2338, against 912 votes cast for Lt Gordon. But despite the clear priority reform received in the election, it evidently was not the candidates' or the electorate's only concern. The intersection of reform politics with religion, particularly as it applied to the favoured position of the church in state, was a great issue. The conservative Lt J.E. Gordon committed himself to protestantism (and for Gordon, this meant Anglicanism) as the surest formula for maintaining British prosperity and pre-eminence; Gen. Gordon and Viscount Duncannon both declared themselves hostile to tithe, critical of abuses in the establishment, and open to widespread reform of the church. Although neither liberal expressly appealed to dissenters or proposed legislation uniquely favourable to them, Ferguson and Duncannon drew attention to their previous parliamentary careers, and their involvement in securing the repeal of the test and corporation acts. It was obvious they represented the party of civil and religious liberty, and Lt Gordon of continued Anglican primacy.

4.3 The July 1834 by-election in Nottingham

General Ferguson retained the representation of the borough until his death in 1841, but Viscount Duncannon's tenure of office lasted only 19 months, until his appointment to the cabinet as home secretary, and elevation to the House of Lords.[29] As Baron Duncannon, he took leave of the electors of the borough in a handbill dated 18 July 1834, and thanked them for the support they had extended him a year-and-a-half earlier, at which point all that was known of him in Nottingham was his devotion to Fox and Grey, 'in asserting the principles of Civil and Religious Liberty and Reform....'[30] The consequent by-election was a week later, on the 25th, and the corporation invited Sir John Cam Hobhouse (1786–1869), the cabinet minister and erstwhile radical MP, to stand for the borough. No conservative bothered to attempt to claim the vacancy, and the expected result might have been an easy and uncontested return for Sir John. But the radicalism of his earlier career in parliament, when he forcefully advocated far-reaching reforms, including those affecting dissent, had faded since 1832, and especially since his taking office in the Grey ministry. Previously he had lambasted '[t]he contemptible Whigs'; now he was one of them.[31] Critics alluded to Hobhouse's support for the coercion bill, his opposition to the ballot and triennial parliaments, and 'charge[d] him with being a political apostate.'[32] Moreover, the corporation, notorious for its tight and corrupt hold on the borough, had invited Hobhouse without consulting the electors. Many resented such highhanded dealings, and opponents requisitioned William Eagle to stand for the borough, and rescue Nottingham from corporation dictation—a condition they claimed was little different from that of Gatton and Sarum.[33]

Eagle's nomination consisted of affirmations of his own radical credentials and attacks on the conduct of his rival candidate. Mr J. Boothby junior seconded him and mentioned a list of reforms Eagle would pursue, including equal rights for religious denominations outside the establishment.

> To the dissenters [Boothby declared], a large and important class, to which I am proud to say I belong, [Mr Eagle] does not give a vague pledge about his willingness to remove practical grievances, but honestly states his intention of endeavouring to do away with all laws, which give any particular privileges to a favored sect, and to leave Christianity to the support bequeathed to it by its Divine founder, the voluntary support of those who love and embrace it....Oh where is the Dissenter, to whom these sentiments are not the very life blood of his religious principles![34]

Eagle's own remarks tackled the practices of the Nottingham corporation, which threatened to render the reform act a dead letter. Whigs had been in office for three-and-a-half years but, Eagle contended, the country had advanced in no substantive way, and had retreated in others. Dissenters' grievances, for instance, remained unresolved. 'Perhaps the tories will not give religious freedom,' he predicted; 'no more will the whigs....' But one goal was a primary concern of Eagle's: he 'object[ed] to all compulsory payment in support of the Ministers of any religion.'[35]

Perhaps to avoid simply reiterating a previous statement, of which no account remains, Sir John spoke only for a short time. His words sought reconciliation, offered only a brief rebuttal of criticism, and did not engage the current plight of dissenters.

A show of hands at the nomination was reported overwhelmingly in favour of Eagle, but the result of the actual contest was the reverse, with Hobhouse polling nearly three votes for every one cast for Eagle.[36] A general election was called less than six months later, and Eagle declined to stand again; Gen. Ferguson and Sir John Cam Hobhouse were returned without contest.[37]

4.4   The 1835 general election in Nottingham

Formal nomination was still necessary, however, and Hobhouse was introduced by Francis Hart esquire, who, perhaps eager to deflect charges of an inadequate record in this respect, plumped Sir John as a 'stern and unflinching advocate of civil and religious liberty.' John Heard esquire— an alderman, a magistrate and a Baptist[38]—seconded the motion and, perhaps with an agenda similar to that of Hart, allowed that the only reproach that could with justice be levelled against the whigs was the cautious speed with which they advanced reform. But, Heard insisted, the Tamworth Manifesto, issued by Sir Robert Peel, the leader of the conservatives, had made one thing clear: 'the Tories were unchanged. [T]he *old* Tories, the *do nothing* Tories,' intended to reform neither the church nor anything else.[39]

4.5   The 1837 general election in Nottingham

The next general election followed the death of William IV and the accession of Victoria, in the summer of 1837. Initially, the two conservative candidates, C.C. Martyn and Horace Twiss (1787–1849), sought to unseat the incumbent liberals. Martyn attributed the achievement of national grandeur to the conservative cause generally, which he deemed best effected by sustaining the well-balanced power of the three estates unimpaired in independence, 'and by steadfastly preserving the connexion of the State with our Established Protestant Church.'[40]

Friendly to the true reform of proven abuses, he would, however, oppose all efforts to degrade or impair the independence of the church, no matter what the pretext.[41] This position, Martyn maintained, was nothing short of the orthodox 'Parliamentary conduct of the most eminent Conservative Statesmen,' and was perfectly 'consistent with a due regard for the religious freedom of all classes of the community.... '[42] But C.C. Martyn withdrew from the contest the third week of July[43] and was replaced by William Henry Chichely Plowden, (1790–1880), FRS. Like Martyn, Plowden was conservative in matters of religion, and strongly opposed any concession to the Roman Catholic clergy.[44]

Horace Twiss, the other conservative candidate, had, while a member for Newport, strongly opposed the reform bill at every stage, although he had earlier supported Roman Catholic emancipation, and continued to entertain certain other liberal measures. The only statement of policy Twiss made in the handbill announcing his candidacy for Nottingham was his earnest support for the Church of England. He promised to address other issues in person.[45]

General Ferguson and Sir John Cam Hobhouse jointly announced their candidacy in a handbill dated from London.[46] Both cited their long association with and continued commitment to reform, especially the securement of equal rights for all classes of British subjects, regardless of local advantage or religious affiliation. Regarding Ireland, Ferguson and Hobhouse insisted that that island could not, with safety or justice, be denied the liberties which previous governments had bestowed on the rest of the kingdom, and they called to bear their parliamentary record on the issue. They highlighted as well their votes in the House of Commons to undo scandalous legislation which maintained disadvantages for Roman Catholics or dissenters.[47] More specifically, Ferguson and Hobhouse were committed to having 'the church rate abolished [and] the blessings of education extended to the Irish poor....'[48]

At the nomination, Mr Alderman Heard esquire, a member of Nottingham's General Baptist Foreign Missionary Society,[49] discussed the importance of the questions which faced the next parliament. These included the abolition of the church rate, and the extension of civil rights to the inhabitants of Ireland, from which they were presently barred on account of the their religion. On both issues, Heard assured his audience, the positions of the liberal candidates were perfectly satisfactory.[50] Thomas Wakefield esquire—ward counsellor, late town mayor, and a nonconformist[51]—acknowledged that some local proponents of reform expressed dissatisfaction with the present ministry, and especially Hobhouse, for the lack of progress, particularly in regard to dissenters' grievances.[52] Perhaps uncomfortable with drawing attention to his more recent record, which evidently a significant bloc of his erstwhile supporters judged inadequate, Sir John dwelt instead on his earlier career: the conflict over the repeal of the test and corporation acts, and the division between whigs and tories over that matter.[53]

In spite of any misgivings on the part of some of the borough's reformers or nonconformists, the town's liberal dominance continued to assert itself: the electorate returned Sir John and Gen. Ferguson with comfortable majorities.[54]

4.6   The April 1841 by-election in Nottingham

But the first effective challenge to the liberal ascendancy in Nottingham was on the horizon. The circumstance that occasioned it was widespread opposition to the new poor laws, and the opportunity was the death of Gen. Ferguson, on 10 April 1841. The general's death meant an election and probably a contest, which the liberal *Nottingham Review* anticipated with unease.[55] John Walter senior (1776–1847), long-time manager and chief proprietor of *The Times*, and George Gerard de Hochepied Larpent (1786–1855), a successful East Indian merchant whose family was ultimately of French Protestant origin and had settled in England after the revocation of the edict of Nantes, contested the borough.

A virtually unknown political novice,[56] Larpent began his address before a meeting of liberal electors of Nottingham answering the question 'Who and what are you?'[57] Larpent answered by focusing first on his commercial background, as a dealer in lace, hosiery and woollen goods, and his consequent familiarity with the interests and concerns of a manufacturing town, as well as his support for free trade in virtually every circumstance. Much of the rest of his answer engaged questions of religious liberty and especially those relevant to dissenters. Larpent identified himself as 'A member of the council for . . . London University, the object of which [wa]s to withdraw from the trammels of bigotry the classes who do not belong to the established church.'[58] He was a churchman, and stoutly attached to the rituals of the Church of England, but altogether objected to the church rates. . . . He stated this strongly, because he did feel . . . that the religious part of the community, dissenting from the Church in principle, had no right to be compelled to support the Church.'[59] Larpent added that he was eager to find a viable substitute to provide for the upkeep of parish churches, but was adamant that any proposed alternative must not 'affect...the principles of the dissenters.'[60]

Walter ran ostensibly as a conservative, although bound in what unfriendly contemporaries called an 'unnatural coalition' with the working classes, to whom his vigorous attacks on the poor law had great appeal.[61] The editors of the *Nottingham Review* reproached him for his silence on most other matters, particularly the question of the church rate. It marvelled that Walter could expect the support of any nonconformist, 'without a word on the rights of Dissenters, or their freedom from church rates!'[62] But Walter's single-minded commitment to attacking the poor law worked in his favour.

The conservative candidate's appeal to the working classes and the division in the liberal ranks, not unnaturally, rather confused expected patterns at the nomination on 23 April. T.B. Charlton esquire, who would himself stand as a conservative at the general election ten weeks later, began his introduction of Walter by invoking the spirit of 'the true Whigs of 1689,' as opposed to 'the false Whigs of 1831.'[63] Walter himself attacked his opponent's position especially on the Church of England, and questioned how a man who claimed to admire and respect the church could conscientiously do everything to weaken it. Singling out his opponent's hostility to the church rate, Walter declared Larpent 'more destructive than Lord John Russell himself,' who at least proposed to find a suitable replacement before implementing abolition.[64] For his part, Walter would not consider abolishing the church rate.[65]

Francis Hart esquire, a recently appointed county magistrate, nominated the liberal candidate, recommending Larpent as a firm friend of civil and religious liberty, 'which is a most important qualification for one who is to make laws for a free country.'[66] Supporters of Walter drowned out Larpent's opening words with hoots, howls, and jeers, but when Larpent was finally able to speak, he drew attention to the fact that Walter's first nominator, William Boworth, had spoken at some length, but addressed only a single matter, the new poor law. That, according to Larpent, was because Mr Boworth, a former mayor of Nottingham, was in many ways a liberal, while Mr Walter opposed reform thoroughly. Walter's own speech, Larpent continued, was an almost unrelieved harangue on the single issue of the poor law, and the only substantive semblance of principle Walter had revealed, as regards the great questions of civil and religious liberty, was wholly unsatisfactory.[67]

Next the liberal candidate engaged the rumour that had circulated the town, and to which Walter had alluded, that Larpent was in reality a Frenchman![68] Larpent responded directly to a demand that he must prove himself an Englishman:

> Gentlemen, I was born and bred an Englishman. My father was born and bred an Englishman. My grandfather was born and bred an Englishman. My great-grandfather, 155 years ago, became an exile from his native country, because he was made a martyr in the great cause of religious freedom. It was because he preferred his religious freedom to the caprices of a tyrant that he became an exile. Persecuted by Louis XIV, he took refuge in this country, which he considered as the refuge of liberty, and it was that which made him adopt as his motto—'Where liberty is, there is my country.'[69]

'[Larpent] felt he still had left some of the blood of the Huguenot, and it boiled with indignation at persecution for religious opinions.'[70] He counted as nothing his opponent's claim to descent from Alfred the Great, if Walter could not demonstrate having ever done anything to advance the civil and religious liberties of Englishmen.[71] Larpent accepted Lord Rancliffe's designation as 'a Whig, and something more,' and claimed to 'have too much of the blood of the old Reformers in [him] to sanction any impost that could be regarded as a tax upon conscience.'[72]

Walter enjoyed a comfortable lead for the duration of the poll, and at the end of the day had claimed 1983 votes against Larpent's 1745.[73] As the *Nottingham Review* lamented, the 'No-workhouse men' and Chartists abandoned their old standards, splitting the liberals into factions, and allowing a tory victory. Notably, '[w]hat remained to [Larpent], faithful under his banners, were the Whigs, the Dissenters, and a small portion of the Radicals. ... [Y]et the other parties being united against them, the battle was lost. ...'[74]

But Walter's tenure as MP for Nottingham would not long interrupt the primacy of the liberals in the borough. As the London *Globe* put it, Mr Walter's political history in Nottingham may be comprised in one line:—

'He went up like a rocket, and fell—like its stick.'[75]

Early in the summer of 1841, the Melbourne ministry lost a vote of confidence, and the nation faced a general election. The incumbents, Hobhouse and Walter, stood again, Larpent presented himself once more, and T.B. Charlton appeared for the first time as a candidate.

4.7   The 1841 general election in Nottingham

The liberal government had fallen partly over issues of free trade, and their decision to go whole-hog with a proposal of a low fixed duty on corn naturally made protection the main issue in the ensuing election.[76] Religion consequently received less attention than in it did in other contests. In a happy coincidence of principle and perceptiveness, however, G.G. de H. Larpent trumpeted the persistence of religion in the struggle between the forces of liberalism and conservatism. In his letter accepting the requisition to stand again for the borough, Larpent asserted that the nation stood divided between two parties, and that he identified himself with the one best representing 'the true principles of civil and religious liberty....'[77]

A more seasoned politician than Larpent, and a cabinet minister,[78] Sir John Cam Hobhouse toed the party line and devoted most of his attention to the desirability of repealing or reducing various tariffs and duties.[79] But Hobhouse's rank and file liberal supporters bore out the reality of Larpent's observation, that 'the great town of Nottingham still [wa]s—as it had been for ages—one of the chief strongholds of that party and of those principles.'[80] At a meeting of liberal supporters, it was moved that, especially in a constituency as large as Nottingham's, it was impossible to have a complete agreement on issues, but that Sir John was nonetheless a good man.[81] Despite his recent apparent insensitivity to the question, they affirmed, Sir John 'had ever stood the firm friend of civil and religious liberty.'[82] This, for liberals of Nottingham, was the touchstone around which they all could rally.[83]

The election that followed was remarkable on several counts, which do not bear directly on the present study. Suffice to say that the two liberals won, although under peculiar circumstances, which included a voter turnout of less than 15 per cent.[84] Many notable nonconformists were present at the chairing of the members, and 'the show of colours and ladies was exceedingly grand' as the procession passed the homes of Dr Alliott and Mr Higginbottom, both dissenters and the latter chair of the Nottingham Tee-total organization.[85]

4.8   Controversy following the general election

Inevitably, the circumstances of the general election prompted a petition, but this was withdrawn, most likely because a committee of investigation would have uncovered incriminating evidence against the activities of Walter and Charlton, as well as Larpent and Hobhouse.

Walter was alleged already to have paid out £15,000 for the April by-election (for a seat, as liberals gleefully pointed out, that he held only seven weeks), and to have laid out close to £5000 more in June. The parties reached a compromise the following summer, whereby the liberal Larpent accepted the Chiltern Hundreds, and agreed not to contest the vacancy created by his resignation, thus giving the conservative Walter an apparently safe seat.

4.9 The August 1842 by-election in Nottingham

In 1842, Walter found that his single-issue approach based on the poor law was no longer adequate. When his nominator on the hustings broached the subject, he was shouted down from the crowd with 'That's all over—it's all up ...'. Therefore, Walter broadened his scope to include defence of the Corn Law, but sweetened with his parliamentary votes on behalf of the people, his advocacy of the Dorchester labourers, and other humanitarian causes.[86]

But at the by-election, on 4 August 1842, Walter faced a contender: the philanthropist, abolitionist, and advocate of peace and temperance, Joseph Sturge (1793–1859).[87]

> [A]s it was the motto of his political creed [Sturge began], that all men are equal, so he beheld it equally his duty to do unto others as he would be done unto, and to endeavour to the utmost of his power to let every man enjoy the social and political privileges to which he was entitled.[88]

From this followed a broad platform of reform, which included complete and universal free trade in all legitimate articles,[89] abolition of the death penalty, and separation of 'the so-called church and state.'

> With regard to the separation of Church and State, he wished to make a clear distinction between the Church Establishment and the Episcopal religion, for very many of the latter objected to and were ashamed of taxing conscientious persons for the maintenance of a religion from which they dissented. It was a violation of the name of justice and the rights of conscience for such a law to be continued.[90]

Sturge drew unfavourable comparisons with the USA, contrasting the happy state of Connecticut, where big churches were built everywhere and everyone could read and write, with the United Kingdom. The former had achieved disestablishment, education, and prosperity in scarcely 50 years, while the latter, despite millions of pounds of annual taxation, spent over several centuries, still had an uneducated and unhappy populace.[91] Joseph Sturge spoke strongly on the subject of the unjust position of the Episcopal church in England as the established religion, and its inadequate and expensive attempts at education, because he was himself a Quaker, and therefore 'belonged to a sect of men that for two centuries had [only] felt the law as far as to allow his goods to be taken out of his house....'[92]

Sturge lost the contest, but the radical candidate made a good showing all the same, polling 1801 votes against Walter's 1885. The *Nottingham Review* observed:

> 3686 voters polled, and out of these 1801 voted for Mr. Sturge without a farthing, or even a breakfast. We will suppose that about 1,000 voted for Mr. Walter also on pure principles[;] that would leave only 885 out of 3686 who were influenced by money or promise, in giving their votes.[93]

The *Review* probably exaggerated a bit, but the conservative interest did resort to illegal tactics, chiefly improper treating or outright bribery, to secure votes. The election was declared void on petition, and a by-election was scheduled the next April.

4.10   The April 1843 by-election in Nottingham

The liberal interest was divided on whom to choose as a candidate. The corporation was eager to bring back Larpent, 'but the Radical Reformers rightly assert[ed] that it [did] not rest with the Whigs to decide, but with the 1801 electors who voted for Mr Sturge.'[94] But Joseph Sturge wrote from near Birmingham to decline a requisition from the electors of the borough.[95] He would promise to stand for Nottingham only if no other viable liberal candidate had been secured by the day of nomination. He reminded voters that he would pay only the barest and most essential costs, and added to these unenthusiastic terms the 'distinct condition' that his 'attendance in Parliament during the remaining part of the present session [be excused], except on occasions which ... appear[ed] to [him] of paramount importance.'[96]

In consequence, a meeting of some '300 or 400 of the most respectable and influential leaders of the Liberal party' was convened by circular.[97] Most of the assembly expressed satisfaction with Larpent, although a large number favoured the nomination of Thomas Gisborne (1794–1852), a radical reformer who had previously represented Stafford, Dervyshire, and Carlow, as well as having contested several other constituencies, including Ipswich.[98] As Gisborne's supporters pointed out, the whigs of Nottingham already had a member in the person of John Cam Hobhouse; therefore the Complete Suffrage Association ought to have its representation, as well. Gisborne was everything Larpent was, his supporters claimed, and something more. The meeting ended with a show of hands 'greatly in favour of Sir George Larpent, and the requisition was ordered to be sent to him.' If he declined, the assembly decided then to seek Thomas Gisborne as a candidate.[99]

Evidently Larpent did decline, and Gisborne was duly requisitioned. On confirming the support of a majority of the liberal electors, he agreed 'to accede to their wishes,' and was soon canvassing the borough.[100] At a liberal meeting in the Exchange Room, the Quaker Anti-Corn Law League agitator, John Bright (who was not yet a candidate for Durham City, but would claim over 44 per cent of the votes for that constituency less than a week later) attacked Mr Walter,[101] and praised Gisborne, whom he introduced as neither a tory nor a whig, the latter 'whom the people had not cause to like for their stand-still doctrines—but he was...a thorough going Radical.'[102] Next Gisborne himself spoke, and declared himself in agreement with John Bright on most issues.

[A]s it was known he did so, many of his own class considered him a sort of suicide, and that he ought to be buried in the high road, and to have a stake through his body. He had been a large farmer for twelve years, and during that period he had been an advocate for the total repeal of the corn laws.[103]

Although the primary referent to this suicide to his class is of course Gisborne's position as a free trader and opponent to the Corn Law, it is notable that his father was a clergyman in Durham, and a 'highly respected Predendary' of the cathedral.[104] In spite of this, the younger Gisborne was advanced in his liberal thinking on religious matters, particularly his determination to abolish the church rate. At a meeting held in Barker Gate Chapel, Gisborne continued his criticism of conservative policies on religion.[105] Abuse of dissenters was sanctioned, he claimed, and the ecclesiastical court was nothing but delay, jargon and injustice. He criticized the conservative government scheme for sending out bishops, at considerable expense, to Malta and Jerusalem, where there were hardly any English or Irishmen—or, indeed, hardly any other protestants.[106]

Gisborne also criticized the conservative position on religion as it related to education policy. He drew attention to an excellent education bill which nonconformists had proposed, but that the conservative government dismissed in its entirety, in favour of one that gave priority to Anglican doctrine.

> He should be glad to help the Tories in giving education to the people, but they must not dogmatize, and say it should be done in their way, and no other. Let the great end be, the real education of the people, and not an attempt of the church to arrogate those doctrines, against which their forefathers struggled, and which he trusted the generation of his day would struggle against successfully.

In this and other respects, Thomas Gisborne censured 'the grasping efforts of the Church of England....'[107]

It is more difficult to gauge the political sentiments of Gisborne's conservative opponent, the 25-year old John Walter junior (1818–1894). Although biographies and other scholarship sum up the career of the younger Walter as liberal-conservative or even liberal,[108] in the 1840s he stood for Nottingham as an undoubted conservative. The admittedly hostile *Nottingham Review* summed up his performance and reception at the nomination in this manner:

> Mr. Walter, jun. [wa]s a young man of very unintelligent appearance, and...a most pitiable speaker. It was evident he had committed a few sentences to memory, probably written by his father, and during his delivery of them, he repeatedly stopped, as if breaking down, amid the most derisive laughter, and cries of 'Does your mother know you're out!' &c.[109]

It appears that his intention was to pursue a manifesto similar to that of his father,[110] which he hoped was acceptable to the electors. Having no parliamentary career of his own to call upon, the son drew attention instead to the political record of the father. Indeed, his introduction and nomination had consisted largely of accounts of the borough's association with John Walter senior and, when the debating got tough, it was the father who stepped up to field questions too difficult for the son.[111]

John Walter junior lost the contest to Gisborne, on 5 April, by a margin of only a hundred votes and three percentage points,[112] and 'NOTTINGHAM,' according to the liberal press, '[WA]S ITSELF AGAIN.' 'Bravely done, Nottingham!' the *Nonconformist* similarly enthused.[113] In Gisborne the electors had returned a man who was 'a REAL FRIEND TO THE WORKING CLASSES, AN ENEMY TO ALL ABUSES, and a STAUNCH ADVOCATE FOR CIVIL AND RELIGIOUS LIBERTY.'[114] Gisborne was praised as 'a THOROUGH RADICAL REFORMER...,' and sympathetic onlookers pronounced themselves 'not without hope, that the election of Mr Gisborne as his [i.e. John Cam Hobhouse's] colleague, will have a salutary influence upon Sir John's conduct. The Honorable Baronet has been too much of a *Whigling* for us....'[115]

4.11   The July 1846 by-election in Nottingham

There was a by-election in the summer of 1846, occasioned by the accession of Lord John Russell's first ministry and the appointment of Hobhouse as president of the board of control for the affairs of India, but there was no challenge and Sir John was returned unopposed on 8 July. His return, however, said 'nothing in favor of either his popularity, or that of the party with which he [stood] connected.'[116] Rather it was the likely imminence of a general election, and the desire of all parties to avoid cost on what would probably prove a short-lived victory. Indeed, already that summer the Anti-Church State Association was preparing vigorously for the general election, and others complained of the return of too many pale-faced mongrel reformers, disappointing to both dissenters and radicals, rather than a strong body of MPs sincerely dedicated to the principles of civil and religious liberty.[117]

4.12   The 1847 general election in Nottingham

The general election was 12 months later, in July 1847. John Walter junior again stood for the conservative interest in the borough, and was joined by the Irish protestant and Chartist agitator Feargus O'Connor (1796?–1855) in challenging the liberal incumbents, Hobhouse and Gisborne. Only a week before the election, the *Nottingham Review* predicted with confidence that the liberals stood to do well in the contest. Of Gisborne, the *Review* stated, 'the Dissenters will rally round him to the man[, and Hobhouse] will probably also be re-elected....'[118] The liberals stood, after all, 'in support of the great and imperishable principles of freedom. . . .' But Hobhouse and Gisborne failed to excite electors, and ran a lacklustre campaign. Perhaps with reason, Sir John dwelt on his early career, his past achievements, and old associations with liberalism; he hardly addressed any current concerns.[119] Similarly, Gisborne's address at the nomination consisted chiefly of a defensive account of his own career.[120] He was more in step than Hobhouse with present matters—addressing in passing a recent education bill, the health of towns bill (particularly relevant for Nottingham), Irish affairs, and the bill for regulating the monetary affairs of the country. But his largely autobiographical self-defence was not received warmly.[121] What he chiefly had in his favour was that he had voted against the education bill, which Hobhouse, in step with the government, had supported.

Feargus O'Connor, on the other hand, supplied the deficiencies of Hobhouse's and Gisborne's lifeless campaign, and stood on a more popular platform, with particular appeal directed at dissent. In addition to a radical agenda in step with the People's Charter (though he had by this time withdrawn support for voting by ballot, which he criticized in the *Northern Star* as putting 'a mask on an honest face'),[122] O'Connor stood unequivocally in support of the separation of church and state, and promised to vote (and agitate) against the endowment of the Roman Catholic priesthood in Ireland, and in support of non-sectarian education generally.[123] He mocked the attention Hobhouse had given to proposals for the appointment of a bishop in the new see Manchester, stating that the people would rather have four new pigs than four new bishops. He also declared his fellow Irishmen too much attached to their Catholic faith to be put off it by any schemes proposed by a liberal government.[124]

Despite his uninspiring performance before the electorate,[125] John Walter junior topped the poll handily with 1683 votes,[126] and Feargus O'Connor followed with 1257. Gisborne and Hobhouse polled 999 and 893, respectively. Thus the strange union first proposed in 1841, by Walter's father, bore fruit, and Nottingham, so long a bastion of liberal politics, returned a tory and a Chartist.[127] The liberal *Nottingham Review* explained the circumstances in this manner:

> A considerable proportion of the Tory voters supported Mr. O'Connor as well as their own candidate, Mr. Walter; to this strange alliance, and to the circumstance that numbers of Dissenters refused to vote for the Minister who had supported the Educational measure, may be ascribed Mr. O'Connor's success.[128]

The tory *Nottingham Journal* likewise drew attention 'to Nonconformist abstentions, a form of protest against the Anglican Church's control over education, which a recent Government proposal upheld.'[129]

4.13 Nottingham: conclusion

Thus through their active involvement in liberal politics, or their passive withdrawal in protest, it is evident that the dissenters of Nottingham were a potent liberal force in Nottingham politics in the mid-nineteenth century.

5
Religion and Politics in an East Anglian Port City: The Case of Ipswich

5.1 Ipswich: Introduction*

The chaos and corruption of Nottingham were closely imitated in Ipswich. A handbill printed in the autumn of 1832 alleged that a bid for election cost candidates and their patrons between £10,000 and £12,000,[1] and although unrest was not as severe as in Nottingham, this was probably due mainly to Ipswich's smaller population. Nevertheless, the borough had had a long history of tumultuous election contests in the century before 1832,[2] and a letter to the *Ipswich Journal* in December of that year bemoaned the fact that '[i]n the last fourteen years, five contests have taken place; and under such circumstances!'[3] The next 15 years would be no kinder: between December 1832 and July 1847, there were a total of nine elections in Ipswich, and every one was contested.

5.2 The 1832 general election in Ipswich

The liberal candidates in 1832 were Rigby Wason[4] (1797/98–1875) and James Morrison (1789–1857), a self-made merchant who would amass over his lifetime a fortune of some three or four millions. Both had been members for the borough since 1831, and they announced their

---

* Located 12 miles from the sea at the junction of the Rivers Gipping and Orwell, the borough of Ipswich was a county-town of Suffolk. Its population increased from 20,454 to 32,914 between 1832 and 1851, and its registered electorate increased from 1219 to 1838 between 1832 and 1852. The town was engaged in the malt, corn, timber, and shipping trades, and in coach-building, brick-, basket- and paper-making, and other light manufactures. No personal influence prevailed in Ipswich, although *Dod's* reported that '[m]oney has long been considered the best friend at Ipswich...'.

candidacy for Ipswich on the same day, in separate handbills dated 30 June. Both expressed the conviction that the recently secured reform bill was only an opening act, setting the stage for extensive reforms in other areas which must follow. Morrison's address was the more explicit of the two.

> The work of Reform in detail is still to be done [he declared]. The task remains of making every part of the government, and every branch of our policy, foreign and domestic, harmonize with the reform in the legislature. The whole of the public establishments must be subjected to a searching revision, that the people may not continue to pay too much for services which are useful, and may not pay at all for any shew of service which is useless or mischievous.[5]

Morrison's demand for 'a searching revision' necessarily included the Church of England, the most ancient of public institutions. He also appealed implicitly to the dissenting interest with his demand that 'The crying scandal of Slavery must be put to an end to [sic],' although he stopped short of the more radical position, favoured by most nonconformists, insofar as Morrison acknowledged the legitimacy of compensating 'those [owners] who are involved in its guilt.' Beyond that, Morrison's appeal to the electorate consisted of a gradual, safe adoption of free trade, and the adjustment and reduction of taxes.[6] Wason's address was shorter, and touched on none of these issues directly; it simply assured the electorate that 'the Reform Bill [wa]s only the means, and not the end,' and that Wason hoped soon to present himself to the borough, and then to answer any questions.[7]

The following autumn, the conservative tory Henry Goulburn[8] (1787–1868) published an address to the borough electorate, in which he informed the constituency 'plainly to which class of Politicians [he] belong[ed].' He was a conservative, he stated, by which he meant

> one who reveres the existing Institutions of his country in Church and State, and who is unwilling to yield them up to rash and random experiments, in the idle hope of erecting upon their ruins some structures of the imagination, undefined and untried.[9]

Thus preservation of the close association of church and state, and the defence of the former by the latter, were key components of Goulburn's version of the conservative agenda.

Also standing for the conservative interest was Fitzroy Kelly (1796–1880) who, although generally milder in his conservatism than Goulburn, nonetheless brought to the fore of his appeal his position as 'a firm and sincere supporter of the Established Church, and of the Monarchy....'[10] Kelly cited natural and religious law as informing his position on colonial slavery, which he desired to end, but like James Morrison, with as equal a regard for those who have 'legal rights and interests involved in the existing system' as for the blacks.[11] Both conservatives claimed openness to reform, but Goulburn stipulated that it must be reform in the true sense of the word (that is 'change from worse to better'), and Kelly would only countenance those measures which promoted the constitution, public or private property, and public faith.[12]

After the formal announcement of the conservatives' candidacy, and less than two weeks before the election, Morrison and Wason issued new handbills, underscoring the position they had stated earlier. Again, Wason's address was brief, and touched on few specifics. He said nothing directly relevant to church or dissent, and justified his disinclination to launch into 'any lengthened detail of [his] Political Principles' on the grounds that he was well known in the borough, had spoken there recently and had, only a year earlier, received the support of many of them.[13]

Morrison's address ranged further. He assessed in a slighting fashion the character and agenda of the newly conceived conservative party, and made clear those institutions—'civil and military, domestic and colonial'—which he aimed to reform. Repeating his call for wide-ranging change, Morrison demanded 'a searching revision of the Public Establishments,... in order to prevent the waste of the public money in offices without duties, or duties without utility....'[14] Next Morrison assessed at length the relationship of church and state, and the position of dissent outside that relationship, and advocated 'A Reform of the Church of England....' Such a reform, he wrote, 'has been demanded by the Nation, [and] is also called for by a large and continually increasing body of the Clergy themselves.'[15]

Morrison avowed himself a sincere churchman, eager to preserve respect for the establishment. To this end, however, he insisted on real reform, especially of the church's sources of income. He judged it necessary that the tithe be commuted to a charge on land rather than a tax on 'the capital employed on its cultivation,' and more significantly— several years before such a goal became a focal point of nonconformist aspirations—James Morrison advocated that the church rate be levied in a manner designed not to offend 'those who conscientiously dissent from its doctrine, or its discipline.'[16] Other church reforms advocated by Morrison were designed to protect and reward the many 'good and efficient Clergymen who devote[d] themselves to the faithful discharge of their Office,' while ridding the establishment and its parishes of persons of inferior quality. In the end, Morrison insisted, liberal ecclesiastical restructuring would aid and strengthen the Church of England, and foster 'the Religion, the Morality, and the good order of Society.'[17]

Two weeks later, Morrison was introduced and nominated on the hustings by Samuel Alexander (d.1838), a leading liberal and senior member of a prominent family of Ipswich Quakers.[18] C.C. Hammond, a surgeon and another nonconformist, seconded the nomination. Speaking for himself, Morrison reviled the concept of so-called conservatism, and chose for himself the label of 'Exterpationist. He was,' he said, 'for exterminating all sinecures in Church and State[, and] Church Reform he considered as necessary as Parliamentary Reform.' Again he drew attention to his allegiance to the church and desire for its preservation as the major motives behind this particular reform; he declared himself its friend, rather than its enemy, and proposed to increase, rather than to diminish, clerical salaries, on the condition that recipients were resident, respectable, and attentive to duty.[19] Curiously, Morrison appears not to have addressed either tithe commutation or the church rate, nor did he mention his opposition to colonial slavery—all issues which he had emphasized in his printed statements, and for which nonconformists were particularly keen.[20] Despite this apparent omission, the force of his expression in his two handbills could hardly have left electors in much doubt how he stood on such matters.

The seed merchant Frederick Francis Seekamp,[21] who as mayor in 1837 would convene an anti-church rate meeting, nominated Rigby Wason.[22] Wason's own statement to the electorate confirmed the candidate's reputation for brevity, as well as displaying what a latter-day critic has called a distinct 'lack of serious political content.'[23] Apparently in response to a charge that 'he did not fear God or honor the King,' Wason conceded with mock humility that he was 'an unworthy member of the Church,' but sarcastically insisted his honour for the king surpassed that of those who declared the reform bill, which had received royal assent, 'a crime to the country.'[24] Wason did not discuss slavery or ecclesiastical income, and addressed no issue particularly concerning the dissenting interest.

While Kelly and Goulburn had managed in their handbills to skirt their position on ecclesiastical restructuring, the latter's sympathy for and unwillingness to reform the church became evident in his statement from the hustings. Henry Goulburn began his speech with the assertion that the 'principles imputed to [the liberal candidates] had a tendency to overthrow the altar and the crown.'[25] In defence of his conservative position, he cited Rigby Wason's praise of David Hume at a recent liberal dinner. Goulburn attacked Hume's religious scepticism, and reminded electors of the occasion when Hume had divided the House of Commons on a motion to remove 'Divine Providence' from the address to the sovereign. Goulburn conceded the usefulness of some ecclesiastical reform, but only on the grounds established in his hand-bill: he would 'not sanction the demolition of the Church under the pretense of reforming it.'[26] He furthermore insisted that 'education and religion should go side by side,' and expressed his belief that education, independent of religious instruction, was a curse, and not a blessing.[27] Here Goulburn was met with cries of 'Shame!' but persisted:

> In a country where the press is free to pour all sorts of books and doctrines into society; to give education, without accompanying it with religious instruction, was like loading a blunderbuss, and placing oneself at the muzzle while it was being discharged. He was not one who thought reading, writing, and arithmetic, the panacea for all evils. Education should be joined with the fear of God.[28]

Though he did not state so directly, it may be inferred that the religious instruction Goulburn favoured was to be strictly in the lens of Anglican orthodoxy.

Unfortunately, the state of preservation of the *Ipswich Journal* rendered Fitzroy Kelly's statement virtually illegible, and useless for analysis.

Ipswich was, as so much of the country, swept up in the liberal tide in the election of the first reformed House of Commons. Morrison and Wason topped the poll with 599 and 593 votes, respectively. Goulburn and Kelly complained bitterly of the interference of a third conservative candidate, Charles Mackinnon (d.1833), which they claimed confused and divided the conservative electorate. The poll does not sustain this position convincingly; however, Goulburn and Kelly received 303 and 267 votes, respectively, and Mackinnon only 94.[29]

5.3   The 1835 general election in Ipswich

The general election of January 1835 witnessed the return of three of the four candidates from the previous contest. The two members for

Ipswich, Morrison and Wason, endorsed the same liberal agenda as in 1832. Kelly was still a moderate or liberal conservative, and again, as in 1832, was paired with a man of decidedly more conservative proclivities: Robert Adam Dundas (1804–1877), who had sat previously for Ipswich (1827–1831) and for Edinburgh (1831–1832).[30] Kelly and Dundas jointly circulated a handbill which stated

> Whilst we announce our determination to maintain to the best of our ability the Protestant Constitution of our Country in Church and State, we are desirous to remove from all classes of our fellow-subjects any grievances which may be found to exist....[31]

As argued in the case of Arthur Trevor's address to the electors of Durham, also in 1835, such language is equivocal. The candidates made clear their partiality for Anglicanism, and their intention to preserve the existing relationship of church and state. But what exactly they were willing to concede was not apparent, since they failed to elaborate their criteria for judging a grievance legitimate. Separately, however, Kelly presented himself as in step with prime minister Peel's recently issued Tamworth Manifesto: he offered the prospect of relief to all, which presumably included dissenters, but stipulated, still evasively, that their grievances must be legitimate.[32]

Nonetheless, Kelly supported a marriage bill for dissenters, and advocated their relief from, although not outright abolition of, the tithe and church rate.[33] But Dundas was more reactionary.[34] In parliament he had strongly opposed the passage of the reform bill and, echoing the fatal expression of the duke of Wellington in November 1830, 'declared the British system of government the most perfect' in history.[35] From such a position, liberals—and dissenters specifically—could hardly expect a progressive programme of reform. On arriving in Ipswich, Dundas declared

> 'The Crown was in danger, the Church was in danger' and... popery might become the established religion [in England] or... the Establishment might be ended altogether.[36]

Shortly afterwards, Kelly and Dundas issued a handbill milder in its sentiments (but no more specific) than their first address, possibly in an effort to palliate dissenters. They reiterated their commitment to preserve 'the Constitution in Church and State,' but also emphasized their intention to relieve the people, no matter what class, of all real burdens or grievances. 'To this end, and to this alone,' they sought the support of the electors of Ipswich.[37]

The liberal campaign, for its part, stigmatized Kelly and Dundas as would-be mutilators and repealers of reform legislation and principles. Both Wason and Morrison declared themselves defenders of civil and religious rights for all, and drew attention to the achievements of the previous ministry, as well as to their own votes in parliament on behalf of dissenters' admission to the universities, and other liberal measures.[38] Morrison made plain his support for the ejected ministry, and emphasized as well his advocacy for non-sectarian state-funded education, the elimination of parishes of the Irish church with no congregation, and the abolition of tithes and pluralism in the English church.[39] Even so, some electors grumbled that James Morrison had not proved himself adequately radical, and was unworthy to stand with Rigby Wason.[40] Some dissenters were evidently included in this category,[41] perhaps roused by what they deemed Morrison's half-hearted commitment on the question of colonial slavery, as evinced in 1832 by his position on the question of compensation. Nevertheless, the Quaker Samuel Alexander, who had nominated Morrison in 1832—and styled himself a radical, desiring that his nominee might incline more in that direction—did not hesitate to stand behind his candidate in 1835.[42]

Kelly and Dundas struck back at the liberals' portrayal of conservatives as adverse to all reforms. On the contrary, they claimed that their 'sentiments [were] in perfect accordance with those of all who desire to see a liberal and just Reform of the evils and abuses which time ha[d] brought upon the Church....' Nevertheless, the conservatives pledged to defend the 'Ancient and Sacred principles of our Constitution' against hateful attacks, and offered no hope of substantive concessions to those who dissented from the establishment.[43]

The conservatives topped the poll in January 1835, with 557 votes for Kelly and 555 for Dundas, respectively, against 531 for Wason and 516 for Morrison. In their address of thanks, the newly returned members simply reiterated their position on church and state: they

> endeavour[ed] to ... maintain ... unimpaired the Religious and Civil Institutions of our Country—our venerated Church Establishment in connection with the State—the Dignity of the Crown—and the Rights and Privileges of all classes of his Majesty's subjects.[44]

Kelly and Dundas continued to promise that, in parliament, they would calmly and dispassionately consider reform measures designed to remove real grievances of any class of society.[45] They hardly had the chance, however. The result of the poll was petitioned against,[46] and a committee of investigation declared that Morrison and Wason had the 'legal majority,' and ought to be returned.[47] The solicitor for Dundas and Kelly was imprisoned, as were six other conservative activists, and the result of the January contest was voided.

5.4 The June 1835 by-election in Ipswich

Morrison and Wason stood in the consequent by-election on 19 June and, to save face in the borough, the conservative interest put up as token resistors two fresh contenders, Lt Col. Horatio George Broke (1790–1860), a local landowner and brother to the county MP, and William Holmes (1779–1851), a former tory whip. Broke and Holmes put forward an uninspiring programme that consisted of supporting Peel, upholding agriculture, and defending the church and crown.[48] They invoked the increasingly dated memory of 1688, as well as the need to resist O'Connellites and papists.[49] The only major pronouncement of policy on the liberal side was Wason's conversion to the ballot, support of which Morrison had already announced.[50] Neither liberal candidate addressed questions of church or dissent.

But the real issue in the contest was tory corruption. The circumstances of the January election gave Rigby Wason a new string to harp on, and in his two subsequent bids for election, he always played up his defence of pure elections. Morrison and Wason polled 542 and 533 votes, respectively, and Broke and Holmes nearly 100 fewer, with 454 and 434.

5.5 The 1837 general election in Ipswich

The next contest in Ipswich was the general election of July 1837, but both parties had been gearing up for a contest as early as the previous autumn. Fitzroy Kelly announced his candidacy for the borough in a handbill which reiterated his position as friendly to just and necessary reform. '[B]ut,' he continued, establishing his principal concern:

I hold that the Protestant Church, as by law established, is the strongest bulwark that protects the Throne; and that the revenues of the Church are sacred to Religious and Ecclesiastical purposes; and that if the Church be endangered, the Throne itself is insecure. When, therefore, I see that the most prominent measures proposed by the present [liberal] Government, involve the spoliation of the Church, both in England and in Ireland, and the application of its property to the purposes of the State:—I feel thus bound publicly to declare that I deem these measures at once unconstitutional and unjust; and that if returned to Parliament I will strenuously oppose them; and I appeal to you as a portion of the people, to testify by your Votes on the day of the Election, whether you approve or condemn these principles which will never cease to guide and regulate my public Conduct.[51]

Thus Kelly's chief priority remained defence of the church in England and Ireland, and specifically, the maintenance of the church rate. Whether he was still inclined to relieve non-Anglicans of compulsory payment of the church rate, the policy he had endorsed in the previous election, is not clear. Certainly he did not mention such a proposal in 1837, perhaps because of the wholesale attack on the church rate by the dissenting and liberal camps, from which he wished to dissociate himself completely. Kelly touched only vaguely on other matters, such as commerce and agriculture, with ambiguous expressions of hope that any government would act rationally, to promote the interests of both industries.

James Morrison temporarily retired from political life after the dissolution following the king's death, perhaps because, as hostile conservatives speculated, he was no longer able to 'supply the secret service money required by his various supporters.'[52] In his stead, Henry Tufnell (1805–1854), a lord of the treasury since 1835, announced his candidacy for the liberal interest. A political novice without a political career by which the electorate could judge him,[53] Tufnell issued a handbill outlining his political creed. He was friendly to various reforms in the spirit of the 1832,[54] and was intent to 'uphold Protestant principles as the firmest bulwarks of civil and religious liberty.'[55] He was a devoted Anglican and declared it in the church's own best interests, as well as those of public peace, that all elements of contention be removed. Therefore, Tufnell approved of the abolition of the church rate, and the better management of church property. Moreover, he advocated reform of the internal discipline of the church, and more equal distribution of ecclesiastical revenue. Specifically in reference to Catholics in Ireland, but with obvious wider application for dissenters everywhere, Tufnell was 'convinced that religious opinions should make no difference in the civil rights of any class of our fellow subjects, and that the principle of self-government and popular control [could] not be too widely diffused.'[56]

Tufnell reiterated several of the same points a few days later at a public meeting of liberal supporters. He promoted reform of tithe in Ireland and challenged the withholding of municipal reform from that kingdom (as had lately been secured for England and Scotland), simply on the unjust grounds that the majority were not Protestant. Other of his sentiments struck chords of hostility to the church's privileged place in the state—for instance his 'wish to see the Church of Ireland reduced to that state in which it will be adequate to meet the wants for the Protestants of that kingdom.'[57] He proposed that excess ecclesiastical revenue in Ireland be directed to education, 'for,' he was convinced, 'that if there be any chance of reclaiming Ireland from the state to which it is reduced, it is by the diffusion of education, and sound political and religious doctrines.' Tufnell confirmed his commitment to challenging unique privileges to any sect and, appropriating rhetoric similar to many opponents of concessions to Catholics, asserted that '[t]o priestly domination, whether from Rome or from Lambeth, I will never bow.'[58] Such equation of the archbishop of Canterbury with the pope in Rome was clearly intended to provoke both conservatives and Anglicans who, in Tufnell's opinion, valued too highly the close association of conservative politics and Anglican religion.

At this meeting, too, Tufnell made explicit his steadfast support of dissent, which his printed address had merely implied. He invoked 'the object of the Reformation [as] not only to establish a Protestant Church, but the introduction of the principle of freedom of opinion,'[59] and denied outright the proposition that dissenters must pay for the upkeep of a church they did not attend and whose doctrines they did not believe. In settling the great question of the day, the church rate, Tufnell demanded a solution that would in no way vex dissenters, or acknowledge any distinction between them and Anglicans.[60]

Rigby Wason, who stood to defend his seat for Ipswich, was also present at the meeting. He spoke only briefly, and engaged mostly in a characteristic effusion championing pure elections. The manner in which he elaborated this theme, however, reflects on the close association in Ipswich, and elsewhere, between conservatism and Anglicanism. Wason asserted that conservatives could only win in Ipswich through recourse to underhanded means. He expected to find them, as he alleged they had done in December of 1834 and January of 1835, telling radicals in one street that they were radical, and churchmen in another that they were committed to tory principles.[61] Wason repeated his support for abolishing the church rate and, in response to a cry from the assembly to 'Pull down the Church,' made the reckless and provocative assertion that he understood the sentiment very well, and hoped it would be reported in the local press, with the observation that every liberal present had applauded the cry.[62]

In the early days of the campaign, it seemed that Kelly's fellow conservative candidate would be the Rt Hon. John Charles Herries (1778–1855), whom the *Ipswich Journal* had 'always... regarded as a most able auxiliar [*sic*] of the Conservative party in Parliament, being a sound practical politician, and a smart debater.'[63] In the event, Kelly was paired with the Rt Hon. Thomas Gibson (1806–1884). Gibson expressed himself willing to reform the church as necessary, but refused to acknowledge any need to abandon an existing source of revenue: the church rate, he insisted, must continue.[64] Both conservatives played up as part of their appeal the alleged threat from Rome to protestant security at home.

One modern account of the 1837 general election in Ipswich has it that the real issue at stake was the new poor law.[65] But the evidence adduced above makes it clear that candidates continued to judge it worthwhile to appeal to electors on issues of church and dissent. This was especially so regarding a candidate's position on the controversy surrounding the church rate. Moreover, unlike the issue of the new poor law of 1834, which had been generally supported by both parties and was therefore likely to be awkward for both,[66] a candidate's position on the church rate provided a strong indication of political affiliation. As we have seen, in this election and elsewhere, and in other boroughs besides Ipswich, conservatives such as Kelly and Gibson championed the cause of the church, while liberals such as Wason and Tufnell came down in favour of dissenting interests.

The resulting contest was very tight, with only eight votes separating first and last place. On the first reading of the poll, Gibson received 601 votes, Tufnell 595, and Kelly and Wason 593 each. After due scrutiny, the two conservatives were declared the legitimate winners, thus commencing nearly a decade of tory representation in parliament for Ipswich.[67]

5.6   The May 1839 by-election in Ipswich

Less than two years later, however, in May 1839, the borough recalled its member Thomas Gibson—who in this year added Milner, previously a forename, to his family name—to account before his constituents for his parliamentary record, particularly his vote in the House of Commons, at variance with most other conservatives, in favour of permitting an

Religion and Politics in Ipswich 79

affirmation as a substitute for an oath in courts of law.[68] Such a position was obviously a boon to Quakers and others whose consciences were troubled by mixing religious matters with secular or legal proceedings. But this apostasy was not the only instance of Milner Gibson's failing to toe the conservative line in parliament. He had converted to Corn Law repeal and free trade generally, supported the ballot, called for an end to the protestant ascendancy in Ireland and, in championing the rights of humanity, drew attention especially to liberty of conscience.[69] The conservative *Ipswich Journal* attacked Milner Gibson's parliamentary conduct, the Wellington Club passed a motion of no confidence in him,[70] and one handbill lambasted him as 'the Judas Gibson[,] an Egotistical, Pragmatical, Turn-coat Hypocriote.'[71] The MP admitted his increasing inclination to vote at variance with other conservatives in the House of Commons, and acknowledged his actions might confuse his constituents, especially those for whom conservative principles had been his strongest recommendation in the summer of 1837. Therefore, he accepted the Chiltern Hundreds, and stood for the vacancy as a liberal, 'thus to afford [his] constituents an immediate opportunity of placing the important charge of their representation in such hands as they may think proper.'[72]

Gibson's opponent in the by-election held 15 July was Captain Sir Thomas John Cochrane (1789–1872), KCB, a captain in the Navy and governor of Newfoundland from 1825–1834, who presented himself to the electorate as open to reform, where it was necessary. In an appeal to the maritime interest of the borough, Cochrane drew attention to his naval career and expressed his belief that any ministry ought to keep alive the name and credit of Britain abroad, as well as tend to the comfort and prosperity of the people at home. He further declared himself a strong defender of the Church of England and, in announcing his support for every wise scheme of education, would 'never consent to delude the appetite of a people craving after wholesome knowledge, with the poisonous food of an adulterated Scripture.'[73] In other words, he believed education must be religious and that religion must be Anglican, in no way tainted by dissent or Catholicism. Standing 'in the long line of Church and King Tories,'[74] Sir Thomas set himself apart from Milner Gibson, whose liberal awakening had led him to champion the rights of dissenters.

The contest was a close one, but Cochrane polled 621 votes, six ahead of Milner Gibson. It seems likely, however, that the result more reflected a determination to punish Milner Gibson, than any endorsement of Cochrane.[75]

5.7   The 1841 general election in Ipswich

As noted previously, and especially in the discussion of Nottingham, the central issue to the 1841 election was free trade: the liberal ministry sought to win electoral support through a programme, which conservatives rejected, of a low fixed duty on corn. In consequence, questions of a politico-religious character might have been expected to slip to the background for the most part. But in Ipswich, as in Nottingham and elsewhere, they were never completely obscured.

In his opening statement after arriving in town, Fitzroy Kelly drew attention to the attempt by the Melbourne government to strike a vital blow at the established church, through the appropriation clause, which measure he had opposed, and the conservatives had succeeded in beating down. It was thanks to conservative electors who had returned such members across the country, claimed Kelly, that the Church of England remained free.[76] Similarly at the nomination, J.C. Cobbold credited Kelly not only as a friend to agriculture and an advocate of the people, but also a constant defender of 'the National Church.'[77] The other conservative contender, the Rt Hon. J.C. Herries, lately MP for Harwich (1823–1841), suffered from a cold during much of the campaign and spoke little. It may be inferred, however, given both his distinction under previous tory ministries—which included tenures as chancellor of the exchequer, secretary at war, and president of the board of trade—and his open coalition with Kelly, that the two conservatives differed little in their respect for the establishment.

The two liberals—Rigby Wason and George Rennie junior (1802–1860)—appear not to have engaged matters of church and state as directly as Kelly but, even in addressing the issue of free trade *v.* protection, the liberals, as well as the conservatives, shaped their respective arguments in a manner plainly designed to attract dissenters. Specifically, they appealed to dissent's ardour for abolishing slavery, even beyond the boundaries of the British empire. The candidates' enthusiasm for the 1834 abolition in the British West Indies was undiminished, and they judged the £20 million paid as compensation to the former owners a worthwhile and noble sacrifice. But they diverged on the wisdom of the tariff on sugar from Brazil, justified by conservatives in part by the persistence of slavery in that country. For the liberals, George Rennie cited the report of the abolitionist Thomas Fowell Buxton (1786–1845),[78] that slavery in the Americas remained as prolific as ever; merely restricting the trans-Atlantic trade and emancipating slaves from British territories was clearly not enough. Rennie argued that the continued policy of British protection against Brazil simply allowed Brazilian merchants to undercut British merchants in their trade with the rest of the world. Moreover, protectionist interference with Anglo-Brazilian commerce reduced British opportunities to exercise leverage on Brazilian policy regarding slavery. Finally, Rennie drew attention to the hypocrisy of condemning Brazilian sugar, while continuing to import cotton and tobacco from the USA.[79] Kelly and Herries challenged Rennie's logic on these points, insisting that the proposal to end duties on Brazilian sugar would wreck the 'noble experiment [of a previous liberal ministry] for the Conversion of a Slave Population into a Free Peasantry in the West Indies,'[80] as well as throw away any advantage gained by the national sacrifice of £20 million.[81]

But other features, besides the formal expression of the candidates' political manifestos, shed light on the persistent connexion between liberalism and dissent, on the one hand, and conservatism and the church, on the other, during the 1841 contest. Present at the meeting to announce the candidacy of Wason and Rennie were the Revd Thomas Middleditch, a Baptist minister; Frederick Alexander, a leading Quaker; and Charles Cowell (d.1842), a dissenter (most likely a Congregationalist).[82] Mr Alexander would second Rennie's nomination at the hustings.[83] Also at the meeting, and identified by the *Ipswich Journal* as a 'supporter...of the Liberal interest,'[84] was F.F. Seekamp esquire, already identified as an opponent of the church rate. Not surprisingly, the Anglican Revd Edward Woolnough was listed among the 'staunch friends of the Conservative cause' who assembled to greet the 'Triumphal entry' of Kelly and Herries into Ipswich,[85] and Kelly's stalwart defence of 'the National Church' was noted by his nominator as an outstanding credential.

The liberals, Wason and Rennie, won what appeared comfortable majorities over the conservatives, Kelly and Herries—659 and 657 votes, respectively, against 611 and 604—but the election was declared void on petition. None of the men would stand again for Ipswich,[86] and at the two ensuing by-elections, in June and August 1842, a total of nine candidates competed for the borough.

5.8 The June and August 1842 by-elections in Ipswich

On 3 June 1842, two conservative candidates, John Otway O'Connor Cuffe, 3rd earl of Desart (1818–1865), and Thomas Gladstone (1804–1889), defeated two liberal candidates, Thomas Gisborne[87] and George Moffat (d.1878) by a margin of over 125 votes. The 'election was probably as pure as that of many other members who kept their seats in other places, but,' according to an obituary of Gladstone nearly a half-century later, 'in those days each defeated party retaliated on the victors with an election petition.'[88] The first by-election was declared void on petition, and a fresh batch of candidates stood in the contest on 17 August: John Neilson Gladstone (1807–1863) and Sackville Walter Lane-Fox (1797–1874) for the conservatives, and George Thornbury (1795–1873) and Henry Vincent (1813–1878) for the liberals. The muddled character of these two contests, the one following close on the heels of the other, makes it useful to consider them together.

George Moffatt presented a typical programme of reform. He proposed free trade, an extended franchise, increased popular education, and he praised previous liberal ministries for their glorious record on behalf of liberty. He invoked particularly the heady days of Charles James Fox,[89] whose battles on behalf of the people, and especially for Catholic emancipation, had defined the outlook for liberal politics earlier in the century. The political programme of Thomas Gisborne has already been assessed above, in the examination of the Nottingham by-election of April 1843, in which he was successful.[90] Let it here suffice to recall that the leaders of the liberal party in Nottingham and the Complete Suffrage Association judged Gisborne all a liberal candidate ought to be, and something more; he championed measures favourable to dissent (including opposition to the church rate), criticized the bishops, and otherwise censured 'the grasping efforts of the Church of England....'[91]

In the joint announcement of their candidacy, the earl of Desart and Thomas Gladstone, older brother of William Ewart Gladstone, mostly promoted their opposition to free trade which, they argued, helped certain classes of society only at the necessary expense of others. They preferred a soberer policy that protected national welfare generally.[92] Desart opposed further parliamentary reform and, indeed, innovation generally; and Gladstone, though he declared his opposition to slavery, was questioned over his family's recent involvement with the practice.[93]

By and large the bugbear of the threat from Rome had temporarily died down in Ipswich and, insofar as the evidence permits, neither conservative directly addressed matters relevant to church or dissent in the spring of 1842. But political interest in religion had far from extinguished in Ipswich, as the appeal of the two liberal candidates evinced, and became more prominent still in the by-election that summer, in which an outright anti-Catholic bigot faced off against a thoroughgoing radical who was intent to disestablish the Church of England.

Sackville Lane-Fox, who had previously sat for Helston (1831–1834) and whose 'main concerns were politico-religious' to the extreme, 'gave notice,' as late as 1843:

of a motion to repeal the Catholic Emancipation Act and when begged in the name of common sense to withdraw it, declared he would not bring up such a motion unless he 'was prepared to prove that it is Popery and nothing but Popery that leads to the disorders now prevailing in Ireland.' Later he announced that 'our glorious Protestant constitution, in which so great a breach was made by the Act of 1829, was as much the law of God as the law delivered to the Israelites on Mount Sinai,' and that war alone could settle the dispute between England and Ireland 'and save the Church from its enemies.' He quoted from Isaiah to prove that the 1688 Protestant Revolution had been foreseen by that prophet. He assured the House of Commons that 'here in these British Isles, where God has planted his true Church, he has also planted a branch of Israel to stand by it in the last days,' and concluded with the prediction that England would overcome the powers of darkness. Fox wrote to Peel informing him of the imminence of the Second Coming and was reported to have told Disraeli that he believed him to be the awaited Messiah—'the branch of Israel'—of the return of Christ. He was satirized by *Punch*, which held a mock commission of lunacy on him, and the *Ipswich Express*, which reported that he flourished a whip in parliament and referred to him as 'Mr. L'âne Fox.'[94]

The other conservative that summer was John Neilson Gladstone, another brother of the future prime minister. In response to the violent anti-Catholic expressions of Lane-Fox, liberals in Ipswich gleefully drew attention to the recent conversion, in May 1842, of the Gladstones' sister, Helen (1814–1880), to Roman Catholicism.[95] As his older brother Thomas had been three months earlier, J.N. Gladstone was harassed for his family's ownership of slaves in the West Indies, and drew particular fire for his attempts to justify the £80,000 compensation received when the slaves were freed, as well as the subsequent use of East Indian coolies.[96] Gladstone championed the close association of church and state and, in a handbill published jointly with Lane-Fox, pledged to pursue any reform designed to fortify the relationship.[97] On the grounds of hostility to state-funded education through any medium other than the Anglican Church, Gladstone proposed decentralizing education altogether, and favoured education by religious or other private charities.[98]

Challenging these conservative defenders of the church were Henry Vincent, Chartist leader of the Newport Riot fame and unsuccessful candidate for Banbury (1841),[99] and George Thornbury. Vincent proposed a six-fold programme, which included 'the separation of the Church from the State, and the abolition of the Church Rate, or any other assessment made for the support of a particular sect'; as well as the provision for more widespread education, ameliorating the plight of women and, in keeping with Vincent's affiliation with the Quakers, opposition to the maintenance of a standing army.[100] George Thornbury was an obscure figure; much of what is known of him is that he was a solicitor and at one point desired his son, also George, to pursue a career in the church.[101]

One other candidate contested both elections in 1842, the somewhat enigmatical Thomas J. Nicholson, who was nominally a third liberal but whose 'politics and motives,' beyond his advocacy of purity of elections, 'remained unclear.'[102] T.J. Nicholson won a total of three votes in June, and only two in August.

5.9   The 1847 general election in Ipswich

The next contest in Ipswich was not until the general election of 1847, nearly five years later. The incumbent Sackville Lane-Fox initially intended to defend his seat after the dissolution of parliament but, on discovering that a strong body of conservatives in Ipswich desired the candidacy of John Chevalier Cobbold (1797–1882), a banker and merchant at Ipswich and Harwich, and chairman of both the Eastern Union Railway Company and Ipswich and Bury St Edmunds Railway Company, the incumbent conservative decided to stand down.[103] Cobbold's chief appeal appears to have been his claim as a 'native son,' as well as his participation in a number of local improvements. He did, however, proclaim his adherence to true constitutional and conservative principles, including the institutions of a protestant church in state, as key to his political credo.[104] Nor was this mere jargon or cant: in 1833, while a councilman and bailiff, he declared certain recent and unspecified reforms

far too dearly purchased by the innovation which has been made upon the integrity of our once excellent and enviable constitution by the too successful attacks that have been directed against the independence of one of the three Estates of the Realm—and the inroads that have been made on the influence of the best religious establishment that any nation was ever blessed with.[105]

Similarly in 1839, he moved a petition which warned the Queen of the dangerous proclivities of the liberal ministry, and emphasized 'his patriotic love of our unrivalled Protestant Institutions....'[106]

Sir Hugh Edward Adair (1815–1902) also claimed personal association with the borough, 'having been born and constantly in residence in the county,' and sitting, with Cobbold, as chairman of the Eastern Union Railways Company.[107] In announcing his candidacy, he identified as the most important issues before the public the government's scheme of education and the possible endowment of the Roman Catholic Church. In respect to the former, Sir Hugh declared it 'the province and duty of government' to extend secular education to all who require it, and such religious knowledge as comes from reading the scriptures, without a compulsory creed or catechism. He favoured total abolition of the church rate and, regarding Catholics, Sir Hugh favoured extending to all the fullest enjoyment of civil rights and liberties, including education, but he opposed the endowment of the Roman Catholic Church, or any legislative act which he deemed 'would tend to offend the religious feelings of the Members of the Church of England and the equally conscientious scruples of our Dissenting Brethren.'[108] Accordingly H.E. Adair opposed the Maynooth grant,[109] and was supported at the hustings by one of the Ransomes, a prominent Quaker family.[110]

Two of the candidates from August 1842 stood again for the borough in 1847, J.N. Gladstone, the remaining sitting member, and Henry Vincent. As it had five years earlier, Vincent's programme ranged well beyond the demands of the People's Charter. Speaking before a political meeting in Ipswich, he espoused additional parliamentary reform, equal rights for all classes, and the abolition of primogeniture. But the first two items he listed were separation of church and state and the termination of all religious endowments by the government.[111] Significantly, the *Ipswich Journal* noted that Vincent's principal supporters at the meeting consisted of 'a large body of Dissenters.'[112]

In the summer of 1842, J.N. Gladstone had topped the poll comfortably, far outstripping either the liberal or Chartist candidate. His position on church and state was in keeping with conservative principles, and he had during the earlier campaign committed himself to strengthening the church as a national institution. He remained steadfast to these and other conservative principles, having sided with the Protectionist, rather than the Peelite, wing of the party in 1846.[113]

Therefore, the conservative credentials of J.N. Gladstone ought to have been as impressive in the run-up to the general election of 1847 as they had been five years earlier, and his bid for conservative support might have seemed secure. But in a single parliamentary division in 1845, on the fate of the government's grant to St Patrick's College, Maynooth, Gladstone had failed to toe the line of many of his conservative colleagues, and voted with the government. For this apostasy, religious as well as political, many conservative electors in Ipswich could not forgive him.

Two weeks after his vote with the government, on 25 April 1845, Gladstone wrote to the Anglican Revd Thomas Henry Lumsden in Ipswich, to account for his vote. Shortly before the 1847 election, Gladstone forwarded a copy of the letter to John E. Sparrowe, a local conservative solicitor and county coroner, with instructions that it should be read publicly at a meeting of the conservative interest, and further circulated among the borough's conservatives.[114] 'If I were of the opinion that the present measure [i.e. increasing and making permanent the grant to Maynooth] must necessarily lead to or hasten the payment of the Roman Catholic Priests,' Gladstone had written to the Revd Lumsden in 1845, 'I would vote against it, but I see no necessary connection between the two.' He reasoned that the government must support the institution—for it was founded by the government and its establishment pre-dated the act of union with Ireland[115]—but must never pay the priests' salaries, as the policy would offend most of the country.[116]

The public letter continued in an effort to re-establish Gladstone's credentials as an orthodox queen and church conservative, and defuse any challenges that he was too much inclined to sympathize with Catholics.

> I voted against the Bill, [Gladstone pointed out] for the Repeal of Statutes affecting the Roman Catholics, because I did not conceive that for the removal of imaginary grievances, it was right to repeal laws which were intended to guard the Protestant Institutions of this Country, and which were still generally deemed essential for that object. When any real grievance is proved, which can be remedied without incurring a greater evil, I should be ready to consider the propriety of its removal, but I am not aware of any of which the Roman Catholics should have a right to complain.[117]

But Gladstone recognized that such efforts were probably insufficient. Eight months after the parliamentary division, and fully 18 months before the 1847 election, John wrote to his brother William that the result of the next election 'will depend ... on the number of Maynooth votes I lose.'[118] His opinion did not change after he lost the contest for, in a farewell address to his former constituents, he noted that 'I attribute my defeat mainly to the neutrality of some, and the opposition of others, who objected to my vote in favour of the increased grant to Maynooth.'[119] Nor is there any evidence that he was wrong in this respect.[120]

Of the four candidates who contested Ipswich in 1847, Gladstone and Vincent evidently held the more extreme religious views. Gladstone, we have seen, rejected education not under the control of the Church of England, and refused equal civil rights for Roman Catholics. Vincent, on the other hand, was hostile to the church establishment. On religious matters, his radical agenda went the whole way to disestablishment. Cobbold and Adair were more moderate. Although a conservative, Cobbold had supported the Maynooth grant, and refused to attack Catholics or dissenters.[121] Adair was mainly a liberal, but could appeal to churchmen on his opposition to the Maynooth grant. (This would attract dissenters, as well, on the different grounds of refusing religious endowment.)[122] The latter two candidates won the contest, thus breaking the pattern in Ipswich, established over the past 30 years or more, whereby voters always returned two candidates from the same party. For the next 21 years, until Cobbold was defeated in his bid for re-election in 1868, he and Adair continued to be returned for the borough.[123]

This change was due in part probably to the fact that both Cobbold and Adair were local men. Prior to 1847, no candidate for MP in Ipswich had boasted a strong local base since the early nineteenth century. Those who contested, and indeed won, Ipswich were uniformly outsiders, and at one point in the late 1820s two Scots and an Irishman stood for the borough.[124] The split representation in Ipswich from 1847 on was also due to the fact that both parties had burned themselves out after 30 years of hard campaigning.[125] Therefore it seems unlikely that it was simply the advanced denominational chauvinism of Gladstone and Vincent that lost them the contest in 1847. On the contrary, Vincent's extreme opinions on church and state almost certainly gained him votes among the dissenting electors, as we shall see in Chapter 9. And of course, it was Capt. Gladstone's break, on religious grounds, from his core support base that resulted in their alienation from him on the hustings.

5.10 Ipswich, 1832–1847: summary and conclusion

A modern historian has written that '[t]he religious division between Anglicans and dissenters was the most important one in Ipswich politics until at least the mid 1830s.'[126] The present research bears this position out in the main, but must extend the terminal date. T.M. Gibson lost the 1839 by-election in large part due to matters of religion; denominational rivalry was clearly present in the 1841 contest and corresponded to political preference; the by-election of August 1842 pitted a fanatical bigot against a thoroughgoing reformer of religion; and it was the Maynooth Grant which ended the political association of J.N. Gladstone with Ipswich. As Professor Gash has observed, the 'general election of 1847—repeal of the Corn Laws notwithstanding—was fought on the religious rather than the economic records of the Peel and Russell ministries in so far as it was fought on any general issue at all.'[127] This was undoubtedly the case in Ipswich where, at least a decade into the reign of Queen Victoria, religion continued to fuel the engine of politics.

6

Religion and Politics in a Southern Midland Agricultural Town: The Case of Bedford

6.1 Bedford: Introduction*

In many ways, it is easier to assess the course of electoral politics in Bedford than it was in Durham, Nottingham, or Ipswich. For one thing, the borough experienced only the five general elections between 1832 and 1847, and there were no by-elections. Additionally, only five men contested Bedford's two parliamentary seats in this period—in contrast to Ipswich's 25!—making it a good deal easier to keep straight various political personalities. With the exception of one man, who contested only a single election, every candidate stood for the borough at least three times, and one candidate stood in every election in the 1830s and 1840s.

In large part, this seems to have been due to reluctance on the part of the inhabitants of Bedford to have dealing with men from outside the region. The consensus was that the electors of Bedford ought to be represented by prominent men, local to the county (or better still, the borough), and preferably of longstanding association. Witness the Russells (which family furnishes the dukes of Bedford) and the

---

* An agricultural county-town in the southern midlands, the borough of Bedford was located on the River Ouse, about 50 miles north of London. Its population increased from 6959 to 11,693 between 1832 and 1851, and its registered electorate was reduced from 1572 to 910 between 1832 and 1852, due to the extinction of potwalloper and other pre-reform franchises. Bedford was a centre for manufacturing agricultural and industrial implements, specifically in the corn and timber trades, and lace-, shoe-, and straw-plait-making. *Dod's* reports that the duke of Bedford could usually expect to return one liberal member, and the Whitbread family (also liberal) had some influence; both were in decline in the decade-and-a-half following the reform act.

Whitbreads, who had by 1832 returned their sons as members of the borough for much of the preceding century, and without interruption since the 1810s. The one genuine outsider who contested the borough in this period came all of 30 miles, from Buckingham, in the adjacent county of Bucks.

The electors of Bedford also seem to have desired for their borough a reputation for order and respectability in political matters. In point of fact, Bedford could be as seedy as other constituencies, and the outcomes of two elections were petitioned against.[1] But in one case, the petition was thrown out and in the other, which a parliamentary committee judged valid, the wrongly elected member was simply unseated and replaced by the true winner, without the ignominy of a by-election.[2] It was even common in Bedford at least to pay lip-service to the advantage of parliamentary representation split between a liberal and a conservative member.[3] On many levels, there was apparently genuine acceptance in Bedford of a balanced status quo.[4] Yet in spite of this complaisance, and in spite of the fact that both liberals and conservatives tried to play a careful game in which they offended the religious sensibilities of no one, controversies between Anglicans and dissenters regularly coloured elections in Bedford.

6.2   The 1832 and 1835 general elections in Bedford

The same three candidates vied for the parliamentary representation of the borough in both 1832 and 1835: Capt. Frederick Polhill (1798–1848) as a conservative, and William Henry Whitbread (1795–1867) and Samuel Crawley (1790–1852) as liberals. All three were local men, although the business interests of Polhill, who was the lessee of the Covent Garden Theatre and Theatre Royal in Drury Lane, and Whitbread, who was partner with his brother of a large brewery in Finsbury, kept them frequently in London. Crawley had sat as a member for Honiton (near Exeter), from 1818 to 1826. The two others were the sitting members for Bedford: Polhill since 1830,[5] Whitbread since 1818.[6]

Frederick Polhill announced his intention to defend his seat for Bedford in a handbill dated 3 September 1832, and rested his appeal chiefly upon his performance in the previous two parliaments. Most importantly, Polhill had given his general support to the cause of reform. But he had not been indiscriminating in this support. 'Looking upon the Irish Reform Bill,' he stated in his handbill, as calculated to throw the whole of the Representative power into the hands of the Roman Catholics, and fearing the increase of that power arising from the increase in the number of the Members proposed by it, [he] voted against it altogether.[7]

In light of this prejudice, Polhill presumably had not favoured Catholic emancipation, and was likely also in favour of maintaining the status quo regarding protestant dissenters.[8] Beyond that, Polhill declared himself independent of any party, and indeed inclined '*not to support the present Administration*, except when their measures appear... expedient and just.'[9] To achieve economy and retrenchment, he advocated the lowering of taxes, and the cessation of the present ministry's meddling policy abroad.

Captain Polhill criticized the ministry's foreign policy in another handbill, posted after the dissolution of parliament. This time he announced the 'two subjects, upon which [he was] anxious to express [his] sentiments,... SLAVERY and WAR.'[10] On the latter issue, he strongly censured the government's siding with France, against the Dutch, on the matter of Belgian independence from the Netherlands. This involvement, he feared, would have no good end, as it would alienate an old and valuable ally, 'aggrandize a Rival, seriously embarrass and injure our Commerce and Trade, increase our National Burdens, and plunge Europe again into general Misery.'[11] On the topic of slavery, Polhill would do all he could to promote the comfort of slaves, and 'to curb and punish the oppression of them in whatever form it may appear.' But he was reluctant to leap from a cliff in the dark. Polhill knew 'that where the British Flag floats Slavery ought not to exist,' but he rejected immediate emancipation as an option. This was due to concern for the interests of the empire, he claimed, as well as for the good of the slaves themselves.

> I would with Freedom [he wrote] give them more than the empty name. I would have them instructed as to the rights which Freedom confers, that they might fully understand it's [*sic*] blessings, without running the risk of suffering from it's [*sic*] too sudden operation.[12]

War and slavery, then, were then two principal subjects of Polhill's appeal to the Bedford electors in the fall of 1832. Besides what can be inferred from the aforementioned reference to his opposition to the already passed reform bill for Ireland, Polhill never once broached questions of the Church of England or dissent. But given his hostility to the proposal for Ireland, which had the effect of giving more representation to Roman Catholics (who made up some seven-eighths of the island's population), it seems unlikely Polhill would have supported any liberal measures of church reform, at least in Ireland.

In the run-up to the election of 1835, Polhill presented himself to the electors of Bedford as 'ever...a determined opposer of dangerous innovations, and a warm supporter of Conservative Principles.' This succinct manifesto, following hard on the heels of the king's recent dismissal of the liberal government over the issue of Irish church reform, must be understood as a commentary on that event. The interests of the church necessarily went hand in hand with 'Conservative Principles,' and the 'dangerous innovations' Polhill opposed were undoubtedly that government's proposed reform of the Irish church and redistribution of its wealth. So far as Frederick Polhill was concerned, the protestant ascendancy in Ireland must remain inviolate.[13]

Samuel Crawley came before the Bedford electorate in 1832 as a self-proclaimed radical reformer.[14] Having been absent from parliament for over half a decade, and therefore having missed the great debates of 1828, 1829, and 1830–1832, Crawley drew attention instead to the achievements of the recently dissolved House of Commons. The triumphant majority, he claimed, was devoted to freedom and good government, and he shared its reforming sympathies. With no recent career of his own to call upon—and with critics alleging that his record as member for Honiton was more in keeping with toryism than liberalism[15]—Crawley declared it his intention to 'emulate their [i.e. the liberal government's] example.'[16]

> There is no question which may be submitted to the Legislature [he continued], having for its object the *Education of the People*, the *Freedom of my Fellow Man*, or the *Abolition of Partial and Oppressive Taxation*, which shall not have in me a constant and steady supporter....

He reckoned the present ministry worthy of gratitude and confidence, and pledged that if elected he would support it warmly.[17]

Beyond the probably suggestive fact that Crawley conducted part of his canvass from a Methodist chapel,[18] no explicit evidence suggests that he or his fellow liberal, Whitbread, either espoused church reform as fundamental to their campaign, or appealed directly to dissenters. As we have seen previously, however, with the passage of the reform bill secured, there was in 1832 as yet no evident pressing issue for dissenters.

But the emphasis on 'the *Freedom of my Fellow Man*'—especially when expressed in 1832—almost certainly indicated Crawley's advocacy of the immediate abolition of colonial slavery.[19] In 1832, as it had been in the previous two general elections, abolition was a key issue around which dissenters rallied.[20] Thus the neglect of specific reference to religion in this case, which appears at firsthand to contrast with the attention to that topic evinced in three contests examined in previous chapters, becomes less striking. Samuel Crawley's vigorous attack on colonial slavery in 1832, along with his conspicuous presence in a Methodists chapel, suggests strongly his deliberate appeal to Methodists, and dissenters generally.

In his address of thanks to the electors after the election, Whitbread said nothing of religion, and announced his and Crawley's first order of business to be cooperation with the government to adjust the system of taxation.[21]

Religion found a more prominent place, at least in Crawley's appeal, in 1835. He described the upcoming election as an opportunity for the electors to reaffirm, by their choice of MPs,

> that they *still* desire to promote every just principle of reform in the CHURCH AND IN THE STATE;—that they are *still* anxious to secure those Reforms in the Church which *her best Interests* require, and will render her what she professes and ought to be,—A reformed Church, adorned by the *purity of her Faith*, and beloved on account of the *Tolerance of her Principles. ...*[22]

Strikingly, Crawley couched his advocacy for ecclesiastical reform strictly in the terms of the own best interests of the church. He argued that the reforms espoused by the late liberal ministry aimed to protect and promote the Anglican establishment by restoring its purity and tolerance, but forbore any notice of the position of dissenters. To be sure, most other would-be church reformers emphasized the positive implications for the church, and it is clear Crawley was eager not to outright offend churchmen. At the same time, no one could have taken his words as a compliment to the church. But it is curious that Crawley wholly disregarded an obvious opportunity to nod in the direction of the evident interests of dissenters, that is the principle of redistribution of ecclesiastical wealth by the state.

Whitbread topped the poll comfortably in December 1832, with 599 votes, while Crawley secured second place only narrowly, with 486 votes against Polhill's 483. The results reversed themselves in January

1835: Capt. Polhill and Crawley split the representation of the borough with 490 and 403 votes, respectively, and Whitbread bottomed out with 383.[23]

6.3   The 1837 general election in Bedford

Crawley's association with dissent was more pronounced in the run-up to the 1837 general election than it had been in either of the previous two contests. In a letter read before the Bedfordshire anti-church rate meeting, nearly four months before the election, Crawley promised that his votes in parliament would always accord with the wishes of nonconformists, and pledged himself specifically to oppose the church rate.[24] Although this commitment can hardly be regarded as secret, since it was reported in the local press, it is striking that Crawley initially chose not to make this part of his general appeal to the electorate three months later, at the end of June. Having sat for the borough twice before, his announcement to stand a third time merely asserted that constituents were already familiar with him and his record, coupled with a sweeping pledge to attend to the welfare of the nation generally, and of every class.[25] But as we have seen, such a position, which vaguely promises everything to everyone, does not necessarily carry any real commitment to anyone. Conservative candidates, in Bedford and elsewhere, readily issued statements very similar to Crawley's handbill of 28 June, but with the intention of maintaining the status quo *vis-à-vis* church and dissent.

But Crawley's more substantial commitment earlier that spring, to abolish the church rate, was used against the liberal candidate, as he learned ten days before the election. Arriving in town on the evening of 15 July, he declared himself shocked to learn that the

> most *outrageous slander* had been industriously circulated against me by my political opponents, *that I am inimical to the* CHURCH ESTAB-LISHMENT OF THIS COUNTRY—and they quote my vote in favor of the abolition of Church Rates in support of this charge.[26]

Crawley repudiated such slander. He yielded to no man in attachment and veneration to the Church of England, 'which [he] consider[ed] the Bulwark of [the] sacred Protestant Faith.' He admitted having voted against the church rate, but had done so, he claimed, 'to remove *from the poor man's shoulders a burden he ought not to labour under,* and at the same time [to] *strengthen . . . the Church,*' by increasing her respect from 'that great portion of the Community who complained of the Rates as a grievance and a fetter to their Consciences.' These were his sentiments, and he shared them with Her Majesty's ministers. '[I]f the present or any future Government should entertain principles hostile to the Church,' Crawley continued, 'no Member of the House of Commons would more decidedly oppose them than myself.'[27] Thus, while Crawley's commitment to ending the church rate was evident, his stated rationale behind abolition was no less striking. As well as granting an obvious concession to dissenters, he sought to give his position greater breadth and inclusiveness—and therefore appeal—by starting with the poor. He admitted the church needed to be strengthened and, to that end, he sought to appease 'that great portion of the Community' for whom the church rate was a conscientious burden.

Samuel Crawley reiterated this position a week later, at a meeting of the local Reform Club.

> His object [he stated] was to reform the Church in time; and delay would only increase public demand for a further reform than that which they [the government] now sought, and which he should not be disposed to grant.[28]

As a further palliative to dissenters, Crawley drew attention to his vote in favour of the marriage act of 1836, popularly known as the dissenters' marriage bill, which he hoped the assembly found satisfactory.[29]

In point of fact, Crawley had, by the time of the 1837 campaign, mustered an impressive parliamentary record on behalf of dissenters. In addition to having voted for the marriage bill in 1835 and 1836, he had supported all the other measures put forward by dissent since the beginning of the decade: he had always championed colonial abolition, and had voted with the minority to abolish the church rate in 1836. His commitment to protestant dissenters in England was strong, and his advocacy for the Irish was equally robust. On the latter topic, he insisted 'there was not a man living on the earth more anxious to afford the Irish equal privileges with the English.' Crawley claimed to have always voted in a manner designed to promote the welfare of the Irish, and promised to continue to do so.[30]

Frederick Polhill announced his intention to defend his seat two days after Crawley, and declared his principles unchanged from the first time he had proclaimed them in Bedford seven years earlier. He pledged to support to the best of his ability '*The Church, the Throne, and the Constitution.*'[31] He was a defender of the status quo, which necessarily favoured the maintenance of the church's place as part of the establishment, and was hostile to rival denominations. He described himself as willing 'to rectify abuses where *they really have* existed' (but the substance of his message essentially rejected the claims of protestant dissenters as illegitimate), and he pledged to preserve the Church of England in its privileged position.[32]

The third contender for Bedford in 1837 was Henry Stuart (d.1852), whose statement of policy was rather vague, but nonetheless fitted best with Polhill and principles of conservatism. He was

> a staunch Supporter of those Institutions which the wisdom of ages ha[d] raised up, and an ardent Admirer of the Glorious Constitution, through which Great Britain ha[d] attained a rank unequalled among nations.[33]

Stuart claimed as his further appeal to the electorate his family's connexion with the county, and his own acquaintance with the inhabitants of the borough, although his critics denied any association, branding him an intruder and an interloper.[34]

At the nomination, Stuart laid out his conservative credentials in a more obvious fashion. He defended the church rate, and called upon electors to '[s]tand forward, therefore, in defence of your church and your country...,' by voting for a man who would champion the rate in parliament.[35] Charles Robinson, a surgeon who seconded Stuart's nomination, raised the spectre of the French Revolution, with the attendant bogey of irreligion, should his nominee fail to be returned for the borough.[36]

Polhill also took up matters of religion at the nomination, and made them more prominent than Stuart had. '[The general election of 1837] is not so much a political as a religious struggle. It is,' he said 'whether we shall have those [who] support the Protestant religion or the O'Connell-rid ministry.' The votes cast in that election, Polhill claimed, would determine whether the people of Great Britain returned a government that supported a protestant or a Catholic establishment.[37] On the subject of the church rate, he declared unwavering support, insisting, with what was now a rather antique argument, that '[e]ven those who may dissent from the Church of England will always find it to their own interest to support mother-church.'[38]

But Sir Charles Frederick Palgrave, a chemist and a nonconformist who seconded Crawley's nomination, derided 'Talk about the Church and the State being in danger and all that nonsense! The time for that war-whoop serving a party,' he said, 'had gone by....'[39] Now Samuel Crawley stepped to the fore in his appeal to and advocacy of dissent with more determination than he had previously shown. First he recalled his role in the first reformed House of Commons, in carrying the act to emancipate the slaves, the measure he knew dissenters cherished especially. Again he plumed himself on his role in passing the dissenters' marriage act, and expressed disgust that the Irish corporation bill, which had passed twice in the lower house, had been twice rejected in the House of Lords, simply because 'the Irish were Catholics,' and were therefore judged unqualified to manage their own affairs. Finally, Crawley tore into the church rate with vehemence. He supported complete abolition and, perhaps in response to Capt. Polhill's dated defence of the measure, Crawley called it 'the grossest robbery. . . .' He compared the legal imposition, on those outside the Church of England, to financially support it, to his 'compel[ling] any of the inhabitants of Luton to repair [his] house at Stockton.'[40]

Samuel Crawley lost the election with 412 votes, seven less than Henry Stuart, who polled 419. Polhill was comfortably ahead with 467.

6.4   The 1837 election in Bedford: remarks during the chairing

After the poll, Crawley ascribed his defeat not so much to a triumph of the tory party in Bedford, but principally to whig defections. He was defeated, he said,

> by the treachery and unfaithfulness of certain Electors who have always professed themselves to be Whigs and voted as such, but have now deserted to the Tory camp,—by the non-exercise of their elective franchise by some who have *thus* aided in our defeat. . . . Had we the Tories only to fight against, I should yesterday have been entitled to the Mayor's return as one of your Representatives.[41]

But in this result Crawley did not wholly dismiss the impact of the church rate question. The defections he railed against had been triggered by 'those bigoted and intolerant' men of the tory interest, 'who ha[d] raised the senseless cry of "Danger to the Church," that bugbear in all periods of our history. . . .'[42] The *Cambridge Independent Press* concurred:

> The Whig interest in this Borough has lost its member entirely by the bug-bear question of Church-rates; the prejudices of two of the most

ancient (and always looked up to be as most respectable) Whigs in the town, having renegaded to the Tories on the above question.[43]

The *Independent* continued, identifying in particular the heads of two families who, 'on the grounds of consistency, ought to have been with the Whigs....' They were Francis Green esquire, coal and timber merchant and banker, and Thomas Barnard, banker, who had, respectively, abstained from polling and plumped for Stuart.[44] The influence of these two gentlemen extended to their dependents—a coachman, a footman, two nephews, a clerk, two brick-makers, three labourers, and a servant—who either voted in manners injurious to Crawley's return, or did not vote at all. Had these electors 'polled as on former occasion it would have given Mr Crawley a majority' of 13 over Mr Stuart.[45] The conduct of Green, the editors contended, was particularly despicable. Green had always called himself a friend of civil and religious liberty, and boasted his friendship with 'the House of Russell, a family that never verged from the principles they professed, of being advocates of civil and religious liberty,' and had made clear their desire for Crawley's return.[46]

In consequence of such apparent use of influence, which might compare, on a milder scale, to the 'thumbing' found in Nottingham and other industrial districts, Crawley was confirmed in his advocacy of the ballot. His critique of the open electoral system reveals particularly the widespread perception (and, as other instances from this study make clear, reality) of the political alignment of the church with toryism. Crawley anticipated with hope the time

> when Clergymen will no longer think it their duty, *as they will then know it will no longer operate to their advantage* to attempt to influence or coerce any Elector,—when they will no longer think it consistent with their Holy Calling to mingle in the profligacy and headstrong recklessness of principle such as this Election has disclosed, and when also they will be convinced that such improper interference goes much further to alienate the People's affection from the Church, then [sic] could possibly be effected by any vote given in Parliament by me, who am most anxious to preserve the Church by reforming existing abuses and making her what she ought to be—*free*, even from SUSPICION *of error*.[47]

Such a statement, added to Crawley's strong feeling on the hustings and his previous commitment always to satisfy dissenters, leaves little room for doubt about his feelings on the close association of liberalism with dissent.

Henry Stuart, for his part, assured his friends assembled for the chairing that 'he hated the d—n—n whigs,' and *'was ready to die for the church.'*[48]

6.5 The 1837 election in Bedford: controversy following the poll

Despite the initial decision of the poll, an investigative committee of the House of Commons declared Stuart's election invalid, and Crawley was seated after due scrutiny, in 1838. (Significantly, all four of the petition's drafters were nonconformists: Charles Frederick Palgrave, James Woodroffe, Henry Mayle, and George Peter Livius.[49]) Crawley retained his seat until the defeat of the ministry in 1841, and thereafter retired from political life on grounds of poor health. On taking leave of Bedford, he recommended to the liberal electors William Henry Whitbread, who had last sat for the borough in 1834, as a suitable replacement.[50]

6.6 The 1841 general election in Bedford

In his acceptance of a requisition to stand, Whitbread declared himself a supporter of the crown and 'yielding to no man in ... sincere attachment to the true interests of the Church....'[51] But as the assessment of Crawley's first electoral address of 1837 has demonstrated, such an expression is too ambiguous to be of much use. Few candidates who were not avowed nonconformists of one or another sect (and they were few in number) did not profess loyalty and devotion to the church, or fail to express respect and admiration for its forms. Indeed, even most nonconformist candidates and members expressed respect for the church; their criticism was only of its privileged position as a state establishment. Virtually no candidate even hinted at a desire for its demise.[52]

Most likely Whitbread's intention with such a statement was to strike a good defence, drawing thoughts away from the spectre of *Church in danger!* This could soothe the fears and thus ease the consciences of liberal electors who were also good churchmen and genuinely shaken by the first attack in England on one of its ancient revenues. In neither the formal address announcing his candidacy nor, so far as the available evidence reveals, on any other occasion, did W.H. Whitbread ever squarely engage issues relevant to dissent in the run-up to the election of 1841. Nor, as we have seen, does he appear to have made a direct appeal to dissenters in his electioneering efforts in 1832 or 1835. Yet in parliament he voted consistently to abolish the church rate and for other measures favourable to nonconformists. Furthermore, the national and local press regularly reported on significant votes in parliament and, in spite of his reticence on the hustings and in other venues, Whitbread's record in these respects would have been known to anyone who read a newspaper.[53]

The proceedings of the local liberal organization in 1841 seem to have been equally silent on dissenting issues. At a crowded meeting of the Bedford whig benefit club, in which several prominent nonconformists took part,[54] dissenting issues were wholly neglected. Nor were such issues on the agenda at another meeting of the borough's liberals, held two weeks later.[55]

Henry Stuart, however, who again stood with Capt. Polhill, raised the issues of church and state directly, as he had done in 1837.[56] He committed himself

> to defend the Church and the Throne from the attacks that are daily made by the present Government; to uphold the ancient institutions of this Country; and to preserve unimpaired that Constitution by the aid of which Great Britain has risen to the highest rank among Nations....[57]

The conservatives won both seats at the election, on 29 June. Polhill and Stuart polled 433 and 421 votes, respectively, and Whitbread brought up the rear with 410. Perhaps because the outcome was undesirable, from the editorial point of view of the *Bedford Mercury*, that newspaper gave little attention to the proceedings of the nomination and election. What little can be gleaned is that Stuart reiterated his support for church and throne, and nothing was said directly relevant to dissent.[58]

6.7   The 1847 general election in Bedford

The next general election was not for another six years, and by that time the issue of established religion was of central concern to the inhabitants of Bedford. Fully two years before the contest, a Bedford weekly ran an advertisement for *The Nonconformist*, which identified as 'the leading question of our age—the question of STATE-ENDOWMENTS OF RELIGION.'[59] A newly established newspaper in the summer of 1845, the *Bedford News* pronounced itself 'a journal of sufficient firmness of tone and independence[, such as had] long been wanting' in the county.[60]

In an early number, the editors 'lay... before [its] readers a plain and unreserved avowal of the political principals [it] intend[ed] to advocate, and of the mode of management [it] purpose[d] to adopt.' This included

> [t]he great principle of Civil and Religious Liberty [which] we shall firmly advocate, and invariably practice.... Religious controversy shall never find any place in these columns, except in those political questions of Church and State where it is impossible altogether to shut out all reference to the peculiarities of the dominant and would-be dominant sects.... Civil and Religious Liberty can never be perfectly attained in any country where there is a State Church establishment.[61]

Sir Harry Verney, Bt (1801–1894), a well-known evangelical and supporter of dissent, who had sat for Buckingham borough from 1832 to 1841, was invited to challenge the incumbent conservatives, Polhill and Stuart.[62] He accepted the requisition and issued a handbill that stated his political manifesto and detailed his career since 1832.[63] Verney presented himself as a supporter of the governments of Grey and Melbourne, a reformer at home and in the colonies, and a friend of free trade. Sir Harry was eager for all classes of society to have access to education, 'and that every member of this great Community may freely participate in the same, without prejudice to his conscientious Religious Opinions.'

> I am very desirous [he stated in his handbill] that all sums disbursed for National Objects, especially for those of a Religious Character, should be administered with a strict view to the advantage of all, and I do not see that any necessity exists for fresh Grants in favor of any Religious Community.[64]

Thus, it may be inferred, he would not challenge the Maynooth grant, but neither would he countenance further measures like it.

Such a reading is consistent with another handbill Verney issued a week later. The electors were evidently unsatisfied with the evasiveness of the previous handbill, and had asked him his position specifically on the grant, and generally on 'the endowment of the Roman Catholic Priesthood in Ireland out of funds of the State.'[65] Verney took a long view of the matter. He judged Pitt foolish in having established the seminary in the first place, and wished he never had. But St Patrick's College, Maynooth, did exist, and was established by the state. Sir Harry, for one, would not vote to abolish it. He made clear his acceptance of state support for the educational institution only, however, and distinguished this legitimate (if unfortunate) use of public funds from the illegitimate payment of the priests' salaries. 'I am hostile,' he said, 'to any endowment of the Roman Catholic Priesthood out of Public Funds.'[66]

Captain Frederick Polhill announced his candidacy the day after Verney had done. 'I shall invariably uphold the Protestant Faith,' he said, and

> resist as I have done on former occasions any Grant or Concession to the Roman Catholic Priesthood, and use my best efforts for the maintenance of the established Religion of our Country, and support the general encouragement of Education.[67]

These were the issues that Polhill judged really to matter; for the rest, he stated simply that he had long been associated with the electorate, and they knew his positions.

Henry Stuart, too, gave priority to the condition of religion and its potential fate in the upcoming sessions of parliament. He was known to the electorate already, he said, and connected not by the railways but by a longstanding unity of interests.[68] He promised, when on the hustings, to answer specific questions and account for past actions, but did want to underscore his determination to protect 'Reformed Religion.' In this endeavour, Stuart claimed, too many of the leading men of both parties had become lax. Therefore, he continued,

> I feel it incumbent upon me to state in the most explicit terms, that whether in Parliament or out of Parliament, I shall always do my utmost to secure the maintenance of those *Protestant Principles* which, by the Blessing of Divine Providence, have been the means of giving this Country the greatest amount of Liberty and Prosperity enjoyed by any People on the face of the Globe, and I have further to add, that I should feel it my duty ... to oppose every measure which may *directly* or *indirectly* countenance or support the engenderment, or encouragement of Popery in this County.[69]

Stuart continued along these lines for the duration of the campaign.

Mr Livius,[70] who introduced Sir Harry Verney at the nomination and whose family probably belonged to the Church of the Moravian Brethren, announced the candidate's mottos as 'Peace all over the world,... Free trade, and free circulation of the Word of God all over the globe.' He further emphasized the role played by religion in influencing the policies and life of Sir Harry, who was an active member of the Bible Society, the Church Missionary Society, and the Evangelical Alliance.[71] The man who seconded the nomination drew attention to the close friendship between Verney and Lord John Russell, an old Bedfordshire neighbour, who also happened to be the prime minister of Great Britain. Verney himself reminded his audience of the positive measures liberal ministries had accomplished during their decade in office. In retort to Henry Stuart's strong words against the Maynooth grant, and his alleged repeated opposition to it, Verney divulged that an examination of parliamentary divisions on three occasions the annual grant went to vote—in 1840, 1842, and 1843—revealed that Stuart had in fact not voted against it.[72]

Next Verney turned his attention to accusations that he favoured Roman Catholicism at the expense of the Church of England. He stressed his own credentials as 'a sincere Churchman.'

> I desire [he said] that the Church should be in the highest degree the means of spiritual usefulness to her members, and I have exerted any influence that I have possessed, in order to render the Church efficient by uniformly promoting the appointment of the most zealous and faithful clergymen on every occasion which has been presented to me....[73]

> I deeply lament the errors of the Roman Catholics. I have striven against the prevalence of their tenets, by co-operating in the distribution of the Holy Scriptures among them, both in Ireland and in foreign countries; it has even been my good fortune to assist in establishing Protestant Chapels and Schools in countries where, before that attempt was made, Protestantism was proscribed.[74]

But he condemned hostility to Catholics or any other sect, and wished all to be treated with access to justice. For dissenters and their 'exertions... in the cause of Christianity,' Verney expressed the most sincere respect and high appreciation, although he denied having ever led them to believe he was himself anything other than a churchman.[75] He also supported the abolition of Jewish disabilities.

Captain Polhill was absent from the hustings on the nomination day, having been advised of 'a writ against him,' and the threat of personal violence. As the returning officer, Alexander Sharman, the mayor, declared a show of hands overwhelmingly in favour of Verney and Stuart, whereupon T.A. Green demanded a poll on behalf of Polhill. Mayor Sharman's judgement was borne out: Sir Harry Verney and Henry Stuart claimed 453 and 432 votes, respectively, and Frederick Polhill 392.[76]

6.8   The 1847 election in Bedford: the chairing of the members

At the chairing, Stuart wondered at and regretted the third-place showing of Capt. Polhill (who, in any event, died the next year), and promised in parliament he would concentrate on preserving the cherished institutions of the state. He was determined 'to maintain inviolate the connexion between Church and State[, and] to resist the public Endowment of Error...,' but, in a clear effort not to offend dissenters, added his determination 'to extend Education to all classes of my fellow subjects, and to interfere with the Religious Liberty, and to deny the Civil Rights, of none.'[77]

6.9   Bedford: conclusion

But his words from the nomination are most revealing of the importance Henry Stuart attached to religion. He acknowledged having presented himself to the borough six years earlier as a supporter of Sir Robert Peel, but now stated that their paths had increasingly diverged. The late prime minister's apostasy from protection had not constituted a critical point in the parting of their ways, for that issue had not, according to Stuart, ever enjoyed the hallmark of true conservative principle its supporters claimed. Stuart had no hesitation in admitting that he had followed the conservative government that had proposed free trade. With a rapidly expanding population and the likelihood of a general blight in the potato crop in Ireland, he 'could not as a man and a Christian...refuse the admission of [foreign] corn into England, without which we must have been reduced to a fearful condition.'[78]

But what was unforgivable, in Stuart's eyes, had been the position of Peel's government on the Maynooth grant. With that measure, Stuart realized that the prime minister's principles on the most vital matters were not his principles. Specifically, he knew that he 'ought not to go with him [Peel] on the Maynooth grant...,' which Stuart opposed and feared as the thin edge of the wedge leading to further endowments outside the establishment.[79] Stuart readily championed the repeal of agricultural protection, even while addressing the electorate of an agricultural borough, but he would never countenance measures he judged hostile to the vital interests of the Church of England. This, for Stuart and many others besides, was the true litmus test for the conservative party in Great Britain.

7
Religion and Politics in a Southwestern City: The Case of Exeter

7.1 Exeter: Introduction*

Exeter, like Bedford, favoured men with local connexions. James Wentworth Buller (1798–1865), the sitting liberal member since 1830, belonged to a prominent political family in the southwest: indeed, no fewer than 16 Bullers (as well as a Buller-Elphinstone and a Buller-Yarde-Buller) sat for constituencies in Cornwall, West Looe, East Looe, North Devon, South Devon, Devonport, Totnes, Launceston, Liskeard, or Exeter in the eighteenth and nineteenth centuries, and one more Buller stood unsuccessfully for Helston.[1] In the last decade of the eighteenth century, the family had also furnished the cathedral city one bishop.[2] The two other candidates for Exeter were local men, as well: Edward Divett (1797–1864) and William Webb Follett (1798–1845), a county magistrate and a successful attorney,[3] respectively, stood for the borough's liberal and conservative interests.

---

* Located on the River Exe in southwestern England, the borough of Exeter was a county town with a cathedral. Its population increased from 28,201 to 40,688 between 1832 and 1851 (due in large measure to extended boundaries), and its registered electorate increased from 3016 to 3550 between 1832 and 1847. Its economic interests included lace-, serge- and coarse cloth-making (which were in decline in the decade-and-a-half following the reform act), and the shipping trade. *Dod's* reports that there was 'little [electoral influence] of a personal kind,' although the earls of Devon and the Buller family were listed among other with 'some slight interest' and, as a distinguished native of Topsham, W.W. Follett possessed a measure of personal influence.

7.2 The 1832 general election in Exeter

The nomination proceedings were straightforward. Each nominator confined himself in large part to his candidate's connexion with, familiarity in, and service to the borough. Interestingly, it was the nominator for the conservative Follett, a Dr Pennell, who most stressed his candidate's willingness to undertake the reform of all national institutions which time or circumstances rendered necessary, and to end all abuses.[4] Presumably, the liberals' credentials in this respect were beyond question, and required no elaboration. None of the nominators addressed topics which were likely to appeal specifically to dissenters, unless the reference by William Kennaway,[5] on Buller's 'anxious[ness] alike for the liberty of the subject..., and the happiness and independence of all' be taken in this light. Issues such as church reform and the abolition of slavery were left untouched.

For the most part, J.W. Buller's speech proposed measures of sober but steady reform. He praised the reform bill at length, but only hinted at some of the changes for which it had laid the groundwork.[6] He was also eager to assuage worries that the reform of 1832 had gone too far, let alone that it was intended to 'overthrow the Throne, and the Church, and destroy all that was august and venerable in the empire.' Still without elaboration, Buller assured his listeners that both the people (by which he meant the humbler classes) and the country could expect positive and striking changes as the result of reform. The first of these changes was 'an immediate examination of all our Establishments and institutions,' with an eye to renovation, not destruction. Wise and periodic adjustment, Buller contended, was no novel or untried approach, but one with precedent, including recent examples: 'after having removed the Test and Corporation Act [sic] from our Statute Books—after the Catholic disabilities had been withdrawn—' Buller judged that parliamentary reform had been all but inevitable. He welcomed suggestions that had been made to repeal certain dated navigation laws, and to ameliorate an inhumane criminal code.[7]

And he indicated that certain other reforms might be necessary. Buller did not, however—aside from an undefined commitment to lowering taxes—express what these might be. But it seems likely that his emphasis on reform with a view 'to giv[ing] new vigour to' certain established institutions meant the Church of England,[8] and it is obvious with which camp he sought to associate himself when he invoked the repeal of the test and corporation acts and Catholic emancipation.

The positions Edward Divett outlined on the hustings supplied the deficiencies of the rather bland remarks of his fellow liberal and their nominators, and he devoted the great bulk of his attention to matters of religion. First, however, he declared his support for the present ministry, on the grounds of its evident commitment to reform.

> As an individual [Divett] had no love for change, merely as such, but when change became necessary in order to [effect] the riddance of great abuses, then did he desire to see it, and any Ministers disposed to lend their aid in this way, would... have his support.[9]

Specifically, he turned to 'one subject that inevitably must come very early before' the next parliament.

> It was a subject, too, on which he knew many excellent persons in this city, of the most pure and philanthropic views, felt very deeply. He meant the subject of Colonial Slavery.[10]

Divett said he wanted to secure abolition as soon as possible, but always with regard for the best way to achieve this end, and with regard for avoiding confusion. Thus, he declared, he was eager to secure abolition by parliamentary legislation. On this important topic, Divett was uncharacteristically obscure, for it remains unclear how else abolition might be effected, and he was silent on the great question, evidently so controversial in other constituencies, of compensation to the slave-owners.

Next he addressed ecclesiastical matters. Vicious rumours had circulated in the town, Divett said, accusing him of being an enemy to the church and endeavouring to effect its ruin. Divett vehemently denied the allegations. 'He [said that he] was no enemy to the Church...,' but 'was one of its sincerest—its best friends; for he desired not to destroy, but to reform its abuses.'[11] Only a true enemy to the church, Divett implied, would wish to block reform, which was inevitable, and safer sooner than later. Although Divett archly refrained from elaborating his exact meaning, he obviously was alluding to the rumble of mounting discontent with the Church of England, and the beginning of open demands for its disestablishment. Having opened up the question, Divett continued apace on the specifics of church reform. On the subject of ecclesiastical revenues, he opposed the present system of inequitable distribution, which had as its chief fruit the proliferation of 'non-resident Rectors and starving Curates.' He desired to 'have these revenues apportioned among the working Clergy[, and] he would have pluralities entirely abolished as inconsistent with the very intention of the priesthood.'[12]

Here Divett seemed to wind down somewhat. Having addressed the important matters of colonial slavery and the reapportionment of church funds, he appeared to be drawing to a close with a general assertion that, in the same spirit of reform, other adjustments to certain national institutions would necessarily follow. But the details, he said, were too complicated to be addressed at present. At this point, however, Divett's enthusiasm was re-ignited, and he launched into a passionate attack on the ecclesiastical courts, which he desired, 'and at once, [to] have completely broken down....'

> [N]or, until this was done [he continued], did he think the country would be satisfied. In lieu of these he would have all proceedings of this kind carried on, as in the other Courts of Law, in the face of day. It was no longer a time to attempt to keep the world in ignorance, for men now required a reason for what they saw done, and who was the man who having a suit of law, was not desirous of seeing and knowing the steps it was carried through? All these things must be removed,—they were the fruits of the times when tyrants of old desired to retain their power through the fears and superstitions of, rather than to reign in the affections of their subjects, and were not fitting for a free and enlightened country.[13]

Divett proceeded to argue for the commutation of tithes and the necessity of ridding the boroughs of abuse at the hands of corrupt corporations as national priorities. Although ecclesiastical reforms of the character Divett addressed were not pressing concerns for dissenters— they could expect no benefits from them—they probably regarded such proposals with enthusiasm, as an extension of their dislike of the church's privileged position in the establishment, and their desire to see it reduced to the footing of one denomination among many. Therefore, reform of the ecclesiastical courts and tithe commutation were most likely popular issues with dissenters.

The unreformed condition of municipal government, on the other hand, did present a practical grievance for many dissenters, if less so in southern corporations than in midland or northern ones— such as Manchester, Birmingham, Leeds, and so on—where dissenters were a majority, but virtually without municipal representation before 1835.[14] Nevertheless, because they certainly resented the Anglican composition of almost all unreformed corporations,[15] virtually all dissenters welcomed municipal reform, and the old association, prior to 1835, of the corporation with the Church of England and conservatism would have been felt keenly in a cathedral city such as Exeter.[16]

Thus four of the five issues—inequitable clerical livings, ecclesiastical courts, tithe commutation, and corporation reform—to which Edward Divett devoted his energies in the election campaign of 1832 bore directly on ecclesiastical concerns, and were matters of consequence to dissenters. The fifth, the abolition of slavery, was certainly a dissenting issue, as well.

In the rest of his remarks, Divett attacked the conservative candidate Follett. His criticism was often highly personal, but one policy issue that did excite Divett was Follett's hostility to the reform act.[17] That measure secured, however, it seemed that what would hereafter divide Divett from Follett—and, by extension, liberals from conservatives— would be matters touching on religion, and the role of dissent outside the establishment. At least as early as the general election of 1832, that was the touchstone of division between the liberal and conservative parties, in Exeter as elsewhere.

Unfortunately, the text of William Webb Follett's speech is largely illegible. Naturally, much of it was an indignant reply to the abuse Divett had delivered. From his closing remarks, however, it is possible to conclude that Follett sought to defend and protect the church, the monarchy, and the constitution from onslaughts by the present ministry and those who supported the reform bill. These sentiments he more or less repeated in his valedictory statement following the close of the poll.

In returning two liberal members to parliament, Follett claimed, Exeter strengthened a threat to 'the Throne and the Altar ... alike,' and in doing so discredited the character of the borough. He said further that he had sought the suffrage only of 'those who will uphold the Church' in all its integrity.[18] In other words, Follett in 1832 made no false effort to ingratiate himself to the dissenters of Exeter.

At the end of the second day's polling, Buller had secured a convincing lead with 1615 votes. Divett, in spite of his fiery oratory on the hustings (or perhaps because of it), had 1121 votes, and Follett was defeated with 985.[19]

7.3   The 1835 general election in Exeter

While arguably much the same in substance, the tenor of W.W. Follett's campaign, in regard to openness to reform, was markedly more conciliatory in December 1834 and January 1835 than it had been two years earlier. On 16 December, he announced his intention to stand again for Exeter as soon as the dissolution of parliament became imminent, and declared himself 'most anxious to see effected those Reforms and Amendments which the lapse of time, and the altered circumstances of Society, have rendered necessary in many of our Institutions.'[20] The sitting liberal members, Buller and Divett, issued announcements two days later, and commenced canvassing on the 18th. Follett's recent appointment by Peel to the 'high and important Office' of solicitor-general kept him in London—it was also at this time that he as knighted—but a committee began canvassing on his behalf that same day.[21] Sir William published another address, similar in the main to the original from the 16th, but more explicit in detail. The discrepancy between the two most probably reflects the fact that the earlier one had preceded by two days the publication of Peel's Tamworth Manifesto—that is, the statement of the conservative party's new programme of commitment to necessary and cautious reform—and, as a member of the government, Follett was eager in his second address to accord with the party's new course. Thus he referred directly to the conservative ministry's policy of improving, rather than destroying, the institutions of the country, and his desire to 'remov[e] from Dissenters...all civil disabilities and exclusions, [and] to secure to everyone the fullest and most unrestricted enjoyment of religious belief.'[22]

Edward Divett's announcement to stand compared the potential of Peel's ministry unfavourably with the achievements made for England and Ireland by the previous government of Melbourne, and emphasized Divett's independence of party and his support for 'your Local Interests' and 'the future prosperity of your City.'[23] J.W. Buller's address simply announced his intention to stand.[24]

The nominations of Buller and Follett were lacklustre, if straight-forward, affairs; their supporters on the hustings emphasized in fairly neutral contours each man's independence and principles. John Tyrell esquire,[25] on the other hand, who introduced Divett, took advantage of his opportunity on the hustings to blast the present—and, in his view, unconstitutional—ministry thoroughly, arguing that any man opposed to it was a credible candidate. He demanded 'religious liberty for injured Ireland,' and proceeded to quote

> several passages from Sir Robert Peel's address [the Tamworth Manifesto], contending that the phrases in themselves were not only vague, but involved a negative.... Sir Robert told the electors of

Tamworth and of England, that the Ministry of which he formed part would not oppose the redress of 'real grievances.'[26]

Tyrell drew attention to the often shallow substance of the manifesto, and took particular issue with Peel's alleged commitment to the 'principles' of legislation favoured by nonconformists. 'In this,' Tyrell allowed, 'there [wa]s a remarkable instance of generosity towards a large, an opulent, and much grieved body of men,' but when it came to any substantial concession—for instance, on dissenters' admission to the universities—Peel opposed it with qualifying and, in Tyrell's view, unsatisfactory language. In all, Tyrell's tirade was a condemnation of Sir Robert Peel, the duke of Wellington, and the new ministry. Only at the end did he mention Exeter, or even remember to nominate Divett.[27]

Buller was the first candidate to speak. He affirmed his faith in the working classes, whom he praised as industrious and useful members of society. He accepted the king's prerogative in having dismissed Melbourne's ministry, but insisted on the primacy of the electorate's prerogative, which now was being consulted. This, Buller believed, embodied the principle of reform: that all interests were entitled to 'a fair trial,' but with the electorate enjoying the final say.[28]

Buller proceeded to discuss the legislation proposed by the late liberal government and, as that ministry had been dismissed in large part for proposing further ecclesiastical reform, he naturally focused heavily on religious matters. Buller was eager to revise the method of collecting tithes, which would, he argued, benefit both the landed classes and the clergy. In an appeal to other interests, he next addressed dissenters and their grievances. He claimed that 'no one was more anxious to bear testimony to their worth' than he, 'or to allow their consequence in the country.... [S]eeing their wealth and great respectability,' Buller understood well dissenters' desire for proportionate influence. He favoured the implementation of a national registry of births, to relieve dissenters from having to seek Anglican baptism, and presumably supported a measure to replace Hardwicke's marriage act, which had made only marriage celebrated in the established church legal, and thus discriminated against dissenters.[29]

There was one, and only one, claim made by the dissenters which Buller regretted the necessity of having to oppose. 'It was from no want of respect for the Dissenting body,' he said, '—it was from no want of a Christian and charitable feeling towards them, as well collectively as individually....' But, Buller contended, dissenters had no claim of right to admission to the universities. (Up to this point, his speech had been met mostly with cheers; this statement prompted 'Hear, cheers, ... signs of disapprobation, great clamour,' and 'Cries of "they have...." ') He acknowledged that all parents, especially wealthy ones, desired for their children the best possible education; this was a particular concern among dissenters, for education helped partially to relieve them from civil disability. But Buller believed that dissenters were abundantly and well provided in respect to institutions of learning. Moreover, he argued, the universities had rights, and their own funds to implement those rights, and no parliamentary legislation could justly interfere with their exercise of them.[30]

Buller conceded the need to strengthen the Church of England through reform. He judged the Church of Ireland a more delicate issue, but pronounced himself in favour of reform where it was needed, so long as the protestant character of the 'these kingdoms' was maintained unimpaired. On the question of the church rate, he stopped short of making payment wholly voluntary or of outright abolition, but desired somehow to relieve dissenters of their burdens.

In short, all of the proposed legislation J.W. Buller addressed was religious in character. Although he campaigned ostensibly on a liberal agenda, Buller promoted a programme that frankly had more in common, including its occasional ambiguity, with the conservative Tamworth Manifesto, than with liberal principles.[31] Towards the beginning of his speech, Buller had expressed general accord with the reforming policies of Lord Grey. This seems curious, for the liberal party had been formally headed by Melbourne since the summer. Perhaps this was a mere slip of the tongue on Buller's part, but perhaps he intended to register wariness of the comparatively advanced liberalism of the party's assertive second-in-command, Lord John Russell.

Divett took a firmer line than Buller, judging that 'whether judicious, salutary, and necessary reform should be carried on, or whether that great cause in which they had struggled so successfully should be abandoned ... was really the question at issue. ...' He turned his attention first to questions relating to the Church of England and the just claims of dissenters. Divett's goal was to reform all abuses present in the church, which otherwise must weaken its efficiency and prestige. 'He desired to see the Church ... broadly and deeply rooted,' and 'on this principle, and as a firm friend to the Church ..., he had moved for the abolition of the Church Rates.' So long as a church rate existed, he maintained, the struggle against it would continue as well, thus blemishing not only the reputation of the Church of England, but the good name of religion generally. Thus Divett employed a conventional, and comparatively neutral, argument against the church rate. But he also affirmed that dissenters, who included 'the most opulent persons,' rightly felt aggrieved at having to pay for the maintenance of buildings they did not use.[32]

Divett did not address the issue of dissenters' admission to the universities, but he did promote measures for the education of all classes of society. As the responses to Buller's statement demonstrated, no dissenters would tolerate a denial of their claim of right in this respect—but the matter would have been of personal interest to very few. The big concern for dissenters was the church rate, and on that point, Divett made his position clear.

Turning to the late crisis and the conservative ministry, Divett criticized the prime minister's waffling approach. Peel claimed to regard municipal reform as a high national priority but had, while serving on the review committee—of which Divett also was a member—attended meetings only once or twice, and never contributed anything of substance to the proceedings. Divett regarded Peel's apparently shallow commitment to this vital issue as very likely reflective of that of the Tamworth Manifesto and the conservative programme generally: 'if stripped of the chaff, the grain would be found to be little indeed.' Finally, in a tactic likely designed to appeal to dissenters, Divett reminded his audience of the role played by liberals in the House of Commons in abolishing colonial slavery, as well as in securing the repeal of the test and corporation acts and Catholic emancipation.

Follett commenced by defending the king's dismissal of the late ministry, in part because of the resignations of Stanley, Graham, Ripon, and Richmond.[33] He denied the allegations by Buller and Divett that the present ministry opposed reform out of hand, and reiterated the government's position, and his, as receptive to cautious and sober reform. He maintained, however, that there had been men in the late ministry who were avowedly hostile to the Church of England, and who sought and acted for its destruction. Such 'reform' Follett would always reject.

Turning to measures of reform that did have his support, Follett advocated the commutation of tithes, since the existing state of things, in which tithes were paid in kind, was obnoxious to all. He was willing to consider some revision of the method of collecting the church rate, in order to satisfy dissenters, but elaborated no further, and stipulated that any alteration must continue to provide for the upkeep of the church. He also favoured a marriage bill for dissenters, while expressing his hope that the time would never come when the act of marriage was stripped of all religious character, and made simply a civil contract. He denied dissenters any right to admission to universities which had been founded for the purpose of training ministers of the church; it was for the governing bodies of the two universities, and not parliament or any other body, to amend these. Follett reiterated his determination always to support those principles on which 'our Constitution in Church and State depends....'[34]

7.4 The 1835 election in Exeter: the outcome and analysis of the poll

In 1832, Buller had aimed to offend neither churchman nor dissenter, and in this he succeeded, principally by avoiding association with contentious positions. He expressed in passing his approval of the repeal of the test and corporation acts and the act for Roman Catholic relief, but committed himself no further—and in 1832 he led the poll. But in 1835 the electorate no longer countenanced such an ambiguous programme, and Buller's strategy of steering a middle course in an effort to offend none, resulted rather in his inability to gain the confidence of any. As they expressed themselves during the latter canvass, Buller and Follett advanced largely similar agendas, and Divett appeared the fringe candidate. In this light, it would have been natural for a radical bloc of voters to plump for Divett, and for the moderates or conservatives to split between Follett and Buller. After all, if anything, Buller was the least extreme candidate.

But times were different, and the politico-religious landscape of England, and the demands of Exeter's electors, had changed, too. Parliamentary reform had been the overarching theme of the 1832 general election. That measure achieved, it was supplanted by questions of church and state and, in 1835, as would be the case afterwards, the electorate wanted strong commitment on religious positions. Follett and Divett were for the most part direct on matters of religion, and therefore claimed the allegiance of conservatives and liberals, respectively. But Buller's moderate course signified lack of commitment on issues evidently of vital importance, and a large body of electors rejected him. The conservative candidate Follett came out at the top of the polls, with 1425 votes, Divett followed with 1176, and Buller with 1029. Buller would not again seek re-election for Exeter.[35] Divett and Follett would both continue to represent it for the rest of their lives.

7.5   The 1837 general election in Exeter: speeches before the poll

Within ten days of the death of William IV in June 1837, both sitting members posted handbills announcing their intentions to stand for re-election,[36] and more than two weeks before the election, the editors of *Trewman's Exeter Flying Post* predicted with confidence that they would be returned without a contest.[37] Addressing his supporters from his brother's house a week before the election, W.W. Follett concurred with the *Post*, but nevertheless considered it incumbent to make a strong stand on behalf of conservative principle. Significantly, Follett revived the memory of the borough's previous election for parliament, and the role played by religion in that contest. He made clear his conviction that unfailing attachment to the Church of England was a *sine qua non*, co-equal with commitment to the crown and the constitution, for true conservative belief.[38]

A few days later, on 19 July, Follett elaborated the position in speeches before the Exeter Central Conservative Association and the Exeter Southern Conservative Association. In addressing the former assembly, Follett reiterated his commitment to existing institutions, in contrast, he said, to the present liberal ministry's penchant for thoughtless and destructive innovation. 'Let...all look into history,' Follett urged his listeners,

> and they will but too clearly see, that the result of an attempt to raise the power of the House of Commons at the expense of the other branches of the Legislature, was the death of the King, and the destroying of the House of Lords....[39]

He continued with this lesson from history, pointing out that the rash experiment of the 1640s and 1650s had not led to any increase in the influence of the House of Commons, but rather its usurpation by military rule. Although Follett did not say as much directly, the corollary views on the established church held by seventeenth-century revolutionaries and nineteenth-century reformers—and the attendant spectres of chaos and war in the event a liberal government continued to act without restraint—are suggestive.[40] And, as Follett proceeded to demonstrate, 'nothing has tended so much to open the eyes of the people of this country, as the attacks which have been made on our venerated Established Church.' In other words, Follett judged the most striking contrast between conservatives and liberals in the decade following the reform act to be the positions those parties took regarding questions of religion.

Follett had heard arguments to the effect that support of the church ought to be on a voluntary basis and, he conceded, such a position had abstract validity. But, he persisted, there were large parts of the country where voluntary contributions alone could not provide for the upkeep of church and clergy,

> —and for these [he said] it broadly and plainly, it [wa]s the duty of the State to provide.... I resist to the utmost the measure that has been introduced into Parliament for interference with the property of the Church, and should it be brought forward again I shall still offer to it my resistance.... It is an essential ingredient in the principles of Conservatism, to resist any attack on the Church....[41]

In a halfhearted appeal to dissenters (who it is doubtful were represented in the ranks of the Exeter Central Conservative Association), Follett insisted that, even outside the Church of England, all who desired the inculcation of morality and religion ought to support a nationally established church. If he could not appeal to reason, Follett desired to appeal on sentiment: if most people loved the church, was it not right to support it nationally?

> If the persons who hold [voluntarist] language had seen as I have seen in another country, the Churches desecrated and turned to unhallowed purposes: the sanctuaries of the dead disturbed and all in a state of unsightly ruin throughout the land, they would surely pause before they were parties to any act by which similar lamentable consequences might be produced here.[42]

It was the duty of the government, Follett insisted, to provide religious instruction and places of worship for the poor, who otherwise surely would face hellfire. He continued:

> Should there be any such, however,—should there be any uninflu-enced by powerful considerations like these, then I do say that my feelings are not in unison with theirs, and I am sure no such feeling influences the breast of any true Conservative, whose desire is to uphold the Established Church, and to govern his life by the principles that are taught in it; and these I am satisfied are the opinions entertained upon this subject by my constituents.[43]

Addressing the Exeter Southern Conservative Association later in the day, Follett pleaded fatigue and exhaustion from the canvass as necessarily limiting his speech.[44] He did, however, muster sufficient energy to turn to what was, in essence, the theme of his campaign. He declaimed the present ministry as hostile to established religion, and again drew attention to the contest of 1835. He continued to blast liberals generally and concluded that only recently, and for the sole expedient of gaining temporary popularity at the polls, had it been liberal policy to attack 'the National Church.'[45] Although Follett did not identify the voting bloc liberals sought to win over by this ploy, the dissenters stand out as the most obvious benefactors, and therefore are the most likely indicated.

7.6   The 1837 election in Exeter: public addresses after the poll

The election was held on the morning of Saturday the 22nd. As he had done in 1835, John Tyrell, who introduced Divett, took a broad view of the duties incumbent on the task of nominator—so much so that his fellow supporters of Divett expressed disapprobation at the lengths his wandering oratory led him. The other nominators confined themselves to emphasizing their respective candidate's votes on various parliamentary divisions and, with no challenger on hand, the high sheriff declared Edward Divett and Sir William Webb Follett duly elected.[46]

Divett spoke first, and addressed his past, present and intended future political conduct. He expressed great pride in his role in supporting Irish, as well as English, corporation reform, and also certain reforms of the Irish church. He valued especially those reforms which established a precedent for bringing Ireland to an equal footing with England. Divett

> believed it impossible in the present day that the Protestant Church of the Minority could be maintained on the footing it now was [in Ireland], against the sense and strength of feeling that existed in the majority, who were Catholics; but when a disposition was shown to do justice and to conciliate, then that Church might be maintained.[47]

Divett also discussed his motives in the case of his votes on two matters which, he regretted, he recognized had been at variance with some of his usual supporters. The first of these was capital punishment. Divett admitted he disliked the death penalty, but was not prepared to oppose it outright until a satisfactory substitute (possibly absolutely permanent transportation) was proposed. The second controversy was 'that of Sabbath legislation.' Divett admitted to having voted in favour of Mr Poulter's measure—that is, in support of some sabbatarian restrictions. But the ridicule the measure had received in parliament convinced Divett that injury rather than improvement must follow the insertion of such religious concerns into politics: consequently he had voted against Sir Andrew Agnew's bill, which Divett judged so monstrous that he could not in Christian spirit support it.[48] He proceeded to clarify his opinions on the matter:

[His] belief on this question of Sunday legislation was, that it was impossible in this country to make things better than they were by any penal measure.... He had been in countries where the Sabbath was loosely observed, and he had been in countries where it was very strictly observed—he objected to both.

In the main, he believed people should not work on Sunday, but they ought not by any means be prevented from picnicking, exercising or otherwise playing on Sunday.

He had considered this subject deeply, nor could he find anything in the Gospel that justified resort to coercion in matters of this kind.... To his mind, such a line of conduct was inconsistent with the Religion of Christ.[49]

For dissent, of course, the wider application of Divett's principle—generally to prefer restraint from secular employment or recreation on Sunday, but never resorting to compulsory religious observance—had obvious appeal. Legislative sabbatarianism was never widespread among most nonconformists; rather it was more a preoccupation for high church tories in England, and for Scots.[50] Divett's attention to capital punishment also seems likely directed at dissenters. Although abolishing the death penalty was not a principal concern of dissenters—except, of course, in the case of Quakers, for whom the practice was repugnant—probably a significant number of non-Quaker dissenters nonetheless gave regular support to the campaign against capital punishment.[51] Most likely, then, it was dissenters whom Divett meant when he alluded to a section of his regular supporters, and he was eager to reassure them that, though he appeared to have wavered on two matters that interested them, he had deliberated the issues, and in the end still represented their views.

For his part, Follett stated his disapproval of the direction in which the policies of the present government were leading the country. He had generally supported corporation reform, but with some outstanding reservations. On the matter of Irish municipal reform, however, Follett 'had voted against it at every stage.' He claimed to wish, 'as much as the most strenuous supporters of that measure did, to see the Irish in possession of every civil right and every civil privilege,' but did not believe the bill had had that design. Rather Follett believed it was calculated to make many things worse, and improve nothing. It is most striking that Follett seemed to have deliberately omitted the '*and religious*' that, in almost universal contemporary usage, appeared in tandem with appeals for *civil* rights or privileges.

From this provocative omission, the conservative member finally turned to the question of the church rate which, he pointed out, Divett had curiously not discussed. Follett's position in this respect was also evasive, if in keeping with charges of ambiguity made in the last elections against Peel's Tamworth Manifesto. Regarding the church rate, Follett had

> declared that he was ready to remove any hardship that pressed upon the Dissenter, and he said so still, but he never said that under any plausible pretence that might be put forth, he would consent to a removal of obligation, where the object was not relief on the score of sincere and conscientious objection, but to get rid of this means of support of the Church altogether.... The measure which had been brought forward by Ministers...was not so much a relief of the Dissenters, as a measure for stripping the Dignitaries of the Church of the possessions of that Church, and...on the grounds of its being an interference with private interests and private property it was impracticable.[52]

Follett repeated the allegation he had expressed before the Exeter Southern Conservative Association, that the ministry had only adopted church rate abolition and other so-called reforms in ecclesiastical affairs as electoral expedients, and closed finally with the reiteration that he had no confidence in the government.

7.7 The 1837 election in Exeter: private addresses after the poll

Afterwards, before friends and supporters at their respective victory dinners, Follett and Divett each spoke more candidly of their politico-religious opinions. Among other things, Follett disparaged the recent appointment under the Melbourne ministry of a registrar-general of births, marriages and deaths.[53] He judged 'any good effect was doubtful.... The only benefit, if that could be called a benefit, was that of removing the solemn sanctions of Religion from the most holy and important contract into which mankind can enter.' He also stated, as a matter of course, 'that no man now could occupy public situation without belonging to one or the other of the two great parties in the state.' Follett rejoiced that the liberal party, which he associated with the destruction of the church and other institutions, had for the past four years steadily been losing ground to the conservative party that defended the establishment.[54]

At the liberal dinner, Divett justified having failed to mention the church rate controversy from the hustings, in order 'to avoid all topics of an irritating' character.[55] In any event, he argued, they all knew his position on the matter already. No longer in the mixed company of the combined electorate, Divett felt uninhibited in unleashing vitriolic invective against the local conservative church interest. Among other things, he referred to Exeter as 'this hitherto priest-ridden city....' He also launched into lengthy diatribes against the duke of Cumberland (1819–1878), now King of Hanover, and the influence of Orange Lodges in Ireland, in the army, and elsewhere. He admitted his personal preference for protestantism, but could not countenance its forced and unnatural imposition on Catholic Ireland. Although a young man,[56] Divett claimed he was an old reformer, and although he had not sat in the House of Commons in 1829, he had nevertheless been 'an early advocate for Catholic Emancipation.'[57]

Touching on the church in England, it was Divett's view that '[a] sufficient reform in the Church Establishment was a most important object,'

and he thought in the forthcoming Parliament much more would be done for making it a better means for the diffusion of genuine Christianity:—that much also would be done for taking away from it political feeling. He sincerely regretted to see so many of the Clergy engaged in political matters. He thought that every man undoubtedly had a right to express his opinions, but when men were paid for functions of a far different nature than political topics, he thought it most inadvisable that such a course should be abstained from. He was sorry to see Reform in our Episcopal Bench was not so rapid as he could wish. Yet there was even now a great improvement. They had now a Bishop put on that Bench—the Bishop of Norwich—who was a sound and serious reformer. He hoped in the future that the Bishops would discourage, not as in many places promote, Political Topics.[58]

In short, virtually everything Follett and Divett addressed in 1837, both publicly and before friends, was of a politico-religious character, and much of it was particular relevance to dissenters or Catholics.[59]

7.8   The 1841 general election in Exeter

By the summer of 1841, Melbourne's control of the House of Commons had become highly problematic, and conservatives had a strong plurality. With its support seriously fragmented, the government decided to call an election. The great issue of the general election of 1841, ostensibly, was free trade—but as the studies of the other boroughs have made clear, what party leaders sought to emphasize did not always animate the electorate. Exeter provides an excellent example of how little, if at all, free trade could matter in 1841, and that what continued to arouse voters and—as a consequence, lead to the victory or defeat of a candidate—was religion.

On 8 June 1841, Edward Divett had handbills posted throughout the borough announcing his intention to stand for a fourth time. He took up the ministerial position, declaring himself a lifelong champion of free trade and hostile to all forms of monopoly. The next day a handful of electors for Exeter resolved to re-elect Divett, although not on the grounds he had recently stated. Instead they recognized his concern for local interests, and particularly his 'uniform and steady exertions for an efficient Reform in our Institutions,—his support of the Principles of Civil and Religious Liberty. . . .'[60] Similarly, notice of Sir William Follett's candidacy, also dated the 8th, made no mention of free trade or protection; it merely asserted that the electorate was already familiar with the candidate's political positions, and that he stood to defend the constitution.[61] The Eastern and Western Conservative Associations of Exeter met the next day to requisition the Right Honourable Algernon George Percy, Lord Lovaine (1810–1899) to stand as well, as 'a staunch

Conservative, [and] a worthy colleague with Sir William Follett....'[62] Lovaine's reply confirmed that his 'Principles [we]re identical with those of Sir William Follett,' which the former elucidated to be advocacy of commercial and agricultural interests alike, zealous attention to the welfare of Exeter, and attachment to the Church of England and the constitution.[63]

The candidates and their supporters began canvassing the borough well in advance of the election, and the *Post* predicted the contest would be severe. Lovaine, they acknowledged, hailed from the northeast and was hitherto unknown in Exeter, but had received a flattering requisition from local conservatives. Follett and Divett could boast local connexions. Although Follett had secured a strong majority in 1835, Divett had, '[w]ithout reference to party...most assiduously sought to comply with the wishes of the Electors.... [Consequently,] men of all political opinions—many indeed his most strenuous opponents—[thought] him worthy the highest approbation.'[64]

At a liberal meeting held two weeks before the election, Divett spent most of his time outlining his opinions on the antagonistic concepts of free trade and monopoly. These were, he said the two great principles facing the country, and he came down decidedly in favour of the former.

[C]ommerce should be free [he declared];...there should be no let or hindrance to the industry of the inhabitants of this country; but...they should be at liberty to carry on trade in all their several lines and callings with every part of the world. [T]he great question in this coming struggle [i.e. the general election] will be whether the empire of Monopoly, or the empire of Free Trade shall prevail.[65]

Divett asserted that England was no longer predominantly an agricultural, but rather a manufacturing country, and proceeded to assess the evils of the Corn Law and the monopoly of West Indian sugar. He concluded with the necessity of voting by ballot, which many liberals saw as a second issue of broad appeal to the electorate.[66]

Divett's liberal audience submitted patiently and graciously to what was, in essence, their candidate's ministerial stump speech. Once control of the meeting's agenda was in their own hands, however, they shifted to rather different concerns. The first resolution moved that

Divett's uniform and steady exertion for an efficient reform in our institutions,—his support of the principles of Civil and Religious liberty,—his undeviating advocacy of the improvement of our

Commercial Code,—and his constant and anxious attention to our Local interests during three successive Parliaments in which he has been our Representative, entitle him to our warmest thanks and continued confidence.[67]

Thus Divett's support for reform generally, and his 'support... of Civil and Religious liberty' in particular—which issues, it should be noted, he had not addressed at all that day—received priority, while his concern for 'the improvement of our Commercial Code' came afterward, and with no reference to free trade or protection.

Next the Revd Dr George Payne (1781–1848), a Congregationalist minister who in 1836 had been chosen as chairman of the Congregational Union of England and Wales, urged the assembly to vote only for men whose actions tended to support national prosperity. Such a proposition had obviously widespread appeal, but Dr Payne continued, indicating specifically those measures demanding 'the gratitude of the great body of Dissenters....'[68] Liberal MPs such as '[o]ur excellent friend Mr Divett,' Dr Payne argued,

> have removed the Corporation and Test Act [*sic*], and I thank them for it. They have permitted us to solemnize marriages in our own places of worship, and by our own pastors—the choice of our own hearts....They gave us too that great and good measure Reform....From the unhappy slave they knocked off his fetters, and taught him to stand erect as a free man.[69]

It is plain that Payne had not the slightest doubt that Divett and the liberal party were the great and especial champions of the dissenters, and that in many cases his use of 'us' or 'our' explicitly applied to those outside the establishment, viewing the liberal party, as it were, as a dissenting mainstay. His list of accomplishments touched on nearly every one of the dissenters' goals that had been achieved through parliamentary legislation in the first half of the nineteenth century. Furthermore, he believed that, had it not been for conservative obstruction, more reforms could have been achieved, and further burdens relieved from dissenters.[70] Dr Payne turned lastly to the question of monopoly, but in a fashion distinctive of his religious preoccupations. Namely, he alluded to the liberal government's having 'abolished...—mainly through the instrumentality of two noble minded men,—one of them a friend of my own,—...the monopoly of printing Bibles.'[71] The application to the monopoly in religion claimed by the Church of England is evident.

The meeting's second resolution pledged the assembly to exert itself to the utmost on behalf of the candidate's return. Divett thanked everyone for their support and, perhaps sensing that his earlier focus solely on free trade and the ballot had been received more politely than enthusiastically, hastened to re-establish his credentials as an outspoken champion of religious liberty and the rights of denominational minorities. Specifically, he drew attention to 'the bill he had the good fortune to carry through the House of Commons, for giving municipal privileges to the persons of the Jewish persuasion....'[72]

The requisition of the Eastern and Western Conservative Associations to Lord Lovaine was formally delivered by Gen. Samuel Mortimer on 10 June. It called upon Lovaine to represent 'the great, sound and noble principles of Conservatism,' which Gen. Mortimer elaborated further as 'support and [maintenance of] the sacred and legitimate rights of the Altar and the Throne.'[73] Divett and other liberals had already poked fun at the weakness of Lovaine's local connexions, claiming he was 'only known as the son of Lord Beverley, whose only connection with the county of Devon..., consisted in his being the patron of the rotten borough of Beeralston....'[74] Lovaine's brief response to the conservative requisition was orthodox party cant, consistent with the charges of Divett et al. that he was a pawn of the Carlton Club, which had subjected Lovaine to involved vetting procedures before endorsing him.

Follett's arrival in Exeter and the ensuing conservative rally proved more lively affairs. As Divett had done, Follett first drew attention to the importance of the upcoming election. It would, he suspected, demonstrate overwhelmingly that the country favoured conservative principles. By this, however, he did not mean protection or the right of monopolies.

[He meant] those principles of genuine loyalty which give birth to feelings of attachment to the Throne,—which give birth to feelings of attachment to the Established Church; and to those free Institutions of our country, out of which springs all national prosperity, and individual happiness and comfort which we enjoy.[75]

For Follett, the conservative agenda remained in 1841, as it had been throughout the 1830s, in large part defined by its defence of the Church of England, and in this respect it contrasted sharply with the present ministry: 'We have saved the Church from attacks which have been made upon it, and have prevented the wild and violent schemes of a section of her Majesty's Government from being carried into effect.'[76]

Follett also denied any particular liberal association with free trade; rather, he claimed, that principle was a smokescreen, designed to provoke the poor with promises of cheap bread, to incite class against class, and thus to divert attention from the government's miserable mishandling of affairs. Perhaps in an effort to tug at the heartstrings of dissenters, Follett further challenged the government's commitment to ameliorate the plight of black slaves, whose condition, he and other conservatives alleged, free trade inevitably imperilled.[77]

The respective canvasses continued into the week preceding the nomination, on 28 June. In introducing Divett, Mark Kennaway esquire,[78] attorney at law, contested the position that the government's proposed policy of free trade in sugar would tend to encourage slavery in Brazil, Cuba, or elsewhere. The preferential duty on sugar, he argued, only profited those West Indian planters for whom the British public had already paid out £20 million compensation for the emancipation of the slaves, and it was ludicrous to suggest that the proposed liberal measures threatened slaves in other places. Who was it, Kennaway demanded, who had laboured for a quarter century

> to extinguish this foul blot of national escutcheon? . . . . [I]t was the liberal interests of the country that ever kept this question alive, and made the cause of suffering humanity their own; and never departed from it until they had accomplished in our colonies the complete emancipation of this dark, and too long degraded portion of our race.

Kennaway accused conservatives of having, in their half-century in government, done little more than to run up expenditure and enact bad legislation. He contrasted this with the accomplishments of liberals over the past dozen years.

> In the first place he would cite to them, although not the first in order of time, that great and memorable act the Emancipation of the Slaves in our Colonies. In the second place they had fought for Catholic Emancipation.

Third and fourth he cited as parliamentary and municipal reform.

> And lastly they put an end to all the bad spirit that was engendered, and those injurious feelings to which the circumstances scarcely ever

failed to give rise, in the exercise of the power of taking Tithes in kind; that barbarous and unholy law which for so many years checked industry and improvement, and pressed most hardly on a most valuable portion of the people.[79]

Kennaway had begun with the observation that the queen had dissolved parliament 'for reasons... of the trade and industry of the country...,' but in addressing the trade in sugar, very rapidly digressed to those issues that really inspired him: the plight of slaves and dissenters, for instance, reform legislation, and reducing the burdens imposed by the church establishment. The other five nominators did not do much more than to endorse their respective candidates, but Kennaway's words from the hustings indicate those concerns which truly fired the electorate of Exeter in 1841, and they were not issues of free trade or the ballot.

Much of Divett's speech, unfortunately, is illegible, but part of it appears to rebut allegations printed and distributed by Follett, against the liberal ministry generally, and specifically its commercial proposals. Evidently, Follett's address alluded to the 'great peril,' followed by 'glorious triumph,' the nation had experienced in 1835. In reply to this evident mention of the controversy of Irish church appropriation, Divett responded:

> He knew of no peril in which the country was placed at that time, unless indeed, it could be said to have been placed in peril by the Orange faction in Ireland. The Orange flag was certainly then unfurled in the sister country, but a wiser and much sounder system of policy prevailed in Ireland now.[80]

Evidently both conservative and liberal camps were much intent on keeping alive the fire of religious debate as the surest way of exploiting the differences between the respective parties and energizing the electorate, even if the strongest recent demonstration of this lay six-and-a-half years in the past.

The bustle and enthusiasm of the assembly prevented anyone from hearing the conservatives, but Follett was able to address his supporters under more favourable circumstances later that day. He addressed many supposed misconceptions that Divett, Kennaway, and others had promulgated, and returned to his theme that liberals favoured free trade only as a means of inciting agitation, not out of principle. Furthermore, Follett insisted that neither he nor the conservative agenda was inherently inimical to free trade.

And, [he continued], these are not Whig doctrines. They are not taught in any Whig School. Who is the man who is universally acknowledged to have been the great author of those principles? Who was Mr. Huskisson? Was he a Whig? The Whigs are undoubtedly fond of claiming a great deal, but I suppose they will hardly attempt to claim him....[81]

Follett continued in this vein:

And while I am on the subject of claims, I am reminded [that whigs claim credit for abolishing the slave trade]. Well, gentlemen, if they claim Mr. Huskisson, as a Whig, do they claim also the best and the greatest friend of the negro—that man whose whole life and energies were devoted to the cause of abolition? Do they claim Mr. Wilberforce also? No, gentlemen, Mr. Wilberforce was no Whig.[82]

In short, Follett denied the liberal party its exclusive claim to the causes of free trade and emancipation. The ministry of the day certainly claimed the former issue, and the liberal party would continue to rally round it even after the Corn Laws were abolished in 1846. But as Follett argued, this simply did not reflect reality. What clearly motivated him and his conservative supporters was championing the cause of the Church of England. He defined liberals in 1841 in terms of their wild and revolutionary doctrines and, although he did not state it directly in this instance, the wildest of liberal doctrines for him were those that pertained to the establishment in church and state.

Follett and Divett were re-elected with 1302 and 1192 votes, respectively (over three-quarters of the votes cast for Divett were plumpers); and Lord Lovaine trailed in third place with 1119. There was a by-election six weeks later, following Follett's appointment as solicitor-general under the new conservative ministry, and Follett was returned unopposed on 13 September.

7.9 The April 1844 and July 1845 by-elections in Exeter

If the outgoing liberal government had intended the general election of 1841 as a showdown between the principles of free trade and protectionism, this dynamic should have been more prominent still in Exeter's two by-elections of 1844 and 1845, which pitted a free trading candidate, Maj. Gen. John Briggs (1785–1875), FRS, backed by the Anti-Corn Law League, against the conservative interest of the borough.[83] The first contest, on 20 April 1844, was occasioned by Follett's appointment as attorney-general. Having been frail much of his life, and tubercular since his 20s, Follett's ill health prevented his presence in Exeter for the election.[84] Naturally, the free trader could anticipate greater support from local liberals than conservatives and, in nominating Gen. Briggs, Samuel Maunder[85] drew notice to the candidate's commitment to the ballot (another liberal issue in 1841), as well as giving particular attention to his position on religion:

> General Briggs is in favour of perfect freedom of conscience in religion: he is also in favour of a wise and liberal plan of education; and these I believe to be essential to the liberty of the people.[86]

Thomas Besley, printer and owner of the *Devonshire Chronicle and Exeter News*, who seconded the nomination of Gen. Briggs, did more service to the cause of free trade than Maunder had done, but even he broadened his appeal as he concluded the nomination, insisting that 'If England would be great and powerful, she must be free,—that is free in the just and proper sense of that term.—She must have freedom of trade as well as freedom in other things.'

If Besley's words imply religious freedom, Briggs's own statement made the concern explicit. Indeed, on his favoured topic of free trade, Gen. Briggs presented himself rather poorly, and even sympathetic listeners smirked at his cloudy calculations whereby, through careful, wise and free management, 'the granite hills of Dartmoor,' which covers 80,000 acres, could sustain 640,000 acres of 'ripening ears of golden grain' and sugar cane![87] On matters of religion, his sense was easier to grasp. Of the 'distinct and most memorable eras' of English history, he cited

> the first of these [wa]s that in which Magna Carta was obtained from King John; the second was the Reformation that took place in matters of religion; the third was the period of the Commonwealth; the fourth that of the Revolution in 1688....[88]

General Briggs's appeal to liberalism and dissent was obvious. Distinct though they were, all four eras to which he had alluded were cherished by posterity as advancing the freedom of the English church, and in all cases save the reformation, were driven by interests intent on restricting the crown's prerogative. Moreover, liberals and dissenters regarded all four eras as stages in the enlarging of English freedom more generally.

Briggs may have stood primarily as a candidate backed by the Anti-Corn Law League but, his position made plain, the goal of freedom in trade was only part of a greater object, cherished by dissenters and liberals everywhere, of perfect freedom in religion and all things else. In case any had missed the sentence of this lesson in history, Briggs in his closing words cast a wider net of appeal, inclining himself to liberalism generally, advocacy of the ballot, 'and, as respects religion, desirous that every man should enjoy the most perfect liberty of conscience.'[89]

Afterwards, Sir Robert Follett, one of Sir William's brothers, addressed conservative supporters, having been forbidden (along with Spencer, another brother) by the high sheriff to speak before the assembly of the special county court, on the grounds that neither man was a borough elector. Free trade supporters also assembled elsewhere, and one of them, Robert R. Moore (1811–1864), sought to allay the concerns of what might follow repeal of protectionist legislation by reminding his listeners of the warnings that preceded Catholic emancipation and the repeal of the test and corporation acts.[90] Evidently 15 years after their passages through parliament, these measures were still regarded by liberals as emblems of what divided them from conservatives, who opposed in principle any reform legislation which tended to detract from the position and prestige of the established religion, by promoting rival denominations.

General Briggs lost overwhelmingly to the absent W.W. Follett, claiming less than 30 per cent of the votes cast. Undeterred, however, he presented himself before the Exeter electorate 14 months later, to contest the vacancy caused by Sir William's death, on 28 June 1845. Two days later, Briggs posted a notice of intent to stand again for the borough as a free trade candidate. 'With respect to legislation in matters of Religion,' he declared himself 'in favour of full liberty of conscience,' albeit, in clear reference to the current controversy over the government's Maynooth College act, in opposition to any extension of state endowments for religious purposes.[91] The local conservative organization was seriously fragmented over the same issue, which had passed into law that day, but the greater part shortly settled on Sir John Thomas Buller Duckworth (1809–1887), a local notable with cathedral connexions, who accepted.

Election proceedings commenced seven days later. Charles Bird esquire rose first at the nomination, to introduce Gen. Briggs, whom he praised as a champion of freedom in trade and 'likewise...the friend of Civil and Religious freedom.' Exeter had already distinguished itself in pursuit of one of these 'two great freedoms,' Bird declared, since in the face of the country it was honoured and distinguished for the struggle it had made in defence of religious freedom.... The electors of Exeter had it now then in their power to complete the work. He would scarcely call it a climax for it was only as the very simple gradation as one and one make two. By their firmness and decision they had secured their religious freedom, and might secure their commercial freedom also.[92]

Bird's rhetoric evinces a widespread belief among liberal reformers in the nineteenth century, that freedom in civil and religious matters were really two sides of the same coin, and that the one must necessarily imply the other. This language and sentiment has appeared throughout this study, and perhaps most recognizably in comments by Gen. Briggs at the previous by-election.[93] Bird closed by reiterating Gen. Briggs's commitment to 'the full liberty of conscience,' and complaining that the conservative Duckworth, in his printed address, had said nothing of substance 'on those great and grand principles as well religious, civil, and commercial....'[94]

Great confusion and dissention accompanied Briggs's attempts to speak, but it seems he confined himself strictly to his chosen topic of free trade, and said nothing of religion. His nominator had, of course, vouched for his credentials in this respect, and Briggs had himself treated the subject on previous public occasions.

For his part, Duckworth countered the charges that he had been unclear on certain important matters. Although Bird claimed not to have found them in his address, they were plainly there, Duckworth insisted, and 'they [we]re CONSERVATIVE PRINCIPLES':

It is upon this basis I shall endeavour to uphold and maintain the Protestant Established Church of England; and if I can, to extend the benefits that Church is calculated to afford to all those who may conscientiously differ from her; but at the same time taking care that neither her rights nor her immunities are surrendered back to those whom the circumstances of the Country required should be taken from them.[95]

In other words, the cornerstone of conservative principles for Sir John Duckworth was close association with and unfailing defence of the established church. Issues of trade or protection found no part in his definition of conservatism and, when he did address these matters, he came forth not in a hostile, but in a sceptical, almost neutral, position.

He declared himself 'not...in support of perfect free trade, but' neither yet opposed to 'well devised measures' to adjust the existing system of duties and restrictions. 'There was,' however

> one other subject and only one which he intended to touch on at present, and that was one on which he was well aware a large body of the people in Exeter did feel most warmly. This was the question of concessions to the Roman Catholics.... And [he] desired now thus publicly and openly to say that he would not pledge himself as to the line of conduct he would pursue on this or that question, or this or that point, and this he would not do even though the issue of the present election were made dependent upon it.[96]

As previous chapters have shown, most tellingly in the contemporary controversy in Ipswich, and to a lesser degree elsewhere, a candidate's position on Maynooth could seriously disrupt his political career. Duckworth was disinclined to commit himself as absolutely opposed to the government's recent decision, but was determined to avoid the fate Capt. Gladstone faced in Ipswich. Thus, if ambiguous on policy, he went on to make manifest his negative sentiments toward Roman Catholics. Duckworth recognized the strength of hostility to Catholicism, which he judged part of the fabric of Englishness, 'and with the exhibition of which he by no means found fault.'

> And while he said this too he would also say further, that he was most fully sensible of the terrors and the dangers of Roman Catholic opinions, and little likely to be in any way assisting in giving undue extension or power to these.

If this were not enough, Duckworth finally directed the unconvinced to inquire of his intimate friends of his lifelong loyalty to the Church of England.[97]

7.10   The 1847 general election in Exeter

General Briggs was defeated by Duckworth by only a slightly smaller margin than he had been by Follett 14 months earlier and, with the Corn Laws repealed in June 1846, did not challenge Divett and Duckworth, the sitting members, in 1847. The two incumbents announced their stands for re-election in separate handbills dated 14 July. The substance of Divett's was to hope that '[t]he present absence of violent political feeling' boded well for future social improvement. Duckworth stood on his independence, and pledged himself to education, health, universal comfort, the improvement of community institutions, and the protestant principles of the country.[98]

The nomination and election took place on the 28th, and Mark Kennaway spoke first. He began by bestowing his approval on the recent great liberal measures achieved in the form of free trade. Then he cast his mind back to Catholic emancipation and the reform act which, he said, had been effected by the force of public opinion alone, in spite of the inclinations of the government.[99] Kennaway's facts and logic ran faulty here. He spoke indiscriminately of various governments, and seemed to imply that liberals had enjoyed uninterrupted ascendancy since 1828 or 1829, and that Lord John Russell had been prime minister since 1841. Moreover, it is most likely that, no matter what the case in 1832, a reformed House of Commons—at least one faithfully reflecting the desires of its constituents—could not have granted Catholic emancipation in 1829. Nevertheless, it merits note that Catholic emancipation remained, almost 20 years after the fact, an important rallying point for liberals at mid-century, regardless how obscured the circumstances of the measure's passage had become in liberal mythology.

'[A]dverting to the present mode of Church government,' Kennaway

condemned it in the most sweeping and unreserved terms. He would have the power of the Church quite distinct from all political power, and such regulations introduced as should prevent Bishops from being political.[100]

He avowed himself attached to the church, but judged its purposes to be higher than the realm of politics. Following this line of reasoning, he commented obscurely on the bible, and from there turned to

pronounc[ing] his detestation of Ecclesiastical Courts, and warned those whom it concerned, that a power would come by and by that would sweep them all away. He declared that the people did not like to see the Bishops at stated periods leave their immense charge, and resort to London for political purposes and pursuits, the end of which is money. He condemned the mode in which Ireland had been governed, and especially the system of Church government in that country, which he declared was characterised by injustice.[101]

Kennaway seemed prepared to carry on in this vein until it was pointed out that he had not yet nominated anyone, whereupon he nominated Edward Divett, and retired. D.B. Davy esquire, who seconded Divett's nomination, limited himself to brief and laudatory commentary on the unrestrained benefits of free trade, not the least being that it had saved hundreds of thousands in Ireland from doom.[102]

John Carew esquire[103] nominated Sir John Duckworth, introducing the candidate as 'allied with a family whose name had been respected from the Episcopal Palace through a variety of honourable stations for the last century.' Samuel Kingdon seconded the nomination, expressing his relief that 'the Corn Laws were done away[;] as a Conservative he felt they ought not, nor did not, stand still in the great career of improvement.'[104]

The nomination process concluded, W.H. Furlong esquire, an attorney, rose to speak. He complimented Kennaway's speech, but observed that it seemed to give 'the go by to one most important question, important alike to the Church of England and the cause of Protestantism. . . .' He continued at length:

> These observations had an equal bearing on Churchmen and on Dissenters[;] it was alike important to them both. They had a right on that day ere they held up their hands for any gentleman, to know if he were likely to maintain those principles and that holy religion,— that religion for which so many had suffered, and for which an army of martyrs had yielded up their lives. He would ask both Sir John Duckworth and Mr. Divett, if according to their views, they thought it right that from Protestant pockets should be drawn money for the purpose of maintaining Roman Catholic principles. . . . He was trying to awaken electors to the importance of knowing what their members would do if the Government should attempt to carry such measures as those to which he had alluded. He would call on Sir John Duckworth and Mr. Divett for a full expression of their opinions.[105]

Bird also interrupted the proceedings, to demand if Duckworth regarded as traitors members in the House of Commons who were nominees of peers. The question prompted great tumult; Duckworth was urged by John Carew not to answer and, in any event, said he did not understand the question. Divett evidently interpreted Bird's question as touching on the controversy of Lionel de Rothschild's admission to the commons, because of the oath, sworn 'on the true faith of a Christian,' and stated that 'he had once himself introduced a bill on the subject and would again vote for any thing which would remove such disabilities as may exist.'[106] Whatever Bird was after, Divett's response is surely suggestive. The phrasing, 'on the faith of a true Christian,' had been instituted in 1828, in accordance with the repeal of the test and corporation acts, to ease the entry of dissenters, rather than solely Anglicans, into political office. Clearly Divett intended to carry the precedent of inclusion a logical step further, to embrace non-Christians, as well.

7.11   The 1847 election in Exeter: the remarks of the returned members

No other candidate present, the sheriff declared Divett and Duckworth duly returned. Divett spoke first.

He opened with a few observations on the advantages of a system of free trade, such as Britain now enjoyed, as compared to protected economies, such as France's, and insisted, contrary to protectionist nay-sayers, that freedom of commerce was beginning to have an effect on undermining slavery, as well. In response to W.H. Furlong's lengthy inquiry, Divett said he believed it best to avoid topics liable to induce excitement. Furlong persisted that constituents ought to know their members' positions on Maynooth, the endowment of Roman Catholic priests, and similar proposals which might face parliament in the future. Divett complied with an answer that ranged from the college's founding a half-century earlier, to the act of union, to the degraded conditions of classrooms and the quality of food provided for faculty and students—all which had been used to justify amending the grant. Finally he admitted having voted in favour of the grant in 1845, in the belief that its extension served to improve the education of the priests and to dissociate them from agitators, and confirmed that he would vote for similar measures in the future. 'Now then as regards endowment of the Catholic Priests—[Divett] would say he should be sorry to see the question discussed.'[107]

Still on the topic of Ireland and religion, Divett maintained that, notwithstanding his love and allegiance for the Church of England, he could not accept that its interests were identical to the interests of the Church of Ireland. He judged, however, that policymakers in England were finally beginning to understand matters in Ireland, which gave good hope for real improvement there. In closing, Divett made some observations on the health of cities and other concerns in which private local bodies were likely to be more informed and efficient than any central board in London.[108]

Duckworth's speech was in most ways vaguer than Divett's had been. He maintained his ambiguous position on free trade from 1845: he was not fully in agreement with, but did not seek to alter, any legislation parliament had recently passed. He was equally uncommitted on Ireland, although seemed in the main to have concurred with Divett, that improvement was on the horizon. He advocated investigation into the navigation laws, on the grounds that nothing should be sustained which could not bear inquiry. Duckworth said the income tax was unfair and the window tax ought to be repealed—but only if other means could be found to continue raising £50 million per annum. On the matter of ecclesiastical law, he stated that he opposed nothing in principle, and welcomed any scheme designed to satisfy all parties. 'For himself,' Duckworth declared (rather disingenuously, given the vacillation evident in virtually every statement of policy),

> he had no desire to conceal any single political opinion, but unless some circumstances were to occur very different from any of which there was prospect at present, he could not give his consent to the endowment of the Roman Catholic Clergy.

Both Divett and Duckworth gave the impression of being reluctant to engage matters of a potentially divisive nature, perhaps especially as the election was uncontested, and the return of both guaranteed. They preferred to address relatively uncontroversial matters, in Exeter at least, such as the health of cities, the competing merits of local or central bodies, and the future of certain antiquated navigation laws.

But this was not good enough for the electorate, who insisted that Divett and Duckworth make known their positions the matters of policy that counted, those concerning questions of church and state. Through meetings and petitions before the election, and in questions directed at candidates on the hustings, electors demanded that these topics be addressed, and willy-nilly, the two candidates complied.

Part II

When you can measure what you are speaking about, and can express it in numbers, you know something about it; but when you cannot measure it, when you cannot express it in numbers, then your knowledge is of a meagre and unsatisfactory kind.

William Thomson, Lord Kelvin (1824–1907)

8
Evidence of Partisan Alignment in Parliament, 1833–1847

8.1 Introduction

In view of the evident importance that candidates, electors and others attached to a member's voting record in the House of Commons, it is reasonable to consider whether a methodical investigation of such divisions has anything to contribute to the present study. In the past, historians have analysed the parliaments that met between 1833 and 1847, but reached no clear consensus. Derek Beales and David Close, for instance, influenced by Norman Gash's view of Peel and party, believed that party discipline was advanced between 1835 and 1845, and the line separating liberals and conservatives strong. To test ('confirm' might be the better word) the hypothesis, Beales turned to a very small number of indisputably outstanding divisions which he identified as 'touchstones' of party, and likely indicative of a strong pattern of party alignment. Perhaps unsurprisingly, under these guidelines, his position appeared to be verified.[1] Ian Newbould found fault with Beales's over-reliance on Gash's methods and conclusions, and convincingly undercut the latter by a rigorous analysis of hundreds of divisions from the same period.[2] Newbould's findings show that party discipline, supposed by Beales and others to be a new phenomenon resulting from the general elections of 1835 and 1837, was neither weaker nor stronger than it had been in the early 1830s and, when compared with the work of Austin Mitchell, much weaker than it had been in the 1810s and 1820s.[3]

Obviously there is much to recommend Newbould's caveat, that any selective approach to such an investigation may skew results, often in favour of the position a researcher has already settled on. A selective analysis of division lists—which tests divisions of a specific category, while dismissing all others—brings with it certain distortion, to say nothing of subjective bias. That must be especially so for an analysis such as Beales's, which extrapolates from a tiny sample—he examined only six divisions, two from the 1835 parliament and four from the 1837 parliament—on literally hundreds as many actual divisions in parliament.

8.2   The criteria and lay-out of the present analyses

But despite the 'obvious pitfalls' that Newbould warns of, and 'the ... problems of subjectivity and preconceived notions,'[4] it need not follow that all selective approaches to analysing divisions are misleading, or at least of little use. The analyses that concern the present chapter derive from those occasions when the House of Commons, between 1833 and 1847, divided on measures concerned with religion—that is, those dealing with the affairs of the church and dissent, and almost always affecting the relationship between the two. This chapter examines 200 divisions on matters as diverse as government spending, parochial boundaries, sabbatarian observance, education and admission to the universities, tithes and livings for clergy and curates, political involvement of bishops, and even military attendance at religious ceremonies. By assessing such diverse policy issues, this chapter tests the strength of such questions, unified by religion, in polarizing party affiliation in the decade-and-a-half following the reform act.

Another difference which sets apart the present analysis from most previous assessments of the divisions of the 1830s and 1840s is that, in contrast to its large sample of divisions, it focuses on a comparatively small number of MPs. Specifically, it traces the voting behaviour of the 35 men who, between 1833 and 1847, sat as members for the boroughs discussed in previous chapters.[5] Such an approach involves certain shortcomings, insofar as it treats on an equal footing, on the one side, members such as Sir W.H. Whitbread (who cast only two votes), the earl of Desart (who cast only one vote), and G.G. de H. Larpent (who cast no votes), and, on the other side, Capt. Sir G.R. Pechell (1789–1860) and Sir J.C. Hobhouse, who cast 113 and 73, respectively, in the same period. Regardless of such discrepancies, focus on a narrow but, for the purpose of the study, inclusive group, in conjunction with the descriptive analyses from previous chapters, opens windows into members' personalities, and the motives behind their votes. Such a view could be little more than anecdotal in an analysis of a much greater number of MPs.

Whereas Beales, Newbould, and others organized their analyses along distinctions of 'ministerial' and 'non-ministerial' votes, such a breakdown is not quite the one that is used here. (For one thing, the ministerial/non-ministerial distinction is not really useful in the period between 1841 and 1846, when the conservative party was in the process of breaking up—but this is not to say that conservative differences on religious issues were not an important part of the explanation of the party's disunity.) Other studies examined the votes of MPs to see how they measured up as party members. This study looks at members identified by themselves and others as liberals or conservatives, to test how they voted on religious issues.

8.3   The analyses: an overview of methods and findings

The following evidence and discussion examine the 200 divisions of the four parliaments of 1833, 1835, 1837, and 1841 that, directly or indirectly, bore on religious matters. Table 8.1, which is taken from Appendix A,[6] demonstrates the manner in which the data were collated.

Along the left are surnames of the twelve MPs who sat in a particular parliament. They are arranged without relation to the constituencies they represented, but grouped by party affiliation, with the liberals, in italics, in the top portion, and the conservatives, in plain type, in the bottom portion. Each subsequent column is a division, and the intersection of a row and a column indicates how an MP divided on a particular decision in the House of Commons. A vote which may be described as one broadening religious freedom (i.e. one favourable to dissenters) is indicated by a plus (+); one tending to favour the establishment

Table 8.1 Sample of results from Appendix A

	44:140	44:248	44:305	44:322	44:372	44:495	44:541	44:543	44:546	44:547
Crawley	+	+	+	+	−	+	+	−	0	0
Divett	+	0	0	0	+	0	0	0	0	0
Ferguson	0	0	0	+	0	0	0	0	0	0
Harland	0	0	0	0	0	0	0	0	0	+
Hobhouse	0	+	0	0	−	0	+	−	+	0
Pechell	+	+	+	+	+	+	+	+	+	0
Dalrymple	−	−	−	0	−	0	−	−	−	−
Dungannon	−	0	0	0	0	0	0	0	0	0
Follett	0	0	0	−	0	+	−	−	−	0
Gibson	+	0	0	−	−	0	−	−	0	0
Kelly	0	−	0	0	0	0	0	0	0	0
Polhill	0	−	0	0	−	0	0	0	0	0

Table 8.1a Votes cast by Pechell and Dalrymple, from Table 8.1

Pechell	+	+	+	+	+	+	+	+	+	0
Dalrymple	−	−	−	0	−	0	−	−	−	−

over dissent is a minus (−); and zero (0) signifies no vote cast at all. In other words, Table 8.1 shows that, of a total 120 votes that could potentially have been cast (12 MPs over ten divisions), 24 registered as +, 24 as −, and 72 as 0. A comparison of the voting record of liberal and conservative MPs reveals that, over this sample of ten divisions, votes cast by liberals registered as + on 22 occasions, as − on four occasions, and liberal members did not vote, or registered as 0, on 34 occasions; figures for conservatives are two, 20, and 38, respectively. On the whole, then, liberals appear to have backed measures favourable to dissent and conservatives to have supported measures favourable to the church, as a close-up of Table 8.1a demonstrates. Only twice did Lord Dalrymple (1784–1866) not vote, Capt. Pechell failed to vote only once, and neither member ever cross-voted.

In the main, this pattern is reflected across the divisions in Appendix A. In both Table 8.1 and Appendix A, it is fairly obvious that most of the liberal votes (indicated by +)—that is, those votes which tend to favour a dissenting political agenda—fall above the heavy line, representing votes cast by liberals, and most of the conservative votes (indicated by −)—that is, those in support of the established church, often at the expense of non-Anglicans—fall below the heavy line, among conservative ranks.

But perhaps the most readily apparent observation from these data is the high frequency of neutral registers (or 0), representing no vote cast at all. In other words, what these data reveal most overwhelmingly is that most MPs did not bother to vote on most divisions most of the time—a fact concealed by narrowly selective analyses such as Beales et al. employ, but one borne out abundantly by Newbould's more exhaustive analysis.[7] In Appendix A, of the total 2400 votes that could have been potentially cast, 1512 registered 0. Thus 63 per cent of the time, the present sample of MPs cast no votes. Such a rate of abstention, which always reflected absenteeism from the house on the occasion of a division, may seem surprising, but attention to parliamentary duties in the first half of the nineteenth century should not be judged by modern standards, and many MPs interpreted their obligations as representatives very loosely. Various instances from previous chapters have suggested that scant regard by MPs for their parliamentary responsibilities was often far from unusual.[8] Indeed, contemporaries recognized, apparently not judgementally, that some members simply never voted.[9] Furthermore, it should be remembered that, although meetings of the lower house usually convened at 4 p.m., many members did not attend until after dinner, and debates regularly ran well past midnight. Therefore, any large sampling almost certainly includes divisions that occurred before dinner or in the small hours of the morning, after many members had retired to their London homes and were in bed. If Beales's comment, that '[p]olitical involvement [i.e. a large turnout for votes on divisions] is more than half-way to political affiliation,'[10] is subjected to these data, it appears the two-party system in the House of Commons was, by most standards, far from maturity.[11]

But more conclusive patterns come to light when we turn to those votes with a more definite meaning—that is, those votes that were cast. From these an important conclusion is evident: that liberals strongly supported measures promoting political agendas favourable to dissenters, while conservatives supported the privileged position of the establishment. The following results tell the story. Taking Appendix A, of the 888 occasions on which members participated (including as tellers and pairs) on these 200 divisions, 526 votes registered a +, or liberal votes favourable to dissenters, and 362 votes registered a −, or conservative votes favourable to the established church. The percentages are 59.5 per cent and 40.5 per cent, respectively, or a ratio of almost exactly 3 to 2 favouring dissent over the church. On comparing these ratios to the composition of liberal and conservative MPs in the same sample, a striking correlation appears. Of the 200 divisions considered here, 119 of the members who could potentially have participated were liberals and 81 were conservative. The percentages are 59.2 per cent and 40.8 per cent, respectively: the ratio of almost exactly 3 to 2 liberal to conservative MPs remains constant when compared to the actual votes cast.

At first glance, the degree of correlation seems hardly possible to credit merely to chance. But a quick scan of the rows and columns of Appendix A, and only a little closer inspection of the figures in Table 8.2, which expresses the same information in a condensed, numerical format, quickly reveal there is more than meets the eye, and suggests the old warning against lies, damned lies, and statistics.

It is clear that, on numerous occasions, votes which may be called conservative were cast within the liberal ranks, and vice versa, but indiscriminate analysis of the aggregate data conceals such variation.

Table 8.2 'Dissenting' and 'establishment' votes cast, by affiliation (tallies)

	Votes cast by liberals	Votes cast By conservatives	Combined votes
'Dissenting' votes	475	51	526
'Establishment' votes	79	283	362
Total	554	334	888

Nevertheless, the extreme nearness of the ratios of liberal and conservative participants and dissenting and Anglican partisan votes suggests a strong overall pattern that indeed exists, and reveals just as strong a relationship, when presented in a more conclusively meaningful fashion.

If we consider only those votes which were cast—a + or a −, or an aye or a no—by MPs participating in these 200 divisions (unlike the previous test, which additionally weighed in the total number of votes which the combined composition of sample MPs *could potentially* have cast), we then are working with a total of 888 votes.[12] The ratio of about 3 to 2, or 119 liberal and 81 conservative MPs, remains constant. Furthermore—and conveniently, because it reduces the likelihood of substantial distortion of overall valid patterns—the ratio of votes actually cast by liberals and conservatives, respectively, remains quite close to the ratio of participants. More specifically, liberal members cast 554 of the votes in this sample (62.4 per cent), and conservative members cast 334 votes (37.6 per cent).[13]

If we further break down the + votes and − votes along lines of MPs' party affiliation, we see that, of the 554 occasions liberal members divided, 475 votes were on the side of religious dissent, and 79 supported the church. The percentages are 85.7 per cent and 14.3 per cent, respectively, or overwhelmingly in favour of a liberal, dissenting political agenda. Examination of the 334 votes cast by conservative members reveals that, on 283 occasions, they divided in favour of the establishment, and only 51 times did they advance liberal or dissenting agendas. The inverse percentages are almost the exact same as for the liberals: 84.7 per cent and 15.3 per cent. Thus the link associating conservatism to Anglicanism (or restricted religious freedom) is only minutely weaker than that aligning liberal MPs with dissent. Table 8.3 presents these data.

Tables 8.2 and 8.3 present averages over four parliaments and, of course, individual parliaments reflect these averages to greater or lesser extents. Table 8.4 breaks down these data by individual parliaments.

Table 8.3 'Dissenting' and 'establishment' votes cast, by affiliation (percentages)

	Votes cast by liberal MPs	Votes cast by conservative MPs
'Dissenting' votes	85.7	15.3
'Establishment' votes	14.3	84.7
Total	100.0	100.0

Table 8.4 'Dissenting' and 'establishment' votes cast in individual parliaments, by affiliation (and tallies and percentages)

1833–1834

	Votes cast by liberal MPs	Votes cast by conservative MPs	Combined votes
'Dissenting' votes	60	0	60
'Establishment' votes	13	1	14
Total	73	1	74

	Votes cast by liberal MPs	Votes cast by conservative MPs
'Dissenting' votes	82.8	0.0
'Establishment' votes	17.2	100.0
Total	100.0	100.0

1835–1837

	Votes cast by liberal MPs	Votes cast by conservative MPs	Combined votes
'Dissenting' votes	175	2	177
'Establishment' votes	15	65	80
Total	190	67	257

	Votes cast by liberal MPs	Votes cast by conservative MPs
'Dissenting' votes	92.1	3.0
'Establishment' votes	7.9	97.0
Total	100.0	100.0

1837–1841

	Votes cast by liberal MPs	Votes cast by conservative MPs	Combined votes
'Dissenting' votes	128	15	143
'Establishment' votes	21	91	112
Total	149	106	255

	Votes cast by liberal MPs	Votes cast by conservative MPs
'Dissenting' votes	85.9	14.2
'Establishment' votes	14.1	85.8
Total	100.0	100.0

1841–1847

	Votes cast by liberal MPs	Votes cast by conservative MPs	Combined votes
'Dissenting' votes	112	34	146
'Establishment' votes	30	126	156
Total	142	160	302

	Votes cast by liberal MPs	Votes cast by conservative MPs
'Dissenting' votes	78.9	21.2
'Establishment' votes	21.1	78.8
Total	100.0	100.0

In considering these figures, an unmistakable pattern is evident. Only in the last parliament, that of 1841, did expected partisan percentages fall below 80 per cent and, even in this case, at 78.9 per cent for liberal members and 78.8 per cent for conservative ones, they never did by more than slightly over a single per cent. In other words, by a consistent ratio of around 4 to 1 or greater, and in one parliament (1835–1837) by more than 10 to 1, liberal MPs cast votes in support of political agendas favouring dissenters, and conservative MPs cast votes in favour of the established church. Of course this also means that liberals and conservatives in the House of Commons crossed party lines, as indicated by religious principles, less than 22 per cent of the time. Sceptics might protest the inclusion of conservative member Frederick Polhill's lone conservative vote cast in the 1833 parliament as anomalous, and skewing overall results for conservative partisanship by producing a dubious 100 per cent partisanship in favour of the church establishment. After all, its apparent strength might be held to rest speciously on a single member who, on 20 other occasions in the same parliament, failed to vote altogether. For example, a comparison based on number rather than percentage of votes cast, indicates only one conservative vote more than a liberal. But comparison with Capt. Polhill's behaviour in other parliaments reveals that his record during 1833–1834 was characteristic of his broader patterns of voting.[14] Tallied across the 200 divisions of the four parliaments, Capt. Polhill voted in a consistently conservative/Anglican manner 90.7 per cent of the time, and cross-voted for liberal/dissenting measures only 9.3 per cent of the time.[15] Moreover, the next parliament—of 1835–1837, when a Melbourne government met parliament for the first time—demonstrated remarkably high ratios of partisan voting, in some cases stronger than during 1833–1834, by liberals and conservatives alike. Of 190 votes cast by liberal MPs, 175, or over 92 per cent, cast votes in favour of religious freedom; on only 15 votes, or less than 8 per cent of the time, did liberals cross over and vote with conservatives for measures promoting the established church. Thus the ratio by which liberal members of the House of Commons favoured liberal legislation or policies on matters pertaining to the relation between church and dissent was 11 to 1. The sample of votes cast by conservative MPs in the same parliament was a third as large,[16] but the results are as convincing. On only two divisions out of 67, or a mere 3 per cent of the time, did conservatives cross over to the liberal ranks and vote for dissenters. On 97 per cent of the remaining occasions, conservatives divided with their own party, for the establishment, and the ratio of conservative MPs voting strictly along party lines was 33 to 1. In that same parliament, between January 1835 and July 1837, Capt. Polhill never once voted against the conservative consensus, and cast 16 votes with fellow conservatives.[17] Thus recourse to a wider set of data argues compellingly for including all the data from 1833 to 1835 on equal footing.

8.4   Detailed analyses of divisions in parliament of 1837–1841

But it is probably most instructive to examine in some detail the parliament of 1837–1841. This is not because it was the parliament with the strongest display of party loyalty (that was 1835–1837), nor had it the largest number of divisions relevant to church and state (that was 1841–1847). It is chiefly useful to study the first parliament of Queen Victoria's long reign because the number of liberal and conservative MPs being sampled remained constant at six apiece, permitting an unusually balanced comparison.[18] Notably, as well, it was in this parliament that the ratios of liberal and conservative partisan voting matched most closely the overall ratios for the period 1833–1847.[19] And this parliament is instructive in its own right because of the interpretative controversy it has generated. For this is the period that Beales's work, with its emphasis on touchstone divisions, identifies as a high water mark, hitherto unknown in parliament, of disciplined political alignment in the House of Commons, unmatched thereafter for another quarter century. At the same time, Newbould, in his research on divisions, concludes that strict partisanship was paltry during the period, at only 10.5 per cent, and that by criteria permitting wide latitude for inclusion.[20] Obviously this is an important and hotly contested period, and our understanding of it will benefit from yet another perspective.

The results for this parliament, summarized in the relevant entries from Table 8.4, are presented in full in Appendix A. But before proceeding to assess the divisions, one disparity should be noted. Despite the balance that existed on one level between liberal and conservative MPs, and consequently the number of potential votes each side could cast,[21] the six liberal MPs in the sample demonstrated higher levels of participation (voting on over a third of the divisions) than their conservative counterparts (voting on just over a quarter of the divisions). Nevertheless, very strong correlations remain evident. Of the 149 votes liberal members cast, 128 of them, or 85.9 per cent, were partisan liberal votes on matters of religion, tending to support a political agenda favourable to dissenters, and on only 21 occasions, or 14.1 per cent of the time, did they cross-vote. The percentages for the smaller sample of votes by conservative members is almost exactly inverse: of a total of 106 votes, they divided 91 times in favour of the establishment, and cross-voted on 15 occasions, or 85.8 per cent and 14.2 per cent, respectively. These percentages are also almost identical to those generated by an analysis of all 200 divisions over all four parliaments, as summed up in Table 8.1—liberal MPs voting liberal 85.7 per cent of the time and conservative MPs voting conservative 84.7 per cent of the time. The ratio of roughly 17 to 3 remains constant throughout, and the tendency to vote along rigorous party lines is unmistakable.

The value of the approach employed by Beales, which examines select-ively only six divisions with uncharacteristically high turnouts by both parties, and extrapolates onto several hundred others, has already been questioned. His judgement, mentioned above, that 'political involve-ment' indicates strong 'political affiliation,' appears to argue for weak partisan alignment for the period 1833–1847 if the present analysis of 200 divisions is any guide: only 37 per cent of the time did any of the sample MPs bother to vote, and 63 per cent of the time they did not.[22] Such being the case, and Beales's evidence relying so heavily on exceptional divisions, it merits investigating whether similar factors could potentially distort the apparent strength of the patterns hitherto developed in this chapter, as regarding religious issues. Again, the parlia-ment of 1837–1841 is exemplary.

8.5 The implications of varying levels of parliamentary participation

As the preceding discussion and the relevant entries for Table 8.4 and Appendix A show, not many of the 68 divisions on religion between 1837 and 1841 attracted a large number of MPs. In only 16 divisions, or less than a quarter, did as many as half the available 12 vote at all. Voter absenteeism was 69.4 per cent, or slightly higher than the average (63 per cent) of the four parliaments. Only four divisions attracted more than eight MPs; of these, only three attracted more than ten MPs and only one attracted 11 MPs. In no case did all 12 members vote. Table 8.5 compares the voting patterns in these few divisions, with exceptional participation, against those with lower, more typical, turnouts.

Clearly the strongest possible correlation—that is, 100 per cent in all cases—occurs in the four divisions with higher than usual voters turnout. But what is also evident is that the inclusion of the outstanding character of those few divisions with exceptionally high—indeed, perfectly predictable—rates of partisanship does not significantly distort the overall results for the 1837 parliament. Calculations based only on divisions in which five or fewer—and in some cases only two—members divided reveal the same basic pattern developed in the analysis of the aggregate, if only a little less strongly. That is to say, even in those divisions with a turnout of less than half, in which 70.5 per cent of

Table 8.5 Parliamentary divisions, broken down according to levels of particip-ation, 1837–1841

	Liberal	Conservative	Combined	Liberal	Conservative
	5 or fewer votes, tallies			5 or fewer votes, percentage of votes cast	
+	79	11	90	85.9	22.9
−	13	37	50	14.1	77.1
0	220	264	484		
Total	312	312	624	100.0	100.0
	6 or more votes, tallies			6 or more votes, percentage of votes cast	
+	49	4	53	86	6.9
−	8	54	62	14	93.1
0	39	38	77		
Total	96	96	192	100.0	100.0
	7 or more votes, tallies			7 or more votes, percentage of votes cast	
+	31	3	34	93.9	8.8
−	2	31	33	6.1	91.2
0	15	14	29		
Total	48	48	96	100.0	100.0
	8 or more votes, tallies			8 or more votes, percentage of votes cast	
+	19	0	19	100	100
−	0	20	20	0	0
0	5	4	9		
Total	24	24	48	100	100
	10 or more votes, tallies			10 or more votes, percentage of votes cast	
+	15	0	15	100	100
−	0	16	16	0	0
0	3	2	5		
Total	18	18	36	100.0	100.0
	11 or more votes, tallies			11 or more votes, percentage of votes cast	
+	5	0	5	100	100
−	0	6	6	0	0
0	1	0	1		
Total	6	6	12	100	100

the liberals and 84.6 per cent of the conservatives failed to participate, liberal MPs who did vote still supported political agendas favourable to dissenters by a ratio of more than 17 to 3, and conservative MPs backed the church by nearly 4 to 1. In these divisions with lower rates of participation, the percentages for conservative MPs dividing with their party for the church and cross-voting for dissent are 77.1 per cent and 22.9 per cent, respectively, or a slightly weaker correlation than for the 1837 parliament overall, or the average of the four parliaments. The percentages for liberal MPs in divisions with five or fewer members voting are *identical* for the aggregate data for 1837—in both cases 85.9 per cent divided for religious freedom and 14.1 per cent voted for the establishment

8.6   The 1841 parliament: implication of the Maynooth and state-funded education

Finally, the last parliament in review, that of 1841–1847, also merits particular attention because—if for no other reasons—it was the longest parliament, it experienced the largest number of relevant divisions (64 in all), and its data show some of the weakest patterns of partisanship. Taken together, these facts might incline sceptics to hearken Newbould's call for more and more varied divisions. After all, as we saw in the case of conservatives in the first reformed House of Commons, extrapolation from small samples can create the appearance of questionable patterns. But as more thorough analyses of the conservative votes in 1833 and 1834 indicated, especially in the wider context of the member's behaviour across all four parliaments, their inclusion was justified. Closer scrutiny of the divisions from this last parliament reveals that there was no great aberration between 1841 and 1847, and that the patterns established by previous analyses were weakened only minutely.

The chief reason these data show weaker partisanship is the high frequency of two particular types of division: those touching on schemes for national education, and provisions for the seminary at St Patrick's College, Maynooth. Both issues were highly contentious, as previous chapters have shown, and tended to produce strange bedfellows. Specifically, nonconformists resented the proposed church monopoly in most schemes of state-supported education brought forward, and opposed them. High church conservatives, inspired by anti-Catholicism and desirous of maintaining the Church of England unspoiled by parliamentary interference, opposed them also.[23] Thus, in pursuit of freedom and voluntarism, nonconformists and liberal MPs who championed them occasionally found themselves lining up with chauvinist Anglicans and conservatives—to the exclusion of more moderate members.

Table 8.6a   Parliamentary divisions on Maynooth grant or national education, 1841–1847 (tallies and percentages)

	Liberal MPs	Conservative MPs	Combined MPs
Liberal votes	34	15	49
Conservative votes	16	43	59
Abstentions	42	30	72
Total	92	88	180

	Votes cast by liberal MPs	Votes cast by conservative MPs
'Dissenting' votes	68.0	25.9
'Establishment' votes	32.0	74.1
Total	100.0	100.0

Table 8.6b   Parliamentary divisions excluding Maynooth grant or national education, 1841–1847 (tallies and percentages)

	Votes cast by liberal MPs	Votes cast by conservative MPs	Combined
'Dissenting' votes	78	19	97
'Establishment' votes	14	83	97
Abstentions	192	202	394
Total	284	304	588

	Votes cast by liberal MPs	Votes cast by conservative MPs
'Dissenting' votes	84.8	18.6
'Establishment' votes	15.2	81.4
Total	100.0	100.0

Table 8.6 (a and b) breaks down the data from Table 8.4, distinguishing those divisions concerning the fate of the government's annual grant to Maynooth and the government's scheme for national education, and all the others—for example, bills for the removal of Jewish disabilities, relief of Roman Catholics, pious and charitable purposes, the bishopric of Manchester, and other matters.

Starting with a comparison of non-participation, it is clear that MPs demonstrated much lower levels of absenteeism on the smaller number of targeted divisions on education and Maynooth than they did over all. The average absenteeism across all four parliaments, it will be recalled, was 63 per cent; in the parliament of 1841 it was slightly lower, at 60.7 per cent. But non-participation rates for divisions on Maynooth and education were substantially lower, at exactly 40 per cent. The rate of absenteeism for divisions on the Maynooth grant was 43.8 per cent, and on schemes of national education it was only 25 per cent. This demonstrates, as Beales inadvertently did in his study, that certain types of divisions fostered exceptional levels of participation. And as the next analyses shows, these 15 exceptional divisions (a dozen on Maynooth and three on education), representing fewer than a quarter of the sample divisions for this parliament, departed from the remaining 76.6 per cent of the votes cast in a sufficiently dramatic manner to perceptibly skew overall patterns.

If the conservative MPs were united in opposing the government scheme of education, registering 100 per cent unanimity, they were more divided on the government grant to Maynooth, showing less than two-thirds (65.9 per cent) partisanship, and crossing over to liberal ranks more than a third (34.1 per cent) of the time. Liberal MPs were more unified than conservatives in regard to Maynooth, supporting it by more than 7 to 3, but their unity fell to only 3 to 2 on national education, with 61.5 per cent voting in a predictable, liberal manner and 38.5 per cent crossing over to conservative ranks. Taking into account only the remaining divisions—that is, those 49 occasions the House of Commons voted on matters relevant to church or dissent, but not including divisions on Maynooth or national education—familiar patterns emerge. Dividing with their party 81.4 per cent of the time, conservative MPs voted by a ratio of more than 4 to 1 for legislation favourable to the church. Liberal MPs showed stronger partisanship, voting on behalf of dissent 84.8 per cent of the time, or by a ratio of nearly 17 to 3. These figures are consistent with broader patterns developed over the period 1833–1847.

Thus it is obvious that it was chiefly the force of the 15 exceptional divisions on Maynooth and national education—the circumstances of which measures tended to make fuzzy the line separating dissenting and Anglican votes—that diminished patterns so strongly evident in other parliaments. It is further noteworthy that even these 15 divisions could not distort overall patterns by substantial margins: liberal partisanship in the 1841 parliament was weaker than it was for all four parliaments by less than 8 per cent, and conservative partisanship by less than 7 per cent. In this sample of 64 divisions between 1841 and 1847, liberal MPs were 776 times more likely than conservatives to cast votes in favour of religious freedom, and conservative MPs were 555 more likely than liberals to vote in defence of the establishment. Across all four parliaments, the figures are 1072 and 2636, respectively.

8.7 Conclusions

These analyses, based on 888 votes cast by 35 MPs representing six boroughs spread across England, make it clear that the House of Commons was, between 1833 and 1847, divided sharply on matters of religion. Newbould's wariness of touchstone divisions is well taken, but does not apply to the present study. By overwhelming numbers, liberal MPs divided on behalf of policy and legislation favourable to religious dissent, and conservatives voted to uphold the privileged position of the church in state.[24]

9
Evidence of Partisan Alignment at the Constituent Level, 1832–1847

> The poll-books will tell the tale, and in those poll-books it should be the duty of all true friends of civil and religious liberty to endeavour by every possible exertion to send the votes.[1]

> Can Catholics vote for a man who is perpetually loading them with virulent abuse, and defaming their church and themselves with the grossest of lies? Will Dissenters support a person who is almost daily in the habit of insulting them, and of trying to load them with heavy extortions? Can Churchmen vote for a person whom they know to be insincere, and whom they must recollect formerly to have been one of their most malignant and unscrupulous antagonists?[2]

9.1 Introduction

Chapter 8 tested the degree to which patterns of liberal and conservative self-identification in the House of Commons lined up with dissenting and Anglican legislation in the four parliaments that met between 1833 and 1847. The evidence developed in that chapter argued strongly for mature organization of parliament along perceptible party lines several decades before the age of Gladstone and Disraeli. The present chapter turns to the other major component of this research that lends itself to numerical analysis, and allows us to test these attitudes at another level of political power, in an assessment of electoral behaviour among the constituents of four of the five boroughs in review. Such analysis is feasible for two reasons: because of the practice of public voting in the United Kingdom until the secret ballot act of 1872 and the consequent printing of poll books indicating how individual electors voted for members of parliament; and because dissenting chapels, especially until the marriage and registration acts of 1836, usually kept their own records of baptisms, marriages, and burials.

9.2   Earlier attempts at quantifying religion and politics: the potentials and pitfalls

John Vincent has demonstrated that the clergy of the Church of England, and church organists, were more likely to vote conservative than not, and that dissenting ministers were more inclined to vote liberal.[3] In view of the evidence from foregoing chapters, such findings are not surprising, nor are they by themselves very useful—although they are a little more instructive than Vincent's findings, confirmed by others, that butchers supported conservatives and grocers supported liberals![4] But can we do better than this? Working from poll books and chapel records, can we draw meaningful conclusions about the role played by religion in the voting behaviour of the electorate?[5]

T.J. Nossiter addressed the same question over a generation ago, and it is worth quoting his conclusion:

> Few historians would doubt that religious affiliation was one of the determinants in voting behaviour after 1832, although they might disagree over the details. Proving it is quite another matter. In principle, it would be possible to go through church and chapel records, and relate individuals to details of polling, but there are many objections, both practical and theoretical, to this approach. It would be not only a Herculean task to gather the data but also, ultimately, Sisyphean, in view of its erratic survival. Even if it was available in some cases, it is doubtful how meaningful it would be, when many married in church but attended other denominations, and when religious attachments were generally so fluid.[6]

In spite of Nossiter's gloomy forecast for the success of such an endeavour, the approach he outlined is more or less the method used in preparing the present chapter. The limitations are real and caveats are necessary; the task may be Herculean, but in no sense is it Sisyphean.

9.3   The model used in the present analyses

Turning first to the method and the caveats, the evidence for this chapter, which is given in full in Appendix B, correlates relevant data from chapel records and relates individuals to their voting record. Church records and other data relating specifically to the establishment were, by and large, ignored and electors who could not be identified positively with any dissenting chapel were rejected for special analysis and considered with the bulk of electorate, most of whom were Anglican.

Of course there are certain hazards to such an approach, and Dr Nossiter outlined some in using poll books as historical documents:

> The possibilities of error are, unfortunately, legion: at the most general level it should not be assumed that what survives—or what survives in readily usable form—is necessarily an accurate reflection of 'How Victorians Voted.'... [I]t is often difficult to be certain whether Tom Smith of Nelson Street is the same Tom Smith who voted in the last election, or his son, his uncle or, worse still, no relation at all. Nor can one be sure that when the electors' occupation is sought in the commercial directories which proliferate after the 1820s that Tom Smith is unquestionably T. Smith, Nelson Street, grocer.[7]

And these are only the difficulties encountered when attempting to make sense of printed material from the early nineteenth century: in the case of handwritten manuscripts, as virtually all chapel records were, fresh perils arise. It was, as George Eliot described it, an age where there existed

> the opinion...that it was beneath a gentleman to write legibly, or with a hand in the least suitable to a clerk...: the vowels were all alike and the consonants only distinguishable as turning up or down, the strokes had a blotted solidity and the letters disdained to keep the line....[8]

Additionally, a majority of the names identified from most chapel registers will not also be those of electors and, therefore, will be useless for analysis. Take two hypothetical cases. One is a wheelwright whose wife gave birth nine times between the years 1832 and 1847, and whose children were baptized in the local nonconformist chapel. Another is a man of wealth and prominence in the community, active in the same chapel, entrusted with its funds and speaking for it publicly. Relying solely on registers of birth, there would be abundant evidence for the existence of the first man, but perhaps none for the second, if he were no longer fathering children, unmarried, or a widower. Furthermore, the latter man would almost certainly have been enfranchised, while his humbler neighbour might have never cast a vote in his life, in which case the evidence of his denominational affiliation would be, for the purposes of this study, useless.

Yet in spite of the evident hazards involved in working with dissenting registers, at least one circumstance argues strongly in favour of such an approach. Recourse to records such as baptismal registers, for instance, yields a much more representative sample of dissenters than could be gleaned through any other means. In the previous hypothetical situation, the politics of the prominent dissenter and probable elector would very likely be similar to those of the minister and other leading members of the congregation, and therefore analysis of his votes would probably do little more than reinforce the conclusion noted above, that dissenting ministers were strongly inclined to vote for liberal candidates. But analysis of a wide cross-section, such as baptismal records offer, provides a far larger sample of men (and possible electors) who shared the common experience of becoming a father, and chose to celebrate the occasion outside the established church.[9]

Thus, possessed of the relevant records, rigorous criteria for inclusion, and patience, the researcher is prepared to test the data from a number of angles. Such analyses comprise the rest of this chapter.

9.4 The findings: overview and of elementary analyses

In large part the data in Appendix B, partially reproduced in Table 9.1, speak for themselves.

The simplest of arithmetical comparisons makes clear that the dissenting electorate voted in a predictable, fairly uniform manner, significantly distinct from the remaining electorate. More specifically, such comparisons show that, while the rest of the electorate's support for the two parties fluctuated significantly over time, dissenters voted consistently in favour of candidates representing liberal interests. In each of the 23 elections examined here, dissenting support was decidedly in favour of the liberals. Indeed, on only three occasions did this support fall below 75 per cent, and in the lowest of these, the Durham by-election of April 1843, the liberal candidate made his first visit to the town less than 24 hours before the polling commenced, and had only two-and-a-half hours to present himself to the town's constituents before the nomination. In more than 30 per cent of these contests, dissenters cast 85 per cent of their votes, or more, for liberal candidates, and in four contests, or more than 17 per cent of the time, they cast more than 90 per cent of their votes for liberals.

Table 9.1 Support for liberal candidate(s), by dissent *v.* Anglicanism (percentages)

		Bedford	Ipswich	Nottingham	Durham
Dec 1832	Dissenting electorate	0.84	0.96	0.93	0.88
	Anglican electorate	0.67	0.62	0.83	0.66
	Combined electorate	0.69	0.64	0.83	0.69
Jan 1835	Dissenting electorate	0.77	0.91	—	0.85
	Anglican electorate	0.59	0.45	—	0.59
	Combined electorate	0.62	0.49	—	0.62
June 1835	Dissenting electorate	—	0.96	—	—
	Anglican electorate	—	0.51	—	—
	Combined electorate	—	0.55	—	—
July 1837	Dissenting electorate	0.81	—	—	0.78
	Anglican electorate	0.66	—	—	0.59
	Combined electorate	0.68	—	—	0.62
May 1839	Dissenting electorate	—	0.83	—	—
	Anglican electorate	—	0.47	—	—
	Combined electorate	—	0.50	—	—
June 1841	Dissenting electorate	0.79	0.86	—	—
	Anglican electorate	0.64	0.50	—	—
	Combined electorate	0.66	0.52	—	—
June 1842	Dissenting electorate	—	0.81	—	—
	Anglican electorate	—	0.42	—	—
	Combined electorate	—	0.44	—	—
Aug 1842	Dissenting electorate	—	0.84	0.79	—
	Anglican electorate	—	0.41	0.48	—
	Combined electorate	—	0.44	0.49	—
Apr 1843	Dissenting electorate	—	—	0.82	0.62
	Anglican electorate	—	—	0.50	0.55
	Combined electorate	—	—	0.52	0.56
July 1843	Dissenting electorate	—	—	—	0.72
	Anglican electorate	—	—	—	0.52
	Combined electorate	—	—	—	0.54
July 1847	Dissenting electorate	0.79	0.77	0.65	0.80
	Anglican electorate	0.68	0.44	0.38	0.71
	Combined electorate	0.69	0.26	0.39	0.71

To be sure, the strength of dissenting support ebbed and flowed over time, but in most cases consideration of the context of a particular contest goes a long way in accounting for such fluctuations. Moreover, it should be noted that, across all 23 contests, these samples of dissenting electors polled an average of 81.7 per cent of their votes for liberal candidates, and supported conservatives less than a fifth of the time. In four contests with particularly close returns, it was clearly the force of the dissenting electorate, united in its support of liberalism, that turned the election and pulled one or more liberal candidates from defeat to victory.[10]

9.5   Change over time and more sophisticated analyses

Unfortunately these data do not permit many useful conclusions regarding change over time. Certainly dissenting support for liberal candidates appears weaker in 1847 than it had been in 1832, in all boroughs, but the results of intermediate elections do not support so simple a pattern as consistent declining enthusiasm over time. The story must be more complex, even when comparing results across boroughs in a single election.

For instance, as presented in Table 9.1, it would appear that dissenters in Bedford and Durham lent comparable support to the liberal interest in 1847, casting 79 per cent and 80 per cent of their votes, respectively, for liberal candidates. But the strength of this simple conclusion stands up only when we overlook the fact that, in Bedford, dissenters polled 79 per cent of their votes for a single liberal candidate who faced two conservatives, while in Durham, dissenters divided 80 per cent of their votes between two liberals who faced a single conservative.[11] In this light, the behaviour of dissenters in Bedford indicates a more robust commitment to liberalism than the behaviour of dissenters in Durham. Nor are these the only potential variations we must consider, for three-way contests such as occurred in Bedford and Durham were not the rule in other boroughs. Table 9.1 analyses in Nottingham one three-way contest, two two-way contests, and one four-way contest; and in Ipswich six four-way contests, one two-way contest, and one five-way contest. (In strictest terms, the Ipswich by-elections of 1842 were five-way contests as well, but the fifth man, whose 'politics and motives... remained unclear,'[12] won the suffrage of only three electors!)[13]

Even if all these factors could be discounted (and they cannot be), any careful, thorough analysis of these contests discredits a statement positing uniformly decreased support by dissenters for liberals. For instance, recourse solely to Table 9.1 suggests that dissenters showed comparable support for liberals in Nottingham and Ipswich in the general election of 1832, and in Ipswich in the by-election of 1835— in each case they polled between 93 per cent and 96 per cent of their votes for liberal candidates. Use of more sophisticated statistical analysis, however, such as a contingency table analysis, reveals different patterns.

In Table 9.2, contingency table analyses have been performed on the dissenting values from Table 9.1. This presentation of data shows the

Table 9.2 Contingency table analysis indicating tendency of nonconformists, in contrast to wider electorate, to vote for liberals and reject conservatives

	Bedford	Ipswich	Nottingham	Durham
Dec 1832	2.58	14.92	3.17	4.04
Jan 1835	2.37	12.20	—	3.59
June 1835	—	23.47	—	—
July 1837	3.55	—	—	2.45
May 1839	—	5.44	—	—
June 1841	3.46	6.04	—	—
June 1842	—	6.07	—	—
Aug 1842	—	7.24	4.18	—
Apr 1843	—	—	4.53	2.18
July 1843	—	—	—	2.31
July 1847	2.40	4.27	2.99	1.66

cross-product ratios of dissenting to Anglican votes, and allows us to analyse the comparative impact of dissenters' tendency, as compared to the wider electorate, to support liberal candidates. The data reveal that, in the general election of 1832, the dissenting electors of Ipswich were 14.9 times more likely than the remaining electors (most of whom we may assume to have been Anglican) to have polled for either of the two liberal candidates. The sample of dissenters from Nottingham, on the other hand, was only 3.2 times more likely than the wider electorate to support the liberal candidates. (Of course, the use of 'only' in this case needs qualification: the extent to which Nottingham's dissenters departed from the rest of the electorate was weak only with reference to the exceptional standard established by the dissenters of Ipswich. In addition, see Table 9.4 below.) If dissenters in Ipswich supported liberal candidates by a ratio of 25 to 1 in 1832, the dissenters in Nottingham supported liberals only slightly less forcefully, by a ratio of 13.3 to 1. Among the wider electorate, the ratios were slightly more than 3 to 2 in Ipswich, and nearly 5 to 1 in Nottingham. What a contingency table analysis indicates, then, is the ratio by which dissenters' voting patterns were distinct from the voting behaviour demonstrated in the wider electorate, and what the comparatively low cross-product ratio for Nottingham reflects is that the electors of this semi-radical borough already overwhelmingly rejected the lone conservative candidate (only 17 per cent of them voted for him, and less than 6 per cent supported him undividedly). Dissenters simply rejected him more decisively—indeed, 3.17 times more so.

The average cross-product ratio in all four boroughs in 1832 indicates that dissenters were 6.18 times more likely than the wider electorate to vote for liberals. The average dropped slightly in January 1835,[14] to 6.05, but the ratio in Ipswich skyrocketed in a by-election held five months later: dissenters were 23.5 times more likely than the wider electorate to support the two liberals than the two conservatives. On average, the dissenters in these twenty-three contests were 5.47 times more likely than the wider electorate to poll for liberal candidates.

In general, levels of partisanship—measured by a tendency to give full support to candidates of one party or the other, rather than to divide support—were higher in Ipswich than in the other three boroughs. In part, no doubt, this is due to the highly politicized nature of that borough's electorate—a fact commented on by contemporaries as well as latter-day observers.[15] But it must also have been due, in large part, to the higher instances of balanced, or four-way contests, in which two liberals faced off against two conservatives to gain the constituents' favour. (The only other four-way contest outside Ipswich was anomalous: the election for Nottingham in 1847 pitted two liberals against a coalition consisting of a conservative and a Chartist.) In three-way contests, which were common in Bedford and Durham, and occurred in Nottingham in 1832, the elector whose party advanced only one candidate faced the option of effectively 'throwing away' half of his vote or, perhaps equally unappealingly, tendering half to a candidate of the opposite party.[16] On the whole, the five relevant by-elections from Table 9.1 suggest that two-way contests tended to produce weaker partisanship, even if, as Table 9.2 shows, cross-product ratios remained substantial. In the two-way by-election in Ipswich in 1839, dissenters were still 5.4 times more likely than the wider electorate to vote for the liberal than the conservative candidate; in the two-way by-elections in Nottingham in 1842 and 1843 they averaged 4.4 times more likely; and in the two-way by-elections in Durham in 1843 they averaged 2.3 times more likely.

But even these two tests mask relevant patterns, as further examination of the Bedford elections makes clear. If only the data in Table 9.1 were consulted, it would appear that dissenting support for a liberal candidate or candidates dropped off from 1832 to 1835, rose in 1837, dropped again in 1841 and remained stable in 1847. Table 9.2 tells much the same story, although the magnitude of change differs, and the cross-product ratio of dissenting to non-dissenting votes dropped strikingly in 1847. Use of contingency table analyses on another presentation of the data from Appendix B reveals very different patterns.

Table 9.3 Contingency table analysis indicating tendency of nonconformists, in contrast to wider electorate, to cast the most partisan liberal vote and reject the most partisan conservative vote

	Bedford	Ipswich	Nottingham	Durham
Dec 1832	3.32	13.23	3.55	9.78
Jan 1835	3.61	12.82	—	6.39
June 1835	—	23.26	—	—
July 1837	4.55	—	—	3.38
May 1839	—	5.44	—	—
June 1841	3.98	6.02	—	—
June 1842	—	6.23	—	—
Aug 1842	—	7.83	4.18	—
Apr 1843	—	—	4.53	2.18
July 1843	—	—	—	2.31
July 1847	2.70	6.60	3.49	1.64

Table 9.3 applies contingency table analyses to the most extreme partisan liberal and conservative votes in these 23 electoral contests. That is, this test has omitted for analysis those occasions when an elector unnecessarily plumped for a candidate when a straight was possible, or when he split his two votes between the two parties, and thus cast a neutral vote. Either type of vote was unusual among the politicized electorate of the 1830s and 1840s, and on only one occasion did a substantial bloc of voters choose either type of vote.[17] The average for the percentages by which dissenting electors plumped or straighted in a manner most inclined to support liberals was 83.8 per cent, and on five occasions it exceeded 97 per cent.

The presentation of data in Table 9.3 shows that the tendency of dissenters in Bedford to favour the most partisan liberal vote over the most partisan conservative vote, as compared against the wider borough electorate, increased over the 1830s, and remained higher in 1841 than it had been in either 1832 or 1835. What this reflects is that, in 1832, nearly half the electorate (48 per cent) cast votes for the two liberal candidates. Dissenters showed this tendency more forcefully— 3.32 times more forcefully than the wider electorate—with 68 per cent of their vote. The same three candidates stood again for the borough in 1835, but this time the electors returned a representation split between a liberal and a conservative. Dissenters, however, stood firm in their determination to vote only for two liberals, and were distinguished from the wider electorate by the increased cross-product ratio of their

behaviour so that they were 3.61 times more likely than the wider electorate to give a straight vote for two liberals. But in 1837, a single liberal
stood for the borough of Bedford, against two conservatives. In this case,
it was necessary for liberal electors determined to show their loyalty to
the fullest extent to forfeit one of their two votes. Liberals who were
dissenters did so cheerfully, voting in this manner 67 per cent of the
time. Mainstream liberals, on the other hand, who lacked the dissenters'
degree of fervour for liberalism, voted in this manner only 39 per cent
of the time. It is also worth pointing out that the general election of
1837 was the first contest in Bedford in which religious controversy, in
the form of the church rate debate, was a central political issue. Thus
dissenters were 4.55 times more likely than the remaining electorate to
favour the most partisan liberal vote over the most partisan conservative
vote, and the paradigm of declining dissenting allegiance to liberalism
over time diminishes further.

9.6   Chi-square analysis

Finally, chi-square analyses allow us to test the significance, from a
statistical perspective, of the values of the dissenting votes, as distinct
from those of the wider electorate, in each contest.[18]

In Table 9.4, the higher the χ^2-value and, consequently, the lower
the p-value, the less representative were the votes of the dissenters of
the entire electorate. In other words, a high χ^2-value and a low p-value
indicate dissent's marked divergence from the behaviour of the wider
electorate and, statistically speaking, the more significant the degree to
which the hypothesis is sustained that dissenters favoured liberal politics
strikingly more so than did Anglicans.

For each contest, the p-value indicates the probability that a bloc the
size of the dissenting sample could produce, by chance, so skewed a
liberal vote. In only one contest, the general election in Durham in
1847, was the probability as much as 5 per cent, and in only two others
(also in Durham) was it as high as one-tenth of a per cent. The odds were
much lower in every other case. On average, the odds were around 1 in
100 billion ($p = 10^{-11}$), and in one case, the Ipswich general election of
January 1835, the probability of such results being produced randomly
was 1.3×10^{-22}, or odds of roughly 1 in 7.7 sextillion.[19]

In spite of the evident change across boroughs and individual
elections, all these data point to one overwhelming conclusion. The
nonconformist electors of England were, in the 1830s and 1840s, highly
politicized, and were more inclined than the wider electorate, most

Table 9.4 χ^2 analysis for comparing dissenting votes against behaviour of the wider electorate

		Bedford	Ipswich	Nottingham	Durham
Dec 1832	χ^2	22.9	62.8	24.4	26.1
	df	2	4	2	2
	p	1.0×10^{-5}	7.5×10^{-13}	5.0×10^{-6}	2.2×10^{-6}
Jan 1835	χ^2	19.6	105.0	—	29.2
	df	2	3	—	2
	p	5.5×10^{-5}	1.3×10^{-22}	—	4.6×10^{-7}
June 1835	χ^2	—	104.0	—	—
	df	—	3	—	—
	p	—	2.1×10^{-22}	—	—
July 1837	χ^2	53.9	—	—	13.9
	df	2	—	—	2
	p	2.0×10^{-12}	—	—	9.6×10^{-4}
May 1839	χ^2	—	38.2	—	—
	df	—	1	—	—
	p	—	6.4×10^{-10}	—	—
June 1841	χ^2	55.2	85.5	—	—
	df	2	3	—	—
	p	1.0×10^{-12}	2.0×10^{-18}	—	—
June 1842	χ^2	—	92.5	—	—
	df	—	3	—	—
	p	—	6.4×10^{-20}	—	—
Aug 1842	χ^2	—	96.6	51.4	—
	df	—	3	1	—
	p	—	8.4×10^{-21}	7.5×10^{-12}	—
Apr 1843	χ^2	—	—	57.4	12.5
	df	—	—	1	1
	p	—	—	3.6×10^{-14}	4.0×10^{-4}
July 1843	χ^2	—	—	—	11.8
	df	—	—	—	1
	p	—	—	—	6.0×10^{-4}
July 1847	χ^2	26.7	62.8	45.1	5.99
	df	2	3	3	2
	p	1.6×10^{-6}	1.5×10^{-13}	8.8×10^{-10}	5.0×10^{-2}

χ^2 = chi-square result
p = probability
df = degree(s) of freedom

of whom we may assume to have been Anglican, to have voted to return liberal candidates as members of parliament. These facts are not surprising, especially in view of earlier chapters, but they do merit note, for they demonstrate the degree to which the dissenters identified for analysis in Appendix B—on average less than a ten-per cent rump of the electorate[20]—contributed, as a bloc, to the liberal vote. In 17 of 18 applicable elections, nonconformists cast a heavy majority of their votes in the most extreme partisan liberal manner, and on two-thirds of these occasions such votes accounted for over 65 per cent of the dissenting vote. In the five two-way by-elections, dissent's majority for liberals averaged 75.6 per cent.

9.7   Old *v.* new dissent: the place of Wesleyan Methodists

At this point it is worth looking within the ranks of nonconformity, to see if useful conclusions can be made regarding individual dissenting denominations and their relative support for liberal politics and, more specifically, to compare the behaviour of old dissent (Congregationalists and Baptists, for the most part) with the various Methodist denominations. The latter question is of particular importance because, by the mid-nineteenth century, Methodists probably accounted for over half of the dissenters in England. Moreover, the political allegiance of Methodists, and especially Wesleyans, has been much debated. One historian has concluded of the Wesleyans that '[m]any of them lacked strong commitment to either party,' and 'that the connexion was unreliable in politics, and...as the spirit of Reform declined in the 1840s, it became increasingly hard to rally its members to the Liberal cause.'[21] It is likewise the judgement of the chief authority on the politics of Methodism in the first half of the nineteenth century that '[t]he political allegiances of the [Wesleyans] were...more complicated' than old dissent or other Methodists.[22]

Present-day historians' ambivalence about nineteenth-century Methodists, as to both their political and religious orientation, was shared by their contemporaries, with the Wesleyans presenting a particular puzzle. A meeting at the Baptist chapel in Park Street (Nottingham), 'for the purpose of appointing a Committee to watch over the interests of the Dissenters,' heard that very question raised. The Revd Messrs Howitt and Gilbert observed that 'for a time they [i.e. Methodists] had stood on a sort of debateable [sic] ground, assumed a neutral character, and were claimed by both Churchmen and Dissenters....' However, the late persecution of J.R. Stephens (1805–1879), a Methodist preacher who opposed the church rate, 'had brought the opinions of the Methodists to the test,' and it was now obvious that they were rightly classified as dissenters.[23] To claim otherwise, the Revd Gilbert said, was to argue a paradox.[24]

In 1842 a body of dissenting ministers in Birmingham recommended to the nonconformist electors of Nottingham the Quaker candidate Joseph Sturge, on the grounds that Baptists, Congregationalists, Unitarians, and 'the liberty-loving Methodists' shared a common outlook, and were virtually one politically.[25] Militant Anglicans who were hostile both to dissent and Methodism also saw them as interchangeable. As one curate wrote to George Henry Law (1761–1845), the Bishop of Bath and Wells, 'Wesleyan teachers... [N.B. the author denied them the distinction of minister or preacher] are like all other dissenting teachers, mere impostors...,' whose doctrines promote *'Illegitimacy, drunkeness* [sic], *and the defrauding of Creditors.'*[26] Similarly, the *Churchman*, described as 'one of the Organs of the Tory Party,' when it spoke of *'Dissenting* and *Methodist Ministers*, refuse[d] to give them the title of *Reverend*, but substitute[d] the word *Rebel....'*[27]

Other evidence from dissenting chapel records indicates a fair degree of collegiality among different nonconformist denominations. The burial register for the Congregationalist meeting house in Tacket Street (Ipswich), for instance, lists one Francis Brown, who died in 1847 and to whose entry was added 'At the Wesleyan Association Chapel, Friar's Street, in this Town,... late Minister of that Place of Worship.' Similarly, Ralph Johnson, of the same congregation, was buried for whatever reason 'In the Burial Ground of the Baptist Congregation....'[28] An elector in Bedford is listed, some years apart, as associated with the Congregationalist Howard Chapel and St Paul's Wesleyan Chapel.[29] There is also the case of the Revd Timothy Richard Matthews (d.1845), a Bedford clergyman of the Church of England who fraternized with Jews and Wesleyans alike, formed his own adult-baptizing Primitive Episcopal Church (of which he appointed himself bishop), and was at one point on the verge of following the Latter-day Saints![30] What these examples might suggest—and there are not enough, of course, to make a firm case—is that as old dissent was taken over by evangelicals, not much was left to divide protestant dissenters.

Based only on the votes they cast, the Methodists of Ipswich demonstrated overwhelming support for liberal politics—although the number of Wesleyan and Primitive Methodists together in Ipswich was admittedly not large.[31] Nonetheless, it is noteworthy that, of the 63 votes the Methodists did cast, in eight elections, every single vote was cast for a liberal candidate or candidates, and not once did a Methodist elector support any conservative. Of the contests for which contingency table analyses are possible (they cannot be performed if any of the values tested is zero), Methodist electors demonstrated, on average, almost identical preference for liberal candidates as did the old dissenters. In fact, the strength of their support differed by less than one-and-a-half per cent: electors who adhered to the Methodist denominations were 1.01 times more likely than Baptists, Congregationalists, and others to favour the most partisan liberal vote over the most partisan conservative vote.

Granted, this average masks significant variation at the level of the individual constituencies. The Methodists in Durham, for instance, were stronger in their support for liberals than were the Methodists of Nottingham or Bedford. In Durham, Methodists were 1.64 times more likely than the wider dissenting electorate to favour a liberal candidate or candidates over any conservative. Indeed, new dissenters in Durham seemed occasionally on the verge of favouring radical politics, as witness their overwhelming support in 1837 for T.C. Granger, who laid out a platform of broad and thoroughgoing reform. Presbyterians and Congregationalists preferred the milder liberal, W.C. Harland, but Methodist support for Granger and his radical agenda, ranging far beyond civil and religious liberty, was enough by itself to push the candidate to the top of the poll among the dissenting electorate.[32] On the other hand, Methodists in Nottingham were only 0.78 times as likely as, or 1.29 times less likely than, the wider dissenting electorate to choose liberal rather than conservative candidates; and in Bedford they were only 0.58 times as liberal as, or 1.73 times more conservative than, other dissenters.

Samples from Primitive Methodists and the New Methodist Connexion are too small to advance any sweeping statement on the significance of their electoral influence. Nor can much be said about other mainstream nonconformist denominations. Baptists in Bedford displayed stronger allegiance to liberalism than did the Congregationalists in the 1830s, but the pattern reversed itself in the 1840s. In Ipswich, the small body of Presbyterians constantly shifted position in this respect with the larger group of Congregationalists. The two large General Baptist Congregations in Nottingham always voted strongly for liberals, but the smaller sample of Congregationalists always outstripped them. The Presbyterians of Durham regularly voted to return liberal candidates, though they were not a large group.[33] We can, however, say with confidence that, in no borough, and not even in any single contest, did any nonconformist denomination ever vote in such a way as to suggest a desire to return a conservative over a liberal candidate. This was as true of the Methodist congregations as it was for the Baptists or Congregationalists.[34]

9.8 Conclusions

In closing, it should be pointed out that the data from Appendix B and their foregoing analyses in this chapter have not by any means included under the category of dissenting elector every nonconformist in Durham, Nottingham, Ipswich, or Bedford who cast a vote in parliamentary elections between 1832 and 1847. Simply too many complicating obstacles must be overcome for this to be possible. For one thing, many committed dissenters, through no fault of their own, were married or buried in an Anglican service.[35] Other limiting circumstances have been discussed already.

The electors who have been used met stringent criteria for inclusion. Those for whom there were not strong grounds were ignored for special analysis, and grouped with the remainder of the electorate, most of whom were Anglicans. The actual figure for dissenting voters in Bedford probably was roughly double what is reflected in Appendix B and has been used in this chapter, and for Durham was perhaps triple. It is harder to say for the two much larger electorates, but in Ipswich it was perhaps also triple. In Nottingham, attendance at dissenting services was twice as high as at parish services on Census Sunday 1851, and the editors of the *Nottingham Review* reckoned that 'dissenters, ... without doubt, form[ed] a majority of the electors' in the borough.[36] What this means is that, in Bedford and Durham, around a fifth of the voters ignored for special analysis were in fact dissenters. The figure stands probably higher in Ipswich (perhaps around a quarter) and vastly more so in Nottingham. Most likely these overlooked electors advocated liberal politics, and therefore contribute to false negatives in the results. In other words, an analysis that was able to include all nonconformist electors in Durham, Nottingham, Ipswich and Bedford would almost certainly reveal even stronger associations between dissent and liberalism on the one hand, and Anglicanism and conservatism on the other.

10
Conclusion: The Legacy of Dissent in English Politics in the Nineteenth Century

When I look back to the history of this country, and consider its present condition, I must say that all that the people possess of liberty has come, not through the portals of the cathedrals and the parish churches, but from the conventicles, which are despised by [the] hon. gentlemen opposite. When I know that if a good measure is to be carried in this House, it must be by men who are sent hither by the Nonconformists of Great Britain,—when I read and see that the past and present State alliance with religion is hostile to religious liberty, preventing all growth and nearly destroying all vitality in religion itself,— then I shall hold myself to have read, thought, and lived in vain, if I vote for a measure which in the smallest degree shall give any further power or life to the principle of State endowment; and, in conclusion, I will only exhort the Dissenters of England to act in the same way, and to stand upon their own great, pure, and unassailable principle; for if they stand by it manfully, and work for it vigorously, the time may come—nay, it will come, when that principle will be adopted by the Legislature of the country.

John Bright (1811–1888), MP for Durham City, speaking in parliament on the Maynooth grant, 1845[1]

Lord John Russell, first earl Russell (1792–1878), prominent leader of the reform movement of the 1820s and 1830s, and later liberal prime minister, once remarked: 'I know the Dissenters. They gave us the emancipation of the slave. They gave us the Reform Bill. They gave us Free Trade.'[2]

Allowing for political hyperbole, there remains much truth in Russell's portrait of dissenters as the chief mainstay of liberal principles in the nineteenth century. From the repeal of the test and corporation acts onwards—from parliamentary and municipal reform to the dissenters' marriage bill, from the abolition of colonial slavery to campaigns for disestablishment, from the Anti-Corn Law League and the push for free trade to the abolition of the church rate and tithes—dissenters involved themselves energetically on behalf of virtually all the liberal aims of the early- to mid-nineteenth century. They were then, as they are recognized to have been later in the century, the backbone of the liberal party. But it is curious that, of the measures Lord John attributed in large part to the efforts of the dissenters, he omitted to mention those reforms which most directly impacted the nonconformists themselves, for dissenters were undoubtedly vigorous campaigners for full civil and religious liberty. Nevertheless, Russell apparently preferred to draw attention to those measures with a wider appeal, and thus identified some of the hallmarks of nineteenth-century English liberal ideology.

Equally striking is the handbill posted by William Eyre, an auctioneer and liberal activist, in the run-up to the Nottingham by-election of April 1841. Eyre made public the contents of a letter he had sent three days earlier to each of the candidates vying for the seat made vacant by the recent death of one of the members of the borough. In the letter, Eyre quizzed the candidates on what he judged to be six of the most important political questions of the day. He indicated that a duplicate had been sent to the other candidate, 'and [made clear] that the answers I receive will decide my vote,' and obviously intended that his preference should influence similarly minded liberals. Tellingly, only one of the six points Eyre demanded touched in the least matters of religion: 'a plan of National Education, unfettered by the doctrines of the Church....' The others were typical liberal, or even radical, goals: repeal of the Corn Law, the ballot, free trade, practical measures to extend the suffrage, and shorter parliaments. And yet in spite of the wide range of topics, Eyre nevertheless reckoned such a programme consistent with the goals of 'every CONSISTENT FRIEND to Civil and Religious Liberty...'—a proposition surely calculated to appeal to dissenters.[3]

As we have seen from previous chapters, nonconformists were in the vanguard of virtually every major liberal campaign between 1832 and 1847. With the exception of certain schemes of national education and the Maynooth grant (on which their principles might dictate opposition),[4] they were on the liberal side of every debate that concerned the relation of the church and state. Nonconformists nominated liberal candidates on the hustings and introduced them in other venues, they assumed prominent roles in liberal political meetings, invited liberal candidates to canvass from their chapels, and regularly turned out *en masse* at liberal political rallies. The *Nottingham Review* made the connexion between nonconformists and liberals all but explicit in reporting on the proceedings of the Nottinghamshire Auxiliary of the London Missionary Society.[5] The two-day gala was poorly attended on the second morning, apparently due to the fact that so many 'members of churches of all [dissenting] denominations' had gone to view the triumphant entry of the liberal member standing for re-election, Sir John Cam Hobhouse.[6]

But English nonconformists eager to advance liberal political agendas did more than merely organize and agitate in behalf of liberal candidates seeking to be members of parliament. An address to the 'Reformers of England' that circulated in Bedford following the king's dismissal of the liberal government in December 1834 urged liberal electors to

> Let each ... independent constituency, without loss of time, prepare for its local struggle without wasting strength in what is called national demonstration. ... The only demonstration worth making is sending such Members to the next Parliament as will dispose of this Duke [i.e. Wellington] and his greedy red-coated adventurers the first day of the next sessions.[7]

In 1837 the *Bedford Beacon* similarly rated the significance of the vote, in referring to 'the present struggle [i.e. the approaching general election]. ..., [as] unquestionably, a fight between the powers of good and evil. ...'

> It is to crush for ever that party [i.e. the conservative party] to which all such mischief is traceable—it is to crush for ever that party, reckless of all consequences whatsoever, so that their lust of power and wealth be indulged, that the Electors are now called upon to come forward. If they neglect their duty in the coming contest, the empire is lost; but if they will only resolve that the battle *shall* be won, they will secure a triumph to the cause of Freedom throughout Europe.[8]

And enfranchised nonconformists used their votes overwhelmingly to return liberal members to the House of Commons.[9] As John McKenzie, a nonconformist preacher in Bedford, said:

> if he were called on to preach one sermon, the text should be, 'Down with the Tories.' There was not one Dissenting minister in the town who will not give his vote for Mr Whitbread [i.e. the liberal candidate], but how many is there of the Established Church who would give him a vote? Not one, save and only a highly educated and benevolent man, the Rector of Stevington....[10]

Chapter 9 proved the truth of McKenzie's words: Bedford nonconformists were nearly four times more likely than their Anglican counterparts to reject conservative and favour liberal candidates, departing from the average voter in this respect by odds of approximately 1.0×10^{-12}, or one in one trillion.[11] The pattern was borne out abundantly, in Bedford as elsewhere, by dissenting laity as well as ministers.

English electors took seriously the proposition that '[t]he poll-books will tell the tale, and in those poll-books it should be the duty of all true friends of civil and religious liberty to endeavour by every possible exertion to' return reformers to the House of Commons.[12] As a Nottingham handbill put it:

> When called upon to vote, you may be threatened with having your Name shown [*sic*] up in the Poll-Book:—remember, there is a Book beyond that, the Book of every Man's Conscience:—there is a Book beyond that, the Book of GOD'S Remembrance, in which every Name, every Action, is registered. Shew then, when you come to vote, whose you are, by shewing whom you serve.[13]

One who identified himself only as 'a Protestant Dissenter' emphasized '[t]he importance of political responsibility being connected with the exercise and profession of *Christian principles*...,' and charged every voter with his obligation to use his vote to honour God and promote the 'sacred cause of freedom....'[14]

Nonconformists did not, of course, command a majority of the votes in most constituencies, and disdainful conservatives taunted them on these grounds, claiming that '[o]f one thing, the Dissenters must be certain,—*they can do nothing alone....*'[15] But as their advocates retorted, 'the Dissenters of ... all ... places, ought to unite together as one man...,' to return only those candidates who would pursue a dissenter's political agenda.[16] Given the reputation of the English political unions established in the early 1830s, it is striking that the Bedford Union Society explicitly rejected correspondence or association with other unions, or forming branches, but that political nonconformists of the same borough evidently had no such reservations.[17] Regionally as well as nationally, 'the protestant Dissenters of Great Britain' organized to discuss the 'Grievances under which Dissenters labour, with a View to their Redress....'[18] Moreover, as the previous chapter demonstrated, nonconformist weight certainly was sufficient to decide an election: in at least four elections in three boroughs, it was indeed clearly the force of the dissenting electors who turned the tide of a contest, and led to the return of one or more liberal candidates.[19]

Liberal MPs clearly recognized their debt to nonconformist electors, and regularly acknowledged them while canvassing, from the hustings, and in other public speeches. In what was plainly more a gesture of obligation than substantial financial assistance, the liberal members for Nottingham each contributed £2 to the Wesleyan Methodist Benevolent Society in 1834.[20] Liberal candidates recognized nonconformist grievances publicly, and made their redress a significant part of their electoral appeal, as in the following recitation:

> 1st. That church rates, and all compulsory payments for the support of religious are a practical grievance.
>
> 2nd. That the not being permitted to marry and bury in their own way, and without the intervention of the established clergy, or any other authority, is a practical grievance.
>
> 3rd. That the want of a registration of births and marriages, independent of the established church, is a practical grievance.
>
> 4th. That not being allowed admission to the universities, and to all their honours and privileges, is a practical grievance.[21]

Liberal MPs could most tangibly demonstrate their attachment to nonconformists, however, in parliament, in their capacities as legislators. As Sir William Follett, conservative MP for Exeter, told his constituents in 1841, the most reliable guide to the rival strength of the parties lay in how members divided in the House of Commons.[22] In considering the numerous and varied divisions on matters touching religion, clear signs exist of consistent partisan behaviour on the part of MPs, with liberals and conservatives alike casting votes on predictable party lines between 80 and 85 per cent of the time. The discipline of a two-party system was, in respect to religion, plainly evident in the decade-and-a-half that followed the first reform bill, and the issues were already broached that would divide parties in the age of Gladstone and Disraeli, and in some cases beyond. This widening divide in politics occurred at both the constituency and the parliamentary levels, and there were liberals and conservatives in a period long before what is usually seen as the beginning of a two-party system. In the famous words of Elie Halévy, only slightly out of context, *This is modern England,* and its foundations lie in the controversies that separated dissenters and Anglicans.

Religious and denominational rivalry permeated most of the great political debates of the 1830s and 1840s. It loomed large in the period of the reform crisis and the run-up to the first general election in 1832, as well as in the campaigns, so sacred to dissent, to abolish colonial slavery and, later, to terminate the so-called apprentice status of the former slaves. All these issues reformers subsumed under the slogan of *civil and religious liberty.* Religion could hardly fail to count in the general election of 1835, precipitated by the king's dismissal of a government, in spite of its backing by a majority of the House of Commons, on grounds of religious reform. These events remained fresh in the minds of electors and the rhetoric of candidates two-and-a-half years later, during the first general election of Queen Victoria's reign, which was also the first contest to elicit strong feeling over the issue of church rates, an issue which repeatedly divided the resulting parliament. Historians have typically regarded the general election of 1841 as being waged over tariffs and duties, but as we have seen, religious controversy could never be wholly removed from the wider demand for 'freedom of trade as well as freedom in other things.'[23] Similarly, emphasis on the disruption within the conservative party following the government's adoption of partial free trade measures in the spring of 1846 has obscured the continuity evident in parliamentary divisions on religion issues. And many, inside parliament and out, clearly judged a member's position on the Maynooth grant a weightier index of his true political convictions than his vote on the Corn Law. Moreover, many regarded conservative apostasy in respect to the Maynooth grant, which occurred fully a year before the repeal of the Corn Law, as an unpardonable breach of conservative principle. This event, as much as conservative realignment following Corn Law repeal, was a principal focal point of the general election of 1847. And religion supplanted other matters commonly identified as 'party issues' in several of the period's by-elections, as well.

No doubt party leaders such as Peel or Russell would have preferred stricter parliamentary discipline, especially in the controversy over protection and free trade. As indicated in Chapter 4, the positions expressed by the two liberal candidates for Nottingham in 1841 are suggestive of this tension. It was Sir John Cam Hobhouse, the seasoned sitting member and cabinet minister, who campaigned energetically on behalf of the government's doomed scheme for rolling back import duties on timber, sugar, and especially foreign grain:[24] 'this,' he told his constituents in Nottingham, '[wa]s the touchstone' that divided the liberal from the conservative party.[25] On the other hand, it was Sir John's fellow liberal candidate, a successful businessman but an amateur politician, George Gerard de Hochepied Larpent, who probably was closer to the mark: in his assessment, what truly divided the liberal and conservative parties, and the nation, was the division over 'the true principles of civil and religious liberty.'[26] Among conservatives, even party men could deviate from their leaders, as in the case of Sir William Follett in Exeter, who had served as solicitor general in Peel's short-lived ministry of 1834–1835, and would be re-appointed to the post on the conservatives' reclaiming the government in 1841. Nevertheless, Sir William dismissed the priority of trade or protection in the general election of 1841 and on other occasions, and campaigned instead on the basis of his defence of conservative Anglicanism. Indeed, nationally, only 60 per cent of the conservative candidates made the unimpaired maintenance of Corn Law the leading issue of their manifestos in 1841,[27] and in many cases, the other 40 per cent were most likely responding to the pressure of the electorate, which was frequently put off by incessant dispute over agricultural protection, and demanded that the debate return to what they reckoned was really relevant to them—religion.

Even when they did not completely trump other political issues, the sentiment and rhetoric of religious issues were easily integrated into wider arguments for reform. Advocates of free trade, for instance, readily slipped into the familiar language of 'perfect freedom of conscience in religion' to serve in their demand for perfect freedom in trade.[28] As one free trader in Exeter put it,

> If England would be great and powerful, she must be free,—that is free in the just and proper sense of that term.—She must have freedom of trade as well as freedom in other things.[29]

Certainly religion was indicated among 'other things' for, as another free trader from Exeter said, the borough had already distinguished itself in pursuit of one of these 'two great freedoms [—i.e. in] the struggle it had made in defence of religious freedom....' He continued:

> The electors of Exeter had it now then in their power to complete the work. He would scarcely call it a climax for it was only as the very simple gradation as one and one make two. By their firmness and decision they had secured their religious freedom, and might secure their commercial freedom also.[30]

Liberals in the 1830s had similarly declared the religious freedom for which they struggled to be the next step in the transformation of English society, following naturally on the heels of the civil freedom embodied in the great reform act. Demands for parliamentary reform subsided over the next decade, but the clamour for religious freedom remained strong, and as we have seen, a new goal—perfect freedom in trade—was added to the agenda of liberal reform. By the mid-nineteenth century, free trade had become so firmly a part of the dissenting and liberal identify that, by the 1840s, the old whig and dissenting slogan of civil and religious liberty had, as a new liberal and dissenting slogan, expanded to include 'those great and grand principles as well religious, civil, and commercial....'[31]

In regard to other issues—the new poor law of 1834, Chartist demands, or the Corn Laws—the parties were often split, and their rival fortunes ebbed and flowed on both national and local levels. Cohesion in the conservative party in Exeter had withered away in the mid-1840s; unity among liberals in Bedford 'had been smashed to atoms,' and they were divided between conservative liberals, radical liberals, church liberals, dissenting liberals, Wesleyan liberals, and more besides.[32] In Ipswich in 1847 both parties had burned themselves out after more than two decades of hard campaigning and, as a result, the borough returned a split representation for the first time in a generation.[33] A contemporary handbill claimed that the labels liberal or conservative no longer made sense as apt descriptions of what divided England politically and otherwise, but acknowledged a potent split along religious lines.[34] Norman Gash's comment on the importance of religion division in the 1847 general election has already been noted:[35] the contest was largely an expression of opinion on the Maynooth grant, and it is telling that we find advertisements in the summer of 1847 for such tracts as 'The Christian's part in the approaching General Election.'[36]

That is why consideration of religion is essential for a proper grasp of the origins and development of the modern political system in nineteenth-century England. And within the realm of religion, and the great and divisive questions of church-state relations, the constructive role played by the dissenters must be especially acknowledged. Granted, those outside the establishment did not in most cases constitute a majority in constituencies, but they were rarely so small as to be negligible—either from the point of view of candidates seeking election, or the perspective of historical inquiry. Nor were their numbers so great as to render the present sort of investigation infeasible, at least not over a sampling of constituencies within a discrete chronological framework, such as this study employs.

Moreover, dissenters spanned a diverse breadth of the English social spectrum in the nineteenth century. As Professor Gash has pointed out, the line that divided dissenters from Anglicans was no ordinary boundary of class or wealth or status or region. Instead there was a *vertical* line, cutting indiscriminately through rich and poor, urban and rural, industrial and agricultural. What they had in common was that they were dissenters—they dissented from the Anglican establishment. They were nonconformists—they did not conform to the doctrines or practices of the Church of England.

The present analysis provides examples. Although the most evident advocates of civil and religious liberty were, unsurprisingly, men of substance, the use of civil registers and poll books permits a far more inclusive portrait of political dissent: the electors identified in Chapter 9 as nonconformists of one variety or another range from labourers and colliers at one end of the social spectrum, to esquires (and the rather vague designation of gentlemen), aldermen, attorneys-at-law, and medical doctors at the other—with shoemakers, barbers, and tailors falling somewhere in between.

If it can be demonstrated in a useful, consistent, and statistically defensible manner that such a range of men—spread over five boroughs, representing a host of different economic, social, professional, regional, and experiential backgrounds (and indeed, including the occasional nonconformist butcher!)—nonetheless voted in the same, predictable manner, election after election, and that the candidates they preferred in turn reflected distinct partisan alignment in parliament in a period before most historians have suspected the existence of significant party organization, something has been achieved in advancing our understanding of England's politics in a formative period of its constitutional history.

Appendix A.1

The arrangement of these tables is explained in Section 8.3 of Chapter 8. Briefly, names above the heavy line and in italics are liberal members of parliament, and those below it in plain type are conservative MPs. Each column is a parliamentary division found in a particular volume and column of *Hansard*. A plus (+) indicates a vote favourable to dissent, a minus (−) is a vote supporting the church establishment at the expense of dissent, and a zero (0) represents a member's absence from the House of Commons, and no vote cast.

1833 parliament

	17: 1337	18: 59	18: 978	18: 1098	19: 282	19: 1033	20: 356	20: 560	20: 782	21: 628
Buller	+	+	0	−	0	0	0	0	0	0
Chaytor	0	+	0	+	0	0	0	0	0	0
Divett	0	+	0	+	+	−	+	0	+	+
Duncannon	0	+	0	−	0	0	−	−	0	0
Faithfull	0	0	0	+	0	+	0	0	0	0
Ferguson	0	+	0	−	0	0	−	0	0	+
Harland	0	0	0	+	+	+	+	+	0	0
Morrison	0	0	+	+	0	0	0	0	+	0
Wason	+	0	+	+	0	0	0	0	0	+
Whitbread	0	0	0	−	0	0	0	0	0	0
Wigney	0	+	0	+	0	0	0	0	0	0
Polhill	0	0	0	0	0	−	0	0	0	0

	21: 1143	22: 153	22: 928	22: 1060	22: 1373	23: 356	23: 1350	24: 86	24: 364	25: 129
Buller	0	0	0	0	+	0	0	0	0	0
Chaytor	0	+	+	−	0	+	0	0	+	0
Divett	0	0	+	+	0	0	+	+	0	0
Duncannon	0	0	0	0	0	0	0	0	0	0
Faithfull	+	+	0	+	0	0	0	+	+	0
Ferguson	0	+	0	−	0	0	0	0	0	0
Harland	0	0	0	0	0	+	0	0	0	−
Morrison	0	0	+	0	0	0	0	+	+	0
Wason	+	0	+	+	+	0	+	+	0	+
Whitbread	0	0	0	−	0	0	0	0	0	0
Wigney	+	0	0	+	0	0	0	+	0	0
Polhill	0	0	0	0	0	0	0	0	0	0

25:199	
Buller	0
Chaytor	0
Divett	+
Duncannon	0
Faithfull	0
Ferguson	0
Harland	+
Morrison	0
Wason	−
Whitbread	0
Wigney	0
Polhill	0

1835 parliament

	27:772	27:83	27:861	27:969	28:161
Crawley	+	+	+	+	0
Divett	+	0	0	+	0
Ferguson	+	+	+	+	0
Harland	+	0	+	0	0
Hobhouse	+	0	0	0	0
Pechell	+	0	0	0	0
Wigney	+	0	0	+	0
Dundas	−	0	0	−	−
Follett	−	0	0	−	0
Kelly	−	0	0	0	0
Polhill	−	0	0	−	0
Trevor	−	0	0	−	−

	29:1067	30:310	31:868
Crawley	0	0	0
Divett	+	+	+
Ferguson	+	+	+
Harland	+	0	+
Hobhouse	+	+	0
Morrison	+	0	+
Pechell	+	+	0
Wason	+	0	+
Wigney	+	0	0
Follett	−	0	0
Polhill	−	0	0
Trevor	−	0	−

	33: 18	33: 831	33: 1078	33: 1236	34: 117	34: 754	34: 979	34: 983	34: 1018	34: 1030
Crawley	+	0	+	0	+	0	+	0	+	+
Divett	+	0	0	0	+	0	0	0	0	0
Ferguson	+	0	+	0	+	0	+	+	0	+
Harland	+	0	0	0	+	0	0	0	0	0
Hobhouse	0	0	0	+	+	0	0	0	+	+
Morrison	0	0	0	0	+	0	0	+	+	+
Pechell	0	+	+	+	+	+	+	0	+	+
Wason	0	+	0	+	+	0	0	−	0	+
Wigney	0	0	0	0	+	−	0	0	+	0
Follett	−	0	0	0	−	0	0	0	−	−
Polhill	−	0	0	0	−	0	0	0	0	0
Trevor	−	0	0	0	−	−	0	0	−	−

	34: 1033	34: 1149	34: 1259	34: 1280	35: 53	35: 149	35: 157	35: 212	35: 218	35: 548
Crawley	+	+	+	0	0	0	0	0	0	0
Divett	0	0	+	0	0	+	+	0	0	0
Ferguson	+	+	+	+	0	+	−	+	+	0
Harland	+	0	+	0	0	−	+	−	0	−
Hobhouse	0	0	+	+	−	+	−	0	+	+
Morrison	0	0	+	0	+	0	0	0	0	0
Pechell	+	0	+	0	0	+	+	+	0	0
Wason	+	0	+	0	0	0	0	0	0	0
Wigney	0	0	+	0	0	0	0	0	0	0
Follett	0	0	−	0	−	0	0	0	0	0
Polhill	0	0	−	0	0	0	0	0	0	0
Trevor	−	0	−	0	0	−	+	−	−	−

	35: 855	35: 874	35: 1129	35: 1140	35: 1143	35: 1210	36: 630	37: 549	38: 461	38: 539
Crawley	+	0	0	0	0	0	+	+	+	0
Divett	+	0	0	0	0	0	0	+	0	0
Ferguson	+	0	0	−	+	0	0	+	0	−
Harland	+	0	0	0	+	0	+	+	0	0
Hobhouse	+	0	0	−	0	0	+	+	0	0
Morrison	+	0	+	+	0	+	0	+	0	+
Pechell	+	0	0	0	0	0	0	+	0	−
Wason	0	0	0	0	0	0	−	+	0	+
Wigney	+	+	0	0	0	0	0	+	0	0
Follett	0	0	0	0	0	0	0	−	0	0
Polhill	−	0	0	0	0	0	0	−	0	−
Trevor	−	−	−	−	−	−	+	−	−	−

	38: 545	38: 652	38: 858	38: 905	38: 1073	38: 1336	38: 1379	38: 1434	38: 1629
Crawley	0	+	0	0	+	0	+	+	0
Divett	+	0	−	+	+	+	+	+	0
Ferguson	−	+	0	+	+	+	+	+	+
Harland	0	0	0	0	+	0	+	+	+
Hobhouse	0	+	0	+	+	0	+	+	0
Morrison	0	+	0	+	+	0	0	0	0
Pechell	+	+	+	+	+	0	0	+	+
Wason	+	0	0	+	+	+	0	+	0
Wigney	0	+	0	0	+	0	0	+	0
Follett	−	−	0	0	−	0	0	−	0
Polhill	−	−	0	−	−	−	−	−	0
Trevor	−	−	0	0	−	−	−	−	0

1837 parliament

	39: 358	41: 1119	42: 755	42: 892	42: 920	42: 924	42: 931	42: 955	42: 1162	42: 1353
Crawley	0	0	0	0	0	0	0	0	0	0
Divett	+	+	0	+	0	0	0	+	0	+
Ferguson	−	+	−	+	0	+	+	+	0	+
Harland	−	0	0	+	−	+	+	0	0	+
Hobhouse	0	0	0	+	0	0	+	0	+	+
Pechell	−	+	+	+	0	0	+	0	+	+
Dalrymple	−	−	0	−	−	0	0	0	0	−
Dungannon	0	0	0	−	0	0	0	0	0	−
Follett	−	0	0	−	0	0	0	0	0	−
Gibson	0	0	−	−	0	0	0	0	0	0
Kelly	0	0	0	−	0	0	0	0	0	−
Polhill	0	0	0	−	0	0	0	0	0	−

	43: 738	43: 786	43: 891	43: 1160	43: 1162	43: 1164	43: 1202	43: 1209	43: 1245	44: 41
Crawley	0	+	0	0	0	0	+	+	0	0
Divett	0	+	0	+	+	+	+	+	+	0
Ferguson	+	+	0	0	+	+	+	+	0	0
Harland	0	0	0	0	0	0	0	+	0	0
Hobhouse	+	0	0	−	0	0	+	+	0	+
Pechell	0	+	+	+	0	0	+	0	+	0
Dalrymple	0	0	0	−	0	0	0	−	0	0
Dungannon	0	+	+	−	−	−	+	−	0	0
Follett	0	0	0	0	0	0	+	−	0	0
Gibson	0	0	0	−	0	0	0	0	0	+
Kelly	0	0	0	0	+	0	0	−	0	0
Polhill	0	0	0	0	0	0	0	−	0	0

	44: 140	44: 248	44: 305	44: 322	44: 372	44: 495	44: 541	44: 543	44: 546	44: 547
Crawley	+	+	+	+	−	+	+	−	0	0
Divett	+	0	0	0	+	0	0	0	0	0
Ferguson	0	0	0	+	0	0	0	0	0	0
Harland	0	0	0	0	0	0	0	0	0	+
Hobhouse	0	+	0	0	−	0	+	−	+	0
Pechell	+	+	+	+	+	+	+	+	+	0
Dalrymple	−	−	−	0	−	0	−	−	−	−
Dungannon	−	0	0	0	0	0	0	0	0	0
Follett	0	0	0	−	0	+	−	−	−	0
Gibson	+	0	0	−	−	0	−	−	0	0
Kelly	0	−	0	0	0	0	0	0	0	0
Polhill	0	−	0	0	−	0	0	0	0	0

	44: 693	44: 1016	45: 581	47: 1226	48: 204
Crawley	–	0	0	0	0
Divett	0	+	+	0	0
Ferguson	0	0	0	0	0
Harland	0	0	0	0	0
Hobhouse	–	0	+	+	+
Pechell	0	+	–	0	0
Dalrymple	–	0	0	–	0
Dungannon	0	0	0	0	0
Follett	–	0	0	0	+
Gibson	0	0	0	0	0
Kelly	0	0	0	0	0
Polhill	0	0	0	0	0

	48:681	49:530	52:116
Crawley	0	0	–
Divett	+	0	0
Ferguson	0	0	0
Harland	+	0	0
Hobhouse	+	–	–
Pechell	+	+	+
Cochrane	0	0	0
Dalrymple	–	0	0
Dungannon	–	0	0
Follett	0	0	–
Kelly	–	0	0
Polhill	–	0	0

	52: 162	52: 1163	53: 618	54: 320	54: 1163	54: 1165	54: 1202	55: 62	55: 114	55: 194
Crawley	0	0	0	0	0	0	0	0	0	0
Divett	0	0	0	+	0	0	0	0	+	+
Ferguson	0	0	0	0	0	0	0	0	+	+
Harland	0	–	0	0	0	0	0	0	0	0
Hobhouse	0	0	+	0	+	+	+	0	0	0
Pechell	+	0	+	–	+	+	+	+	0	+
Cochrane	–	0	0	–	0	0	0	0	–	–
Dalrymple	0	–	0	–	0	0	0	–	–	0
Dungannon	0	0	0	0	0	0	0	0	–	+
Follett	0	0	0	0	0	0	0	0	–	0
Kelly	0	0	0	0	0	0	0	–	0	–
Polhill	0	0	0	0	0	0	0	0	–	–

	55: 218	55: 220	55: 221	55: 358	55: 373	55: 426	55: 428	55: 432	55: 452	55: 576
Crawley	0	0	0	0	0	0	0	0	–	0
Divett	0	0	0	+	0	0	0	0	0	0
Ferguson	0	0	0	0	0	0	0	0	0	0
Harland	+	+	+	0	0	+	+	+	0	0
Hobhouse	+	0	0	0	0	0	0	0	0	0
Pechell	+	+	+	+	0	+	0	0	0	+
Cochrane	0	0	0	0	0	0	0	0	0	–
Dalrymple	–	0	0	–	0	0	0	0	+	–
Dungannon	–	–	–	–	–	0	–	–	0	0
Follett	–	–	–	–	0	0	0	0	0	0
Kelly	0	0	0	0	–	0	0	0	0	0
Polhill	0	0	0	–	–	–	0	0	–	–

	55: 580	55: 581	55: 730	55: 837	55: 849	55: 1106	55: 1161	57: 99	57: 767	57: 801
Crawley	0	0	0	0	0	0	0	0	0	0
Divett	0	0	0	0	0	0	0	0	+	0
Ferguson	0	0	0	+	0	0	0	0	0	0
Harland	0	0	0	0	0	0	0	0	0	0
Hobhouse	+	−	0	+	−	0	0	+	0	0
Pechell	+	0	+	0	+	+	+	+	+	+
Cochrane	0	−	0	0	0	0	0	0	0	0
Dalrymple	0	0	−	0	0	+	0	0	0	+
Dungannon	0	0	0	0	0	0	0	0	0	0
Follett	0	0	0	0	0	0	0	0	0	0
Kelly	0	0	0	0	0	0	0	0	0	0
Polhill	0	0	0	0	0	0	+	+	0	0

1841 Parliament

59:671		63:1627	63:1666		68:24	68:32
Divett 0	*Divett*	+	0	*Pechell*	+	+
Granger +	*Granger*	0	+	*Granger*	0	0
Hobhouse 0	*Hobhouse*	0	0	*Divett*	0	0
Larpent 0	*Larpent*	0	0	*Hobhouse*	0	0
Pechell +	*Pechell*	+	+	Polhill	0	0
Rennie 0	Desart	0	−	Stuart	−	0
Wason 0	Fitzroy	−	−	Hervey	−	−
Wigney 0	Follett	0	0	Fitzroy	0	0
Fitzroy +	Gladstone	−	0	Follett	0	0
Follett 0	Hervey	−	0	Gladstone	0	−
Polhill 0	Polhill	0	0	Lane Fox	0	0
Stuart +	Stuart	−	0	Walter	0	0

	68:728	68:816	68:1089	69:565		71:74	71:76	71:530	73:387
Divett	0	0	0	+	*Bright*	0	0	0	+
Gisborne	0	+	+	+	*Divett*	0	0	0	0
Granger	0	0	0	0	*Gisborne*	0	0	0	0
Hobhouse	0	0	0	0	*Granger*	0	0	0	0
Pechell	0	0	+	+	*Hobhouse*	0	0	0	0
Dungannon	0	0	−	0	*Pechell*	0	0	+	+
Follett	0	0	+	0	Follett	−	0	0	0
Gladstone	−	−	+	−	Gladstone	−	−	−	−
Hervey	−	−	+	0	Hervey	−	−	0	0
Lane Fox	0	+	+	0	Lane Fox	0	0	0	0
Polhill	0	+	−	0	Polhill	0	0	0	0
Stuart	0	0	−	−	Stuart	−	0	0	0

	74: 184	74: 762	75: 106	75: 121	75: 122	75: 128	75: 130	75: 391	75: 667	75: 1098
Bright	0	0	+	0	0	0	0	+	0	0
Divett	0	0	0	0	0	0	0	+	0	+
Gisborne	+	0	0	0	0	0	0	+	+	0
Granger	−	+	0	+	+	−	+	−	+	0
Hobhouse	+	+	0	+	+	0	0	+	+	0
Pechell	+	0	+	0	0	+	+	+	+	+
Follett	0	0	0	0	0	0	0	0	0	0
Gladstone	−	+	−	−	−	−	−	0	−	0
Hervey	−	0	0	0	0	0	0	0	0	0
Lane Fox	0	0	0	0	0	0	0	0	−	0
Polhill	0	0	0	−	0	0	0	−	−	0
Stuart	−	0	0	0	0	0	0	0	−	0

	75: 1234	75: 1236	76: 116	76: 986	79: 109	79: 1042	79: 1311	79: 1429	79: 1432	80: 113
Bright	0	0	0	0	0	+	+	+	0	0
Divett	0	0	0	0	+	−	0	0	0	−
Gisborne	+	0	+	0	0	+	0	0	0	0
Granger	0	0	−	0	+	−	+	+	+	0
Hobhouse	+	+	+	0	0	−	+	+	0	0
Pechell	+	+	0	+	+	0	+	−	+	0
Follett	0	+	0	0	0	−	0	0	0	0
Gladstone	0	+	+	−	0	−	−	+	−	−
Hervey	+	+	+	0	+	−	−	+	−	−
Lane Fox	0	0	−	0	−	+	−	−	0	0
Polhill	0	−	−	0	0	−	−	−	−	0
Stuart	0	0	0	0	−	+	−	+	0	0

	79: 1429	79: 1432	80: 113	80: 123	80: 140	80: 651	80: 745	80: 750	80: 1102	81: 1339
Bright	+	0	0	0	0	+	−	−	+	0
Divett	0	0	−	0	0	0	+	+	0	0
Gisborne	0	0	0	0	0	0	0	0	0	0
Granger	+	+	0	+	−	−	+	+	+	0
Hobhouse	+	0	0	0	0	+	+	+	+	0
Pechell	−	+	0	0	+	0	−	−	0	0
Follett	0	0	0	0	0	0	0	0	0	0
Gladstone	+	−	−	+	−	0	+	+	−	−
Hervey	+	−	−	0	−	−	+	+	+	0
Lane Fox	−	0	0	0	+	+	−	−	0	0
Polhill	−	−	0	−	0	−	−	−	+	0
Stuart	+	0	0	0	0	−	−	0	0	−

	82: 117	82: 118	82: 223	82: 277	82: 377	82: 642	86: 161	87: 935	88: 633	90: 496
Bright	+	0	0	+	+	+	0	0	0	+
Divett	0	0	0	0	0	+	0	+	0	0
Gisborne	0	0	0	0	0	0	0	0	0	+
Granger	+	−	+	0	0	0	+	0	0	0
Hobhouse	0	0	0	0	0	0	0	0	0	0
Pechell	0	0	+	+	0	−	+	+	+	+
Duckworth	0	0	0	−	0	0	0	−	0	−
Gladstone	−	−	−	−	−	0	0	0	−	−
Hervey	0	0	0	0	0	0	0	−	0	+
Lane Fox	0	0	−	−	0	0	−	−	0	−
Polhill	+	0	0	0	0	−	0	0	0	0
Stuart	+	−	−	0	−	0	0	0	0	−

	91: 807	91: 847	91: 1236	91: 1313	91: 1412	92: 718	92: 1093	94: 275	94: 405	94: 478
Bright	+	0	+	+	+	0	0	0	0	0
Divett	0	0	−	0	0	+	0	0	0	0
Gisborne	0	0	+	+	0	+	+	0	0	0
Granger	+	0	−	+	0	0	0	0	0	0
Hobhouse	0	−	−	−	−	0	−	−	−	−
Pechell	+	+	+	+	0	+	0	0	0	0
Duckworth	−	0	−	−	0	0	0	−	−	−
Gladstone	−	0	−	−	−	+	0	0	0	0
Hervey	0	0	−	0	0	−	0	0	0	0
Lane Fox	−	0	−	−	−	0	0	0	0	0
Polhill	−	0	−	−	0	0	0	0	0	−
Stuart	−	0	−	−	−	0	0	0	0	0

	94:550	94:496	94:499	94:566
Bright	0	0	0	0
Divett	0	0	0	0
Gisborne	0	0	0	0
Granger	0	0	0	0
Hobhouse	−	−	−	+
Pechell	+	0	0	0
Duckworth	−	−	−	−
Gladstone	0	0	0	0
Hervey	0	0	0	0
Lane Fox	0	0	0	0
Polhill	0	0	0	0
Stuart	0	0	0	0

Appendix A.2

Bright		Divett		Follett		Gladstone		Rennie	
+	17	+	61	+	5	+	9	+	0
−	2	−	5	−	31	−	35	−	0
0	36	0	134	0	119	0	19	0	1
Σ	55	Σ	200	Σ	155	Σ	63	Σ	1
Buller		Duckworth		Gisborne		Kelly		Stuart	
+	3	+	0	+	14	+	1	+	4
−	1	−	13	−	0	−	9	−	20
0	17	0	11	0	45	0	63	0	40
Σ	21	Σ	24	Σ	59	Σ	73	Σ	64
Chaytor		Duncannon		Gibson		Lane Fox		Trevor	
+	6	+	1	+	2	+	5	+	6
−	1	−	3	−	7	−	16	−	48
0	14	0	17	0	26	0	40	0	64
Σ	21	Σ	21	Σ	35	Σ	61	Σ	118
Cochrane		Dundas		Granger		Larpent		Walter	
+	0	+	0	+	20	+	0	+	0
−	6	−	3	−	9	−	0	−	0
0	27	0	2	0	35	0	3	0	3
Σ	33	Σ	5	Σ	64	Σ	3	Σ	3
Crawley		Faithfull		Harland		Morrison		Wason	
+	30	+	7	+	37	+	23	+	26
−	5	−	0	−	7	−	0	−	3
0	80	0	14	0	92	0	40	0	35
Σ	115	Σ	21	Σ	136	Σ	63	Σ	64
Dalrymple		Ferguson		Hervey		Pechell		Whitbread	
+	3	+	49	+	10	+	105	+	0
−	26	−	9	−	17	−	8	−	2
0	39	0	77	0	36	0	66	0	19
Σ	68	Σ	135	Σ	63	Σ	179	Σ	21
Desart		Fitzroy		Hobhouse		Polhill		Wigney	
+	0	+	1	+	59	+	61	+	17
−	1	−	2	−	23	−	5	−	1
0	1	0	2	0	97	0	134	0	51
Σ	2	Σ	5	Σ	179	Σ	200	Σ	69

Appendix B

Abbreviations

B	Baptist (General or particular, unspecified)
GB	General Baptist
I	Independent/Congregationalist
Jew	Jewish
M	Methodist Circuit
MNC/NMC	Methodist New Connexion
Mor	Moravian Brethren
P	Presbyterian
PM	Primitive Methodist
Prim E	Primitive Episcopalian
RC	Roman Catholic
WM	Wesleyan Methodist

Note: In all of the tables in Appendix B, columns are arranged in a manner indicating relative degrees of political partisanship, moving left to right from the strongest partisan liberal behaviour, through neutral behaviour (where applicable), to the strongest partisan conservative behaviour.

Bedford, 1832: Breakdown of dissenting votes by denomination (tallies)

C = Crawley (Liberal)
P = Polhill (Conservative)
W = Whitbread (Liberal)

	WC	W	C	WP	CP	P	Total
St Peter's Chapel (Mor)	3	1	0	1	0	6	11
Church of Christ, New Meeting (I)	4	0	0	1	0	1	6
Howard Chapel (I)	16	0	0	2	0	3	21
Old Meeting House (I)	10	0	0	1	0	0	11
Baptisms and Burials (I)	8	0	0	2	0	2	12
Mill St Chapel (B)	7	0	0	0	0	0	7
St Paul's Chapel (W)	27	0	2	6	0	8	43
Harpur St Chapel (W)	5	0	1	1	0	1	8
Other dissenters	2	0	0	0	0	0	2
Total	82	1	3	14	0	21	121

Bedford, 1832: Breakdown of dissenting votes by denomination (percentages)

	WC	W	C	WP	CP	P	Total
St Peter's Chapel (Mor)	0.27	0.09	0	0.09	0	0.55	1
Church of Christ, New Meeting (I)	0.67	0	0	0.17	0	0.17	1.01
Howard Chapel (I)	0.76	0	0	0.1	0	0.14	1
Old Meeting House (I)	0.91	0	0	0.09	0	0	1
Baptisms and Burials (I)	0.67	0	0	0.17	0	0.17	1.01
Mill St Chapel (B)	1	0	0	0	0	0	1
St Paul's Chapel (W)	0.63	0	0.05	0.14	0	0.19	1.01
Harpur St Chapel (W)	0.63	0	0.13	0.13	0	0.13	1.02
Other dissenters	1	0	0	0	0	0	1
Total	0.68	0	0.02	0.12	0	0.17	0.99

Bedford, 1832: Comparison of breakdown between dissent and Anglicans (tallies)

	WC	W	C	WP	CP	P	Total
Dissenting electorate	82	1	3	14	0	21	121
Anglican electorate	379	8	4	108	13	322	834
Combined electorate	461	9	7	122	13	343	955

Bedford, 1832: Comparison of breakdown between dissent and Anglicans (percentages)

	WC	W	C	WP	CP	P	Total
Dissenting electorate	0.68	0.01	0.02	0.12	0	0.17	1
Anglican electorate	0.45	0.01	0	0.13	0.02	0.39	1
Combined electorate	0.48	0.01	0.01	0.13	0.01	0.36	1

Bedford, 1832: Comparison of type of vote between dissent and Anglicans (tallies)

	Straight +	Plump −	Split +/−	Plump −	Total
Dissenting electorate	82	4	14	21	121
Anglican electorate	379	12	121	322	834
Combined electorate	461	16	135	343	955

Bedford, 1832: Comparison of type of vote between dissent and Anglicans (percentages)

	Straight +	Plump −	Split +/−	Plump −	Total
Dissenting electorate	0.68	0.03	0.12	0.17	1
Anglican electorate	0.45	0.01	0.15	0.39	1
Combined electorate	0.48	0.02	0.14	0.36	1

Bedford, 1832: Comparison of candidates' votes between dissent and Anglicans (tallies)

	W	C	P	Total
Dissenting electorate	97	85	35	217
Anglican electorate	502	401	448	1351
Combined electorate	599	486	483	1568

Bedford, 1832: Comparison of candidates' votes between dissent and Anglicans (percentages)

	W	C	P	Total
Dissenting electorate	0.45	0.39	0.16	1
Anglican electorate	0.37	0.3	0.33	1
Combined electorate	0.38	0.31	0.31	1

Bedford, 1832: Comparison of old and new dissent (tallies)

	WC	W	C	WP	CP	P	Total
Old dissent	48	1	0	7	0	12	68
New dissent	32	0	3	7	0	9	51
Total	80	1	3	14	0	21	119

Bedford, 1832: Comparison of old and new dissent (percentages)

	WC	W	C	WP	CP	P	Total
Old dissent	0.71	0.01	0	0.1	0	0.18	1
New dissent	0.63	0	0.06	0.14	0	0.18	1.01
Total	0.67	0.01	0.03	0.12	0	0.18	1.01

Bedford, 1832: Other non-Anglicans

	WC	W	C	WP	CP	P	Total
Prim. E	*0*	*0*	*0*	*0*	*1*	*0*	*1*
Jews	*1*	*0*	*0*	*1*	*0*	*0*	*2*

Bedford, 1835: Breakdown of dissenting votes by denomination (tallies)

C = Crawley (Liberal)
P = Polhill (Conservative)
W = Whitbread (Liberal)

	CW	C	W	PC	PW	P	Total
St Peter's Chapel (Mor)	1	0	0	0	3	5	9
Church of Christ, New Meeting (I)	4	0	0	1	0	1	6
Howard Chapel (I)	12	5	0	2	1	3	23
Old Meeting House (I)	7	0	0	2	2	0	11
Baptisms and Burials (I)	6	0	0	0	1	2	9
Mill St Chapel (B)	5	1	0	0	0	0	6
St Paul's Chapel (W)	23	3	1	5	3	12	47
Harpur St Chapel (W)	0	2	1	0	2	1	6
Other dissenters	2	0	0	0	0	0	2
Total	60	11	2	10	12	24	119

Bedford, 1835: Breakdown of dissenting votes by denomination (percentages)

	CW	C	W	PC	PW	P	Total
St Peter's Chapel (Mor)	0.11	0	0	0	0.33	0.56	1.01
Church of Christ, New Meeting (I)	0.67	0	0	0.17	0	0.17	1.01
Howard Chapel (I)	0.52	0.22	0	0.09	0.04	0.13	1
Old Meeting House (I)	0.64	0	0	0.18	0.18	0	1
Baptisms and Burials (I)	0.67	0	0	0	0.11	0.22	1
Mill St Chapel (B)	0.83	0.17	0	0	0	0	1
St Paul's Chapel (W)	0.49	0.06	0.02	0.11	0.06	0.26	1
Harpur St Chapel (W)	0	0.33	0.17	0	0.33	0.17	1
Other dissenters	1	0	0	0	0	0	1
Total	0.5	0.09	0.02	0.08	0.1	0.2	0.99

Bedford, 1835: Comparison of breakdown between dissent and Anglicans (tallies)

	CW	C	W	PC	PW	P	Total
Dissenting electorate	60	11	2	10	12	24	119
Anglican electorate	211	33	17	69	70	305	715
Combined electorate	281	44	19	79	82	329	834

Bedford, 1835: Comparison of breakdown between dissent and Anglicans (percentages)

	CW	C	W	PC	PW	P	Total
Dissenting electorate	0.5	0.09	0.02	0.08	0.1	0.2	0.99
Anglican electorate	0.3	0.05	0.02	0.1	0.1	0.43	1
Combined electorate	0.34	0.05	0.02	0.1	0.1	0.39	1

Bedford, 1835: Comparison of type of vote between dissent and Anglicans (tallies)

	Straight +	Plump +	Split +/−	Plump −	Total
Dissenting electorate	60	13	22	24	119
Anglican electorate	221	50	139	305	715
Combined electorate	281	63	161	329	834

Bedford, 1835: Comparison of type of vote between dissent and Anglicans (percentages)

	Straight +	Plump +	Split +/−	Plump −	Total
Dissenting electorate	0.5	0.11	0.18	0.2	0.99
Anglican electorate	0.3	0.07	0.19	0.43	0.99
Combined electorate	0.34	0.08	0.19	0.39	1

Bedford, 1835: Comparison of candidates' votes between dissent and Anglicans (tallies)

	C	W	P	Total
Dissenting electorate	81	74	46	201
Anglican electorate	322	309	444	1075
Combined electorate	403	383	490	1276

Bedford, 1835: comparison of candidates' votes between dissent and Anglicans (percentages)

	C	W	P	Total
Dissenting electorate	0.4	0.37	0.23	1
Anglican electorate	0.3	0.29	0.41	1
Combined electorate	0.32	0.3	0.38	1

Bedford, 1835: Comparison of old and new dissent (tallies)

	CW	C	W	PC	PW	P	Total
Old dissent	35	6	0	5	7	11	64
New dissent	23	5	2	5	5	13	53
Total	58	11	2	10	12	24	117

Bedford, 1835: Comparison of old and new dissent (percentages)

	CW	C	W	PC	PW	P	Total
Old dissent	0.55	0.09	0	0.08	0.11	0.17	1
New dissent	0.43	0.09	0.04	0.09	0.09	0.25	0.99
Total	0.5	0.09	0.02	0.08	0.1	0.21	1

Bedford, 1835: Other non-Anglicans

	CW	C	W	PC	PW	P	Total
Prim. E	0	0	0	0	0	0	0
Jews	0	0	0	2	0	0	2

Bedford, 1837: Breakdown of dissenting votes by denomination (tallies)

C = Crawley (Liberal)
P = Polhill (Conservative)
S = Stuart (Conservative)

	C	PC	SC	P	S	PS	Total
St Peter's Chapel (Mor)	1	2	0	0	0	6	9
Church of Christ, New Meeting (I)	3	0	0	0	0	1	4
Howard Chapel (I)	22	2	0	0	0	4	28
Old Meeting House (I)	12	1	1	0	0	1	15
Baptisms and Burials (I)	10	0	0	0	0	2	12
Mill St Chapel (B)	6	0	0	0	0	0	6
St Paul's Chapel (W)	28	4	3	1	0	13	49
Harpur St Chapel (W)	4	0	0	0	0	3	7
Other dissenters	4	0	0	0	0	1	5
Total	90	9	4	1	0	31	135

Bedford, 1837: Breakdown of dissenting votes by denomination (percentages)

	C	PC	SC	P	S	PS	Total
St Peter's Chapel (Mor)	0.11	0.22	0	0	0	0.67	1
Church of Christ, New Meeting (I)	0.75	0	0	0	0	0.25	1
Howard Chapel (I)	0.79	0.07	0	0	0	0.14	1
Old Meeting House (I)	0.8	0.07	0.07	0	0	0.07	1.01
Baptisms and Burials (I)	0.83	0	0	0	0	0.17	1
Mill St Chapel (B)	1	0	0	0	0	0	1
St Paul's Chapel (W)	0.57	0.08	0.06	0.02	0	0.27	1
Harpur St Chapel (W)	0.57	0	0	0	0	0.43	1
Other dissenters	0.8	0	0	0	0	0.2	1
Total	0.67	0.07	0.03	0.01	0	0.23	1.01

Bedford, 1837: Comparison of breakdown between dissent and Anglicans (tallies)

	C	CP	CS	P	S	PS	Total
Dissenting electorate	90	9	4	1	0	31	135
Anglican electorate	228	61	18	7	6	357	677
Combined electorate	318	70	22	8	6	388	812

Bedford, 1837: Comparison of breakdown between dissent and Anglicans (percentages)

	C	CP	CS	P	S	PS	Total
Dissenting electorate	0.67	0.07	0.03	0.01	0	0.23	1.01
Anglican electorate	0.34	0.09	0.03	0.01	0.01	0.53	1.01
Combined electorate	0.39	0.09	0.03	0.01	0.01	0.48	1.01

Bedford, 1837: Comparison of type of vote between dissent and Anglicans (tallies)

	Plump +	Split +/−	Plump −	Straight −	Total
Dissenting electorate	90	13	1	31	135
Anglican electorate	228	79	13	357	677
Combined electorate	318	92	14	388	812

Bedford, 1837: Comparison of type of vote between dissent and Anglicans (percentages)

	Plump +	Split +/−	Plump −	Straight −	Total
Dissenting electorate	0.67	0.1	0.01	0.23	1.01
Anglican electorate	0.34	0.12	0.02	0.53	1.01
Combined electorate	0.39	0.11	0.02	0.48	1

Bedford, 1837: Comparison of candidates' votes between dissent and Anglicans (tallies)

	C	P	S	Total
Dissenting electorate	103	41	35	179
Anglican electorate	309	426	384	1119
Combined electorate	412	467	419	1298

Bedford, 1837: Comparison of candidates' votes between dissent and Anglicans (percentages)

	C	P	S	Total
Dissenting electorate	0.58	0.23	0.2	1.01
Anglican electorate	0.28	0.38	0.34	1
Combined electorate	0.32	0.36	0.32	1

Bedford, 1837: Comparison of old and new dissent (tallies)

	C	PC	SC	P	S	PS	Total
Old dissent	54	5	1	0	0	14	74
New dissent	32	4	3	1	0	16	56
Total	86	9	4	1	0	30	130

Bedford, 1837: Comparison of old and new dissent (percentages)

	C	PC	SC	P	S	PS	Total
Old dissent	0.73	0.07	0.01	0	0	0.19	1
New dissent	0.57	0.07	0.05	0.01	0	0.29	0.99
Total	0.66	0.07	0.03	0.01	0	0.23	1

Bedford, 1837: Other non-Anglicans

	C	PC	SC	P	S	PS	Total
Prim. E	0	0	0	0	0	0	0
Jews	0	1	0	0	0	1	2

Bedford, 1841: Breakdown of dissenting votes by denomination (tallies)

P = Polhill (Conservative)
S = Stuart (Conservative)
W = Whitbread (Liberal)

	W	PW	SW	P	S	PS	Total
St Peter's Chapel (Mor)	2	0	2	0	0	5	9
Church of Christ, New Meeting (I)	8	0	0	0	0	1	9
Howard Chapel (I)	18	2	0	0	0	6	26
Old Meeting House (I)	18	0	0	0	0	0	18
Baptisms and Burials (I)	13	0	0	0	0	1	14
Mill St Chapel (B)	5	0	0	0	0	1	6
St Paul's Chapel (W)	30	2	0	0	0	18	50
Harpur St Chapel (W)	4	0	0	0	0	4	8
Other dissenters	4	0	0	0	0	1	5
Total	102	4	2	0	0	37	145

Bedford, 1841: Breakdown of dissenting votes by denomination (percentages)

	W	PW	SW	P	S	PS	Total
St Peter's Chapel (Mor)	0.22	0	0.22	0	0	0.56	1
Church of Christ, New Meeting (I)	0.89	0	0	0	0	0.11	1
Howard Chapel (I)	0.69	0.08	0	0	0	0.23	1
Old Meeting House (I)	1	0	0	0	0	0	1
Baptisms and Burials (I)	0.93	0	0	0	0	0.07	1
Mill St Chapel (B)	0.83	0	0	0	0	0.17	1

Continued

	W	PW	SW	P	S	PS	Total
St Paul's Chapel (W)	0.6	0.04	0	0	0	0.36	1
Harpur St Chapel (W)	0.5	0	0	0	0	0.5	1
Other dissenters	0.8	0	0	0	0	0.2	1
Total	0.7	0.03	0.01	0	0	0.26	1

Bedford, 1841: Comparison of breakdown between dissent and Anglicans (tallies)

	W	PW	SW	P	S	PS	Total
Dissenting electorate	102	4	2	0	0	37	145
Anglican electorate	247	35	20	0	5	357	664
Combined electorate	349	39	22	0	5	394	809

Bedford, 1841: Comparison of breakdown between dissent and Anglicans (percentages)

	W	PW	SW	P	S	PS	Total
Dissenting electorate	0.7	0.03	0.01	0	0	0.26	1
Anglican electorate	0.37	0.05	0.03	0	0.01	0.54	1
Combined electorate	0.43	0.05	0.03	0	0.01	0.49	1.01

Bedford, 1841: Comparison of type of vote between dissent and Anglicans (tallies)

	Plump +	Split +/−	Plump −	Straight −	Total
Dissenting electorate	102	6	0	37	145
Anglican electorate	247	55	5	357	664
Combined electorate	349	61	5	394	809

Bedford, 1841: Comparison of type of vote between dissent and Anglicans (percentages)

	Plump +	Split +/−	Plump −	Straight −	Total
Dissenting electorate	0.7	0.04	0	0.26	1
Anglican electorate	0.37	0.08	0.01	0.54	1
Combined electorate	0.43	0.08	0.01	0.49	1.01

Bedford, 1841: Comparison of candidates' votes between dissent and Anglicans (tallies)

	W	P	S	Total
Dissenting electorate	108	41	39	188
Anglican electorate	302	392	382	1076
Combined electorate	410	433	421	1264

Bedford, 1841: Comparison of candidates' votes between dissent and Anglicans (percentages)

	W	P	S	Total
Dissenting electorate	0.57	0.22	0.21	1
Anglican electorate	0.28	0.36	0.36	1
Combined electorate	0.32	0.34	0.33	0.99

Bedford, 1841: Comparison of old and new dissent (tallies)

	W	PW	SW	P	S	PS	Total
Old dissent	64	2	2	0	0	14	82
New dissent	34	2	0	0	0	22	58
Total	98	4	2	0	0	36	140

Bedford, 1841: Comparison of old and new dissent (percentages)

	W	PW	SW	P	S	PS	Total
Old dissent	0.78	0.02	0.02	0	0	0.17	0.99
New dissent	0.59	0.03	0	0	0	0.38	1
Total	0.7	0.03	0.01	0	0	0.26	1

Bedford, 1841: Other non-Anglicans

	W	PW	SW	P	S	PS	Total
Prim. E	*0*	*0*	*0*	*0*	*1*	*0*	*1*
Jews	*1*	*1*	*0*	*0*	*0*	*1*	*3*

Bedford, 1847: Breakdown of dissenting votes by denomination (tallies)

P = Polhill (Conservative)
S = Stuart (Conservative)
V = Verney (Liberal)

	V	PV	SV	P	S	PS	Total
St Peter's Chapel (Mor)	3	0	0	0	0	6	9
Church of Christ, New Meeting (I)	7	0	0	0	0	2	9
Howard Chapel (I)	15	1	0	0	0	4	20
Old Meeting House (I)	12	0	0	0	0	2	14
Baptisms and Burials (I)	9	0	1	0	0	1	11
Mill St Chapel (B)	3	0	0	0	0	1	4
St Paul's Chapel (W)	28	0	6	0	1	15	50
Harpur St Chapel (W)	4	0	0	0	0	3	7
Other dissenters	7	0	0	0	0	3	10
Total	88	1	7	0	1	37	134

Bedford, 1847: Breakdown of dissenting votes by denomination (percentages)

	V	PV	SV	P	S	PS	Total
St Peter's Chapel (Mor)	0.33	0	0	0	0	0.67	1
Church of Christ, New Meeting (I)	0.78	0	0	0	0	0.22	1
Howard Chapel (I)	0.75	0.05	0	0	0	0.2	1
Old Meeting House (I)	0.86	0	0	0	0	0.14	1
Baptisms and Burials (I)	0.82	0	0.09	0	0	0.09	1
Mill St Chapel (B)	0.75	0	0	0	0	0.25	1
St Paul's Chapel (W)	0.56	0	0.12	0	0.02	0.3	1
Harpur St Chapel (W)	0.57	0	0	0	0	0.43	1
Other dissenters	0.7	0	0	0	0	0.3	1
Total	0.66	0.01	0.05	0	0.01	0.28	1.01

Bedford, 1847: Comparison of breakdown between dissent and Anglicans (tallies)

	V	PV	SV	P	S	PS	Total
Dissenting electorate	88	1	7	0	1	37	134
Anglican electorate	285	27	45	3	18	324	702
Combined electorate	373	28	52	3	19	361	836

Bedford, 1847: Comparison of breakdown between dissent and Anglicans (percentages)

	V	PV	SV	P	S	PS	Total
Dissenting electorate	0.66	0.01	0.05	0	0.01	0.28	1.01
Anglican electorate	0.41	0.04	0.06	0	0.03	0.46	1
Combined electorate	0.45	0.03	0.06	0	0.02	0.43	0.99

Bedford, 1847: Comparison of type of vote between dissent and Anglicans (tallies)

	Plump +	Split +/−	Plump −	Straight −	Total
Dissenting electorate	88	8	1	37	134
Anglican electorate	285	72	21	324	702
Combined electorate	373	80	22	361	836

Bedford, 1847: Comparison of type of vote between dissent and Anglicans (percentages)

	Plump +	Split +/−	Plump −	Straight −	Total
Dissenting electorate	0.66	0.06	0.01	0.28	1.01
Anglican electorate	0.41	0.1	0.03	0.46	1
Combined electorate	0.45	0.1	0.02	0.43	1

Bedford, 1847: Comparison of candidates' votes between dissent and Anglicans (tallies)

	V	S	P	Total
Dissenting electorate	96	45	38	179
Anglican electorate	357	387	354	1098
Combined electorate	453	432	392	1277

Bedford, 1847: Comparison of candidates' votes between dissent and Anglicans (percentages)

	V	S	P	Total
Dissenting electorate	0.54	0.25	0.21	1
Anglican electorate	0.33	0.35	0.32	1
Combined electorate	0.35	0.34	0.31	1

Bedford, 1847: Comparison of old and new dissent (tallies)

	V	PV	SV	P	S	PS	Total
Old Dissent	49	1	1	0	0	16	67
New Dissent	32	0	6	0	1	18	57
Total	81	1	7	0	1	34	124

Bedford, 1847: Comparison of old and new dissent (percentages)

	V	PV	SV	P	S	PS	Total
Old Dissent	0.73	0.01	0.01	0	0	0.24	0.99
New Dissent	0.56	0	0.1	0	0.02	0.32	1
Total	0.65	0.01	0.06	0	0.01	0.27	1

Bedford, 1847: Other non-Anglicans

	V	PV	SV	P	S	PS	Total
Prim. E	0	0	0	0	0	0	0
Jews	1	0	0	0	0	2	3

Ipswich, 1832: Breakdown of dissenting votes by denomination (tallies)

G = Goulburn (Conservative)
K = Kelly (Conservative)
M = Morrison (Liberal)
W = Wason (Liberal)
∗ = Mackinnon (Third party, nominal Liberal)

	Strt +	Plump +						Split +/*		Strt −	Total
Ebenezer Chapel (W)	1	0	0	0	0	0	0	0	0 0	0	1
St Mary's Elms (PM)	1	0	0	0	0	0	0	0	0 0	0	1
St Nicholas St Old Meeting House (P)	6	0	0	0	0	0	0	0	0 0	0	6
Nicholas New Chapel (I)	14	0	0	0	0	0	0	0	0 0	0	14
Tacket St Chapel (I)	44	0	0	0	0	0	0	1	0 0	2	47
Others	3	1	0	0	0	0	0	0	0 0	0	4
Total	69	1	0	0	0	0	0	1	0 0	2	73

Ipswich, 1832: Breakdown of dissenting votes by denomination (percentages)

	Strt +	Plump +						Split +/*		Strt −	Total
Ebenezer Chapel (W)	1	0	0	0	0	0	0	0	0 0	0	1
St Mary's Elms (PM)	1	0	0	0	0	0	0	0	0 0	0	1
St Nicholas St Old Meeting House (P)	1	0	0	0	0	0	0	0	0 0	0	1
Nicholas New Chapel (I)	1	0	0	0	0	0	0	0	0 0	0	1
Tacket St Chapel (I)	0.94	0	0	0	0	0	0	0.02	0 0	0.04	1
Others	0.75	0.25	0	0	0	0	0	0	0 0	0	1
Total	0.95	0.01	0	0	0	0	0	0.01	0 0	0.03	1

Ipswich, 1832: Comparison of breakdown between dissent and Anglicans (tallies)

	M	W	*	K	G	Total
Dissenting electorate	70	69	1	2	3	145
Anglican electorate	529	524	93	265	300	1711
Combined electorate	599	593	94	267	303	1856

Ipswich, 1832: Comparison of breakdown between dissent and Anglicans (percentages)

	M	W	*	K	G	Total
Dissenting electorate	0.48	0.48	0.01	0.01	0.02	1
Anglican electorate	0.31	0.31	0.05	0.15	0.18	1
Combined electorate	0.32	0.32	0.05	0.14	0.16	0.99

Ipswich, 1832: Comparison of type of vote between dissent and Anglicans (tallies)

	Straight +Plump	+Split +/*/	–Split +/	–Plump	–Straight	–Total
Dissenting electorate	69	1	1	0	0	2	73
Anglican electorate	513	7	93	0	2	262	877
Combined electorate	582	8	94	0	2	264	950

Ipswich, 1832: Comparison of type of vote between dissent and Anglicans (percentages)

	Straight +	Plump +	Split +/*/	– Split +/	– Plump	– Straight	– Total
Dissenting electorate	0.95	0.01	0.01	0	0	0.03	1
Anglican electorate	0.58	0.01	0.11	0	0	0.3	1
Combined electorate	0.61	0.01	0.1	0	0	0.28	1

Ipswich, 1832: Comparison of candidates' votes between dissent and Anglicans (tallies)

	M	W	*	K	G	Total
Dissenting electorate	70	69	1	2	3	145
Anglican electorate	529	524	93	265	300	1711
Combined electorate	599	593	94	267	303	1856

Ipswich, 1832: Comparison of candidates' votes between dissent and Anglicans (percentages)

	M	W	*	K	G	Total
Dissenting electorate	0.48	0.48	0.01	0.01	0.02	1
Anglican electorate	0.31	0.31	0.05	0.15	0.18	1
Combined electorate	0.32	0.32	0.05	0.14	0.16	0.99

Ipswich, 1832: Comparison of old and new dissent (tallies)

	Straight +							Split *			Straight −	Total
Old dissent	64	0	0	0	0	0	0	1	0	0	2	67
New dissent	2	0	0	0	0	0	0	0	0	0	0	2
Total	66	0	0	0	0	0	0	1	0	0	2	69

Ipswich, 1832: Comparison of old and new dissent (percentages)

	Straight +							Split *			Straight −	Total
Old dissent	0.96	0	0	0	0	0	0	0.01	0	0	0.03	1
New dissent	1	0	0	0	0	0	0	0	0	0	0	1
Total	0.96	0	0	0	0	0	0	0.01	0	0	0.03	1

Ipswich, Jan 1835: Breakdown of dissenting votes by denomination (tallies)

	Straight +	Plump +	Split								Straight −	Total
Ebenezer Chapel (W)	1	0	0	0	0	0	0	0	0		0	1
St Mary's Elms (PM)	1	0	0	0	0	0	0	0	0		0	1
St Nicholas St Old Meeting House (P)	7	2	0	0	0	0	0	0	0		0	9
Nicholas New Chapel (I)	12	0	0	0	0	0	0	0	0		1	13
Tacket St Chapel (I)	38	1	0	0	1	0	0	0	0		4	44
Others	5	0	0	0	0	0	0	0	0		1	6
Total	64	3	0	0	1	0	0	0	0		6	74

Ipswich, Jan 1835: Breakdown of dissenting votes by denomination (percentages)

D = Dundas (Conservative)
K = Kelly (Conservative)
M = Morrison (Liberal)
W = Wason (Liberal)

	Straight +	Plump +	Split							Straight −	Total
Ebenezer Chapel (W)	1	0	0	0	0	0	0	0	0	0	1
St Mary's Elms (PM)	1	0	0	0	0	0	0	0	0	0	1
St Nicholas St Old Meeting House (P)	0.78	0.22	0	0	0	0	0	0	0	0	1

	Straight +	Plump +			Split					Straight −	Total
Nicholas New Chapel (I)	0.92	0	0 0	0	0 0 0 0					0.08	1
Tacket St Chapel (I)	0.86	0.02	0 0	0.02	0 0 0 0					0.09	0.99
Others	0.83	0	0 0	0	0 0 0 0					0.17	1
Total	0.86	0.04	0 0	0.01	0 0 0 0					0.08	0.99

Ipswich, Jan 1835: Comparison of breakdown between dissent and Anglicans (tallies)

	MW	M	W	MK	MD	WK	WD	K	D	KD	Total
Dissenting electorate	64	0	3	1	0	0	0	0	0	6	74
Anglican electorate	439	1	3	1	0	8	4	7	11	528	1002
Combined electorate	503	1	6	2	0	8	4	7	11	534	1076

Ipswich, Jan 1835: Comparison of breakdown between dissent and Anglicans (percentages)

	MW	M	W	MK	MD	WK	WD	K	D	KD	Total
Dissenting electorate	0.86	0	0.04	0.01	0	0		0	0	0	0.08	0.99
Anglican electorate	0.44	0	0	0	0	0.01		0	0.01	0.01	0.53	1
Combined electorate	0.47	0	0.01	0	0	0		0	0.01	0.01	0.5	1

Ipswich, Jan 1835: Comparison of type of vote between dissent and Anglicans (tallies)

	Straight +	Plump +	Split +/−	Plump −	Straight −	Total
Dissenting electorate	64	3	1	0	6	74
Anglican electorate	439	4	13	18	528	1002
Combined electorate	503	7	14	18	534	1076

Ipswich, Jan 1835: Comparison of type of vote between dissent and Anglicans (percentages)

	Straight +	Plump +	Split +/−	Plump −	Straight −	Total
Dissenting electorate	0.86	0.04	0.01	0	0.08	0.99
Anglican electorate	0.44	0	0.01	0.01	0.53	0.99
Combined electorate	0.47	0.01	0.01	0.02	0.5	1.01

Ipswich, Jan 1835: Comparison of candidates' votes between dissent and Anglicans (tallies)

	W	M	K	D	Total
Dissenting electorate	67	65	7	6	145
Anglican electorate	466	449	550	549	2014
Combined electorate	531	516	557	555	2159

Ipswich, Jan 1835: Comparison of candidates' votes between dissent and Anglicans (percentages)

	W	M	K	D	Total
Dissenting electorate	0.46	0.45	0.05	0.04	1
Anglican electorate	0.23	0.22	0.27	0.27	0.99
Combined electorate	0.25	0.24	0.26	0.26	1.01

Ipswich, Jan 1835: Comparison of old and new dissent (tallies)

	Straight +	Plump +	Split							Straight −	Total
Old dissent	57	3	0	0	1	0	0	0	0	5	66
New dissent	2	0	0	0	0	0	0	0	0	0	2
Total	59	3	0	0	1	0	0	0	0	5	68

Ipswich, Jan 1835: Comparison of old and new dissent (percentages)

	Straight +	Plump +	Split							Straight −	Total
Old dissent	0.86	0.05	0	0	0.02	0	0	0	0	0.08	1.01
New dissent	1	0	0	0	0	0	0	0	0	0	1
Total	0.87	0.04	0	0	0.01	0	0	0	0	0.07	0.99

Ipswich, June 1835: Breakdown of dissenting votes by denomination (percentages)

	Straight +									Straight −	Total
Ebenezer Chapel (W)	2	0	0	0	0	0	0	0	0	0	2
St Mary's Elms (PM)	1	0	0	0	0	0	0	0	0	0	1
St Nicholas St Old Meeting House (P)	9	0	0	0	0	0	0	0	0	0	9
Nicholas New Chapel (I)	17	0	0	0	0	0	0	0	0	1	18
Tacket St Chapel (I)	40	0	0	0	0	0	0	0	0	2	42
Others	5	0	0	0	0	0	0	0	0	0	5
Total	74	0	0	0	0	0	0	0	0	3	77

Ipswich, June 1835: Breakdown of dissenting votes by denomination (percentages)

	Straight +									Straight −	Total
Ebenezer Chapel (W)	1	0	0	0	0	0	0	0	0	0	1
St Mary's Elms (PM)	1	0	0	0	0	0	0	0	0	0	1
St Nicholas St Old Meeting House (P)	1	0	0	0	0	0	0	0	0	0	1
Nicholas New Chapel (I)	0.94	0	0	0	0	0	0	0	0	0.06	1
Tacket St Chapel (I)	0.95	0	0	0	0	0	0	0	0	0.05	1
Others	1	0	0	0	0	0	0	0	0	0	1
Total	0.96	0	0	0	0	0	0	0	0	0.04	1

Ipswich, June 1835: Comparison of breakdown between dissent and Anglicans (tallies)

B = Broke (Conservative)
H = Holmes (Conservative)
M = Morrison (Liberal)
W = Wason (Liberal)

	WM	W	M	MB	MH	WB	WH	B	H	BH	Total
Dissenting electorate	74	0	0	0	0	0	0	0	0	3	77
Anglican electorate	457	3	0	8	0	2	0	10	0	431	911
Combined electorate	531	3	0	8	0	2	0	10	0	434	988

Ipswich, June 1835: Comparison of breakdown between dissent and Anglicans (percentages)

	WM	W	M	MB	MH	WB	WH	B	H	BH	Total
Dissenting electorate	0.96	0	0	0	0	0	0	0	0	0.04	1
Anglican electorate	0.5	0	0	0.01	0	0	0	0.01	0	0.47	0.99
Combined electorate	0.54	0	0	0.01	0	0	0	0.01	0	0.44	1

Ipswich, June 1835: Comparison of type of vote between dissent and Anglicans (tallies)

	Straight +	Plump +	Split +/−	Plump −	Straight −	Total
Dissenting electorate	74	0	0	0	3	77
Anglican electorate	457	3	10	10	431	911
Combined electorate	531	3	10	10	434	988

Ipswich, June 1835: Comparison of type of vote between dissent and Anglicans (tallies)

	Straight +	Plump +	Split +/−	Plump −	Straight −	Total
Dissenting electorate	0.96	0	0	0	0.04	1
Anglican electorate	0.5	0	0.01	0.01	0.47	0.99
Combined electorate	0.54	0	0.01	0.01	0.44	1

Ipswich, June 1835: Comparison of candidates' votes between dissent and Anglicans (tallies)

	M	W	B	H	Total
Dissenting electorate	74	74	3	3	154
Anglican electorate	468	459	451	431	1809
Combined electorate	542	533	454	434	1963

Ipswich, June 1835: Comparison of candidates' votes between dissent and Anglicans (percentages)

	M	W	B	H	Total
Dissenting electorate	0.48	0.48	0.02	0.02	1
Anglican electorate	0.26	0.25	0.25	0.24	1
Combined electorate	0.28	0.27	0.23	0.22	1

Ipswich, June 1835: Comparison of old and new dissent (tallies)

	Straight +								Straight −	Total
Old dissent	66	0	0	0	0	0	0	0	0	3	69
New dissent	3	0	0	0	0	0	0	0	0	0	3
Total	69	0	0	0	0	0	0	0	0	3	72

Ipswich, June 1835: Comparison of old and new dissent (percentages)

	Straight +								Straight −	Total
Old dissent	0.96	0	0	0	0	0	0	0	0	0.04	1
New dissent	1	0	0	0	0	0	0	0	0	0	1
Total	0.96	0	0	0	0	0	0	0	0	0.04	1

Ipswich, 1839: Breakdown of dissenting votes by denomination (tallies)

C = Cochrane (Conservative)
G = Gibson (Liberal)

	Plump +	Plump −	Total
Ebenezer Chapel (W)	5	0	5
St Mary's Elms (PM)	1	0	1
St Nicholas St Old Meeting House (P)	5	2	7
Nicholas New Chapel (I)	13	5	18
Tacket St Chapel (I)	43	6	49
Others	6	2	8
Total	73	15	88

Ipswich, 1839: Breakdown of dissenting votes by denomination (percentages)

	Plump +	Plump −	Total
Ebenezer Chapel (W)	1	0	1
St Mary's Elms (PM)	1	0	1
St Nicholas St Old Meeting House (P)	0.71	0.29	1
Nicholas New Chapel (I)	0.72	0.28	1
Tacket St Chapel (I)	0.88	0.12	1
Others	0.75	0.25	1
Total	0.83	0.17	1

Ipswich, 1839: Comparison of candidates' votes between dissent and Anglicans (tallies)

	Plump +	Plump −	Total
Dissenting electorate	73	15	88
Anglican electorate	542	606	1148
Combined electorate	615	621	1236

Ipswich, 1839: Comparison of candidates' votes between dissent and Anglicans (percentages)

	Plump +	Plump −	Total
Dissenting electorate	0.83	0.17	1
Anglican electorate	0.47	0.53	1
Combined electorate	0.5	0.5	1

Ipswich, 1839: Comparison of old and new dissent (tallies)

	Plump +	Plump −	Total
Old dissent	61	13	74
New dissent	6	0	6
Total	67	13	80

Ipswich, 1839: Comparison of old and new dissent (percentages)

	Plump +	Plump −	Total
Old dissent	0.82	0.18	1
New dissent	1	0	1
Total	0.84	0.16	1

Ipswich, 1841: Breakdown of dissenting votes by denomination (tallies)

H = Herries (Conservative)
K = Kelly (Conservative)
R = Rennie (Liberal)
W = Wason (Liberal)

	Straight +									Straight −	Total
Ebenezer Chapel (W)	5	0	0	0	0	0	0	0	0	0	5
St Mary's Elms (PM)	2	0	0	0	0	0	0	0	0	0	2
St Nicholas St Old Meeting House (P)	9	0	0	0	0	0	0	0	0	2	11
Nicholas New Chapel (I)	9	0	0	0	0	0	0	0	0	6	15
Tacket St Chapel (I)	48	0	0	0	0	0	0	0	0	5	53
Others	9	0	0	0	0	0	0	0	0	1	10
Total	82	0	0	0	0	0	0	0	0	14	96

Ipswich, 1841: Breakdown of dissenting votes by denomination (percentages)

	Straight +									Straight −	Total
Ebenezer Chapel (W)	1	0	0	0	0	0	0	0	0	0	1
St Mary's Elms (PM)	1	0	0	0	0	0	0	0	0	0	1
St Nicholas St Old Meeting House (P)	0.82	0	0	0	0	0	0	0	0	0.18	1
Nicholas New Chapel (I)	0.6	0	0	0	0	0	0	0	0	0.4	1
Tacket St Chapel (I)	0.91	0	0	0	0	0	0	0	0	0.09	1
Others	0.9	0	0	0	0	0	0	0	0	0.1	1
Total	0.85	0	0	0	0	0	0	0	0	0.15	1

Ipswich, 1841: Comparison of breakdown between dissent and Anglicans (tallies)

	WR	W	R	WK	WH	RK	RH	K	H	KH	Total
Dissenting electorate	82	0	0	0	0	0	0	0	0	14	96
Anglican electorate	570	1	3	2	4	2	0	7	0	586	1175
Combined electorate	652	1	3	2	4	2	0	7	0	600	1271

Ipswich, 1841: Comparison of breakdown between dissent and Anglicans (percentages)

	WR	W	R	WK	WH	RK	RH	K	H	KH	Total
Dissenting electorate	0.85	0	0	0	0	0	0	0	0	0.15	1
Anglican electorate	0.49	0	0	0	0	0	0	0.01	0	0.5	1
Combined electorate	0.51	0	0	0	0	0	0	0.01	0	0.47	0.99

Ipswich, 1841: Comparison of type of vote between dissent and Anglicans (tallies)

	Straight +	Plump +	Split +/−	Plump −	Straight −	Total
Dissenting electorate	82	0	0	0	14	96
Anglican electorate	570	4	8	7	586	1175
Combined electorate	652	4	8	7	600	1271

Ipswich, 1841: Comparison of type of vote between dissent and Anglicans (percentages)

	Straight +	Plump +	Split +/−	Plump −	Straight −	Total
Dissenting electorate	0.85	0	0	0	0.15	1
Anglican electorate	0.49	0	0.01	0.01	0.5	1.01
Combined electorate	0.51	0	0.01	0.01	0.47	1

Ipswich, 1841: Comparison of candidates' votes between dissent and Anglicans (tallies)

	W	R	K	H	Total
Dissenting electorate	82	82	14	14	192
Anglican electorate	577	575	597	590	2339
Combined electorate	659	657	611	604	2531

Ipswich, 1841: comparison of candidates' votes between dissent and Anglicans (percentages)

	W	R	K	H	Total
Dissenting electorate	0.43	0.43	0.07	0.07	1
Anglican electorate	0.25	0.25	0.26	0.25	1.01
Combined electorate	0.26	0.26	0.24	0.24	1

Ipswich, 1841: Comparison of old and new dissent (tallies)

	Straight +									Straight −	Total
Old dissent	66	0	0	0	0	0	0	0	0	13	79
New dissent	7	0	0	0	0	0	0	0	0	0	7
Total	73	0	0	0	0	0	0	0	0	13	86

Ipswich, 1841: Comparison of old and new dissent (percentages)

	Straight +									Straight −	Total
Old dissent	0.84	0	0	0	0	0	0	0	0	0.16	1
New dissent	1	0	0	0	0	0	0	0	0	0	1
Total	0.85	0	0	0	0	0	0	0	0	0.15	1

Ipswich, June 1842: Breakdown of dissenting votes by denomination (tallies)

D = Desart (Conservative)
Gis = Gisborne (Liberal)
Gl = Gladstone (Conservative)
M = Moffat (Liberal)

	Straight +						Split			Straight −	Total
Ebenezer Chapel (W)	4	0	0	0	0	0	0	0	0	0	4
St Mary's Elms (PM)	1	0	0	0	0	0	0	0	0	0	1
St Nicholas St Old Meeting House (P)	7	0	0	0	0	0	0	0	0	2	9
Nicholas New Chapel (I)	6	0	0	0	0	0	0	0	0	5	11
Tacket St Chapel (I)	39	0	0	0	0	0	1	0	0	6	46
Others	10	0	0	0	0	0	0	0	0	2	12
Total	67	0	0	0	0	0	1	0	0	15	83

Ipswich, June 1842: Breakdown of dissenting votes by denomination (percentages)

	Straight +						Split			Straight −	Total
Ebenezer Chapel (W)	1	0	0	0	0	0	0	0	0	0	1
St Mary's Elms (PM)	1	0	0	0	0	0	0	0	0	0	1
St Nicholas St Old Meeting House (P)	0.78	0	0	0	0	0	0	0	0	0.22	1
Nicholas New Chapel (I)	0.55	0	0	0	0	0	0	0	0	0.45	1
Tacket St Chapel (I)	0.85	0	0	0	0	0	0.02	0	0	0.13	1
Others	0.83	0	0	0	0	0	0	0	0	0.17	1
Total	0.81	0	0	0	0	0	0.01	0	0	0.18	1

Ipswich, June 1842: Comparison of breakdown between dissent and Anglicans (tallies)

	Gis.M	Gis.	M	Gis.D	Gis.Gl.	MD	M.Gl.	D	Gl	DGl.	Total
Dissenting electorate	67	0	0	1	0	0	0	0	0	15	83
Anglican electorate	469	1	0	2	0	1	0	3	0	654	1130
Combined electorate	536	1	0	3	0	1	0	3	0	669	1213

Ipswich, June 1842: Comparison of breakdown between dissent and Anglicans (percentages)

	Gis.M	Gis.	M	Gis.D	Gis.Gl.	MD	M.Gl.	D	Gl	DGl.	Total
Dissenting electorate	0.81	0	0	0.01	0	0	0	0	0	0.18	1
Anglican electorate	0.42	0	0	0	0	0	0	0	0	0.58	1
Combined electorate	0.44	0	0	0	0	0	0	0	0	0.55	0.99

Ipswich, June 1842: Comparison of type of vote between dissent and Anglicans (tallies)

	Straight +	Plump +	Split +/−	Plump −	Straight −	Total
Dissenting electorate	67	0	1	0	15	83
Anglican electorate	469	1	3	3	654	1130
Combined electorate	536	1	4	3	669	1213

Ipswich, June 1842: Comparison of type of vote between dissent and Anglicans (percentages)

	Straight +	Plump +	Split +/−	Plump −	Straight −	Total
Dissenting electorate	0.81	0	0.01	0	0.18	1
Anglican electorate	0.42	0	0	0	0.58	1
Combined electorate	0.44	0	0	0	0.55	0.99

Ipswich, June 1842: Comparison of candidates' votes between dissent and Anglicans (tallies)[1]

	Gis.	M	D	Gl.	Total
Dissenting electorate	68	67	16	15	166
Anglican electorate	475	474	664	658	2271
Combined electorate	543	541	680	673	2437

---

[1] This does not include a fifth candidate, Charles Nicholson, who polled a total of three votes in June and two votes in August. No dissenter cast any of these five votes.

Ipswich, June 1842: Comparison of candidates' votes between dissent and Anglicans (percentages)

	Gis.	M	D	Gl.	Total
Dissenting electorate	0.41	0.4	0.1	0.09	1
Anglican electorate	0.21	0.21	0.29	0.29	1
Combined electorate	0.22	0.22	0.29	0.28	1.01

Ipswich, June 1842: comparison of old and new dissent (tallies)

	Straight +						Split			Straight −	Total
Old dissent	52	0	0	0	0	0	1	0	0	13	66
New dissent	5	0	0	0	0	0	0	0	0	0	5
Total	57	0	0	0	0	0	1	0	0	13	71

Ipswich, June 1842: comparison of old and new dissent (percentages)

	Straight +						Split			Straight −	Total
Old dissent	0.79	0	0	0	0	0	0.02	0	0	0.2	1.01
New dissent	1	0	0	0	0	0	0	0	0	0	1
Total	0.8	0	0	0	0	0	0.01	0	0	0.18	0.99

Ipswich, Aug 1842: Breakdown of dissenting votes by denomination (tallies)

F = Fox (Conservative)
G = Gladstone (Conservative)
T = Thornbury (Liberal)
V = Vincent (Liberal / Chartist)

	Straight +	Plump +								Straight −	Total
Ebenezer Chapel (W)	4	0	0	0	0	0	0	0	0	0	4
St Mary's Elms (PM)	1	0	0	0	0	0	0	0	0	0	1
St Nicholas St Old Meeting House (P)	5	0	1	0	0	0	0	0	0	3	9
Nicholas New Chapel (I)	9	0	0	0	0	0	0	0	0	4	13
Tacket St Chapel (I)	31	0	1	0	0	0	0	0	0	3	35
Others	10	0	1	0	0	0	0	0	0	2	13
Totalm	60	0	3	0	0	0	0	0	0	12	75

Ipswich, Aug 1842: Breakdown of dissenting votes by denomination (percentages)

	Straight +		Plump +							Straight −	Total
Ebenezer Chapel (W)	1	0	0	0	0	0	0	0	0	0	1
St Mary's Elms (PM)	1	0	0	0	0	0	0	0	0	0	1
St Nicholas St Old Meeting House (P)	0.56	0	0.11	0	0	0	0	0	0	0.33	1
Nicholas New Chapel (I)	0.69	0	0	0	0	0	0	0	0	0.31	1
Tacket St Chapel (I)	0.89	0	0.03	0	0	0	0	0	0	0.09	1.01
Others	0.77	0	0.08	0	0	0	0	0	0	0.15	1
Total	0.8	0	0.04	0	0	0	0	0	0	0.16	1

Ipswich, Aug 1842: Comparison of breakdown between dissent and Anglicans (tallies)

	VT	V	T	VG	VF	TG	TV	G	F	GF	Total
Dissenting electorate	60	0	3	0	0	0	0	0	0	12	75
Anglican electorate	403	6	65	0	0	8	0	6	1	631	1120
Combined electorate	463	6	68	0	0	8	0	6	1	643	1195

Ipswich, Aug 1842: Comparison of breakdown between dissent and Anglicans (percentages)

	VT	V	T	VG	VF	TG	TV	G	F	GF	Total
Dissenting electorate	0.8	0	0.04	0	0	0		0	0	0	0.15	0.99
Anglican electorate	0.36	0.01	0.06	0	0	0.01	0	0.01	0	0.56	1.01
Combined electorate	0.39	0.01	0.06	0	0	0.01	0	0.01	0	0.54	1.02

Ipswich, Aug 1842: Comparison of type of vote between dissent and Anglicans (tallies)

	Straight +	Plump +	Split +/−	Plump −	Straight +	Total
Dissenting electorate	60	3	0	0	12	75
Anglican electorate	403	71	8	7	631	1120
Combined electorate	463	74	8	7	643	1195

Ipswich, Aug 1842: Comparison of type of vote between dissent and Anglicans (percentages)

	Straight +	Plump +	Split +/−	Plump −	Straight +	Total
Dissenting electorate	0.8	0.04	0	0	0.15	0.99
Anglican electorate	0.36	0.06	0.01	0.01	0.56	1
Combined electorate	0.39	0.06	0.01	0.01	0.54	1.01

Ipswich, Aug 1842: Comparison of candidates' votes between dissent and Anglicans (tallies)

	T	V	G	F	Total
Dissenting electorate	63	60	12	12	147
Anglican electorate	485	413	639	629	2166
Combined electorate	548	473	651	641	2313

Ipswich, Aug 1842: Comparison of candidates' votes between dissent and Anglicans (percentages)

	T	V	G	F	Total
Dissenting electorate	0.43	0.41	0.08	0.08	1
Anglican electorate	0.22	0.19	0.3	0.29	1
Combined electorate	0.24	0.2	0.28	0.28	1

Ipswich, Aug 1842: Comparison of old and new dissent (tallies)

	Straight +		Plump +							Straight −	Total
Old dissent	45	0	2	0	0	0	0	0	0	10	57
New dissent	5	0	0	0	0	0	0	0	0	0	5
Total	50	0	2	0	0	0	0	0	0	10	62

Ipswich, Aug 1842: Comparison of old and new dissent (percentages)

	Straight +		Plump +							Straight −	Total
Old dissent	0.79	0	0.04	0	0	0	0	0	0	0.18	1.01
New dissent	1	0	0	0	0	0	0	0	0	0	1
Total	0.81	0	0.03	0	0	0	0	0	0	0.16	1

Ipswich, 1847: Breakdown of dissenting votes by denomination (tallies)

A = Adair (Liberal)
C = Cobbold (Conservative)
G = Gladstone (Conservative)
V = Vincent (Liberal / Chartist)

	Straight +	V	A	VC	AC	GV	GA	C	G	Straight −	Total
Ebenezer Chapel (W)	4	0	0	0	0	0	0	0	0	0	4
St Mary's Elms (PM)	0	1	0	0	0	0	0	0	0	0	1

	Straight +	V	A	VC	AC	GV	GA	C	G	Straight −	Total
St Nicholas St Old Meeting House (P)	2	0	1	0	0	0	0	0	1	2	6
Nicholas New Chapel (I)	12	2	0	0	1	0	0	0	0	3	18
Tacket St Chapel (I)	24	3	2	1	6	0	0	1	0	6	43
Others	8	1	0	1	3	0	1	0	0	0	14
Total	50	7	3	2	10	0	1	1	1	11	86

Ipswich, 1847: Breakdown of dissenting votes by denomination (percentages)

	Straight +	V	A	VC	AC	GV	GA	C	G	Straight −	Total
Ebenezer Chapel (W)	1	0	0	0	0	0	0	0	0	0	1
St Mary's Elms (PM)	0	1	0	0	0	0	0	0	0	0	1
St Nicholas St Old Meeting House (P)	0.33	0	0.17	0	0	0	0	0	0.17	0.33	1
Nicholas New Chapel (I)	0.67	0.11	0	0	0.06	0	0	0	0	0.17	1.01
Tacket St Chapel (I)	0.56	0.07	0.05	0.02	0.14	0	0	0.02	0	0.14	1
Others	0.57	0.07	0	0.07	0.21	0	0.07	0	0	0	0.99
Total	0.58	0.08	0.03	0.02	0.12	0	0.01	0.01	0.01	0.13	0.99

Ipswich, 1847: Comparison of breakdown between dissent and Anglicans (tallies)

	Straight +	V	A	VC	AC	GV	GA	C	G	Straight −	Total
Dissenting electorate	50	7	3	2	10	0	1	1	1	11	86
Anglican electorate	403	45	70	27	156	12	15	36	37	585	1386
Combined electorate	453	52	73	29	166	12	16	37	38	596	1472

Ipswich, 1847: Comparison of breakdown between dissent and Anglicans (percentages)

	Straight +	V	A	VC	AC	GV	GA	C	G	Straight −	Total
Dissenting electorate	0.58	0.08	0.03	0.02	0.12	0	0.01	0.01	0.01	0.13	0.99
Anglican electorate	0.29	0.03	0.05	0.02	0.11	0.01	0.01	0.03	0.03	0.42	1.01
Combined electorate	0.31	0.04	0.05	0.02	0.11	0.01	0.01	0.03	0.03	0.4	1.01

Ipswich, 1847: Comparison of type of vote between dissent and Anglicans (tallies)

	Straight +	Plump +	Split +/−	Plump −	Straight −	Total
Dissenting electorate	50	10	13	2	11	86
Anglican electorate	403	115	210	73	585	1386
Combined electorate	453	125	223	75	596	1472

Ipswich, 1847: Comparison of type of vote between dissent and Anglicans (percentages)

	Straight +	Plump +	Split +/−	Plump −	Straight −	Total
Dissenting electorate	0.58	0.12	0.15	0.02	0.13	1
Anglican electorate	0.29	0.08	0.15	0.05	0.42	0.99
Combined electorate	0.31	0.08	0.15	0.05	0.4	0.99

Ipswich, 1847: Comparison of candidates' votes between dissent and Anglicans (tallies)

	A	V	C	G	Total
Dissenting electorate	64	59	24	13	160
Anglican electorate	644	487	805	648	2584
Combined electorate	708	546	829	661	2744

Ipswich, 1847: Comparison of candidates' votes between dissent and Anglicans (percentages)

	A	V	C	G	Total
Dissenting electorate	0.4	0.37	0.15	0.09	1.01
Anglican electorate	0.25	0.19	0.31	0.25	1
Combined electorate	0.26	0.2	0.3	0.24	1

Ipswich, 1847: Comparison of old and new dissent (tallies)

	Straight +	V	A	VC	AC	GV	GA	C	G	Straight −	Total
Old dissent	38	5	3	1	7	0	0	1	1	11	67
New dissent	4	1	0	0	0	0	0	0	0	0	5
Total	42	6	3	1	7	0	0	1	1	11	72

Ipswich, 1847: Comparison of old and new dissent (percentages)

	Straight +	V	A	VC	AC	GV	GA	C	G	Straight −	Total
Old dissent	0.57	0.07	0.04	0.01	0.1	0	0	0.01	0.01	0.16	0.97
New dissent	0.8	0.2	0	0	0	0	0	0	0	0	1
Total	0.58	0.08	0.04	0.01	0.1	0	0	0.01	0.01	0.15	0.98

Nottingham, 1832: Breakdown of dissenting votes by denomination (tallies)
D = Duncannon (Liberal)
F = Ferguson (Liberal)
G = Gordon (Conservative)

	Straight +	Split 1	Split 2	Plump −	Total
Fletcher Gate (I)	15	0	0	0	15
St Mary's (I)	5	0	0	0	5
Castle Gate (I)	17	1	0	2	20
Stoney St (GB)	28	1	0	3	32
Broad St (GB)	26	1	0	5	32
Halifax and Hockley (WM)	43	0	0	5	48
Parliament St (NMC)	2	0	0	1	3
Others	3	0	0	0	3
Total	139	3	0	16	158

Nottingham, 1832: Breakdown of dissenting votes by denomination (percentages)

	Straight +	Split 1	Split 2	Plump −	Total
Fletcher Gate (I)	1	0	0	0	1
St Mary's (I)	1	0	0	0	1
Castle Gate (I)	0.85	0.05	0	0.1	1
Stoney St (GB)	0.88	0.03	0	0.09	1
Broad St (GB)	0.81	0.03	0	0.16	1
Halifax and Hockley (WM)	0.9	0	0	0.09	0.99
Parliament St (NMC)	0.67	0	0	0.33	1
Others	1	0	0	0	1
Total	0.88	0.02	0	0.1	1

Nottingham, 1832: Comparison of breakdown between dissent and Anglicans (tallies)

	FD	F	D	FG	DG	G	Total
Dissenting electorate	139	0	0	3	0	16	158
Anglican electorate	2186	5	4	39	1	894	3129
Combined electorate	2325	5	4	42	1	910	3287

Nottingham, 1832: Comparison of breakdown between dissent and Anglicans (percentages)

	FD	F	D	FG	DG	G	Total
Dissenting electorate	0.88	0	0	0.02	0	0.1	1
Anglican electorate	0.7	0	0	0.01	0	0.29	1
Combined electorate	0.71	0	0	0.01	0	0.28	1

Nottingham, 1832: Comparison of type of vote between dissent and Anglicans (tallies)

	Straight +	Plump +	Split +/−	Plump	Total
Dissenting electorate	139	0	3	16	158
Anglican electorate	2186	9	40	894	3129
Combined electorate	2325	9	43	910	3287

Nottingham, 1832: Comparison of type of vote between dissent and Anglicans (percentages)

	Straight +	Plump +	Split +/−	Plump	Total
Dissenting electorate	0.88	0	0.02	0.1	1
Anglican electorate	0.7	0	0.01	0.29	1
Combined electorate	0.7	0	0.01	0.28	0.99

Nottingham, 1832: comparison of candidates' votes between dissent and Anglicans (tallies)

	F	D	G	Total
Dissenting electorate	142	139	19	300
Anglican electorate	2257	2210	957	5424
Combined electorate	2399	2349	976	5724

Nottingham, 1832: Comparison of candidates' votes between dissent and Anglicans (percentages)

	F	D	G	Total
Dissenting electorate	0.47	0.46	0.06	0.99
Anglican electorate	0.42	0.41	0.18	1.01
Combined electorate	0.42	0.41	0.17	1

Nottingham, 1832: Comparison of old and new dissent (tallies)

	Straight +	Split 1	Split 2	Plump −	Total
Old dissent	91	3	0	10	104
New dissent	45	0	0	6	51
Total	136	3	0	16	155

Nottingham, 1832: Comparison of old and new dissent (percentages)

	Straight +	Split 1	Split 2	Plump −	Total
Old Dissent	0.88	0.03	0	0.1	1.01
New Dissent	0.88	0	0	0.12	1
Total	0.88	0.02	0	0.1	1

Nottingham Aug 1842: Breakdown of dissenting votes by denomination (tallies)
S = Sturge (Chartist)
W = Walter (Conservative)

	Plump +	Plump −	Total
Fletcher Gate (I)	10	0	10
St Mary's (I)	2	1	3
Castle Gate (I)	14	2	16
Stoney St (GB)	23	9	32
Broad St (GB)	23	6	29
Halifax and Hockley (WM)	37	10	47
Parliament St (NMC)	3	2	5
Others	2	0	2
Total	114	30	144

Nottingham Aug 1842: Breakdown of dissenting votes by denomination (percentages)

	Plump +	Plump −	Total
Fletcher Gate (I)	1	0	1
St Mary's (I)	0.67	0.33	1
Castle Gate (I)	0.88	0.13	1.01
Stoney St (GB)	0.72	0.28	1
Broad St (GB)	0.8	0.21	1.01
Halifax and Hockley (WM)	0.79	0.21	1
Parliament St (NMC)	0.6	0.4	1
Others	1	0	1
Total	0.79	0.21	1

Nottingham Aug 1842: Comparison of breakdown between dissent and Anglicans (tallies)

	Plump +	Plump −	Total
Dissenting electorate	114	30	144
Anglican electorate	1687	1855	3542
Combined electorate	1801	1885	3686

Nottingham Aug 1842: Comparison of breakdown between dissent and Anglicans (percentages)

	Plump +	Plump −	Total
Dissenting electorate	0.79	0.21	1
Anglican electorate	0.48	0.52	1
Combined electorate	0.49	0.51	1

Nottingham Aug 1842: Comparison of old and new dissent (tallies)

	Plump +	Plump −	Total
Old dissent	72	18	90
New dissent	40	12	52
Total	112	30	142

Nottingham Aug 1842: Comparison of old and new dissent (percentages)

	Plump +	Plump −	Total
Old dissent	0.8	0.2	1
New dissent	0.77	0.23	1
Total	0.79	0.21	1

Nottingham, Apr 1843: Breakdown of dissenting votes by denomination (tallies)
G = Gisborne (liberal)
W = Walter (conservative)

	Plump +	Plump −	Total
Fletcher Gate (I)	10	1	11
St Mary's (I)	3	2	5
Castle Gate (I)	14	0	14
Stoney St (GB)	28	7	35
Broad St (GB)	31	8	39
Halifax and Hockley (WM)	39	8	47
Parliament St (NMC)	3	3	6
Others	4	0	4
Total	132	29	161

Nottingham, Apr 1843: Breakdown of dissenting votes by denomination (percentages)

	Plump +	Plump −	Total
Fletcher Gate (I)	0.91	0.09	1
St Mary's (I)	0.6	0.4	1
Castle Gate (I)	1	0	1
Stoney St (GB)	0.8	0.2	1
Broad St (GB)	0.79	0.21	1
Halifax and Hockley (WM)	0.83	0.17	1
Parliament St (NMC)	0.5	0.5	1
Others	1	0	1
Total	0.82	0.18	1

Nottingham, Apr 1843: Comparison of breakdown between dissent and Anglicans (tallies)

	Plump +	Plump −	Total
Dissenting electorate	132	29	161
Anglican electorate	1707	1699	3406
Combined electorate	1839	1728	3567

Nottingham, Apr 1843: Comparison of breakdown between dissent and Anglicans (percentages)

	Plump +	Plump −	Total
Dissenting electorate	0.82	0.18	1
Anglican electorate	0.5	0.5	1
Combined electorate	0.52	0.48	1

Nottingham, Apr 1843: Comparison of old and new dissent (tallies)

	Plump +	Plump −	Total
Old dissent	86	18	104
New dissent	42	11	53
Total	128	29	157

Nottingham, Apr 1843: Comparison of old and new dissent (percentages)

	Plump +	Plump −	Total
Old dissent	0.83	0.17	1
New dissent	0.79	0.21	1
Total	0.82	0.18	1

Nottingham, 1847: Breakdown of dissenting votes by denomination (tallies)
G = Gisborne (Liberal)
H = Hobhouse (Liberal)
O = O'Connor (Chartist)
W = Walter (Conservative)

	Straight +	Plump +(1)	Plump +(2)	Split (1)	Split (2)	Split (3)	Split (4)	Plump -(1)	Plump -(2)	Straight -	Total
Fletcher Gate (I)	2	0	2	0	0	0	0	0	1	0	5
Castle Gate (I)	7	2	0	0	0	0	0	0	0	0	9
Stoney St (GB)	11	1	0	0	1	0	0	5	0	2	20
Broad St (GB)	10	0	4	0	0	0	1	6	0	7	28
Halifax and Hockley (WM)	10	0	3	0	1	0	4	7	1	4	30
Parliament St (NMC)	1	0	0	0	0	0	0	0	0	1	2
Others	0	0	1	0	0	0	0	0	0	0	1
Total	41	3	10	0	2	0	5	18	2	14	95

Nottingham, 1847: Breakdown of dissenting votes by denomination (percentages)

	Straight +	Plump +(1)	Plump +(2)	Split (1)	Split (2)	Split (3)	Split (4)	Plump –(1)	Plump –(2)	Straight –	Total
Fletcher Gate (I)	0.4	0	0.4	0	0	0	0	0	0.2	0	1
Castle Gate (I)	0.78	0.22	0	0	0	0	0	0	0	0	1
Stoney St (GB)	0.55	0.05	0	0	0.05	0	0	0.25	0	0.1	1
Broad St (GB)	0.36	0	0.14	0	0	0	0.04	0.21	0	0.25	1
Halifax and Hockley (WM)	0.33	0	0.1	0	0.03	0	0.13	0.23	0.03	0.13	0.98
Parliament St (NMC)	0.5	0	0	0	0	0	0	0	0	0.5	1
Others	0	0	1	0	0	0	0	0	0	0	1
Total	0.43	0.03	0.11	0	0.02	0	0.05	0.19	0.02	0.15	1

Nottingham, 1847: Comparison of breakdown between dissent and Anglicans (tallies)

	HG	H	G	HO	HW	GO	GW	O	W	OW	Total
Dissenting electorate	41	3	10	2	0	5	0	2	18	14	95
Anglican electorate	682	35	104	48	30	51	22	151	617	812	2552
Combined electorate	723	38	114	50	30	56	22	153	635	826	2647

Nottingham, 1847: Comparison of breakdown between dissent and Anglicans (percentages)

	HG	H	G	HO	HW	GO	GW	O	W	OW	Total
Dissenting electorate	0.43	0.03	0.1	0.02	0	0.05	0	0.02	0.19	0.15	0.99
Anglican electorate	0.27	0.01	0.04	0.02	0.01	0.02	0.01	0.06	0.24	0.32	1
Combined electorate	0.27	0.01	0.04	0.02	0.01	0.02	0.01	0.06	0.24	0.31	0.99

Nottingham, 1847: Comparison of type of vote between dissent and Anglicans (tallies)

	Straight +	Plump +	Split +/−	Plump −	Straight −	Total
Dissenting electorate	41	13	7	20	14	95
Anglican electorate	682	139	151	768	812	2552
Combined electorate	723	152	158	788	826	2647

Nottingham, 1847: Comparison of type of vote between dissent and Anglicans (percentages)

	Straight +	Plump +	Split +/−	Plump −	Straight −	Total
Dissenting electorate	0.43	0.14	0.07	0.21	0.15	1
Anglican electorate	0.27	0.05	0.06	0.3	0.32	1
Combined electorate	0.27	0.06	0.06	0.3	0.31	1

Nottingham, 1847: Comparison of candidates' votes between dissent and Anglicans (tallies)

	G	H	W	O	Total
Dissenting electorate	56	46	32	23	157
Anglican electorate	943	847	1651	1234	4675
Combined electorate	999	893	1683	1257	4832

Nottingham, 1847: Comparison of candidates' votes between dissent and Anglicans (percentages)

	G	H	W	O	Total
Dissenting electorate	0.36	0.29	0.2	0.15	1
Anglican electorate	0.2	0.18	0.35	0.26	0.99
Combined electorate	0.21	0.18	0.35	0.26	1

Nottingham, 1847: Comparison of old and new dissent (tallies)

	Straight +	Plump +(1)	Plump +(2)	Split (1)	Split (2)	Split (3)	Split (4)	Plump −(1)	Plump −(2)	Straight −	Total
Old Dissent	30	3	6	0	1	0	1	11	1	9	62
New Dissent	11	0	3	0	1	0	4	7	1	5	32
Total	41	3	9	0	2	0	5	18	2	14	94

Nottingham, 1847: comparison of old and new dissent (percentages)

	Straight +	Plump +(1)	Plump +(2)	Split (1)	Split (2)	Split (3)	Split (4)	Plump −(1)	Plump −(2)	Straight −	Total
Old Dissent	0.48	0.05	0.1	0	0.02	0	0.02	0.18	0.02	0.15	1.02
New Dissent	0.34	0	0.1	0	0.03	0	0.13	0.22	0.03	0.16	1.01
Total	0.44	0.03	0.1	0	0.02	0	0.05	0.18	0.02	0.15	0.99

Durham, 1832: Breakdown of dissenting votes by denomination (tallies)
C = Chaytor (Liberal)
H = Harland (Liberal)
T = Trevor (Conservative)

	Straight +	Plump +	Split +/−	Plump −	Total
Claypath / FramwellgateChapel (I)	32	0	6	4	42
Bethel Chapel, Chester-le-Street (I)	7	1	3	1	12

	Straight +	Plump +	Split +/−	Plump −	Total
Houghton-le-Spring Presbyterian Chapel (P)	3	0	0	0	3
Methodist Chapel, Old Elvet (W)	5	0	0	0	5
Houghton-le-Spring Methodist Circuit (M)	8	0	1	0	9
Total	55	1	10	5	71

Durham, 1832: Breakdown of dissenting votes by denomination (percentages)

	Straight +	Plump +	Split +/−	Plump −	Total
Claypath / Framwellgate Chapel (I)	0.76	0	0.14	0.1	1
Bethel Chapel, Chester-le-Street (I)	0.58	0.08	0.25	0.08	0.99
Houghton-le-Spring Presbyterian Chapel (P)	1	0	0	0	1
Methodist Chapel, Old Elvet (W)	1	0	0	0	1
Houghton-le-Spring Methodist Circuit (M)	0.89	0	0.11	0	1
Total	0.77	0.01	0.14	0.07	0.99

Durham, 1832: Comparison of type of vote between dissent and Anglicans (tallies)

	Straight +	Plump +	Split +/−	Plump −	Total
Dissenting electorate	55	1	10	5	71
Anglican electorate	307	19	95	273	694
Combined electorate	362	20	100	278	765

Durham, 1832: Comparison of type of vote between dissent and Anglicans (percentages)

	Straight +	Plump +	Split +/−	Plump −	Total
Dissenting electorate	0.77	0.01	0.14	0.07	0.99
Anglican electorate	0.44	0.03	0.14	0.39	1
Combined electorate	0.47	0.03	0.13	0.37	1

Durham, 1832: Comparison of candidates' votes between dissent and Anglicans (tallies)

	H	C	T	Total
Dissenting electorate	63	63	16	142
Anglican electorate	376	340	367	1083
Combined electorate	439	403	383	1225

Durham, 1832: Comparison of candidates' votes between dissent and Anglicans (percentages)

	H	C	T	Total
Dissenting electorate	0.44	0.44	0.11	0.99
Anglican electorate	0.35	0.31	0.34	1
Combined electorate	0.36	0.33	0.31	1

Durham, 1832: Comparison of old and new dissent (tallies)

	Straight +	Plump +	Split +/−	Plump −	Total
Old Dissent	42	1	9	5	57
New Dissent	13	0	1	0	14
Total	55	1	10	5	71

Durham, 1832: Comparison of old and new dissent (percentages)

	Straight +	Plump +	Split +/−	Plump −	Total
Old dissent	0.74	0.02	0.16	0.09	1.01
New dissent	0.93	0	0.07	0	1
Total	0.77	0.01	0.14	0.07	0.99

Durham, 1832: Other non-Anglicans

	Straight +	Plump +	Split +/−	Plump −	Total
St Cuthbert's Chapel (RC)	*2*	*0*	*1*	*0*	*3*

Durham, 1835: Breakdown of dissenting votes by denomination (tallies)
G = Granger (Liberal)
H = Harland (Liberal)
T = Trevor (Conservative)

	Straight +	Plump +	Split +/−	Plump −	Total
Claypath / Framwellgate Chapel (I)	24	5	3	7	39
Bethel Chapel, Chester-le-Street (I)	6	1	2	1	10
Houghton-le-Spring Presbyterian Chapel (P)	2	1	0	0	3
Methodist Chapel, Old Elvet (W)	7	1	2	1	11
Houghton-le-Spring Methodist Circuit (M)	7	0	1	1	9
Old Elvet Chapel (NMC)	1	0	0	0	1
Total	47	8	8	10	73

Durham, 1835: Breakdown of dissenting votes by denomination (percentages)

	Straight +	Plump +	Split +/−	Plump −	Total
Claypath / Framwellgate Chapel (I)	0.62	0.13	0.08	0.18	1.01
Bethel Chapel, Chester-le-Street (I)	0.6	0.1	0.2	0.1	1
Houghton-le-Spring Presbyterian Chapel (P)	0.67	0.33	0	0	1
Methodist Chapel, Old Elvet (W)	0.64	0.09	0.18	0.09	1
Houghton-le-Spring Methodist Circuit (M)	0.78	0	0.11	0.11	1
Old Elvet Chapel (NMC)	1	0	0	0	1
Total	0.64	0.11	0.11	0.14	1

Durham, 1835: Comparison of type of vote between dissent and Anglicans (tallies)

	Straight +	Plump +	Split +/−	Plump −	Total
Dissenting electorate	47	8	8	10	73
Anglican electorate	231	70	141	314	756
Combined electorate	278	78	149	324	829

Durham, 1835: Comparison of type of vote between dissent and Anglicans (percentages)

	Straight +	Plump +	Split +/−	Plump −	Total
Dissenting electorate	0.64	0.11	0.11	0.14	1
Anglican electorate	0.31	0.09	0.19	0.42	1.01
Combined electorate	0.34	0.09	0.18	0.39	1

Durham, 1835: Comparison of old and new dissent (tallies)

	Straight +	Plump +	Split +/−	Plump −	Total
Old dissent	32	7	5	8	52
New dissent	15	1	3	2	21
Total	47	8	8	10	73

Durham, 1835: Comparison of old and new dissent (percentages)

	Straight +	Plump +	Split +/−	Plump −	Total
Old dissent	0.62	0.13	0.1	0.15	1
New dissent	0.71	0.05	0.14	0.1	1
Total	0.64	0.11	0.11	0.14	1

Durham, 1835: Comparison of candidates' votes between dissent and Anglicans (tallies)

	H	G	T	Total
Dissenting electorate	58	54	21	133
Anglican electorate	375	296	452	1123
Combined electorate	433	350	473	1256

Durham, 1835: Comparison of candidates' votes between dissent and Anglicans (percentages)

	H	G	T	Total
Dissenting electorate	0.44	0.41	0.16	1.01
Anglican electorate	0.33	0.26	0.4	0.99
Combined electorate	0.34	0.28	0.38	1

Durham, 1835: Other non-Anglicans

	Straight +	Plump +	Split +/−	Plump −	Total
St Cuthbert's Chapel (RC)	*1*	*0*	*0*	*1*	*2*

Durham, 1837: Breakdown of dissenting votes by denomination (tallies)
G = Granger (Liberal)
H = Harland (Liberal)
T = Trevor (Conservative)

	Straight +	Plump +	Split +/−	Plump −	Total
Claypath / Framwellgate Chapel (I)	10	21	6	5	42
Bethel Chapel, Chester-le-Street (I)	2	4	3	3	12
Houghton-le-Spring Presbyterian Chapel (P)	0	4	0	0	4
Methodist Chapel, Old Elvet (W)	2	4	2	2	10
Houghton-le-Spring Methodist Circuit (M)	5	2	1	2	10
Old Elvet Chapel (NMC)	0	2	2	0	4
Total	19	37	14	12	82

Durham, 1837: Breakdown of dissenting votes by denomination (percentages)

	Straight +	Plump +	Split +/−	Plump −	Total
Claypath / Framwellgate Chapel (I)	0.24	0.5	0.14	0.12	1
Bethel Chapel, Chester-le-Street (I)	0.17	0.33	0.25	0.25	1
Houghton-le-Spring Presbyterian Chapel (P)	0	1	0	0	1
Methodist Chapel, Old Elvet (W)	0.2	0.4	0.2	0.2	1
Houghton-le-Spring Methodist Circuit (M)	0.5	0.2	0.1	0.2	1
Old Elvet Chapel (NMC)	0	0.5	0.5	0	1
Total	0.23	0.45	0.17	0.15	1

Durham, 1837: Comparison of type of vote between dissent and Anglicans (tallies)

	Straight +	Plump +	Split +/−	Plump −	Total
Dissenting electorate	19	37	14	12	82
Anglican electorate	106	230	213	226	775
Combined electorate	125	267	227	238	857

Durham, 1837: Comparison of type of vote between dissent and Anglicans (percentages)

	Straight +	Plump +	Split +/−	Plump −	Total
Dissenting electorate	0.23	0.45	0.17	0.15	1
Anglican electorate	0.14	0.3	0.27	0.29	1
Combined electorate	0.15	0.31	0.26	0.28	1

Durham, 1837: Comparison of candidates' votes between dissent and Anglicans (tallies)

	G	H	T	Total
Dissenting electorate	49	42	25	116
Anglican electorate	322	331	440	1093
Combined electorate	371	373	465	1209

Durham, 1837: Comparison of candidates' votes between dissent and Anglicans (percentages)

	G	H	T	Total
Dissenting electorate	0.42	0.36	0.22	1
Anglican electorate	0.29	0.3	0.4	0.99
Combined electorate	0.31	0.31	0.38	1

Durham, 1837: Comparison of old and new dissent (tallies)

	Straight +	Plump +	Split +/−	Plump −	Total
Old dissent	12	29	9	8	58
New dissent	7	8	5	4	24
Total	19	37	14	12	82

Durham, 1837: Comparison of old and new dissent (percentages)

	Straight +	Plump +	Split +/−	Plump −	Total
Old dissent	0.21	0.5	0.16	0.14	1.01
New dissent	0.29	0.33	0.21	0.17	1
Total	0.23	0.45	0.17	0.15	1

Durham, 1837: other non-Anglicans

	Straight +	Plump +	Split +/−	Plump −	Total
St Cuthbert's Chapel (RC)	1	0	0	1	2

Durham, Apr 1843: Breakdown of dissenting votes by denomination (tallies)

	Plump +	Plump −	Total
Claypath / Framwellgate Chapel (I)	29	21	50
Bethel Chapel, Chester-le-Street (I)	6	6	12
Houghton-le-Spring Presbyterian Chapel (P)	3	0	3
Methodist Chapel, Old Elvet (W)	14	3	17
Houghton-le-Spring Methodist Circuit (M)	5	4	9
Old Elvet Chapel (NMC)	1	2	3
Total	58	36	94

Durham, Apr 1843: Breakdown of dissenting votes by denomination (percentages)

	Plump +	Plump −	Total
Claypath / Framwellgate Chapel (I)	0.58	0.42	1
Bethel Chapel, Chester-le-Street (I)	0.5	0.5	1
Houghton-le-Spring Presbyterian Chapel (P)	1	0	1
Methodist Chapel, Old Elvet (W)	0.82	0.18	1
Houghton-le-Spring Methodist Circuit (M)	0.56	0.44	1
Old Elvet Chapel (NMC)	0.33	0.67	1
Total	0.62	0.38	1

Durham, Apr 1843: Comparison of type of vote between dissent and Anglicans (tallies)

	Plump +	Plump −	Total
Dissenting electorate	58	36	94
Anglican electorate	348	471	819
Combined electorate	406	507	913

Durham, Apr 1843: Comparison of type of vote between dissent and Anglicans (percentages)

	Plump +	Plump −	Total
Dissenting electorate	0.62	0.38	1
Anglican electorate	0.42	0.58	1
Combined electorate	0.44	0.56	1

Durham, Apr 1843: comparison of old and new dissent (tallies)

	Plump +	Plump −	Total
Old dissent	38	27	65
New dissent	20	9	29
Total	58	36	94

Durham, Apr 1843: comparison of old and new dissent (percentages)

	Plump +	Plump −	Total
Old dissent	0.58	0.42	1
New dissent	0.69	0.31	1
Total	0.62	0.38	1

Durham, Apr 1843: other non-Anglicans

	Plump +	Plump −	Total
St Cuthbert's Chapel (RC)	*0*	*1*	*1*

Durham, July 1843: Breakdown of dissenting votes by denomination (tallies)

	Plump +	Plump −	Total
Claypath / Framwellgate Chapel (I)	31	15	46
Bethel Chapel, Chester-le-Street (I)	6	5	11
Houghton-le-Spring Presbyterian Chapel (P)	5	0	5
Methodist Chapel, Old Elvet (W)	13	2	15
Houghton-le-Spring Methodist Circuit (M)	9	3	12
Old Elvet Chapel (NMC)	2	1	3
Total	66	26	92

Durham, July 1843: Breakdown of dissenting votes by denomination (percentages)

	Plump +	Plump −	Total
Claypath / Framwellgate Chapel (I)	0.67	0.33	1
Bethel Chapel, Chester-le-Street (I)	0.55	0.45	1
Houghton-le-Spring Presbyterian Chapel (P)	1	0	1
Methodist Chapel, Old Elvet (W)	0.87	0.13	1
Houghton-le-Spring Methodist Circuit (M)	0.75	0.25	1
Old Elvet Chapel (NMC)	0.67	0.33	1
Total	0.72	0.28	1

Durham, July 1843: Comparison of type of vote between dissent and Anglicans (tallies)

	Plump +	Plump −	Total
Dissenting electorate	66	26	92
Anglican electorate	422	384	806
Combined electorate	488	410	898

Durham, July 1843: Comparison of type of vote between dissent and Anglicans (percentages)

	Plump +	Plump −	Total
Dissenting electorate	0.72	0.28	1
Anglican electorate	0.52	0.48	1
Combined electorate	0.54	0.46	1

Durham, July 1843: Comparison of old and new dissent (tallies)

	Plump +	Plump −	Total
Old dissent	42	20	62
New dissent	24	6	30
Total	66	26	92

Durham, July 1843: Comparison of old and new dissent (percentages)

	Plump +	Plump −	Total
Old dissent	0.68	0.32	1
New dissent	0.8	0.2	1
Total	0.72	0.28	1

Durham, Apr 1843: Other non-anglicans

	Plump +	Plump −	Total
St Cuthbert's Chapel (RC)	*0*	*1*	*1*

Durham, 1847: Breakdown of dissenting votes by denomination (tallies)
G = Granger (Liberal)
S = Spearman (Liberal)
W = Wood (Conservative)

	Straight +	Plump +	Split +/−	Plump −	Total
Claypath / Framwellgate Chapel (I)	27	2	4	14	47
Bethel Chapel, Chester-le-Street (I)	8	0		6	15
Houghton-le-Spring Presbyterian Chapel (P)	5	0	0	0	5
Methodist Chapel, Old Elvet (W)	11	0	2	3	16
Houghton-le-Spring Methodist Circuit (M)	8	0	0	2	10
Old Elvet Chapel (NMC)	1	0	2	1	4
Total	60	2	9	26	97

Durham, 1847: Breakdown of dissenting votes by denomination (percentages)

	Straight +	Plump +	Split +/−	Plump −	Total
Claypath / Framwellgate Chapel (I)	0.57	0.04	0.09	0.3	1
Bethel Chapel, Chester-le-Street (I)	0.53	0	0.07	0.4	1
Houghton-le-Spring Presbyterian Chapel (P)	1	0	0	0	1
Methodist Chapel, Old Elvet (W)	0.69	0	0.13	0.19	1.01
Houghton-le-Spring Methodist Circuit (M)	0.8	0	0	0.2	1
Old Elvet Chapel (NMC)	0.25	0	0.5	0.25	1
Total	0.62	0.02	0.09	0.27	1

Durham, 1847: Comparison of type of vote between dissent and Anglicans (tallies)

	Straight +	Plump +	Split +/−	Plump −	Total
Dissenting electorate	60	2	9	26	97
Anglican electorate	423	30	114	301	868
Combined electorate	483	32	123	327	965

Durham, 1847: Comparison of type of vote between dissent and Anglicans (tallies)

	Straight +	Plump +	Split +/−	Plump −	Total
Dissenting electorate	0.62	0.02	0.09	0.27	1
Anglican electorate	0.49	0.03	0.13	0.37	1.02
Combined electorate	0.5	0.03	0.13	0.34	1

Durham, 1847: Comparison of candidates' votes between dissent and Anglicans (tallies)

	G	S	W	Total
Dissenting electorate	71	62	34	167
Anglican electorate	525	457	416	1398
Combined electorate	596	519	450	1565

Durham, 1847: Comparison of candidates' votes between dissent and Anglicans (percentages)

	G	S	W	Total
Dissenting electorate	0.43	0.37	0.2	1
Anglican electorate	0.38	0.33	0.3	1.01
Combined electorate	0.38	0.33	0.29	1

Durham, 1847: Comparison of old and new dissent (tallies)

	Straight +	Plump +	Split +/−	Plump −	Total
Old Dissent	40	2	5	20	67
New Dissent	20	0	4	6	30
Total	60	2	9	26	97

Durham, 1847: Comparison of old and new dissent (percentages)

	Straight +	Plump +	Split +/−	Plump −	Total
Old Dissent	0.6	0.03	0.07	0.3	1
New Dissent	0.67	0	0.13	0.2	1
Total	0.62	0.02	0.09	0.27	1

Durham, 1847: Other non-Anglicans

	Straight +	Plump +	Split +/−	Plump −	Total
St Cuthbert's Chapel (RC)	1	0	0	1	2

Notes

1 Introduction: the politics of dissent at the time of the great reform bill

1. NPLLSL, EC, Dec 1832.
2. E. Halévy, *The Birth of Methodism in England* [1906], (Bernard Semmel, trans.), (reprint, Chicago: University of Chicago Press, 1971); idem, *England in 1815* [1913] (E.I. Watkin and D.A. Barker, trans), (New York: Barnes & Noble, 1961), pp. 389–485, esp. p. 425.
3. J.C.D. Clark brought religion back to a central role in interpreting English history in the long eighteenth century which, due to the influence of the Church of England, lasted for Clark almost to the fourth decade of the nineteenth century, *English Society 1688–1832: Ideology, Social Structure, and Political Practice During the Ancien Regime* (Cambridge: Cambridge University Press, 1985). B. Hilton identified evangelicalism as the driving force informing social and especially economic thought in England into the second half of the nineteenth century, *The Age of Atonement: The Influence of Evangelicalism on Social and Economic Thought, 1795–1865* (Oxford: Clarendon Press, 1988). R. Brent also recognized the importance of religion in shaping ministerial policy during the whigs' years in office in the 1830s, *Liberal Anglican Politics: Whiggery, Religion, and Reform, 1830–1841* (Oxford: Clarendon Press, 1987). A number of local studies have examined the significance of dissent at the local level, and may be found in the Bibliography; particularly relevant works are mentioned note 26, below.
4. M.R. Watts's magisterial two-volume *The Dissenters* (Oxford: Clarendon Press, 1979 [Vol. 1], 1995 [Vol. 2]) has done much to synthesize disparate existing monographic and local scholarship, and its over 200 pages of maps, figures and appendices indicate the regional prevalence of various denominations of dissent. K.D.M. Snell and P. Ell, in their *Rival Jerusalems* (Cambridge: Cambridge University Press, 2000), have also assessed the comparative strengths and activities of dissent and the establishment, through the lens of their study of the 1851 census of religion. These studies should lay the groundwork to suggest other avenues for investigating the different denominations in England and Wales. See notes 22 and 23, below, for an assessment of two other recent works. Older works include J. Stoughton, *History of Religion in England from the Opening of the Long Parliament to 1850*, vol. 8 (London: Hodder and Stoughton, 1901), which examines dissent as well as the Church of England; A. Lincoln, *Some Political & Social Ideas of English Dissent, 1763–1800* (Cambridge: The University Press, 1938); and R.G. Cowherd, *The Politics of English Dissent* (New York: New York University Press, 1956).
5. The expression is generally attributed to William E. Gladstone, although C.E. Freyer credits the historian Sir Richard Lodge (1855–1936) with virtually the same phrase: that is, dissent had proved the 'backbone of the Whig party'

since 1688; Freyer, 'The Numerical Decline of Dissent in England previous to the Industrial Revolution' in *The American Journal of Theology*, 17 (1913): 233.

6. M.R. Watts reckons they had sunk to slightly over 6 per cent of the population for the period 1715–1718, *The Dissenters*, vol. II, p. 29.

7. Lord Brougham (1778–1868) estimated that nine Englishmen out of ten belonged to the establishment, and George Croly (1780–1860), writing in *Blackwood's Magazine*, put the figure slightly lower, at 85 per cent. The *Monthly Repository* quoted the bishop of London as reporting the ratio of churchmen to dissenters as three to one. The *Repository*'s own calculation— based on a single diocese, supposedly representative of the nation as a whole—reported that only person in seven attended Anglican services, that only one in 38 took communion and, according to these criteria, less than 3 per cent of the population was under the full meaning of 'conformity'! *Hansard*, 3rd ser. xxx (18 Aug 1835): 626–628; 'The Marriage and Registration Bills,' in *Blackwood's Magazine*, 39, 247 (1836): 599–604; 'The Case of the Dissenters,' in *Monthly Repository*, 2nd ser., 8 (1834): 63–70.

8. J. Parry, *Democracy and Religion: Gladstone and the Liberal Party, 1867–1875* (Cambridge: Cambridge University Press, 1986), p. 7.

9. Horace Mann, the original compiler of the census data, reckoned the best estimate for numbers of individuals attending at a place of worship on census Sunday was the sum of those present at the morning service, half present at the afternoon service, and one-third present in the evening. To correct Mann's obvious under-representation of dissent, who often turned out in the strongest numbers to attend evening worship, M.R. Watts in *The Dissenters* preferred a formula of the best attended service of the day, added to one-third the totals present for other services. Snell and Ell derived fully a dozen different calculations from the original data—including attendance, sittings, and occupancy—depending on what type of analysis they applied!

10. This figure is from Watts's recalculations.

11. Ibid.

12. Valid excuses included youth, sickness or debility, 'attendance upon the two preceding classes,' inescapable household duties, and involvement with public transportation. *Parliamentary Papers, 1852–1853*, p. 213.

13. As one historian has written of France in the nineteenth century:

> The apprehension of religious mentalities is full of pitfalls. In often relying on statistics of church attendance, vocations to the priesthood, confraternities, altarpieces, etc., can the historian really claim that he is quantifying faith? One can admit the necessity for quantification in religious history, and still hold that faith and love will always retain a certain preternatural quality. At best, one measures signs of faith and of collective attitudes, not the state of the soul
> J. Delumeau, *Chaire d'Histoire des Mentaliées Relieuses dans l'Occident Moderne* (Paris: Collège de France, 1975), p. 14, cited in R. Gibson, *A Social History of French Catholicism, 1789–1914* (London: Routledge, 1989), p. 3

14. Based on these calculations, 9,811,176 English men, women and children could theoretically have attended a service on 31 March 1851; of these,

3,192,638 attended no service, 3,415,861 attended an Anglican church, and 3,202,677 attended a nonconformist chapel. The respective percentages are 32.5 per cent, 34.8 per cent, and 32.6 per cent. The ratio of Anglican to nonconformist attendances, of course, is still slightly more than one to one.

15. H. McLeod has reviewed the relevant historiography in *Religion and Irreligion in Victorian Britain: How Secular was the Working Class?* (Bangor: Headstart History, 1993), esp. pp. 1–12. Some of the works he considers are E.R. Wickham, *Church and People in an Industrial City* (London: Lutterworth Press, 1957); K.S. Inglis, *Churches and the Working Classes in Victorian England* (London: Routledge and K. Paul, 1963); J. Obelkovich, *Religion and Rural Society: South Lindsey, 1825–1875* (Oxford: Clarendon Press, 1976); A.D. Gilbert, *Religion and Society in Industrial England: Church, Chapel and Social Change, 1740–1914* (London: Longmans, 1976); and S. Yeo, *Religion and Voluntary Organisations in Crisis* (London: Croom Helm, 1976).

16. In spite of many hardships, it seems evident that church and chapel activity continued to touch the lives of the working classes in the nineteenth century. This is perhaps seen most strikingly in the case of the Sunday schools, through whose influence virtually everyone grew up familiar with the Bible, certain hymns and doctrines. Such individuals were certainly nominal, if occasionally passive, Christians.

17. E.J. Evans, *The Great Reform Act of 1832* (London: Methuen, 1983), p. 3.

18. R. Antsey, 'Religion and British slave Emancipation,' in D. Eltis and J. Walvin (eds), *The Abolition of the Atlantic Slave Trade: Origins and Effects in Europe, Africa, and the Americas* (Madison: University of Wisconsin Press, 1981), pp. 51–53.

19. The test act of 1673 was also repealed in 1828.

20. There was no reform of the municipal corporations, for instance, until 1834: this was a real political grievance that had preceded 1832, and survived it.

21. Owen Chadwick, *The Victorian Church, part I, 1829–1859* (New York: Oxford University Press, 1967), pp. 3–4, emphasis added.

22. J.R. Vincent's compilations of evidence of dissenting ministers (1830–1847 and 1848–1872) indicates clear preference for liberal politics, although he is in general sceptical of the usefulness of poll books to sustain such findings from a broader cross-section. Nonetheless, his tables of Wesleyan Methodist voting behavior in 1841 demonstrates strong commitment to liberal MPs among the rank and file; *Pollbooks: How Victorians Voted* (London: Cambridge University Press, 1967), pp. 67–68, 5–6, 69–70. J.A. Phillips also noted that, in the eighteenth and well into the nineteenth centuries, denominational preference, especially for dissenters, was the single best index of an elector's political sentiments; *The Great Reform Bill in the Boroughs* (Oxford: Clarendon Press, 1992), pp. 272–294, and passim. G.I.T Machin concurs: on the whole, dissenters in the middle of the nineteenth century tended to vote liberal and, although the ratios are less significant, Anglicans tended to vote conservative, *Politics and the Churches in Great Britain, 1832–1868* (Oxford: Clarendon Press, 1977), p. 40. Mostly in regard to elections in the period after the principal concern of the present study, K.D. Snell and P. Ell have written that 'nobody could be in any doubt that religious conformism or dissent carried as their corollaries strong voting predispositions,' *Rival Jerusalems*, p. 27.

23. T. Larsen, *Friends of Religious Equality: Nonconformist Politics in Mid-Victorian England* (Woodbridge: The Boydell Press, 1999), p. 3.
24. K.D. Wald, *Crosses on the Ballot* (Princeton: Princeton University Press, 1983), pp. 150, 157, 163–167, and passim.
25. For the whig or even radical inclination of dissent during much of the eighteenth century, see J.A. Phillips, mentioned in note 22, and idem, *Electoral Behavior in Unreformed England* (Princeton: Princeton University Press, 1982), esp. pp. 159–168 and 286–305. J.E. Bradley questioned the strength of such a relationship, especially one involving 'rank and file,' rather than 'elite,' nonconformity, but nevertheless provided a through overview of previous scholarship linking dissent and whiggery, 'Whigs and Nonconformists: "Slumbering Radicalism" in English Politics, 1739–89,' in *Eighteenth-Century Studies*, 9, 1 (1975): 1–27. A dozen years later, Bradley had come to recognize that 'Nonconformity was perhaps the most potent and predictable forces in the electorate,' even in the early decades of the eighteenth century, and that 'Dissenters were always a potential threat' to Tory electoral interests, 'Nonconformity and the Electorate in Eighteenth-Century England,' in *Parliamentary History*, 6 (1987): 246, 250. See also idem, *Popular Politics and the American Revolution in England: Petitions, the Crown, and Public Opinion* (Macon, Georgia: Mercer, 1986); idem, *Religion, Revolution, and English Radicalism: Nonconformity in Eighteenth-Century Politics and Society* (Cambridge: Cambridge University Press, 1990).
26. R.W. Davis, *Political Change and Continuity, 1760–1885: A Buckinghamshire Study* (Newton Abbot: David & Charles, 1972); W.B. Maynard, 'The Response of the Church of England to Economic and Demographic Change: The Archdeaconry of Durham, 1800–1851,' in *Journal of Ecclesiastical History*, 42, 3 (1991): 437–462; R.J. Olney, *Lincolnshire Politics, 1832–1885* (London: Oxford University Press, 1973); and D.C. Moore, *The Politics of Deference: A Study of the Mid-Nineteenth-Century English Political System* (Aldershot: Gregg Revivals, 1994) all looked at poll books with an eye to denominational affiliation and political preferences. T.J. Nossiter questioned outright the usefulness of poll books as historical evidence, especially when combined with evidence of electors' denominational preference; *Influence, Opinion, and Political Idioms in Reformed England: Case Studies from the North-east, 1832–74* (New York: Barnes & Noble Books, 1975); see also idem, 'Elections and Political Behavior in County Durham and Newcastle, 1832–74' (PhD thesis, Oxford University, 1968. A. Everett, 'Country, County and Town: Patterns of Regional Evolution in England,' in *Transactions of the Royal Historical Society*, 29 (1979): 79–108; A.M. Urdank, *Religion and Society in a Cotswold Vale: Nailsworth, Gloucestershire, 1780–1865* (Berkeley: University of California Press, 1990), and others examined the connection between politics and religion, although without recourse to poll books. M.R. Watts, *The Dissenters*, vol. II is, of course, an exhaustive synthesis in virtually every respect, but politics, at least as measured by voting behavior, is not one of the author's key points of focus. Snell and Ell, *Rival Jerusalems* provide some light on this point, too, but their specific studies are on Sunday schools, denominational influence on landownership, urbanization and secularization, and other matters.
27. The boroughs are Durham, Nottingham, Ipswich, Bedford, and Exeter. It was originally intended to include a sixth borough, Brighton, but an ongoing

preservation project of the British Library Newspaper Library (Colindale) and
other unforeseen circumstances made this unfeasible.

2 'A Free Trade—a Free Vote—and a Free Religion...': the politico-religious landscape of reformed England, 1832–1847

1. NAO, DD 568/45: 'The "Bearwood" Chronicle,' 24 Apr 1841.
2. SufRO, GC, n.d. [1847?].
3. See Chapter 3.
4. Their interests included, among other things, iron and corn trade, insurance and railway projects, the cattle market, and the gas company. K.J. Atton, 'Municipal and Parliamentary Politics in Ipswich, 1818–1847' (PhD thesis, University of London, 1979), p. 413. They were related by marriage to the abolitionist T.F. Buxton.
5. Especially after corporation reform in 1835, various Alexanders held municipal positions, including as aldermen, and were members of a range of commissions.
6. Some of the details for the Alexanders and Ransomes are from K.J. Atton, 'Municipal and Parliamentary Politics in Ipswich,' Appendix III, 'Some leading Ipswich politicians,' pp. 413–420. Atton's organization of the appendix reinforces the position that dissenters were liberal and Anglicans were conservative: Quaker or nonconformist individuals are indicated as such, and a note points out that 'All Blues/Conservatives mentioned here are Anglicans,' p. 413. A few liberals, however, are specified as Anglicans, suggesting that such alignment was anomalous.
7. *IJ*, 26 June 1841.
8. For details of their actions, see J.W. Sweet and E. Ombler, *Cases of Controverted Elections* (London: S. Sweet, 1837), pp. 332–337.
9. *SC*, 4 July 1835, from K.J. Atton, 'Municipal and Parliamentary Politics in Ipswich,' p. 196.
10. *SC*, 4 July 1835. Elsewhere the ringing of parish church bells did not always convey so clear a political partisanship. In Exeter, for instance, the cathedral and parochial bells were rung to celebrate any high occasion. They were rung on the day of the nomination in 1841, before the poll had been taken (this coincided with the third anniversary of the queen's coronation) and, more strikingly, their ringing accompanied the reading of the poll in 1832, after a lone conservative had been defeated and two liberals returned. *TEFP*, 1 July 1841, 12 Dec 1832.
11. *IJ*, 19 May 1832.
12. *BM*, 1 Apr 1837; *BT*, 14 Aug 1847.
13. *NR*, 7 Dec 1832.
14. *NR*, 2 July 1841, 16 Apr 1841.
15. NAO, Acc # 12, 432/2: to Arthur Wells, 1842.04.27; NPLLSL, EC, 15 Apr 1841, reprinted from *NR*, n.d. Dissenting associations with the name Alliott are commemorated in Hertfordshire in Alliott House, the girls' house of Bishop's Stortford College (formerly the Nonconformist Grammar School),

founded in 2003 and named after the Congregationalist Revd Richard Alliott.

16. This was in turn followed with the singing of 'With a jolly full bottle'! At a meeting of the Exeter Central Conservative Association, three days earlier, the toasts had been 'Church and State' and 'The Bishop and Clergy of the Diocese.' The same toasts were proposed at a conservative dinner two-and-a-half years earlier, after the 1835 general election. Conversely, the toast that received the widest acclaim at the rival liberal dinner had been 'The People, the source of all power.' *TEFP*, 27 July 1837; 15 Jan 1835.

17. *TEFP*, 27 July 1837. Interestingly, and as discussed below, in Chapter 7, Kingdon was probably a Unitarian. That he should be a Unitarian and a conservative is curious. It may be significant that Kingdon identified Phillpotts as a legislator, not a churchman—as the bishop was exceptionally active in and out of the House of Lords.

18. As far away as Nottingham, the name Phillpotts was a byword for priestly privilege, intolerance, and meddling. *NR*, 4 June 1841.

19. *TEFP*, 27 July 1837.

20. *TEFP*, 29 July 1847. Divett also took the opportunity to rail against the priesthood, in a probable reference to the role of the cathedral in the close corporation prior to 1835, and decried other ecclesiastical abuses generally.

21. *NPB 1832*, p. x.

22. *TEFP*, 25 Apr 1844, 17 June 1841, 27 July 1837. As Anthony Trollope observed in chapter 3 of *Barchester Towers* [1857]: 'Some few years since, even within the memory of many who are not yet willing to call themselves old, a Liberal clergyman was a person not frequently to be met with.'

23. Additionally, dissenters were barred by religious tests from taking university degrees at Oxford and Cambridge. See below, Chapters 4, 5, 6, 7, 8, and 10.

24. While campaigning on behalf of Lord Lovaine in 1841, Gen. Mortimer appropriated military imagery, urging conservatives to stand at their guns, and 'to the utmost of their power, support and maintain the sacred and legitimate rights of the Altar and the Throne'. *TEFP*, 17 June 1841.

25. NAO, DD 1440/73.

26. NPLLSL, EC, 28 Nov 1832; *NR*, 7 Dec 1832; *NJ*, 1 May 1835, qtg *The Standard*; *DPB 1837*; NPLLSL, EC, 15 Apr 1841; *NR*, 30 Apr 1841; *TEFP*, 27 July 1837; 25 Apr 1844.

27. NAO, DD 1440/73, 1828; *NPB 1832*, p. vii; *NR*, 4 July 1834; NPLLSL, EC, 18 July 1834; NAO, DD 568/44/2, 26 July 1837; NPLLSL, EC, n.d. [1841]; *TEFP*, 1 July 1841.

28. 'As the nineteenth century progressed, it became obvious that Dissenters viewed the repeal of the Test and Corporation Acts as the beginning of a campaign to remove their grievances...,' T. Larsen, *Friends of Religious Equality*, p. 43.

29. *TEFP*, 15 Jan 1835. Lord John Russell (1792–1878), younger son of the 6th duke of Bedford, sat for London and a half-dozen other seats for nearly a half-century before being created 1st earl Russell in 1861. He formed parts of numerous Whig and liberal ministries, and was prime minister, 1846–1852 and 1865–1866. The *ODNB* writes that Lord John 'valued the historic role of the dissenting sects in the creation of a pluralistic and tolerant

society,' and he had involved himself energetically on behalf of repeal of the test and corporation acts, as well as other major liberal pursuits.

30. Reprinted in SufRO, GC, 1 Jan 1835.
31. *NR*, 4 Jan 1833.
32. Other goals, not uniquely favouring dissent, were advocacy of free trade and especially opposition to the Corn Law, elections by secret ballot, and an extended franchise. The *Review* did not judge universal suffrage realizable in 1841, and gave priority to practical and possible goals, 6 Apr 1841. Disenchanted with the vague language, too much open to various interpretations, the *Review* would acknowledge only five years later that 'The great political want of the present age is a *new Reform Bill*,' 10 July 1846.
33. *NJ*, 2 Jan 1835, qtg *Nottingham Mercury*. In a similar vein, Matthew Henry Barker (1790–1846) repeatedly castigated the *Journal's* editor, John Hicklin as 'Mr Chuchwarden Hicklin,' NPLLSL, EC, 1 July 1837. Barker's father 'had attained some distinction as a dissenting minister.' *ODNB*. Sir Robert Peel (1788–1850), 2nd Baronet, sat for Oxford University, Tamworth, and other seats in the first half of the nineteenth century, and was conservative prime minister briefly during 1834–1835 and again from 1841 to 1846. An ardent opponent to Catholic emancipation in the 1820s, he was ultimately persuaded to support the measure in 1829. The Tamworth Manifesto (Dec 1834) was his government's statement accepting cautious, necessary, and moderate reform in ecclesiastical and other matters. His positions on corn law repeal and, as we shall see in subsequent chapters, the Maynooth grant, split conservative ranks.
34. *NJ*, 2 Jan 1835.
35. Bor.B.G10/1/47, 8 Sep 1832; Bor.B.G10/1/61, 22 Sep 1832.
36. Indeed, W.W. Follett seemed to deny dissent, or any group, any special association with the movement, when he drew especial attention to the credentials of William Wilberforce as an abolitionist, a conservative, and a churchman. *TEFP*, 1 July 1841 (see also Chapter 7). In point of fact, Wilberforce had been a very independent tory, who favoured repeal of the test act and Catholic emancipation.
37. Evangelicals were, of course, important opponents of slavery but, like their leader Wilberforce, were a suspect minority in Anglicanism.
38. BRO, Bor.B.G10/1/74, 24 Nov 1832; BRO, Bor.B.G10/1/75, 26 Nov 1832; *NR*, 7 Dec 1832.
39. *TEFP*, 13 Dec 1832 (see Chapter 7).
40. *NPB 1832*, p. vii.
41. SufRO, GC, 1 Jan 1835.
42. NPLLSL, EC, n.d. [1841]. W.E. Gladstone's book *The State in Its Relations with the Church* had been published in 1838.
43. Qtd in *NJ*, 2 Jan 1835.
44. The liberal Quaker John Bright, in his various tirades linking clerical greed to the fortunes of West Indian planters (among other things), followed in the same tradition. See esp. DuRO, BC, 17 July 1843.
45. *DPB 1835; DPB 1837; BM*, 29 July 1837; *NR*, 12 Aug 1842.
46. NAO, DD.WR 42/18, 3 Mar 1838; NAO, DD.WR 42/19, 17 Mar 1838; NAO, DD.WR 42/20, 8 Apr 1838; NAO, DD.WR 42/21, 22 May 1838.
47. *DPB 1837*.

48. NPLLSL, EC, n.d [1841]; *TEFP*, 15 July 1847.
49. Thus K.J. Atton has written of Ipswich in 1833 and 1834, although the expression probably accurately applies to much of England, as well. 'Municipal and Parliamentary Politics in Ipswich,' p. 189.
50. The crisis can also be seen as a chapter in the long-running Irish question.
51. Daniel O'Connell (1775–1847), Irish nationalist known as the 'Liberator,' had founded the Catholic Association in 1823 as the chief instrument in the campaign for Catholic emancipation, which issue he forced in 1829, by being elected MP for County Clare the year before. O'Connell instructed fellow Irish MPs to cooperate with the liberal governments in the 1830s, and in the 1840s he agitated to repeal the act of union.
52. K.J. Atton, 'Municipal and Parliamentary Politics in Ipswich,' p. 189.
53. *TEFP*, 13 Dec 1832.
54. *IJ*, 15 Dec 1832.
55. *TEFP*, 13 Dec 1832 and passim.
56. *TEFP*, 27 July 1837.
57. *IJ*, 1 Dec 1832, 7 Dec 1832.
58. DuRO, n.d. [1833].
59. SufRO, GC, n.d. [1837 or 1839]; NPLLSL, EC, n.d. [1837].
60. *IJ*, 1832.12.07.
61. DuRO, n.d. [prob. after 17 Nov 1834].
62. As MP for Northumberland, Charles Grey (1764–1845) had introduced a bill for parliamentary reform as early as the 1790s, and in 1807 he resigned as foreign secretary because of the king's opposition to Catholic emancipation. As 2nd earl Grey, he led the whig opposition for much of the next quarter century, and as prime minister was responsible for the reform act and witnessed the abolition of colonial slavery and other reforms of the early 1830s. Grey resigned in 1834, and was succeeded by William Lamb (1779–1848), 2nd Viscount Melbourne, liberal prime minister briefly in 1834 and from 1835–1841, when his government fell to Peel's conservatives.
63. *IJ*, 1837.07.01; SufRO, GC, n.d. [prob. 1841].
64. BRO, Bor.B.G10/1/157, n.d. [1835]; *NJ*, 1 May 1835.
65. *NR*, 7 Dec 1832; *NPB 1832*, p. iii.
66. Addressing the electors of Nottingham, the Quaker Joseph Sturge stated that '[w]ith regard to the separation of Church and State, he wished to make a clear distinction between the Church Establishment,' which he opposed, 'and the Episcopal religion,' which he did not. *NR*, 5 Aug 1842.
67. *IJ*, 1 July 1837. This was the same expression, we shall see in the next chapter, the conservative F.D. Johnson was gratified to find no longer current in Durham in 1835. *DPB 1835*. The invective launched by John Bright against greed and splendour as often as not seemed directed at the Church of England itself rather than the privileges it enjoyed or the abuses it tolerated. Nor was it always clear whether the liberal *Durham Chronicle*, in labelling Arthur Trevor as 'the minion of corruption in its worst form' and '[t]he creature of an unprincipled, reckless, and despicable oligarchy,' intended to single out his aristocratic or his ecclesiastical patrons; *The Elector's Scrap Book*, p. 5. Indeed, on more than one occasion Bright alleged there was no real difference between the two.

68. In many ways, it seems more appropriate to describe the position and tone of the *Beacon* as 'Whig' than 'liberal.' Bedford really did not have a liberal newspaper until 1845, when the *Bedford News* (which described itself as radical) was launched. See also Chapter 6, note 4.

69. *BB*, 8 or 15 July 1837, extracted and reprinted in BRO, Bor.B.G10/1/138.

70. Ibid.

71. *DPB 1847*.

72. The United Committee had been established in 1833.

73. Events leading up to these acts do not appear to have generated much excitement in any of the five boroughs in review, although the liberal press in Nottingham and Bedford reported triumphantly on the first nonconformist marriages solemnized under the terms of the dissenters' marriage act. *NR*, 14 July 1837; *BM*, 29 July 1837. Opponents to the marriage act minimized or outright criticized the likely effects of the legislation, on religious and other grounds. A poem circulated in Nottingham condemned the measure largely because of the predicament in which it placed pregnant and disgraced young women who, because of the new legislation, could not marry until they were 21. NAO, DD.MI 58, 'On the New Marriage Act.' W.W. Follett questioned the wisdom of a marriage act in 1835, on the grounds it tended to separate religion from marriage altogether, and stopped short of outright condemning it two-and-a-half years later. *TEFP*, 8 Jan 1835; 27 July 1837. A third grievance, exempting dissenting chapels from the poor rate, had been realized in John Wilks's bill of 1833, which Grey's government supported. Wilks (c.1776–1854), radical MP for Boston (1830–1837), had been an avowed enemy of the test and corporation acts, and had earlier served as secretary of the Protestant Society for the Protection of Religious Liberty.

74. M.R. Watts, *The Dissenters*, vol. 2, p. 470.

75. The other unresolved grievance was non-anglican exclusion from taking degrees from Cambridge or Oxford.

76. T. Larsen, *Friends of Religious Eequality*, ch. 2; J.P. Ellens, *Religious Routes to Gladstonian Liberalism: The Church Rate Conflict in England and Wales, 1832–1868* (University Park, Pennsylvania: The Pennsylvania State University Press, 1994) p. 75.

77. T. Larsen, *Friends of Religious Equality*, p. 44.

78. *IJ*, 1 Dec 1832.

79. *NR*, 4 July 1834.

80. Ibid. This almost certainly means participation with the United Committee. The similarity of these tactics with those employed by the London Corresponding Society 40 years earlier, as well as the Committees of Correspondence in colonial America, is of course suggestive. It is particularly striking that organized dissent was willing to engage in such activities—after all, the actions of the LCS had been criminalized and the revolutionary tendency of the American bodies was unmistakable—while the rules of the Bedford Union Society, 'for the purpose of supporting and giving effect to the great cause of Parliamentary Reform' (BRO, Bor.B.G10/1/39, n.d. [June 1832]), strictly rejected any organization on a regional, let alone national, scale.

81. *IJ*, 20 Aug 1836.

82. Ibid.

83. *BM*, 1 Apr 1837.
84. *IJ*, 26 June 1847.
85. *NR*, 16 Apr 1841.
86. *NR*, 30 Apr 1841. Unfortunately, the bizarre circumstances of the looming election (for details, see Chapter 4, especially, note 84) do not permit confirmation in this respect.
87. *NR*, 16 Apr 1841.
88. NPLLSL, EC, 23 June 1837.
89. SufRO, GC, 1 Apr 1837.
90. *NR*, 18 July 1834.
91. J.P. Ellens, *Religious Routes to Gladstonian Liberalism*, p. 75. Use of the archaic term 'recusant'—with its evocative suggestion of the Catholic and protestant martyrs who refused the dictates of the Church of England in the heroic age of the 16th and 17th centuries—was of course intentional. Post-reformation era recusants had faced penalties ranging from fines to imprisonment to death.
92. T. Larsen, *Friends of Religious Equality*, pp. 46–47.
93. *NR*, 16 Apr 1841.
94. *TEFP*, 27 July 1837. The Revd Bartholomew probably referred to Follett's defense of the rate both in parliament and in his office as attorney general.
95. *TEFP*, 27 July 1837.
96. BRO, Bor.B.G10/1/137, 15 July 1837, repeated in *BM*, 22 July 1837; *TEFP*, 27 July 1837; *NR*, date misplaced, prob. 30 Apr 1841.
97. *TEFP*, 27 July 1837.
98. *NR*, 4 July 1834.
99. Ibid. As the *Review* further commented:

> The separation of Church and State was an entirely religious question on the part of the Dissenters, but it was a political question on the part of those who opposed them. The Dissenters disavowed any political authority on subjects which related to man's duty to God, or the welfare of his soul, and they disclaimed the right of any political persons to interfere in matters of religion.

100. *BN*, 30 Aug 1845.
101. *NR*, 14 July 1837.
102. *BM*, 5 June 1841. The bracketed text is illegible, but the gist of the sentence is plain.
103. *BM*, 5 June 1841.
104. *BM*, 26 June 1841.
105. *BN*, 6 Aug 1845.
106. *TEFP*, 3 July 1845.
107. Reprinted in *TEFP*, 3 July 1845.
108. *TEFP*, 3 July 1845.
109. *TEFP*, 10 July 1845.
110. Ibid.
111. Ibid.
112. Hockin and Palk abstained from the election held the next day. Earlier they had moved to nominate Sir Culling Eardley (1805–1863), 3rd Bart. Bacon

cast a vote for Duckworth. *TEFP*, 3 July 1845; 10 July 1845; 17 July 1845. Hockin's and Palk's sponsorship of Eardley (whose surname after 1847 was styled Eardley Smith) suggests the lengths to which anti-Catholicism drove English protestants in the mid-19th century. A 'lay leader of inter-denominational and international evangelicalism' and a thorough evan-gelical with French Huguenot and Jewish ancestry, Sir Culling remained technically a churchman, although his position on church and state relations made him anti-establishmentarian. *ODNB*. In this voluntarist capacity, he chaired the Anti-Maynooth Committee and Conference. As such he could attract liberal anti-monopolists, dissenters, conservative anglicans, and anti-establishmentarians of any stripe. For more on the implications of these curious combinations, see Chapter 8.
113. *BT*, 17 July 1847.
114. *DPB 1847.*

3 Religion and politics in a northeastern cathedral town: the case of Durham

1. *DC*, 4 May 1832, reprinted in *The Electors' Scrap Book* (Durham: George Walker, 1832), p. 4.
2. 'To the electors of the city of Durham,' signed W.C. Harland, 2 May 1832, reprinted in *The Electors' Scrap Book*, p. 3. Harland's father (whose surname had originally been Hoar or Hoare) was venerated among liberals in Durham as one 'who, through the night of Tory misrule,' was among 'the most unswerving supporters of those great principles which are at length recog-nized and acted upon in the government of the country.' Ibid, p. 4. Harland's liberal leanings may have been reinforced by his marriage to Catherine Shafto, daughter of Robert Eden Duncombe Shafto (1776–1848)—himself the son of Robert Shafto (c.1732–1797), celebrated as 'Bonny Bobby Shafto'— who sat briefly for the borough (1804–1806) as an ally of Fox and Grenville and an opponent to Pitt.
3. A long-term project at the BLNL, mentioned in Chapter 1, rendered access to certain relevant issues of the *Durham Chronicle* and *Durham Advertiser*— respectively, the borough's liberal and conservative newspapers—impossible, and circumstances at the Durham Record Office were not much better. Fortu-nately, the poll books published by George Walker junior of Sadler Street furnished detailed accounts of canvasses and nomination and other election proceedings, often including reprinted extracts from the *Chronicle* or the *Advertiser*. These, with the collection of contemporary handbills reposed in the in the Durham Record Office, adequately supplied the deficiency from 1835 onward. *The Electors' Scrap Book*, also published by Walker, provides coverage only through the end of July 1832.
4. *DA*, 29 June 1832, reprinted in *The Electors' Scrap Book*, p. 16. In fact, the actual poll, almost six months later, bore out this position: 362 electors voted for both liberals.
5. *DC*, 1 June 1832, reprinted in *The Electors' Scrap Book*, p. 5.
6. Technically the name was *Hill*-Trevor—his great grandfather, whose surname had originally been Trevor, took on an additional name, after inheriting the

property of his father's half-brother, Marcus Hill—but he was always referred to simply as *Trevor* during his career in Durham.

7. *DC*, 1 June 1832. A month earlier, on 4 May 1832, the *Chronicle* had accused Trevor of being the sitting member for Lord Londonderry rather than the electors of Durham. Both reprinted in *The Electors' Scrap Book*, pp. 4, 3. Additionally, the *Chronicle* called Trevor 'a groveller of the flesh-pots of Egypt,' and reported that he had been 'in a state of absolute inebriation' at the close of one day's canvass! *DC*, 15 June 1832; 29 June 1832. Trevor and the conservative *Durham Advertiser* dismissed all the allegations as lies, slander and 'a bundle of rubbish.' *DA*, 29 June 1832; 7 July 1832; all reprinted in *The Electors' Scrap Book*, pp. 11, 16, 18, 22.

8. The passage is from Scott's poem, *Harold the Dauntless* (1817), and is inscribed in the Prebends Bridge in Durham. The full inscription reads:

> Grey towers of Durham
> Yet well I love thy mixed and massive piles
> Half church of God half castle 'gainst the Scot
> And long to roam these venerable aisles
> With records stored of deeds long since forgot.

9. As Owen Chadwick has commented (*The Victorian Church*, vol. I, p. 39):

> Among all cathedrals...Durham [was, before the reforms of the late 1830s,] uniquely scandalous. With rich lands and coal Durham attained preeminent abundance among ecclesiastical corporations. Each of the twelve canons received about £3,000 a year; but the Dean was Bishop of St. David's, and among the canons were Bishops Gray of Bristol, Sumner of Chester and Phillpotts of Exeter. [Nor had] Durham...forgotten the eighth Earl of Bridgewater, who held a prebend for forty-nine years while he lived in Paris.

10. W.B. Maynard, 'Pluralism and Non-Residence in the Archdeaconry of Durham, 1774–1856: The Bishop and Chapter as Patrons,' in *Northern History*, 26 (1990): 437 and passim.

11. Ibid, pp. 440–441.

12. *DPB 1835*.

13. Qtd in *ODNB*.

14. *DC*, 1 June 1832, reprinted in *The Electors' Scrap Book*, p. 6.

15. Ibid, p. 6.

16. *DC*, 29 June 1832, reprinted in *The Electors' Scrap Book*, p. 17.

17. Fortunately, from this point onward, it is possible to appraise the candidates and their positions from their own words, rather than relying on necessarily limited, albeit colorful, depictions from the local press.

18. N. Gash, *Peel* (London: Longmans, 1976), p. 168.

19. *DPB 1835; DPB 1837*.

20. *DPB 1835*.

21. *DPB 1837*.

22. Ibid.

23. Ibid.

24. Ibid.
25. Ibid.
26. *DPB 1835.*
27. Ibid; *DPB 1837.*
28. *DPB 1835.*
29. Ibid.
30. *DPB 1837.*
31. Ibid.
32. *DPB* 1835; *DPB 1837.*
33. *DPB 1835.*
34. Ibid.
35. *DPB 1837.*
36. Harland's return in 1835 was without controversy, but was justifiably questioned in 1837. For one thing, he surpassed T.C. Granger by an exceedingly narrow margin, 373 *v.* 371, and the defeated candidate attributed this 'colourable majority of two,' with apparent justification, to impropriety during the canvass and at the polls, and other illegal actions. In one case, an elector who intended to vote for both liberals was muffled up and hurried off the hustings after having announced his vote only for Harland. Another case involved an elector who had been pressured into voting only for Harland, although that had not been his original choice. The returning officer refused to alter the records. Furthermore, at least 12 electors who had polled for Harland had changed their residences after the electoral register had been updated, and should therefore have been disqualified from voting. This could not have affected Trevor's place at the top of the poll, but would have knocked Harland from second place, giving Granger a safe majority of some dozen votes. *DPB 1837.* A petition against Harland's return was dismissed by a parliamentary committee of investigation, and he remained member for Durham until 1841, by which time he had become increasingly conservative, and refused to divide with the liberal government on a vote of no-confidence. A. Heesom, *Durham City and its MPs, 1678–1992* (Durham: Durham County Local History Society, 1992), p. 54.
37. Chapter 9 and the relevant tables of Appendix B.
38. Granger was no stranger to anti-slavery agitation in Durham: in 1830, he had delivered a speech 'for the purpose of petitioning Parliament for the abolition of colonial slavery,' which the office of the liberal *Durham Chronicle* reprinted the same year (Goldsmiths' Library, University of London).
39. *DPB 1837.*
40. DuRO, BC, 27 June 1841 (a) The controversy involved Sheppard's mistrust of certain of Lord Londonderry's dealings with Russia. Londonderry had been named ambassador to St Petersburg under Peel's first ministry, although violent opposition in parliament forced him to resign—evidently his enemies believed him too despotically inclined already! Sheppard, through the influence of his friend, 'the notorious Russophobe' David Urquhart (1805–1877), MP for Sheffield, apparently regarded himself as a champion of Poland. DuRO, BC, 27 June 1841 (b) Sheppard 'was not seen in Durham again[, which] precipitated challenges to a duel from [the other conservative candidate], and much correspondence and considerable hilarity in the press!' A. Heesom, *Durham City and its MPs*, p. 61.

41. Contemporaries occasionally styled the name Fitz-Roy or Fitz-roy.
42. 24 Mar 1843, reprinted in *DPB Apr 1843*. The colonists were not happy with FitzRoy, and he was superseded in the autumn of 1845. As it turned out, his lasting fame was neither as a politician or a colonial official, but rather as a hydrographer and 'the first professional weatherman, who founded the Met[eorological] Office in 1853, becoming director in 1855.' *The Times*, 5 Feb 2002. He is also celebrated as captain of the *Beagle* during Darwin's voyage in the Pacific. FitzRoy's uncle, Viscount Castlereagh (1769–1822), had cut his throat in 1822, and his predecessor as captain of the *Beagle* had shot himself in 1828. FitzRoy, in turn, committed suicide in 1865.
43. 25 Mar 1843, reprinted in *DPB Apr 1843*.
44. For Gisborne's candidacy in Nottingham, see Chapter 4. He had also stood unsuccessfully for Ipswich the previous June; see Chapter 5.
45. This was probably the same James Williams (1811–1868) who lived in nearby Sunderland and, with George Binns (1815–1847), had established the Mechanics' Institute, to promote the dissemination of radical and Chartist newspapers. (Binns's parents were Quakers.) In 1840, the two men had been found guilty of attending an illegal meeting, 'and were sentenced to six months imprisonment in Durham Gaol.' Robert Gammage, *History of the Chartist Movement, 1837–1854* [1894] (rev. ed.: London, 1969).
46. *DPB Apr 1843*.
47. Asa Briggs, *Victorian People: A Reassessment of Persons and Themes, 1851–1867* (Chicago: University of Chicago Press, 1954), p. 197. Later, W.E. Gladstone acknowledged Bright to be 'the great, standing, habitual bugbear of the country,' H.J. Leech (ed.), *The Public Letters of the Right Hon. John Bright*, 2nd edn [1895] (New York: Kraus Reprint Co., 1969), p. xxxii.
48. Williams withdrew from the race on the arrival of a suitable liberal.
49. 3 Apr 1843, reprinted in *DPB Apr 1843*.
50. This was in 1847. G.B. Smith, *The Life and Speeches of the Right Hon. John Bright, MP* (two vol.) (London: Hodder and Stoughton, 1881), pp. 288–289. As Briggs observed: 'The Quaker origins of his liberalism and his lifelong sympathy with nonconformity explain the religious core of his conception of government—liberal government grounded in responsibility, self-respect, and justice,' A. Briggs, *Victorian People*, p. 203.
51. The Revd Townsend had published *Accusations of History Against the Church of Rome* in 1825, a 'Life and Vindication of John Foxe' in 1836, and in 1850 would visit Rome, having undertaken a mission to convert Pope Pius IX to Protestantism! Curiously, his father (also George) had been an independent minister. *ODNB*.
52. *DPB Apr 1843*. Tellingly, in the 1839 session Dungannon had, while still the Hon. Arthur Trevor, opposed an Irish Municipal Corporation Bill, on the grounds it aimed to 'put down protestantism.' *ODNB*.
53. *DPB Apr 1843*.
54. Ibid.
55. Ibid.
56. Ibid.
57. Ibid.
58. Ibid.
59. G.B. Smith, *The Life and Speeches*, pp. 65–66.

60. He had left every elector a league tract.
61. Perhaps, Dungannon was echoing the argument, by now quite anti-quated, that all protestants must stand fast against potential Catholic onslaughts.
62. 4 Apr 1843, *DPB Apr 1843*.
63. He was elected a representative peer for Ireland in 1855.
64. DuRO, BC, 15 July 1843, reprinted in *DPB July 1843*.
65. DuRO, BC, 17 July 1843.
66. The queen had been married for more than three years, and there were no English princesses of a suitable age for marriage in the summer of 1843. Nonetheless, Bright's point is clear.
67. As Asa Briggs has written of John Bright: 'In his appeal to the electorate, and more dangerously to the nonelectors, he seemed to play deliberately on class antagonisms.' *Victorian People*, p. 199.
68. Two days after the first speech, and five days before the nomination, Bright addressed a crowd of perhaps twelve or thirteen hundred, and stuck more closely to the theme of free trade as the solution to economic instability. DuRO, BC, 19 July 1843.
69. DuRO, BC, 24 July 1843.
70. G.B. Smith, *The Life and Speeches*, p. 79.
71. DuRO, BC, 24 July 1843. A few years later (probably in 1847), John Bright observed that 'The Established Churches in England and Scotland had done little good and much evil....' G.B. Smith, *The Life and Speeches*, p. 119.
72. A. Heesom, *Durham City and its MPs*, p. 59.
73. 14 July 1843, reprinted in *DPB July 1843*.
74. DuRO, BC, 24 July 1843.
75. Of course, many factors conspired to make Durham a bastion of liberalism, so the *Advertiser* must have in mind the overweening influence of the cathedral in shaping the character of the borough.
76. In fact, there had probably been only two, although admittedly one was a dean of the cathedral. See the following note.
77. *DA*, 28 July 1843. It seems this tirade was against the votes of only two men, a dean of Durham and Mr Prebendary Ogle, who had cast their votes for Bright instead of Purvis. See *DPB July 1843*, and also G.B. Smith, *The Life and Speeches*, pp. 84–85. It is possible these two electors were protégés of Bishop Maltby (1770–1859). No doubt the *Advertiser* and likeminded conservative Anglicans considered his appointment by the liberal government a particularly bitter gall, especially after the cathedral's association with the conservatives, Henry Phillpotts and William van Mildert (1765–1836). For more on Phillpotts, see Chapter 2.
78. *DPB 1847*.
79. As Granger put it, 'I think there are exceptions to these principles of free trade....' *DPB 1847*.
80. *DPB 1847*.
81. This confidence was well founded, as we shall see in Chapter 9.
82. *DPB 1847*.
83. Ibid.
84. Ibid.
85. Ibid.

86. Ibid.
87. The poll was 595 for Granger, 519 for Spearman, and 450 for Wood.

4   Religion and politics in an industrial Midland city: the case of Nottingham

1. Three of these contests—one general election and two by-elections—were concluded without formal polls.
2. The precise meaning of the term 'to spencer' is unclear. Indeed, the *OED* (2nd edn) defines it inexactly as 'Meaning obscure,' with only a single citation, from 1831. However, in view of the contemporary popularity of a short waist-length jacket known as a spencer—derived from George John, 2nd earl Spencer (1758–1834), who presumably made the item fashionable—the present author judges it most likely that the term means to mutilate, by cutting off, with scissors or a knife or simply by pulling, the coattails from a formal coat or jacket: that is, to make it resemble a spencer. The suggestion has been taken under advisement by a Senior Editor of the *OED*, in consideration for a revised entry. Strikingly, all of the cited instances of the term are from Nottingham or nearby Newark, which suggests the abuse (or at least its name), was practiced only regionally.
3. *NR*, 2 July 1841, 20 July 1841.
4. *NR*, 2 July 1841.
5. R.E. Zegger, *John Cam Hobhouse: A Political Life, 1819–1852*. (Columbia: University of Missouri Press, 1973), p. 233.
6. The phrase was used by Lord Rancliffe on the nomination day, 26 Apr 1841, from *NR*, 30 Apr 1841. The liberal contender, G.G. de H. Laprent similarly called the alliance an 'unnatural union,' *NR*, 16 Apr 1841; reprinted in NPLLSL, EC, n.d. [Apr 1841].
7. NPLLSL, EC, 28 Nov 1832. There was evidently some controversy over which military rank applied to Gordon. The contemporary liberal press ridiculed Gordon and his supporters for preferring *Captain*—derived from his brief command of the schooner *St Lawrence*—but nonetheless used the distinction. Modern scholarship consistently identifies him as *Lieutenant*.
8. NPLLSL, EC, 28 Nov 1832. Of course, as we shall see in subsequent chapters, the appeal to the principles of 1688 was problematic, especially when used by conservatives.
9. *ODNB*.
10. NPLLSL, EC, 28 Nov 1832.
11. *NPB 1832*, p. xiv.
12. As noted, however, he supported a policy of 'adequate and just remuneration' for former owners. In an effort to deflect criticism from his advocacy of compensation, Gordon compared the plight of poor workers in England with that of black slaves in the West Indies. 'I am also an enemy, not only to black slavery, but also to that of the whites; do we hear nothing of slaves in our manufactories working 16 or 18 hours a day?' He opposed both conditions equally. *NR*, 7 Dec 1832; *NPB 1832*, p. xvi.

13. *NPB 1832*, p. xvi.
14. Close alliances between candidates were also judged to be acceptable in Ipswich; see Chapter 5.
15. Contemporary and even modern spellings of Gen. Ferguson's name vary. Specifically, the middle name is occasionally styled Craufurd, and the surname with an additional *s*: Fergusson. For purposes of consistency, the more conventional spelling is preferred here.
16. NPLLSL, EC, 5 Dec 1832 (a).
17. Ibid.
18. Wakefield was an influential whig-liberal electoral agent and prominent local manufacturer, R.G. Zegger, *John Cam Hobhouse*, pp. 232–233. At one point he was mayor of the city and counsellor for Park Ward, *NR*, 28 July 1837.
19. *NPB 1832*, pp. iv–vii.
20. Ibid, p. vii.
21. Ibid.
22. This statement met with cries of 'Jewish emancipation' from the assembled crowd.
23. *NPB 1832*, p. viii. General Ferguson's use of the term 'salary' in this instance (as opposed to 'living' 'benefice,' or even 'stipend') would probably have been regarded as questionable taste, if not outright offensive—implying a paid official of the state rather than a member of the clerical establishment. Other liberal candidates in other boroughs used the term under similar circumstances but, significantly, the one occasion it was used by a conservative candidate (J.N. Gladstone in Ipswich), it was used to refer not to Anglican priests, but to Roman Catholic ones!
24. Lord Rancliffe (1785–1850) had been MP for Minehead (1806–1807) and for Nottingham borough (1812–1820, 1826–1830). The name occasionally appears as Randcliff.
25. *NPB 1832*, p. ix.
26. He had previously sat for Knaresborough, Higham Ferrers, Malton, and Kilkenny County.
27. *NPB 1832*, p. xii.
28. Ibid, p. xiii.
29. Baron Duncannon would succeed his father as 4th earl of Bessborough on 3 Feb 1844.
30. NPLLSL, EC, 18 July 1834.
31. He also had abandoned his nonconformist antecedents: his father, Sir Benjamin Hobhouse (1757–1831) had been a Unitarian minister and an active critic of the test and corporation acts, and his mother was also a dissenter. As a young man, Sir John went to a Unitarian school in Bristol, but was able to conform to Anglican doctrine and graduate from Trinity College, Cambridge. The *ODNB* sums up his religious views this way: 'A sceptic when young, he became a comfortable churchgoer when older.'
32. *NR*, 25 July 1834.
33. Ibid.
34. Ibid. George Gill, who introduced Eagle on the hustings, was also a nonconformist.
35. *NR*, 25 July 1834.

36. Hobhouse polled 1591 votes and Eagle 566 votes.
37. This was the general election of 1835—discussed further in Chapters 2, 3, 5, 6, 7, and 10—made necessary by the king's dismissal of liberal government on the grounds of religious reform. In his address following the nomination, Gen. Ferguson drew specific attention to the circumstances of the late dismissal, and affirmed his commitment to the liberal tendencies of the ejected ministry.
38. He also had served as town mayor in 1832, and would again in 1837 and 1847.
39. *NJ*, 9 Jan 1835.
40. NPLLSL, EC, 30 June 1837, reprinted in *NR*, 7 July 1837.
41. Ibid.
42. NPLLSL, EC, 30 June 1837.
43. 'The martin has flown!' the *Nottingham Review* gleefully announced, 21 July 1837. They had predicted as much the previous week, 14 July 1837.
44. M. Stenton (ed.), *Who's Who of British Members of Parliament: A Biographical Dictionary of the House of Commons based on Annual Volumes of Dod's Parliamentary Companion and Other Sources* (vol. 1) (Hassocks: Harvester Press, 1976).
45. *NR*, 30 June 1837.
46. 29 June 1837, reprinted in the *NR*, 7 July 1837.
47. *NR*, 7 July 1837.
48. *NR*, 21 July 1837.
49. *NR*, 4 June 1841.
50. *NR*, 28 July 1837.
51. He would serve again as major in 1842. M.R. Watts identifies Wakefield as a Unitarian (*The Dissenters*, vol. II, p. 282), although the present author finds grounds as well for linking him to the Stoney Street congregation of General Baptists. See Chapter 9 for details of similar instances.
52. *NR*, 28 July 1837.
53. Ibid.
54. They polled 2056 and 2052, respectively, against 1397 and 1396 for Plowden and Twiss.
55. *NR*, 16 Apr 1841.
56. He had stood unsuccessfully for Ludlow the previous spring.
57. 15 Apr 1841; *NR*, 16 Apr 1841; reprinted in NPLLSL, EC, n.d. [Apr 1841].
58. Ibid.
59. Ibid. On an earlier occasion, Larpent had declared himself 'here to support the Rights of Conscience—that no man shall be compelled to pay to a Church, the doctrines of which he does not believe,' NAO, DD 568/45: 'The "Bearwood" Chronicle,' 24 Apr 1841.
60. *NR*, 16 Apr 1841; reprinted in NPLLSL, EC, n.d. [Apr 1841].
61. This alliance was first urged in a handbill dated 6 Apr 1841. Its poster, who signed himself simply 'an elector,' called on 'Tories and Radicals ... [to] "*Unite*," and free the Town from the domination of self-interested Whig leaders, who have too long had their sway ...,' NPLLSL, EC, 6 Apr 1841.
62. *NR*, 23 Apr 1841.
63. *NR*, 30 Apr 1841.

64. Of course, Walter conveniently forgot that Larpent was also insistent on this point.
65. *NR*, 30 Apr 1841.
66. Ibid.
67. Ibid.
68. The allegation further had it that Larpent's sole desire for a seat in parliament was to lure Britain into a war with France; *NR*, 23 Apr 1841, 30 Apr 1841. He also had Hungarian antecedents, on his mother's side, and had acquired the Hungarian title of Baron de Hochepied in 1819.
69. *NR*, 30 Apr 1841. It is striking that religious freedom was fundamental to Larpent's definition of what it means to be English.
70. NAO, DD 568/45: 'The "Bearwood" Chronicle,' 24 Apr 1841.
71. *NR*, 30 Apr 1841. Walter also drew attention to the spoliation of 'our Alfred-established Parishes' under the terms of the new poor law, NPLLSL, EC, n.d. [Apr 1841].
72. *NR*, 30 Apr 1841.
73. Ibid.
74. *NR*, 4 June 1841, 30 Apr 1841.
75. Reprinted in *NR*, 2 July 1841.
76. Of course, electors could often effectively force candidates into addressing other agendas, including religious ones. For outstanding examples of this, see the circumstances of the canvasses and post-election addresses in Exeter in 1841 and 1847; below, Chapter 7.
77. NAO, DD 568/46/2; also *NR*, 18 June 1841.
78. Hobhouse had been president of the board of control since 29 Apr 1835.
79. *NR*, 18 June 1841, 25 June 1841, 2 July 1841.
80. NAO, DD 568/46/2; also *NR*, 18 July 1841.
81. *NR*, 11 June 1841. The same assembly did not find it necessary to qualify in this manner their support for Larpent.
82. *NR*, 11 June 1841.
83. See also the open letter from Samuel Renshaw, hosier, to the framework-knitters of Nottingham: 'Sir John respects the religion of others as he values his own. . . .' He represents '[t]he Roman Catholic and the Dissenter as well as Churchman . . .,' reprinted in the *NR*, 25 June 1841.
84. Larpent and Hobhouse received 529 and 527 votes, and Walter and Charlton 144 and 142 votes. Charlton remained active on behalf of Nottingham's conservative interest, nominating Walter's son, also named John, for the borough at a by-election in April 1843. As the conservative press in Ipswich reported:

> The contest for [Nottingham] was terminated by the resignation of Messrs. Walter and Charlton, the Conservative candidates, at the opening of the poll. The riotous and lawless mobs which the Whigs had organized in the town and neighbourhood for the purpose of intimidating and abducing the Conservative electors,—the powerful influence of Treasury gold and Ministerial patronage, diffused by various conduits through all ranks and classes of Whig voters,—the coercion practised in every direction by the large manufacturers to put down the independent feelings of their workmen,—above all the dread of a civil conflict in the

streets between the honest portion of the labouring classes, and that dishonest and ruffianly portion of them which had been bought over to act against their fellows,—together with the apprehension that such conflict could only be terminated by calling in the military power to act against both parties, to the great danger of the peaceable, and to the almost certain loss of life among the disorderly, inhabitants of the town,—these circumstances formed some of the reasons which induced the Conservative candidates to come to the resolution which we have already described. Under the peculiar circumstances of the case there was no other course to be adopted, except an equally lavish expenditure of money with the other party, which could not fairly be expected from any person unsupported by the Government purse.

(*IJ*, 3 July 1841)

The *Nottingham Review* reported in less detail:

This outrage upon order, this renewal of the olden times, the days of terror, in 1792, when the Tories were the cock of the walk, provoked retaliation, and many other windows were broken on Wednesday night; the state of the town was extremely dangerous and alarming, and at ten o'clock the military were obliged to be called out, to show these infatuated men that property was not thus to be destroyed with impunity.

(*NR*, 18 June 1841)

85. *NR*, 2 July 1841.
86. *NR*, 5 Aug 1842.
87. F.S.W. Craig, *British Parliamentary Election Results, 1832–1885*, 2nd edn (Dartmouth: Parliamentary Research Services, 1989), identifies Sturge as a Chartist, but the designation of liberal, favoured in *Dod's*, or perhaps radical, seems more appropriate, as he admitted only four of the six points. He advocated manhood suffrage, equal electoral districts, the removal of property qualifications for MPs, and presumably the ballot, but rejected salaries for MPs, and was committed only to triennial parliaments. One source says that Sturge espoused five of the six points, R.E. Zegger, *John Cam Hobhouse*, p. 237.

   For more on Sturge, see Alex Tyrrell, *Joseph Sturge and the Moral Radical Party in Early Victorian Britain* (London: Christopher Helm, 1987).
88. *NR*, 5 July 1842.
89. This emphasis may be a barb at the late member, Larpent, whom *The Nonconformist* denigrated earlier that year as 'Opium-smuggling Larpent,' 11 May 1842, reprinted in NPLLSL, EC, n.d. [May 1842]. Larpent was an East India agent, partner in the house of Cockerell and Larpent, and chairman of the East India and China Association. Elsewhere Sturge condemned trade 'in articles ... not conducive to ... health and morals ...,' *NR*, 5 Aug 1842.
90. *NR*, 5 Aug 1842.
91. Ibid.
92. Ibid.
93. *NR*, 12 Aug 1842.
94. *NR*, 31 Mar 1843.
95. 29 Mar 1843, reprinted in *NR*, 31 Mar 1843.

96. *NR*, 31 Mar 1843.
97. Ibid.
98. He also was requisitioned the same week to stand for Durham; see Chapter 3. For Gisborne's unsuccessful bid for Ipswich (June 1842), see Chapter 5.
99. *NR*, 31 Mar 1843.
100. Ibid, 7 Apr 1843.
101. *NR*, 7 Apr 1843. It is unclear which Walter is indicated here. John Walter senior had recently been unseated, and the *Review* does not state how early his son, John Walter junior, was chosen as his intended successor.
102. *NR*, 7 Apr 1843.
103. Ibid.
104. *DPB Apr 1843*. His father, also named Thomas (1758–1846), was a central figure of the Clapham Sect, and close friend to Babbington and Wilberforce. *ODNB*.
105. In 1843, at least three dissenting congregations worshipped in buildings in Barker Gate. Congregationalists and Arminian Methodists shared Salem Chapel, and Baptist services were held at Bethesda Meeting (Paradise Place), both located in Barker Gate. Whatever the case, the political meeting described above was almost certainly in a nonconformist place of worship, evidently a prominent meeting house for liberal interests. A Quaker named Thomas Hopkins was mentioned as in attendance and contributing to the proceedings, *NR*, 31 Mar 1843.
106. *NR*, 7 Apr 1843. For details of Jerusalem's 'little congregation of six inhabitants [who,] with a few visitors, gathered illegally' under the auspices of the London Society for promoting Christianity among the Jews, see O. Chadwick, *The Victorian Church*, vol. I, pp. 189 ff.
107. *NR*, 7 Apr 1843.
108. *ODNB; McCalmont's; Who's Who of British Members of Parliament*.
109. *NR*, 7 Apr 1843.
110. Like his father, Walter junior was powerfully attached to Anglicanism, and on one occasion wrote that 'popery [was] not a fit religion for an Englishman.' *History of The Times*, 2.46, qtd in *ODNB*. Earlier flirtations with Tractarianism—which had briefly alienated father and son—had disappeared.
111. *NR*, 7 Apr 1843.
112. Gisborne gained 1839 votes, and Walter 1728.
113. Qtd in *NR*, 14 Apr 1843.
114. *NR*, 7 Apr 1843.
115. *NR*, 14 Apr 1843.
116. *NR*, 10 July 1846.
117. Ibid.
118. *NR*, 23 July 1847.
119. R.E. Zegger, *John Cam Hobhouse*, p. 238.
120. *NR*, 30 July 1847.
121. Ibid.
122. Evidently O'Connor was not alone in this opposition, and it was due to his influence that the ballot was struck off the final Charter, introduced in

1848. B.L. Kinzer, 'The un-Englishness of the secret ballot,' in *Albion*, 10, 3 (1979): 249.
123. *NR*, 30 July 1847; R.E. Zegger, *John Cam Hobhouse*, pp. 238–239.
124. *NR*, 30 July 1847.
125. Ibid. Indeed, before the poll, he had not even made a personal appearance in the borough since his unsuccessful stand more than four years earlier.
126. In London, the father succumbed to throat cancer the very day the son was first returned for Nottingham.
127. The return of Walter seems to have genuinely reflected the inclination of the Nottingham electorate, rather than merely to have expressed their dissatisfaction with an inactive liberal government: he continued to sit for the borough until 1859, when he stood as a liberal for Berkshire, whose seat he would hold for much of the next quarter century, until retiring from politics in 1885. But it is not so easy to judge the actual appeal of O'Connor. At any rate, insanity crept steadily upon him after 1847, he was committed to an asylum in 1852, and died of syphilis three years later.
128. *NR*, 30 July 1847.
129. *NJ*, n.d. [July 1842], qtd in R.E. Zegger, *John Cam Hobhouse*, p. 238.

5 Religion and politics in an East Anglian Port City: the case of Ipswich

1. SufRO, GC, 27 Sep 1832.
2. K.J. Atton, 'Municipal and Parliamentary Politics in Ipswich,' p. 169.
3. *IJ*, 1 Dec 1832.
4. Wason's actual given name was Peter, but he seems never to have used it in public life.
5. SufRO, GC, 30 June 1832 (a).
6. Ibid.
7. SufRO, GC, 30 June 1832 (b).
8. K.J. Atton, in his study of mid-nineteenth-century municipal and parliamentary politics in Ipswich, designates Goulburn an 'ultra-tory' ('Municipal and parliamentary politics in Ipswich,' p. 188), but this probably puts it too strongly. He had been a member of all tory governments in the period, and had consequently voted for Catholic Emancipation in 1829. Atton further ascribes intense anti-Catholicism as part of Goulburn's conservative appeal in 1832, although other evidence does not support this.
9. SufRO, GC, 27 Oct 1832 (a).
10. SufRO, GC, 31 Oct 1832.
11. Ibid.
12. SufRO, GC, 27 Oct 1832, 31 Oct 1832.
13. 24 Nov 1832, reprinted in *IPB 1832*.
14. 28 Nov 1832, reprinted in *IJ*, 1 Dec 1832, and *IPB 1832*.
15. 24 Nov 1832, reprinted in *IPB 1832*.
16. 28 Nov 1832, reprinted in *IJ*, 1 Dec 1832, and *IPB 1832*.
17. Ibid.
18. *IJ*, 15 Dec 1832.
19. Ibid.

20. The state of preservation of the relevant issue of the *Ipswich Journal* does not, however, permit perfect confidence in this respect; much of Morrison's speech was illegible, and it is therefore possible he addressed the topics of ecclesiastical income or slavery in the obscured lines of text.
21. The name occasionally appears as Seekkamp.
22. *IJ*, 15 Dec 1832; SufRO, GC, 1 Apr 1837.
23. K.J. Atton, 'Municipal and Parliamentary Politics in Ipswich,' p. 236.
24. *IJ*, 15 Dec 1832.
25. Ibid. Elsewhere Goulburn repeated the conviction that those 'principles [had] a tendency ... of destroying the altar and the crown'.
26. *IJ*, 15 Dec 1832.
27. 'The first subject in giving education to the poor' Goulburn stated, 'should be based on principles contained in the Bible....' *IJ*, 15 Dec 1832.
28. *IJ*, 15 Dec 1832.
29. Charles Mackinnon had stood as an official tory candidate for the borough in the previous four elections, but was cast off in 1832. Based on a printed address, his parliamentary career, and his address following the nomination, his principles were moderately conservative; he never explicitly engaged matters of the church or dissent. SufRO, GC, 6 Nov 1832; *IJ*, 15 Dec 1832.
30. Later in life Dundas changed his surname first to *Christopher* and later still to *Nisbet-Hamilton*.
31. SufRO, GC, 2 Dec 1834 (b).
32. K.J. Atton, 'Municipal and Parliamentary Politics in Ipswich,' p. 232.
33. Ibid, p. 191. All three points had been conceded in the Tamworth Manifesto, which had been reprinted in the *Ipswich Journal* [date misplaced; prob. 18 Dec 1835], and would have been familiar to Ipswich conservatives.
34. Indeed, K.J. Atton designates his position as ulta-tory as late as 1835, 'Municipal and parliamentary politics in Ipswich,' p. 232.
35. K.J. Atton, 'Municipal and Parliamentary Politics in Ipswich,' p. 232. Arthur Wellesley (1769–1852), 1st duke of Wellington, had opposed Catholic emancipation, but conceded the measure out of necessity as prime minister in 1829. His refusal to entertain any measure of parliamentary reform led to his government's downfall in 1830.
36. Qtd in K.J. Atton, 'Municipal and Parliamentary Politics in Ipswich,' p. 191.
37. *SC*, 13 Dec 1834.
38. Ibid.
39. K.J. Atton, 'Municipal and Parliamentary Politics in Ipswich,' p. 192.
40. *SC*, 13 Dec 1834. Conversely, his former constituents of St Ives, which lost a member and had many of its electors disenfranchised by the reform act—which Morrison had of course supported—judged his proclivities as too radical!
41. *SC*, 13 Dec 1834.
42. K.J. Atton, 'Municipal and Parliamentary Politics in Ipswich,' pp. 191–192.
43. *SC*, 3 Jan 1835.
44. 9 Jan 1835, reprinted in *IPB Jan 1835*.
45. Ibid.
46. At least one of the drafters of the petition, Robert Gill Ranson, was a Quaker. SufRO, GC, Apr or May 1835. See also K.J. Atton, 'Municipal and

Parliamentary Politics in Ipswich,' p. 194. Ranson was at one point a town alderman.

47. J.W. Sweet and E. Ombler, *Cases of Controverted Elections*, pp. 332–337. The charges against the conservatives' supporters ranged from bribery and illegal votes to various other improprieties that 'otherwise interfered with the freedom of the election,' p. 335.

48. The *ODNB* describes Broke as a 'fanatical protestant, [who] by special permission from the duke of Wellington...was allowed in 1829 to vote against the ministerial Roman Catholic Relief Bill.'

49. SufRO, GC, [18 June] 1835; K.J. Atton, 'Municipal and Parliamentary Politics in Ipswich,' p. 194.

50. His radical credentials were never again questioned in Ipswich, K.J. Atton, 'Municipal and Parliamentary Politics in Ipswich,' pp. 196, 234.

51. SufRO, GC, 26 June 1837.

52. *IJ*, 1 July 1837. He later represented the Inverness burghs (1840–1847).

53. He had unsuccessfully contested Colchester, for which his father had been an MP, in 1835.

54. SufRO, GC, 28 June 1837.

55. *Who's Who of British Members of Parliament*.

56. SufRO, GC, 28 June 1837.

57. *IJ*, 1 July 1837.

58. Ibid. The latter allusion is to Lambeth Palace, the London residence of the archbishop of Canterbury.

59. *IJ*, 1 July 1837.

60. Ibid.

61. Ibid.

62. Ibid.

63. Ibid. Herries had sat for Harwich since 1823.

64. K.J. Atton, 'Municipal and Parliamentary Politics in Ipswich,' pp. 199–200.

65. Ibid, p. 200. Its importance in Nottingham undoubtedly persisted at least until 1841.

66. Certainly it hurt the liberals more, since the act had been introduced and enacted under a liberal ministry. In Ipswich, this action alienated some of the working classes, who had previously formed part of the liberal interest, and induced them to turn to Chartist activity, K.J. Atton, 'Municipal and Parliamentary Politics in Ipswich,' p. 197. Chartist activity is often generalized as being irreligious or outright anti-religious, but the account of it in Ipswich and surrounding regions in Suffolk belies so straight-forward a dynamic. See note 100, below.

67. This was interrupted briefly between 1841 and 1842.

68. K.J. Atton, 'Municipal and Parliamentary Politics in Ipswich,' p. 203.

69. *IJ*, 18 May 1839.

70. K.J. Atton, 'Municipal and Parliamentary Politics in Ipswich,' p. 203.

71. SufRO, GC, n.d. [1839].

72. SufRO, GC, 2 July 1839.

73. SufRO, GC, 4 July 1839 (b).

74. K.J. Atton, 'Municipal and Parliamentary Politics in Ipswich,' p. 203.

75. Ibid, p. 223. According to *Trewman's Exeter Flying Post*, 'Sir Thomas Cochrane...had a quarrel with the electors of Ipswich touching some small

matter of account...' and, having been rejected by the conservatives of Exeter, ran in 1841 for Greenock. He was unsuccessful.

76. *IJ*, 26 June 1841.
77. *IJ*, 3 July 1841.
78. Both T.F. Buxton's mother and his wife belonged the Society of Friends, and the Quaker influence was important in shaping his abolitionist and other philanthropic views.
79. *IJ*, 26 June 1841.
80. SufRO, GC, 9 June 1841.
81. *IJ*, 3 July 1841.
82. *IJ*, 26 June 1841.
83. *IJ*, 3 July 1841.
84. *IJ*, 26 June 1841.
85. *IJ*, 26 June 1841.
86. Rennie, who is probably better remembered as a sculptor and patron of the arts than as an MP, was appointed governor of the Falklands shortly after the general election of 1847. Kelly was returned for Cambridge (1843–1847), and for East Suffolk (near Ipswich) after 1852.
87. For further details on Gisborne, see Chapters 3 and especially 4.
88. *EADT*, 21 Mar 1889. Thomas Gladstone concurred: 'a more stern interpretation of the Law, and a more severe application of it, has been administered in this instance than has ever yet deprived members of their seats...,' SufRO, GC, 9 Aug 1842. A contemporary handbill, signed Mopit and countersigned Filch, satirized the liberal petitioners, resolving 'That henceforth it shall not be lawful for any Elector to rejoice or make merry on the day of Election, and they are hereby commanded to look and conduct themselves demurely and with sanctity.' The bill continued in a similar tone, and ended with a resolution that inns, taverns, and all other places of merriment be closed during an election, and that parish clerks and insuring offices provide drinking water. SufRO, GC, 8 Aug 1842.
89. K.J. Atton, 'Municipal and Parliamentary Politics in Ipswich,' p. 209.
90. See chapter 4.
91. See Chapter 4.
92. 26 May 1842, reprinted in the *SC*, 28 May 1842.
93. K.J. Atton, 'Municipal and Parliamentary Politics in Ipswich,' pp. 209–210.
94. Ibid, pp. 242–243.
95. Ibid, p. 257.
96. Ibid, pp. 211–212.
97. SufRO, GC, 9 Aug 1842.
98. K.J. Atton, 'Municipal and Parliamentary Politics in Ipswich,' p. 212.
99. Subsequently he would stand for Tavistock (1843), Kilmarnock (1844), Plymouth (1846), and York (1848 and 1852)—in each instance without success. Vincent did not initially secure the enthusiasm of the Chartists of Ipswich, who preferred the prospects of Joseph Sturge, but allowed that, 'in default..., there can be no objection to Mr Vincent.' *SC*, 13 Aug 1843, qtd in Hugh Fearn, 'Chartism in Suffolk,' in Asa Briggs (ed.), *Chartist Studies* (London: Macmillan and Co. Ltd, 1959), pp. 166–167. It is striking that the Chartists should reject Vincent—a powerful orator whose credentials as a stanch champion of the cause had been confirmed through

two years' imprisonment—for a man of milder stamp who disclaimed the very label of Chartist and who was, as we have seen, an open Quaker. A year earlier, the Ipswich National Charter Association had backed John Goodwyn Barmby (1822–1881), the socialist and sometimes-communist who, after 1848, became 'one of the best-known [Unitarian] ministers in the West Riding of Yorkshire.' At the time of his association with the Ipswich NCA, Barmby favoured 'wearing his light brown hair parted in the middle after the fashion of the Concordist brethren.' *ODNB*. Such preferences, along with the prominent place of Robert Booley, a dissenter and chairman of the first meeting of he Ipswich Working Men's Association in December 1837, must bring into question any notion that hostility to religion was a necessary hallmark of Chartist opinion.

100. His programme was laid out in the *Suffolk Chronicle*, 13 Aug 1842, Hugh Fearn, 'Chartism in Suffolk,' p. 167. *See* also K.J. Atton, 'Municipal and Parliamentary Politics in Ipswich,' p. 211. Vincent usually attended meetings of the Society of Friends, although he was never a member. As a lay preacher, he frequently conducted services among free church congregations. *ODNB*.

101. In the event, George junior (1828–1876) became a writer and 'one of Charles Dickens's most valuable contributors' to *All the Year Round*. Dickens, *Letters*, iii, p. 239, from *DNB* (1st edn).

102. K.J. Atton, 'Municipal and Parliamentary Politics in Ipswich,' pp. 208–209. Even the designation of 'nominal liberal' is problematic. Nicholson attacked the '*Whigs of the present race of Whigs*,' also known as liberals, and 'offer[ed him]self as a BONA FIDE RADICAL.' He praised Peel's achievements in a mere six months as outweighing 'what the *Whigs ought to have done ten years since*,' and proposed entering the house of commons to support the prime minister in every good measure he undertook. SufRO, GC, Aug 1842. Nicholson apparently attributed the defeat in Nottingham of Joseph Sturge (1793–1859), a Quaker and liberal candidate in a recent by-election in Nottingham, to the united forces of whigs, tories, and '*the* COMBINATION OF THE DISSENTERS *with the Old Rotten Corporation*.' This rather bewildering proposition is the only indication of Nicholson's position on the role of church and dissent, besides a similarly vague appeal to Christianity, in his assertion that the new poor law was an 'ATHEISTICAL *Bill*...,' SufRO, GC, 1 June 1842.

103. *IJ*, 3 July 1847.

104. Ibid.

105. SufRO, GC, 5 Sep 1833.

106. SufRO, GC, 23 May 1839.

107. SufRO, GC, 1 July 1847; *IJ*, 3 July 1847.

108. SufRO, GC, 1 July 1847.

109. *IJ*, 3 July 1847; SufRO, GC, 1 July 1847.

110. *IJ*, 10 July 1847.

111. *IJ*, 26 June 1847.

112. Ibid.

113. The *Ipswich Journal* praised this action, observing that Gladstone had 'preferred...honour and consistency to the smiles of a prime minister,' 3 July 1847.

114. SufRO, GC, 21 June 1847, *IJ*, 26 June 1847.

115. The seminary was founded in 1795.
116. SufRO, GC, 21 June 1847; *IJ*, 26 June 1847.
117. Ibid.
118. 18 Dec 1845, qtd in K.J. Atton, 'Municipal and Parliamentary Politics in Ipswich,' p. 245.
119. 3 Aug 1847, reprinted in *IPB 1847*.
120. See especially the analyses in Chapter 8.
121. K.J. Atton, 'Municipal and Parliamentary Politics in Ipswich,' p. 247.
122. The position could also appeal the anti-Catholic streak some dissenters held. See Chapter 8 for a further discussion.
123. Adair held onto his seat until his defeat in 1874.
124. K.J. Atton, 'Municipal and Parliamentary Politics in Ipswich,' pp. 227–228.
125. Ibid, p. 216.
126. Ibid, p. 250.
127. N. Gash, *Reaction and reconstruction in English politics, 1832–1852* (Oxford: The Clarendon Press, 1965), p. 98.

6 Religion and politics in a Southern Midland Agricultural Town: the case of Bedford

1. The 6th duke of Bedford (1766–1839) wrote to his son, Lord John Russell, that a liberal and a conservative candidate had spent £28,000 between them in 1832, PRO 30/20/1C/155-6 (7 Dec 1834). A young woman wrote in her diary that riots associated with election proceedings kept ladies indoors in 1832, and that the 'windows of both inns were broken'; qtd in Isobel Thompson (ed.), 'Some Bedfordshire diaries—Catherine Young (later Maclear) of Bedford, 1832–45 & 1846,' in *Publications of the Bedfordshire Historical Record Society*, 40 (1960): 144–162. One candidate was threatened with personal harm in 1847, and avoided the nomination, and the while the mayor

   was engaged at [his] own risk in attempting to preserve the peace in another part of the Town, a mob destroyed all the front Windows in [his] House. To some[, he observed,] it may have afforded satisfaction to know that [his] Property has been damaged and the Females of [his] family terrified.... (*BT*, 7 Aug 1847; BRO, Bor.B.G10/1/177, 5 Aug 1847).

2. The successful petition charged that over 300 men who were not entitled to the franchise had nonetheless voted. BRO, Bor.B.G10/1/158, n.d. [1837].
3. Certainly there is grist for the mill of suspicion of sour grapes, for instance in the case of 1837, when the liberals, who in previous elections had run two candidates against a single conservative, and now found the tables reversed, complained of unfair competition and disturbance of the borough's peace by an unnecessary contest.
4. Indeed, into the 1830s and 1840s, candidates and constituents alike in Bedford seemed to have preferred the older labels of 'tory' and 'whig' which, in other districts, had been largely superceded by the more modern 'conservative' and 'liberal.'
5. He had beat out Lord John Russell by a single vote.

6. William Whitbread's father, Samuel (c.1764–1815), had been MP for Bedford from 1790 to 1815, as had his grandfather, also Samuel (1726–1796), with only a brief hiatus, from 1768 to 1790. Thus by 1832, some member of the house of Whitbread had served as MP for the borough for nearly 60 of the previous 65 years.

    William's younger brother, yet another Samuel (1796–1879), had been MP for Middlesex, 1820–1830.

7. BRO, Bor.B.G10/1/40, 3 Sep 1832.

8. Although this does not necessarily follow—for example, some 20 ultras voted for Catholic emancipation in 1828, and afterwards, a large number of evangelical dissenters regularly opposed concessions to Catholics.

9. BRO, Bor.B.G10/1/40, 3 Sep 1832.

10. BRO, Bor.B.G10/1/77, 4 Dec 1832.

11. Ibid. Final agreement on the Dutch–Belgian frontier was only settled with the Treaty of London (Apr 1839), by which Britain and other signatory powers guaranteed Belgian independence. Ironically, Capt. Polhill's fears were borne out, although not as he imagined them, 75 years after the treaty.

12. BRO, Bor.B.G10/1/77, 4 Dec 1832.

13. BRO, Bor.B.G10/1/112a, 20 Nov 1834.

14. BRO, Bor.B.G10/1/50, 11 Sep 1832. Although his position was not overtly radical in 1832, it became more so subsequently, when he added the ballot to his appeal.

15. BRO, Bor.B.G10/1/50, 11 Sep 1832.

16. BRO, Bor.B.G10/1/69, 30 Oct 1832.

17. Ibid.

18. BRO, Bor.B.G10/1/50, 11 Sep 1832.

19. BRO, Bor.B.G10/1/74, 24 Nov 1832; Bor.B.G10/1/76, n.d. [Nov or Dec 1832].

20. See also Crawley's comments from the hustings during the 1837 campaign. *BM*, 29 July 1837.

21. BRO, Bor.B.G10/1/81, 12 Dec 1832.

22. BRO, Bor.B.G10/1/116, 21 Dec 1834.

23. Electoral proceedings in Bedford and the place of religion in them may be examined with greater clarity from the 1837 contest onwards. The Bedfordshire Record Office has no collection of provincial newspapers for the period 1832–1835, and a project at the BLNL (Colindale) made relevant issues unavailable. Consequently the Record Office's collection of election handbills, posters, and so on—which spans much of the nineteenth century and all of the period 1832–1847—proved indispensable.

24. *BM*, 1 Apr 1837.

25. BRO, Bor.B.G10/1/127, 28 June 1837; reprinted in *BM*, 8 July 1837.

26. BRO, Bor.B.G10/1/137, 15 July 1837; reprinted in *BM*, 22 July 1837.

27. Ibid.

28. *BM*, 22 July 1837.

29. Ibid.

30. Ibid.

31. BRO, Bor.B.G10/1/128, 30 June 1837; reprinted in *BM*, 8 July 1837.

32. Ibid.

33. BRO, Bor.B.G10/1/129, 1 July 1837; reprinted in *BM*, 7 July 1837.

34. *BM*, 22 July 1837.

35. *BM*, 29 July 1837. It is striking that Stuart equated the country, and perhaps full citizenship, with Anglicanism. See also J.E. Gordon in Nottingham in 1832.
36. Curiously, both Stuart's nominators were medical men. He was introduced on the hustings by Nicholas Fitzpatrick, a physician.
37. *BM*, 29 July 1837.
38. Ibid. Though Polhill did not elaborate, his position went back to 1688 and the argument that only protestant solidarity could resist the Catholic threat from without. See also Chapters 4 and 5.
39. *BM*, 29 July 1837. Cf. the previous note. Palgrave would later serve as mayor of Bedford, in 1849 and 1850.
40. *BM*, 29 July 1837.
41. BRO, Bor.B.G10/1/144, 26 July 1837; reprinted in *BM*, 29 July 1837.
42. Ibid.
43. *CIP*, 29 July 1837, extracts reprinted as a handbill, BRO, Bor.B.G10/1/146, n.d. [July or Aug 1837]); also reprinted in *BM*, 5 Aug 1837.
44. Green had earlier been an alderman and had served as mayor of Bedford in the first three decades of the century. Barnard would serve the same office in 1854, and sat as MP for the borough, 1857–1859.
45. *CIP*, 29 July 1837, extracts reprinted as a handbill, BRO, Bor.B.G10/1/146, n.d. [Aug or Sep 1837]; also reprinted in *BM*, 5 Aug 1837.
46. Ibid. The *Independent* further alleged that other electors—for example, Alexander Sharman, the agent of Lord Charles Russell and future mayor of the borough, who withheld his vote in 1837—had behaved in an ungrateful and inconsistent manner. As mayor of the borough, in 1847, Sharman would announce 'that I am in principle an avowed, a decided, an uncompromising Whig,' BRO, Bor.B.G10/1/177, 5 Aug 1847.
47. BRO, Bor.B.G10/1/144, 26 July 1837, reprinted in *BM*, 29 July 1837. Cf. Crawley's sentiments with the expressions of John Bright on the same matter, Chapter 3.
48. *BM*, 29 July 1837. The *Mercury* also reports that, on the occasion of the chairing, Stuart referred to 'those d——Whigs....'
49. BRO, Bor.B.G10/1/158, n.d. [1837]. G.P. Livius (c.1793–1856), brother of the playwright Barham John Livius (1787–1853), and occasional chairman of the Bedford committee of whigs and president of the Bedford whig benefit club, may have been a Moravian. If so, his politics were somewhat anomalous; see Chapter 9, note 33.
50. 5 June 1841; reprinted in *BM*, 12 June 1841.
51. *BM*, 5 June 1841.
52. Rigby Wason, MP for Ipswich, who reluctantly admitted having not always regarded the church with its due respect, is a curious exception; see Chapter 5.
53. See Chapter 8 and Appendix A, as well as Chapter 2, which discuss local nonconformist organization in this election.
54. The *Bedford Mercury* mentioned specifically Messrs Woodroffe, Crisp, and Lovell; 5 June 1841. Mr Forster may also have been a nonconformist.
55. *BM*, 19 June 1841.
56. Indeed, sections of the handbill issued in 1841 duplicate *verbatim* the text of the 1837 address. BRO, Bor.B.G10/1/166, 1 June 1841, reprinted in *BM*, 5 June 1841. Cf. BRO, Bor.B.G10/1/129, 1 July 1837, reprinted in *BM*, 8 July 1837.

57. BRO, Bor.B.G10/1/166, 1 June 1841, reprinted in *BM*, 5 June 1841.
58. *BM*, 3 July 1841.
59. *BN*, 6 Aug 1845. The *Bedford News* would draw heavily from *The Nonconformist* hereafter, and advertise publications such as *The Dissenter's Plea for His Nonconformity*.
60. *BN*, 30 Aug 1845. See Chapter 2, note 69 for more on the editorial tone of the *Bedford News*.
61. *BN*, 30 Aug 1845.
62. His original surname had been Calvert but, on inheriting the property of his cousin, adopted the name Verney. As member for Buckingham, Verney was outspoken in his support for abolitionism, full free trade, dissenters' admission to the universities, Jewish disabilities, Irish Church disestablishment, and more. *ODNB*.
63. BRO, Bor.B.G10/1/173, 8 July 1847.
64. Ibid.
65. 13 July 1847, reprinted in *BT*, 17 July 1847.
66. Ibid.
67. Ibid, 17 July 1847, 14 July 1847.
68. Ibid. This last statement, which concluded Stuart's handbill, was a pointed barb at Sir Harry Verney's pretension to represent borough. Verney had ended his handbill, issued the previous day, expressing his pleasure that his own home in Buckinghamshire was connected by rail to Bedford, thus permitting him the opportunity to visit the latter constituency regularly.
69. 9 July 1847, reprinted in *BT*, 10 July 1847, 16 July 1847, 24 July 1847.
70. This is most likely George Peter Livius (for whom see note 49), although it could possibly be his brother, Barham J. Livius. George was at various times believed to aspire to the borough's representation in parliament.
71. *BT*, 7 Aug 1847. Later in his career, Verney would support the disestablishment of the Church of Ireland, *ODNB*.
72. In other respects, Stuart's attention to parliamentary duty appears to have been slightly higher (at 40 per cent) than the average revealed in Appendix A.2 and analysed in Chapter 8.
73. He was a patron of five livings.
74. *BT*, 7 Aug 1847. This may refer to his adventures earlier in life, in South America, which included a chance encounter with an obscure young Catholic priest he would meet later in life as Pope Pius IX.
75. *BT*, 7 Aug 1847.
76. BRO, Bor.B.G10/1/174, n.d. [3 Aug 1847].
77. BRO, Bor.B.G10/1/178, 11 Aug 1847; reprinted in *BT*, 14 Aug 1847.
78. *BT*, 7 Aug 1847.
79. Ibid.

7   Religion and politics in a Southwestern City: the case of Exeter

1. Other nineteenth-century scions of the Buller line sat for North Stafford and South Stafford. Data compiled from G.P. Judd, *Members of Parliament, 1734–1832* (New Haven: Yale University Press, 1955) and *McCalmont's*.

2. This was J.W. Buller's maternal grandfather, William (1735–1800), bishop of Exeter, 1792–1796. The other late member, L.W. Buck (1784–1858), incumbent since 1826, declined to contest Exeter in the 1832 election, citing parliament's decision for Catholic emancipation, in 1829, as setting politics on the downward course they had followed since. *TEFP*, 6 Dec 1832. Later he would sit for North Devon, 1839–1857.
3. Indeed, the *ODNB* calls Follett 'the greatest advocate of his generation.'
4. *TEFP*, 13 Dec 1832. Dr Pennell was a substantrial landowner in South Cheriton, some nine-and-half miles west of Exeter.
5. Kennaway served as mayor of the city three times.
6. *TEFP*, 13 Dec 1832.
7. Ibid.
8. Ibid.
9. Ibid.
10. Ibid.
11. Ibid.
12. Ibid.
13. Ibid.
14. Exeter is a case in point of the limited impact of municipal reform on southern corporations:

> Liberals and Conservatives won an equal number of council seats, but the Liberal contingent was reduced by one when a Quaker declined to take the qualifying oath . . ., and the Conservatives went on to fill 11 of the 12 aldermanic seats with their supporters.
>
> (M.R. Watts, *The Dissenters*, vol. 2, p. 473)

15. The corporation of Nottingham was an exception, and had been for over a century.
16. See Chapter 2 for a discussion of the national importance of municipal reform for dissent.
17. *TEFP*, 13 Dec 1832.
18. Ibid.
19. Contemporary accounts—for example, *Trewman's Exeter Flying Post*—have Divett's poll as 1120. Curiously, Divett's statement after the poll established as the priorities of the new parliament, first, the war with Holland and, second, national expenditure. He spoke in detail on each of these themes, and said nothing on ecclesiastical affairs or dissent.
20. 16 Dec 1834; reprinted in *TEFP*, 25 Dec 1834.
21. *TEFP*, 25 Dec 1834.
22. Ibid.
23. Ibid.
24. Ibid. Buller had, however, been brought before the public eye the previous week, when he defended himself against a rumour circulating in Exeter, that he had, in the House of Commons, stated that the scale of wages paid to labourers and mechanics well surpassed the level necessary for their and their families' maintenance. In response, 192 inhabitants of the parish of Crediton asserted that Buller had '*always paid more than the accustomed rate of Wages to [his] Labourers*, and ha[d] to the utmost of [his] power,

endeavoured to ameliorate the condition of the Poor in the Parish.' Thus, *ipso facto*, Buller, too, drew attention to his service and commitment to local concerns. 10 Dec 1834; reprinted in *TEFP*, 25 Dec 1834.

25. Tyrell would later serve on the corporation board, holding office as judge and treasurer. The name occasionally appears with Tyrrell, and the family may have had Quaker associations.

26. *TEFP*, 1 Jan 1835.

27. Ibid.

28. Ibid.

29. The Marriage Act of 1753 (26 Geo. II. c.33) made exceptions for Jews and Quakers.

30. *TEFP*, 8 Jan 1835.

31. Perhaps in part because of these ambiguities, the *ODNB* persists in labelling Buller a whig rather than a liberal, long after the former designation had become largely obsolete in British political discourse.

32. *TEFP*, 8 Jan 1835.

33. Edward Stanley (1799–1869), eldest son and heir to the 13th earl of Derby, Sir James Graham (1792–1861), the 1st earl of Ripon (1782–1859), and the 5th duke of Richmond (1791–1860) were aristocratic members of Grey's government who had resigned earlier in May chiefly because of the prime minister's proposals to appropriate Irish church funds for secular purposes. Out of government, they constituted the core of the short-lived 'Derby Dilly,' which sought to steer a course between what they perceived as the increasing radical turn of the liberal party (due especially to the influence of Lord John Russell) and the intransigent Toryism of the conservatives.

34. 8 Jan 1835; reprinted in *TEFP*, 15 Jan 1835.

35. In 1839 he made an unsuccessful bid in a by-election for North Devon, for which constituency he was ultimately returned in 1857, and represented until his death eight years later.

36. Follett's handbill was posted on 27 June 1837, and Divett's on 29 June 1837; both were re-printed in the *TEFP*, 6 July 1837.

37. *TEFP*, 6 July 1837.

38. *TEFP*, 20 July 1837. Tellingly, his first significant speech in the commons as member for Exeter had been on Lord John Russell's Irish church motion. *ODNB*.

39. *TEFP*, 27 July 1837.

40. Other champions of conservative politics and a strong association of church and state, in Nottingham and Ipswich, did not hesitate to make the connexion explicit.

41. *TEFP*, 27 July 1837.

42. Ibid.

43. Ibid.

44. Follett had suffered tuberculosis for more than a decade, and *The Times* described him as having a 'feeble constitution' (30 June 1845).

45. *TEFP*, 27 July 1837.

46. Ibid.

47. Ibid.

48. As MP for Wigantownshire (1830–1837), Sir Andrew Agnew (1793–1849), 7th baronet, led the charge in the House of Commons to secure the goal of

the Lord's Day Society: to prohibit 'all open labour on Sunday, excepting works of necessity and mercy.' *ODNB*. The measure Divett supported, proposed by John Sayer Poulter esquire (d.1847), liberal MP for Shaftesbury (1832–1838), claimed to be less ambitious, aiming only to suppress trade on Sunday—although critics argued it went a good deal further. *Hansard*, 3rd ser., 25 (18 July 1834): 194.

49. *TEFP*, 27 July 1837.
50. T. Larsen, *Friends of Religious Equality*, pp. 189ff.
51. The present author is grateful to Professor Timothy Larsen, of Wheaton College, Illinois, for clarifying dissenting attitudes on capital punishment— he describes them as probably 'enthusiastic (albeit ideologically soft)'—and supporting this interpretation of Divett's agenda.
52. *TEFP*, 27 July 1837.
53. In 1834, it will be recalled—and in keeping with the moderate reform proposed in the Tamworth Manifesto—Follett had expressed cautious enthusiasm for a dissenters' marriage bill.
54. Ibid.
55. Ibid.
56. Perhaps Divett was somewhat exaggerating his youth: in fact he was 39 or 40 years old.
57. *TEFP*, 27 July 1837.
58. Ibid. The reference is to Edward Stanley (1779–1849), who had been installed as bishop earlier that year. A thoroughgoing reformer in ecclesiastical and other matters, Bishop Stanley espoused several projects 'which brought together on neutral ground churchmen and nonconformists.' *ODNB*.
59. *TEFP*, 27 July 1837.
60. At least one of the signatories to the statement, the Revd Dr Payne, was a nonconformist minister. Both statements were reprinted in *TEFP*, 17 June 1841.
61. Reprinted in *TEFP*, 17 June 1841.
62. *TEFP*, 17 June 1841. According to the *Ipswich Journal*, it was speculated, as late as the second week of June, that one of the Barings, a politically active family in the southwest and particularly Devon, would stand with Follett for the conservative interest, 12 June 1841.
63. 10 June 1841; reprinted in *TEFP*, 17 June 1841. In fact, Lovaine's credentials as a 'queen and church' conservative would become questionable—at least in the latter respect—after 1845 when, upon marriage, he adopted the beliefs (which he held for the rest of his life) of the millenarian Catholic Apostolic church. His obituary note in *Illustrated London News* reported simply 'he was a nonconformist' Qtd in *ODNB*.
64. *TEFP*, 17 June 1841.
65. Ibid.
66. Ibid.
67. Ibid.
68. Ibid.
69. Ibid.
70. Ibid.
71. Ibid.

72. Ibid.
73. Ibid.
74. These are Divett's words, before a body of liberal supporters. *TEFP*, 17 June 1841.
75. *TEFP*, 17 June 1841.
76. Ibid.
77. Ibid.
78. Kennaway would later serve as borough and country distributor for the revenue office.
79. *TEFP*, 1 July 1841.
80. Ibid.
81. William Huskisson (1770–1830) had, as liberal-tory president of the board of trade (1823–1827) under Lord Liverpool, taken steps in the direction of free trade.
82. *TEFP*, 1 July 1841. Philanthropist, MP, and evangelical reformer, William Wilberforce (1759–1833) was, for nearly half a century, one of the leading advocates in the campaign to end slavery in the British empire.
83. See Maj. Evans Bell, *Memoir of Gen. John Briggs* (n.d. [before 1887]).
84. He had complained of undue exhaustion during both the 1837 and 1841 canvasses.
85. This may have been the same Samuel Maunder (1785–1849), the editor of reference works, whose family hailed from north Devon. *ODNB*.
86. *TEFP*, 25 Apr 1844.
87. The phrasing is Robert Follett's, one of Sir William's brothers.
88. *TEFP*, 25 Apr 1844.
89. Ibid.
90. Moore had earlier been a member of the Irish anti-slavery society.
91. 30 June 1845; reprinted in *TEFP*, 3 July 1845.
92. *TEFP*, 10 July 1845.
93. For example, the same idea was expressed only a little less directly by Gen. Ferguson in Nottingham in 1832. Such language is also a consistent (and early) expression of what Prof Larsen identifies as the overarching political goals of dissent in the years immediately after the present study—that is, the period between the general elections of 1847 and 1867. Of this period he argues that, motivated by principle and informed by biblical and theological convictions, nonconformists at mid-century were determined to create a free, just and equal England. T. Larsen, *Friends of Religious Equality*. Larsen suggests these sentiments are best associated with the later period, but the same claim—that is, the repeal of the test and corporation acts would bring 'civil equality'—had been a chief argument for the repeal of those acts from the beginning of the century.
94. *TEFP*, 10 July 1845.
95. Ibid.
96. Ibid.
97. Ibid.
98. Both reprinted in *TEFP*, 22 July 1847.
99. *TEFP*, 29 July 1847.
100. Ibid.
101. Ibid.

102. Ibid. In fact the repeal of the Corn Law was a belated move by the late conservative government, and probably had little effect in Ireland.
103. Carew was appointed JP the next year.
104. *TEFP*, 29 July 1847. This seems to have been the same Sam Kingdon who was an ironmonger and a Unitarian, and had been elected by conservatives as first mayor of the reformed corporation, M.R. Watts, *The Dissenters*, p. 473. However, another Samuel Kingdon, roughly contemporary and living around Exeter, had graduated from Cambridge, so was presumably an Anglican.
105. *TEFP*, 29 July 1847.
106. Ibid. Lionel de Rothschild (1808–1879) was eldest son to Nathan Mayer Rothschild (1777–1836), and had succeeded as head of the family's banking business after his father's death. In 1847, he was elected to the House of Commons as liberal member for the City of London, but was barred from taking his seat on technical grounds mentioned above. He stood and was elected a half-dozen times before finally entering parliament more than a decade later. 'However, having achieved his aim of advancing the Jewish cause by entry into parliament, Rothschild never spoke in the Commons during his entire parliamentary career.' *ODNB*.
107. *TEFP*, 29 July 1847.
108. Ibid.

8 Evidence of partisan alignment in parliament, 1833–1847

1. D.E.D. Beales, 'Parliamentary Parties and the Independent Member,' in R. Robson (ed.), *Ideas and Institutions of Victorian Britain* (London: Barnes & Noble, 1967), pp. 17, 10–19, passim. See also D.H. Close, 'The Formation of a Two-Party Alignment in the House of Commons between 1830 and 1841,' in *English Historical Review*, 84 (1969): 257–277.
2. I. Newbould, 'The Emergence of a Two-Party System in England from 1830–1841: Roll Call and Reconsideration,' in *Parliaments, Estates and Representation*, 5, 1 (1985): 25–31.
3. A.V. Mitchell, *The Whigs in Opposition, 1815–1830* (Oxford: Clarendon, 1967).
4. I. Newbould, 'The Emergence of a Two-Party System in England': 26.
5. Additionally, this chapter analyses voting record for MPs from Brighton. It was originally intended that this study would examine that borough, as well, although its inclusion was not possible. Nonetheless, certain data from Brighton were collected, and are used. In a sense, Brighton can be seen as a foil, permitting us to see if larger numerical and statistical patterns exist, even if they are not confirmed by the more conventional historical documentation.
6. This represents divisions from July 1838.
7. I. Newbould, 'The Emergence of a Two-Party System in England': 26.
8. Viscount Dungannon and T.C. Granger in Durham and Edward Divett in Exeter all drew especial attention to their exemplary records of attendance and participation, in contrast to other MPs, who were more lax in their sense of duty. Handbills in Nottingham blasted Horace Twiss and John Walter

senior for their rare attendance and careless attention to parliamentary matters. Chaytor also was criticized in Durham for neglecting his duties.

9. See the discussion of Sir Gilbert Heathcote (1773–1851), D.E.D. Beales, 'Parliamentary Parties and the Independent Member,' p. 11.

10. D.E.D. Beales, 'Parliamentary Parties and the Independent Member,' p. 17.

11. Another fairly obvious fact from Appendix A is that, although the combined total remains constant at 12, the distribution of MPs above and below the heavy line varies from parliament to parliament and, indeed—after certain by-elections—within an individual parliament. The ratios, it might be pointed out, broadly reflect the distribution of seats in the commons: very strongly liberal after 1832, weaker thereafter until nearly balanced between 1837 and 1841, and then in the hands of the conservatives.

12. The figure is actually 870 but, for the purpose of the analysis, it was most meaningful to include MPs who either paired off (a total often) or served as tellers (a total of eight) on particular divisions as casting definitive votes with the sides for which they paired off or served as tellers.

13. Notably, these ratios are within a few percentage points of those of the aggregate data, given above.

14. The breakdown of Polhill's (and the other 35 candidates') + votes, − votes and 0 votes is in Appendix A.1.

15. The actual numbers, from Appendix A, are 49 conservative and five liberal votes; Polhill did not vote on 146 divisions.

16. This was because, most of the time, the sample of conservative MPs was three and the liberals nine.

17. On 31 further divisions, he did not vote at all.

18. This division is fairly representative of the House of Commons at the time. After the general election of 1837, the liberal ministry and its radical and Irish allies had a majority of hardly more than 30 out of a house of 658 members. By the spring of 1839, the ministry won what was in effect a vote of confidence, on the suspension of Jamaica's constitution, by a mere five votes, thus setting the stage for the 'bedchamber crisis.' By the end of the parliament, support for Melbourne had dwindled so low that the ministry lost a vote of confidence on repeal of the Corn Law. The general election of 1841 returned 367 conservatives and 291 liberals.

19. Cf. Table 8.3 and the relevant entries for Table 8.4.

20. I. Newbould, 'The Emergence of a Two-Party System in England': 29.

21. The present analysis considers 68 divisions, or 816 possible votes: 408 by liberals and 408 by conservatives.

22. The actual disparity is slightly greater, since the present study ignored those divisions in which either none of the sample MPs cast a vote, or only one did—since, in either contingency, it was not possible to assign affiliation by comparison.

23. As previous chapters have shown, hostility to Catholicism also could inspire liberal and nonconformist electors. Liberal candidates and MPs seem not to have adopted anti-Catholic rhetoric, and many, for example, T.C. Granger in Durham, actively censured it. The *Bedford Mercury* also identified the occasional anti-Catholic streak to dissent, and condemned it. *BM*, 6 Aug 1845.

24. The present data do not do much to clarify the further controversy between Newbould and Beales—that is, whether or not party discipline was substan-

tially weaker or much the same before 1835. Such a position might be inferred from the results for liberal MPs (although on an exceedingly modest scale), but there is insufficient data to make the case either way for conservatives. At any rate, in so short a parliament, with relatively few relevant divisions, it seems best to reserve judgement. It is also noteworthy that the evidence in this chapter in no way challenges Newbould's position that touchstones, or other selective analyses of divisions, 'say... nothing of organization' in the period. Indeed, the previous chapters' assessments of the general election of 1841 square nicely with 'Peel's complaint... that too many candidates spoke on the hustings for themselves rather than the party,' I. Newbould, 'The Emergence of a Two-Party System in England': 30. Lord John Russell probably felt the same frustrations at many of his liberal colleagues.

9 Evidence of partisan alignment at the constituent level, 1832–1847

1. *NR*, 18 June 1841.
2. NPLLSL, EC, 23 Apr 1841.
3. As Vincent has written: 'With clergy and dissenting ministers, who were necessarily sparsely distributed, very small numbers in each locality accumulate nationally to give a very strong indication of party preference,' *Pollbooks: How Victorians Voted*, p. 10.
4. The former preference can be explained, in most cases, by the fact that butchers were reliant for what they sold (and therefore often for credit) upon farmers, and it was in the interest of both groups to support the party associated with the land and agricultural protection. Of course, even these categories cannot serve as absolute, as in the case of the Bedford Congregationalist, John Carter, who was listed on some entries and poll books as a grocer, and others as a butcher. His voting record reflects some of this ambiguity: he split his votes between a liberal and a conservative in the general elections of 1832 and 1841, cast plumpers for the lone liberal in 1837 and 1847, and did not vote in 1835.
5. See Owen Chadwick's comment on this point, quoted in Chapter 1.
6. T.J. Nossiter, *Influence, Opinion, and Political Idioms in Reformed England: Case Studies from the North-east, 1832–74* (New York: Barnes & Noble Books, 1975), p. 174. Writing a decade-and-a-half later, J. Bradley was only slightly more sanguine: 'Valuable as they are, poll books turn out to be too blunt an instrument to discern abiding economic and religious divisions in society,' *Religion, Revolution, and English Radicalism*, p. 13.
7. T.J. Nossiter. *Influence, Opinion, and Political Idioms*, p. 4. J.A. Phillips addresses some further complicating factors involved in attempting such analyses, *Electoral Behavior in Unreformed England*, pp. 35–36.
8. George Eliot, *Middlemarch* [1871–1872], chapter 56. It was also an age where spelling conventions were not as clearly established as they are today. Following is a cavalcade of only some of the names encountered with various spellings in different, or sometimes even the same, poll books or registers: Ayres/Eayres, Bithray/Bithrey, Cook/Cooke, Dazeley/Daizley/Dazley, Frazer/

Frazier, Green/Greene, Jeffries/Jeffreys, Malden/Maulden, Matheson/ Mathiason, M'Cleod/McCloud, Odell/O'Dell, Osborn/ Osborne/Osbourne, Pearce /Pierce, Rawlins/Rawlings, Sharp/Sharpe, Sheppard/ Shepperd/ Shepherd, Stewart/ Stuart, Swannel/Swannell, and Wootten/Wootton.

9. As suggested above, baptismal records and the like are potentially unwieldy sources of information and, on the face of it, chapel membership lists might appear to be more useful tools in reconstructing the denominational identity of electors. In fact, the present analysis does draw on limited use of membership lists and similar items, as well as some secondary literature. But in the former case, the state of preservation was often poor: occasionally a single notebook was used over several years or even decades—with entries scratched out, squeezed in, amended, and so on—in whatever manner was most convenient to the transcriber. Records of baptism, marriage, and death, by contrast, seem to have been kept with greater care and with an eye for posterity.

10. Crawley would have lost to Polhill in Bedford in 1832; Wason and Rennie would have lost to Kelly and Herries in Ipswich in 1841; Adair would have lost to Capt. Gladstone in Ipswich in 1847; and Chaytor would have lost to Trevor in Durham in 1832. See relevant tables in Appendix B for details.

11. The significance of such permutations, with emphasis on Bedford but in wider contexts, is assessed more thoroughly below.

12. See Chapter 5.

13. None of these three appear to have been a nonconformist.

14. This not does include Nottingham, where the general election of 1835 went unopposed.

15. For example, *IJ*, 1 Dec 1832; K.J. Atton, 'Municipal and Parliamentary Politics in Ipswich,' passim.

16. The idiosyncrasies of the English electoral system were occasionally perverse. For accounts of the character of these procedures and the curious language used by contemporaries to describe (as well as the methods employed by modern scholars to study) them, see J.A. Phillips, *Electoral Behavior in Unreformed England*, passim and esp. p. 20; and P.J. Salmon, *Electoral Reform at Work: Local Politics and National Parties, 1832–1841* (Woodbridge: Royal Historical Society, 2002).

17. The unusual occasion was the general election for Durham in 1837, discussed in Chapter 3 and in passing in Chapter 5. It should be noted, however, that the borough's dissenters continued in that contest to vote more than two-thirds of the time for the liberal candidates.

18. These chi-square values are derived from the votes cast for each candidate, as an individual and without reference to party, rather than any other breakdown. The rationale for the organization is two-fold. First, this produces a manageable range in terms of degree(s) of freedom—between one and four. By comparison, consideration of every possible combination in the Ipswich election in 1832 would produce 13 degrees of freedom. Second, in all but two instances (see next note), this approach involves sufficiently large values for all expected frequencies.

19. The odds may have been even lower in the by-election held that June, but the data set included small numbers, which have the potential to produce inaccurate p-values. The results for the 1832 general election in Ipswich are also questionable on the same grounds.

20. The actual average is 9.07 per cent.
21. R.J. Olney, *Lincolnshire Politics*, pp. 63, 61.
22. D. Hempton, 'Methodism' in D.G. Paz (ed.), *Nineteenth-Century English Religious Traditions: Retrospect and Prospect* (Westport, Connecticut: Greenwood Press, 1995), p. 135. G.I.T. Machin agrees: 'The voting of Wesleyans was less predictable than that of older Dissenters,' *Politics and the Churches in Great Britain, 1832 to 1868*, p. 40. David L. Holmes junior, Professor of Religious Studies at The College of William and Mary in Virginia, has described the theological and social positions of mid-nineteenth century Wesleyans as 'hemi-demi-semi-Episcopalian'!
23. The son of a prominent Methodist minister, Joseph Rayner Stephens championed a wide range of liberal and even radical causes, including opposition to the new poor law, education, trade unionism, and unemployment. *ODNB*. Reporting on the unveiling of a monument to his memory, *The Times* called Rayner 'one of the first and most earnest of those whose labours secured the passing of the Factory Acts,' 21 May 1888. He stood unsuccessfully as a member for Ashton in the 1837 general election. He was also famous for his involved with Chartism, although he rejected being labelled a Chartist. Rayner's support of disestablishment brought him into conflict with the Wesleyan hierarchy, whereupon he resigned from the connexion and became minister to a congregation of separatists. For details, see D.A. Johnson, 'Between evangelicalism and a social gospel: The case of Joseph Rayner Stephens,' in *Church History*, 42 (1973): 229–242.
24. *NR*, 4 July 1834. R.J. Olney suggests that Methodists in this period should be labelled as 'nonconformists' but not 'dissenters,' although the distinction he intends is not clear.
25. *NR*, 12 Aug 1842.
26. *BM*, 15 July 1837. Bishop Law, a conservative high churchman and a critic of the 'morbid liberality' of his day, had opposed extending liberties to Catholics and dissenters alike (*ODNB*), and presumably required little persuasion to suspect Wesleyans, as well.
27. BRO, Bor.B.G10/1/135 (12 July 1837).
28. FRC, RG4 1795.
29. FRC, RG4 271; BRO, MB2,5.
30. This most likely was the father of hymn-writer clergyman of the same name (1826–1910). Matthews senior 'very frequently preached in the public streets of the town,' but despite these 'irregularities,' the *Bedford Times* wrote in his obituary, he was nonetheless well respected. A Wesleyan minister read the service at his funeral, and at least one other nonconformist minister was present. *BT*, 13 Sep 1845.
31. In all cases, Methodists were less than 10 per cent of the total dissenting electorate in Ipswich, and they were only 3 per cent in the general elections of 1832 and 1835.
32. Although some of them were associated with the New Methodist Connexion, most of these Methodists in Durham were Wesleyan.
33. The Presbyterians of Durham were of Scots origin, not traditional English Presbyterians, who had for the most part drifted to Unitarianism by the mid-nineteenth century.

34. The Moravians of Bedford are the only non-anglican group of whom we cannot say their politics were liberal—but Moravians are not generally considered part of dissent. On average across the five elections, the Moravian electors were 7.7 times more likely than the wider dissenting electorate to cast votes for a conservative candidate or candidates. Indeed, they were, on average, 2.4 times more likely than the remaining electorate as a whole, dissenting or Anglican, to support conservative candidates. The synods of the Moravian churches in England exercised what has been called a 'controlling influence' over individuals and, '[u]ntil [the mid-nineteenth century] it had been unlawful for a member to publish any literary work without the permission of the Unity Elder's Conference.' E.M. Griffin, 'An examination of some nonconformist congregations in Bedfordshire during the nineteenth century' (Unpublished thesis, Bedford College of Education, 1967), pp. 66, 73. This might strengthen the notion of a conservative bent to the sect, and the occupation of one prominent Moravian of Bedford, Charles Frederick Timæus, a printer, may be suggestive. Not only did Mr Timæus vote for conservative candidates in every general election and engage himself in the conservative affairs of the town, he also served regularly as printer for conservative handbills. Thus the evident conservatism of Bedford's Moravians might be seen as reflecting Moravian political preference nationally, if their numbers were not insignificant, making up less than five one-hundredths of a per cent of the population of England, according to the 1851 census. Perhaps 5 per cent of Bedford was Moravian in the 1830s and 1840s, in which case they are slightly over-represented in the present sample, at an average of 7.19 per cent. But this was not enough to have much of an impression on the overall liberal character of the dissenters of Bedford who, as we have seen, clearly favoured liberal politics.
35. Their last great battle, which they won in 1880, was for the right to be buried in their parish churchyard.
36. *NR*, 16 Apr 1841. In the parish of St Mary, nonconformists outnumbered churchmen by 6 to 1, J. Beckett and B.H. Tolley, 'Church, chapel and school,' in J. Becket (ed.), *A Centenary History of Nottingham* (Manchester and New York: Manchester University Press, 1997), p. 358.

10   Conclusion: the legacy of dissent in english politics in the nineteenth century

1. Qtd in G.B. Smith, *The Life and Speeches*, pp. 119–120.
2. Qtd in E.M. Griffin, 'Nonconformist Congregations in Bedfordshire,' p. 101.
3. NPLLSL, EC, 20 Apr 1841. The original letter to the candidates was delivered 17 Apr 1841. Larpent, the liberal candidate, declared himself in favour of all the measures, while Walter, the conservative, mentioned his previous votes in the House of Commons in respect to two of the proposals, but refused any statement regarding future conduct.
4. The division in this regard—which was based on whether the principle of voluntarism, and therefore precluded government aid—also divided conservative Anglicans. Indeed, in the 1830s, some of the most stalwart Anglicans had even favoured disestablishment on these very grounds.

5. The LMS was the union of dissenting denominations involved in overseas missions. (By this date its membership was largely Congregational.) The Church Missionary Society (CMS) was the mission society of the Anglican establishment.

6. *NR*, 18 June 1841. Circumstances suggesting the same link between dissent and liberalism occurred seven years earlier, when the *Review* reported that the same persons inclined to celebrate the appointment of Viscount Duncannon, liberal MP, as home secretary were likely as well to take keen interest in the public sale of property seized for refusal to pay the church rate. See Chapter 2 for details.

7. BRO, Bor.B.G10/1/111, n.d. [1834]. The handbill accused the duke, among other things, of having 'resisted the demands of the Dissenters until beaten by the votes even of an unreformed Parliament' and, equally galling from a dissenter's perspective, having resisted the abolition of the slave trade.

8. *BB*, 8 July 1837 or 15 July 1837; extracted and reprinted in BRO, Bor.B.G10/1/138.

9. Even those without the vote took up the cause of political liberalism. In Ipswich in 1832, a man who identified himself only as one 'who has not yet attained his just rights as a Citizen' called upon the borough's free burgesses and £10 householders '[n]either [to] be deluded with half measures, nor trifling affairs; play not with pebbles when mountains demand your attention....' He urged all electors, before pledging themselves to any candidate, to question him on matters of national importance, including the abolition of all tithes, to 'leave the Clergyman of the Church of England ... maintained by the free contributions of the members of their own communion,' and the eradication of the national debt by 'reduc[ing] the interest one-quarter every half year, and ... sell[ing] the whole of the property, commonly called Church Property, ... with the proceeds pay[ing] a composition to the fundholders.' SufRO, GC, 1832b.

10. *BM*, 26 June 1841.

11. See Tables 9.3 and 9.4.

12. *NR*, 18 June 1841.

13. NPLLSL, EC, 7 Dec 1832. Evidence for several elections sustains the position that poll books were regarded seriously, and regularly consulted by 'all those interested in electioneering matters....' Richard Sutton, a printer of Bridlesmith Gate, prepared for Nottingham a poll book, 'with preface, analysis, &c.,' within four weeks of the general election of 1832, in which contest more than 3000 electors had polled. The price was 2s. for subscribers and 2s. 6d. for non-subscribers. A year-and-a-half later, following the by-election of July 1834, Sutton promised to have the poll books ready for sale '*in a fortnight*' after the contest, and advertised poll books from earlier contests could be purchased for 6d. Poll books were printed as private ventures, for profit, and were not official documents in any sense, but nevertheless were used as legal evidence, even before parliamentary committees of investigation. (See the opening section of J.R. Vincent, *Pollbooks*, for a discussion of circumstances which influenced printers to produce poll books.) Even those who did not participate in elections consulted them, and in at least one case, in Bedford in 1832, a candidate's fitness for office was challenged, on the grounds of a vote he had cast six years earlier, as an elector

in another constituency! *NR*, 4 Jan 1833; 25 July 1834; 29 July 1842; 28 May 1841; 7 Dec 1832; BRO, Bor.B.G10/1/50, 11 Sep 1832.

14. NPLLSL, EC, Dec 1832.12(b); *DPB 1835*.
15. *IJ*, 20 Aug 1836.
16. *BM*, 5 June 1841.
17. BRO, Bor.B.G10/1/39 (n.d., June or July 1832).
18. *NR*, 14 July 1837.
19. See Chapter 9, note 9.
20. *NJ*, 9 Jan 1835.01.09. These were the smallest donations listed in the *Journal*.
21. *NR*, 25 July 1834. The candidate would not go so far as to concede that 'that the *separation of church and state [was] a practical grievance of dissenters*[; rather it was] a national question.'
22. *TEFP*, 1 July 1841.
23. *TEFP*, 25 Apr 1844.
24. Similarly, Sir John's major theme had been defence of the government's poor law in 1837, in which election many other candidates gave priority to the church rate.
25. *NR*, 18 June 1841.
26. NAO, DD 568/46/2; also *NR*, 18 June 1841.
27. D. Eastwood, 'The Corn Laws and their Repeal 1815–1846,' in *History Review*, 25 (1996): 6–10.
28. *TEFP*, 25 Apr 1844; *DPB Apr 1843*.
29. *TEFP*, 25 Apr 1844.
30. *TEFP*, 10 July 1845.
31. *TEFP*, 10 July 1845.
32. *TEFP*, 3 July 1845; *BT*, 3 July 1847.
33. K.J. Atton, 'Municipal and Parliamentary Politics in Ipswich,' p. 216 and passim. Nevertheless, the dissenting electorate remained united in its determination to return liberal men to parliament: 70 per cent of them rejected conservatives wholly, and only 15 per cent failed to either plump split for a liberal. We also see something along these lines in Durham in 1837: despite the wider electorate's irregular voting behaviour—most likely influenced by certain local shenanigans (see Chapter 3, esp. note 32)— the dissenters of Durham, and especially the Wesleyans, remained the one predictable bloc of voters, throwing their support resoundingly behind the liberal, and more particularly the semi-radical, candidates.
34. *BT*, 17 July 1847.
35. Chapter 5, note 127.
36. *BT*, 17 July 1847.

Bibliography

Note: Provincial newspapers, poll books, and other relevant primary sources are listed under 'Abbreviations,' at the beginning of the work.

Reform, electoral and party politics, and legislation

Books

Acland, James. *The Imperial Poll Book of All Elections from the Passing of the Reform Act in 1832 to June, 1869.* Brighton: R. Clarke, 1865.

Alderman, Geoffrey. *British Elections: Myth and Reality.* London: Batsford, 1978.

Bellamy, Richard, ed. *Victorian Liberalism: Nineteenth-Century Political Thought and Practice.* London: Routledge, 1990.

Brock, Michael. *The Great Reform Act.* London: Hutchinson, 1973.

Butler, J.R.M. *The Passing of the Great Reform Bill.* New York: A.M. Kelly, 1963.

Cannon, John A. *Parliamentary Reform 1640–1832.* Cambridge: Cambridge University Press, 1973.

Craig, Fred W.S. *British Parliamentary Election Results, 1832–1885.* 2nd edn. Aldershot: Parliamentary Research Services, 1989.

——. *British Electoral Facts, 1832–1987.* 5th edn. Aldershot: Parliamentary Research Services, 1989.

Davis, Richard W. *Dissent in Politics, 1780–1830: The Political Life of William Smith, MP.* London: Epworth Press, 1971.

——. *Political Change and Continuity, 1760–1885: A Buckinghamshire Study.* London: Newton Abbot, 1972.

Dinwiddy, John R. *From Luddism to the First Reform Bill: Reform in England, 1810–1832.* Oxford: B. Blackwell, 1987.

Evans, Eric J.*The Great Reform Act of 1832.* London: Methuen, 1983.

Finlayson, Geoffrey B.A.M. *Decade of Reform: England in the Eighteen Thirties.* New York: Norton, 1970.

Gash, Norman. *Politics in the Age of Peel: A Study in the Technique of Parliamentary Representation, 1830–1850.* London: Longmans, Green, 1953.

——. *Reaction and Reconstruction in English Politics, 1832–52.* Oxford: Clarendon Press, 1965.

Gibson, Jeremy S.W. and Colin Rogers. *Poll Books, c.1696–1872: A Directory to Local Holdings in Great Britain.* 2nd edn. Baltimore, MD: Genealogical Pub. Co, 1990.

Grego, Joseph. *A History of Parliamentary Elections and Electioneering, from the Stuarts to Queen Victoria.* London: Chatto & Windus, 1892.

Hamer, David A. *The Politics of Electoral Pressure: A Study in the History of Victorian Reform Agitations.* Hassocks: Harvester Press, 1977.

Jaggard, Edwin. *Cornwall Politics in the Age of Reform, 1790–1885.* Woodbridge: Royal Historical Society, 1999.

Judge, David, ed. *The Politics of Parliamentary Reform.* Rutherford, NJ: Fairleigh Dickinson University Press, 1984.

Jupp, Peter. *British Politics on the Eve of Reform: The Duke of Wellington's Adminis-tration, 1828–30*. Houndmills: Macmillan, 1998.

Lawrence, Jon and Miles Taylor, eds. *Party, State, and Society: Electoral Behaviour in Britain Since 1820*. Aldershot: Scolar Press, 1997.

Mandler, Peter. *Aristocratic Government in the Age of Reform: Whigs and Liberals, 1830–1852*, Oxford: Clarendon Press, 1990.

Moore, David C. *The Politics of Deference: A Study of the Mid-Nineteenth-Century English Political System*. Aldershot: Gregg Revivals, 1994.

Newbould, Ian. *Whiggery and Reform, 1830–41: The Politics of Government*. Basing-stoke: Macmillan, 1990.

Nossiter, Thomas J. *Influence, Opinion, and Political Idioms in Reformed England: Case Studies from the North-east, 1832–74*. New York: Barnes & Noble Books, 1975.

O'Gorman, Frank. *The Emergence of the British Two-Party System, 1760–1832*. New York: Holmes & Meier, 1982.

——. *Voters, Patrons, and Parties: the Unreformed Electoral System of Hanoverian England, 1734–1832*. Oxford: Clarendon Press. 1989.

Olney, R.J. *Lincolnshire Politics, 1832–1885*. London: Oxford University Press, 1973.

Parry, Jonathan P. *The Rise and Fall of Liberal Government in Victorian Britain*. New Haven: Yale University Press, 1993.

Phillips, John A. *Electoral Behavior in Unreformed England: Plumpers, Splitters, and Straights*. Princeton: Princeton University Press, 1982.

——. *The Great Reform Bill in the Boroughs: English Electoral Behaviour, 1818–1841*. Oxford: Clarendon Press, 1992.

Stewart, Robert M. *Party and Politics, 1830–1852*. New York: St Martin's, 1989.

Turner, Michael J. *British Politics in an Age of Reform*. Manchester: Manchester University Press, 1999.

Woodbridge, George. *The Reform Bill of 1832*. New York: Crowell, 1970.

Wright, D.W. *Democracy and Reform 1815–1885*. Harlow: Longmans, 1970.

Articles and chapters

Aspinall, A. 'English Party Organization in the Early Nineteenth Century.' *English Historical Review*, 41, 163 (1926): 389–411.

Aydelotte, William O. 'Constituency Influence on the British House of Commons, 1841–1847.' *The History of Parliamentary Behavior*. Idem, ed. Princeton: Princeton University Press (1976), pp. 225–246.

——. 'Voting Patterns in the British House of Commons in the 1840s.' *Comparative Studies in History and Society*, 5, 2 (1963): 134–163.

Beales, D.E.D. 'Parliamentary Parties and the "Independent" Member, 1810–1860.' *Ideas and Institutions of Victorian Britain*. Robert Robson, ed. New York: Barnes and Noble (1967), pp. 1–19.

Best, Geoffrey F.A. 'The Whigs and the Church Establishment in the Age of Grey and Holland.' *History*, 45 (1963): 103–118.

Briggs, Asa. 'Middle-Class Consciousness in English Politics, 1780–1846.' *Past and Present*, 9 (1956): 65–74.

Close, D.H. 'The Formation of a Two-Party Alignment in the House of Commons Between 1830 and 1841.' *English Historical Review*, 84, 331 (1969): 257–277.

Davis, Richard W. 'Buckingham, 1832–1846: A Study of a "Pocket Borough".' *Huntington Library Quarterly*, 34, 2 (1971): 159–182.

——. 'Deference and Aristocracy in the Time of the Great Reform Act.' *American Historical Review*, 81, 3 (1976): 532–539.

——. 'The Whigs and the Idea of Electoral Deference: Some Further Thoughts on the Great Reform Act.' *Durham University Journal*, 67, 1 (1974): 79–91.

——. 'The Mid-Nineteenth Century Electoral Structure.' *Albion*, 8, 2 (1976): 142–153.

——. 'The Politics of the Confessional State, 1760–1832.' *Parliamentary History*, 9, 1 (1990): 38–49.

——. 'The Strategy of "Dissent" in the Repeal Campaign, 1820–1828.' *Journal of Modern History*, 38, 4 (1966): 374–393.

——. 'The Tories, the Whigs, and Catholic Emancipation, 1827–1829.' *English Historical Review*, 97, 382 (1982): 89–98.

——. 'Toryism to Tamworth: The Triumph of Reform, 1827–1835.' *Albion*, 12, 2 (1980): 132–146.

Drake, M. 'The Mid-Victorian Voter.' *Journal of Interdisciplinary History*, 1, 3 (1970): 473–490.

Dreyer, F.A. 'The Whigs and the Political Crisis of 1845.' *English Historical Review*, 80, 316 (1965): 514–537.

Finlayson, G.B.A.M. 'The Politics of Municipal Reform, 1835.' *English Historical Review*, 81, 321 (1966): 673–692.

——. 'The Municipal Corporation Commission Report, 1833–35.' *Bulletin of the Institute of Historical Research*, 36, 93 (1963): 36–52.

Flick, Carlos. 'The Fall of Wellington's Government.' *Journal of Modern History*, 37, 1 (1965): 62–71.

Gash, Norman. 'The Organization of the Conservative Party 1832–1846: Part I: The Parliamentary Organization.' *Parliamentary History*, 1 (1982): 137–159.

——. 'The Organization of the Conservative Party 1832–1846: Part II: The Electoral Organization.' *Parliamentary History*, 2 (1983): 131–152.

——. 'Peel and the Party System, 1830–1850.' *Transactions of the Royal Historical Society*, 5th series, 1 (1951): 47–69.

Heesom, Alan. ' "Legitimate" Versus "Illegitimate" Influence: Aristocratic Electioneering in Mid-Victorian Britain.' *Parliamentary History*, 7, 2 (1988): 282–305.

Jordan, Henry D. 'The Political Methods of the Anti-Corn Law League.' *Political Science Quarterly*, 42, 1 (1927): 58–76.

Kemnitz, Thomas M. 'The Chartist Convention of 1839.' *Albion* 10, 2 (1978): 152–170.

Kinzer, B.L. 'The Un-Englishness of the Secret Ballot.' *Albion* 10, 3 (1979): 237–256.

Kitson Clark, George. 'The Electorate and the Repeal of the Corn Laws.' *Transactions of the Royal Historical Society*, 5th series, 1 (1951): 109–126.

——. 'Hunger and Politics in 1842.' *Journal of Modern History*, 25, 4 (1953): 355–374.

——. 'The Repeal of the Corn Laws and the Politics of the Forties.' *Economic History Review*, 4, 1 (1951): 1–13.

Newbould, Ian. 'The Emergence of a Two-Party System in England from 1830 to 1841: Roll Call and Reconsideration.' *Parliaments, Estates and Representation*, 5, 1 (1985): 25–31.

——. 'William IV and the Dissolution of the Whigs, 1834.' *Canadian Journal of History*, 11 (1976): 311–330.

O'Gorman, Frank. 'Campaign Rituals and Ceremonies: the Social Meaning of Elections in England, 1780–1860.' *Past and Present*, 135 (1992): 79–115.

——. 'Response—The Electorate Before and After 1832.' *Parliamentary History*, 12, 3 (1993): 171–83.

Phillips, John A. 'The Many Faces of Reform: The Reform Bill and the Electorate.' *Parliamentary History*, 1 (1982): 115–135.

—— and Charles Wetherell. 'The Great Reform Act of 1832 and the Political Modernization of England.' *American Historical Review*, 100, 2 (1995): 411–436.

Spring. D. 'Earl Fitzwilliam and the Corn Laws.' *American Historical Review*, 59, 2 (1954): 287–304.

Woolley, S.F. 'The Personnel of the 1833 Parliament.' *English Historical Review*, 53, 210 (1938): 240–262.

Religion and society

Books

Bebbington, David W. *Evangelicalism in Modern Britain: A History from the 1730s to the 1980s*. London: Unwin Hyman, 1989.

——. *Victorian Nonconformity*. Bangor: Headstart History, 1992.

Binfield, Clyde. *So Down to Prayers: Studies in English Nonconformity, 1780–1920*. London: Dent, 1977.

Bradley, James E. *Popular Politics and the American Revolution in England: Petitions, the Crown, and Public Opinion*. Macon, Georgia: Mercer, 1986.

——. *Religion, Revolution and English Radicalism: Nonconformity in Eighteenth Century Politics and Society*. Cambridge: Cambridge University Press, 1990.

Brent, Richard. *Liberal Anglican Politics: Whiggery, Religion, and Reform, 1830–1841*. Oxford: Clarendon Press, 1987.

Briggs, John and Ian Sellers, eds. *Victorian Nonconformity*. London: Edward Arnold, 1973.

Brown, Kenneth D. *A Social History of the Nonconformist Ministry in England and Wales, 1800–1930*. Oxford: Clarendon Press, 1988.

Brownell, K.G. 'Voluntary Saints: English Congregationalism and the Voluntary Principle, 1825–1862,' PhD thesis, St Andrews University, 1982.

Chadwick, Owen. *The Victorian Church*, 2 vols. New York: Oxford University Press, 1966–1970.

Clark, J.C.D. *English Society, 1688–1832: Ideology, Social Structure, and Political Practice During the Ancien Regime*. Cambridge: Cambridge University Press, 1985.

Close, D.H. 'The Elections of 1835 and 1837 in England and Wales,' Unpublished DPhil thesis, Oxford, 1977.

Coleman, Bruce I. *The Church of England in the Mid-Nineteenth Century: A Social Geography*. London: Historical Association, 1980.

Cowherd, Raymond G. *The Politics of English Dissent*. New York: New York University Press, 1956.

Cunningham, Valentine. *Everywhere Spoken Against: Dissent in the Victorian Novel*. Oxford: Clarendon Press, 1975.

Davis, Richard W. and R.J. Helmstadter, eds. *Religion and Irreligion in Victorian Society: Essays in Honor of R.K. Webb*. London: Routledge, 1992.

Ellens, J.P. *Religious Routes to Victorian Liberalism: The Church Rate Conflict in England and Wales, 1832–1868*. University Park: Pennsylvania State University Press, 1994.

Halévy, Elie. *The Birth of Methodism in England*. [1906] Bernard Semmel, ed. and trans. Chicago: University of Chicago Press, 1971.

Helmstadter, Richard, ed. *Freedom and Religion in the Nineteenth Century*. Stanford: Stanford University Press, 1997.

Hempton, David. *Methodism and Politics in British Society, 1750–1850*. London: Hutchinson, 1984.

———. *The Religion of the People: Methodism and Popular Religion c.1750–1900*. London: Routledge, 1996.

Hilton, Boyd. *The Age of Atonement: The Influence of Evangelicalism on Social and Economic Thought, 1795–1865*. Oxford: Clarendon Press, 1988.

Hylson-Smith, Kenneth. *Evangelicals in the Church of England, 1734–1984*. Edinburgh: T. & T. Clark, 1988.

Inglis, Kenneth S. *Churches and the Working Classes in Victorian England*. London: Routledge and K. Paul, 1963.

Isichei, Elizabeth A. *Victorian Quakers*. London: Oxford University Press, 1970.

Jones, R. Tudur. *Congregationalism in England, 1662–1962*. London: Independent Press, 1962.

Larsen, Timothy. *Friends of Religious Equality: Nonconformist Politics in Mid-Victorian England*. Woodbridge: The Boydell Press, 1999.

Lovegrove, Deryck W. *Established Church, Sectarian People: Itinerancy and the Transformation of English Dissent, 1780–1830*. Cambridge: Cambridge University Press, 1988.

Machin, G.I.T. *Politics and the Churches in Great Britain, 1832–1868*. Oxford: Clarendon Press, 1977.

———. *The Catholic Question in English Politics, 1820 to 1830*. Oxford: Clarendon Press, 1964.

Martin, H.R. 'The Politics of the Congregationalists, 1830–1856.' Unpublished PhD thesis, Durham University, 1971.

McLeod, Hugh. *Religion and Irreligion in Victorian England: How Secular was the Working Class?* Bangor: Headstart History, 1993.

Moore, Robert S. *Pit-men, Preachers & Politics: The Effects of Methodism in a Durham Mining Community*. London: Cambridge University Press, 1974.

Norman, Edward R. *Anti-Catholicism in Victorian England*. London: Allen & Unwin, 1968.

Obelkevich, James. *Religion and Rural Society: South Lindsey, 1825–1875*. Oxford: Clarendon Press, 1976.

Paz, D.G., ed. *Nineteenth-Century English Religious Traditions: Retrospect and Prospect*. Westport, CT: Greenwood Press, 1995.

Snell, K.D.M. and Paul S. Ell. *Rival Jerusalems: The Geography of Victorian Religion*. Cambridge: Cambridge University Press, 2000.

Soloway, Richard A. *Prelates and People: Ecclesiastical Social Thought in England, 1783–1852*. London: R. Routledge & K. Paul, 1969.

Thompson, David M., ed. *Nonconformity in the Nineteenth Century*. London: Routledge and K. Paul, 1972.

Tyrrell, Alexander. *Joseph Sturge and the Moral Radical Party in early Victorian Britain*. London: Christopher Helm, 1987.

Urdank, Albion M. *Religion and Society in a Cotswold Vale: Nailsworth, Gloucester-shire, 1780–1865.* Berkeley: University of California Press, 1990.

Vincent, John R. *Pollbooks: How Victorians Voted.* London, Cambridge University Press, 1967.

Virgin, Peter. *The Church in an Age of Negligence: Ecclesiastical Structure and Problems of Church Reform, 1700–1840.* Cambridge: James Clarke, 1988.

Wald, Kenneth D. *Crosses on the Ballot: Patterns of British Voter Alignment Since 1885.* Princeton: Princeton University Press, 1983.

Ward, W. Reginald. *Religion and Society in England, 1790–1850.* London: Batsford, 1972.

Waterman, Anthony Michael C. *Revolution, Economics, and Religion: Christian Political Economy, 1798–1833.* Cambridge: Cambridge University Press, 1991.

Watts, Michael R. *The Dissenters,* Vol. 2. Oxford: Clarendon Press, 1995.

Wolffe, John R. *The Protestant Crusade in Great Britain, 1829–1860.* Oxford: Clarendon Press, 1991.

Articles

Anderson, John A. 'The Incidence of Civil Marriage in Victorian England and Wales.' *Past and Present,* 69 (1975): 50–87.

Bebbington, David W. 'Baptist MPs in the Nineteenth Century.' *Baptist Quarterly Review,* 29 (1981): 3–24.

——. 'The Dissenting Political Upsurge of 1833–34.' *Modern Christianity and Cultural Aspirations.* Idem et al., eds. London: Sheffield Academic Press, 2003.

——. 'Nonconformity and Electoral Sociology, 1967–1918.' *The Historical Journal,* 27, 3 (1984): 633–655.

Bradley, James E. 'Nonconformity and the Electorate in Eighteenth-Century England.' *Parliamentary History,* 6 (1987): 236–261.

——. 'Religion and Reform at the Polls: Nonconformity in Cambridge Politics, 1774–1784.' *Journal of British Studies,* 23 (1984): 55–78.

——. 'Whigs and Nonconformists: "Slumbering Radicalism" in English Politics, 1739–89.' *Eighteenth-Century Studies,* 9, 1 (1975): 1–27.

Brent, Richard. 'The Whigs and Protestant Dissent in the Decade of Reform: The Case of the Church Rates, 1833–1841.' *English Historical Review,* 102, 405 (1987): 887–910.

Brown, C.G. 'Did Urbanization Secularize Britain?' *Urban History Yearbook.* (1988): 1–14.

Caplan, N. 'A Nonconformist View of Sunday Railway Excursions.' *Journal of the United Reformed Church History Society,* 1, 3 (1974): 91–93.

Cox, Jeffery. 'Religion and Imperial Power in Nineteenth-Century Britain.' *Freedom and Religion in the Nineteenth Century.* Richard Helmstadter, ed. Stanford: Stanford University Press (1997), pp. 339–374.

Ellens, J.P. 'Which Freedom for Early Victorian Britain?' *Freedom and Religion in the Nineteenth Century.* Richard Helmstadter, ed. Stanford: Stanford University Press (1997), pp. 87–119.

Evans, Eric J. 'Some Reasons for the Growth of English Rural Anti-Clericalism, c.1750–1830.' *Past and Present,* 66 (1975): 84–109.

Gibson, W.T. ' "Unreasonable and Unbecoming": Self Recommendation and Place-Seeking in the Church of England, 1700–1900.' *Albion,* 27, 1 (1995): 43–63.

Hempton, David. 'Wesleyan Methodism and Educational Politics in Early Nineteenth-Century England.' *History of Education*, 8, 3 (1979): 207–221.

Inglis, Kenneth S. 'Patterns of Religious Worship in 1851.' *Journal of Ecclesiastical History*, 11, 1 (1960): 74–87.

Lea, John. 'Secularising Dissent—The Early History of Lancashire Independent College.' *Durham University Journal*, 49, 1 (1987): 38–51.

Marwick, W.H. 'Some Quaker Firms of the Nineteenth century: II.' *Journal of the Friends' Historical Society*, 50, 1 (1962): 17–35.

Masson, Margaret J. 'D.H. Lawrence and Congregationalism.' *Journal of the United Reformed Church History Society*, 4, 2 (1988): 146–157.

Paz, D.G. 'Another Look at Lord John Russell and the Papal Aggression, 1850.' *The Historian*, 45, 1 (1982): 47–64.

Piggin, Stuart. 'Halévy Revisited: The Origins of the Wesleyan Methodist Missionary Society: An Examination of Semmel's Thesis.' *Journal of Imperial and Commonwealth History*, 9, 1 (1980): 17–37.

Rack, H.D. 'Domestic Visitation: A Chapter in Early Nineteenth–Century Evangelicalism.' *Journal of Ecclesiastical History*, 24, 4 (1973): 357–376.

Salter, Frank R. 'Political Nonconformity in the 1830s.' *Transactions of the Royal Historical Society*, 5th series, 3 (1953): 125–143.

———. 'Congregationalism and the "Hungry Forties".' *Transactions of the Congregational Historical Society*, 17, 4 (1955): 107–116.

Short, K.R.M. 'London's General Body of Protestant Ministers: Its Disruption in 1836.' *Journal of Ecclesiastical History*, 24, 4 (1973): 377–393.

———. 'English Baptists and the Corn Laws.' *Baptist Quarterly*, 21 (1965–1966): 309–320.

Tillyard, F. 'The Distribution of the Free Churches in England.' *Sociological Review*, 27 (1935): 1–18.

Walker, R.B. 'The Growth of Wesleyan Methodism in Victorian England and Wales.' *Journal of Ecclesiastical History*, 24, 3 (1973): 267–284.

Webb, R.K. 'The Limits of Religious Liberty: Theology and Criticism in Nineteenth-Century England.' *Freedom and Religion in the Nineteenth Century*. Richard Helmstadter, ed. Stanford: Stanford University Press (1997), pp. 120–149.

Boroughs

Bedford

Bell, Patricia L. 'Bedford's Second Jewish Community, 1787–1883.' Unpublished thesis, N.p. [Bedford] (1994).

Bushby, D.W., ed. 'Bedfordshire Ecclesiastical Census, March 1851.' *Publications of the Bedfordshire Historical Record Society*, 54 (1975).

Griffin, E.M. *An Examination of Some Nonconformist Congregations in Bedfordshire during the Nineteenth Century*. Unpublished thesis, Bedford College of Education, 1967.

Tibbutt, H.G. 'The Bedford Congregational Academy.' *Transactions of the Congregational Historical Societ*, 20, 3 (1966): 114–118.

———. *Mill Street Baptist Church, Bedford, 1792–1963*. N.p., 1963.

———. *A History of Howard Congregational Church, Bedford*. N.p. [Bedford]: Howard Congregational Church, 1961.

Durham

Allen, Louis. 'Tract 90 and Durham University.' *Notes and Queries*, 14, 2 (1967): 43–47.

Beynon, Huw and Terry Austrin. *Masters and Servants: Class and Patronage in the Making of a Labour Organisation: The Durham Miners and the English Political Tradition.* London: Rivers Oram Press (1994).

Gooch, Leo. 'Lingard *v.* Barrington, et al.: Ecclesiastical Politics in Durham, 1805–1829.' *Durham University Journal*, 85, 1 (1993): 7–26.

Heesom, Alan. 'The Enfranchisement of Durham.' *Durham University Journal*, 80, 2 (1988): 265–285.

Jaffe, James A. 'The "Chiliasm of Despair" Reconsidered: Revivalism and Working-Class Agitation in County Durham.' *Journal of British Studies*, 28, 1 (1989): 23–42.

——. 'Religion, Gender, and Education in a Durham Parish during the Early Nineteenth Century.' *Journal of Ecclesiastical History*, 48, 2 (1997): 282–301.

Klienberger, H.R. *Durham Elections: A List of Material Relating to Parliamentary Elections in Durham, 1675–1874.* Durham: University Library, 1956.

Large, David. 'The Election of John Bright as Member for Durham City in 1843.' *Durham University Journal*, 47 (1954–1955): 17–23.

Maynard, W.B. 'Pluralism and Non-residence in the Archdeaconry of Durham, 1774–1856: The Bishop and Chapter as Patrons.' *Northern History*, 26 (1990): 103–130.

——. 'The Response of the Church of England to Economic and Demographic Change: the Archdeaconry of Durham, 1800–1851.' *Journal of Ecclesiastical History*, 42, 3 (1991): 437–462.

McCord, Norman. 'Some Aspects of Change in the Nineteenth-Century Northeast.' *Northern History*, 31 (1995): 241–266.

Newton, J.S. 'Edward Miall and the Diocese of Durham: The Disestablishment Question in the North-east in the Nineteenth Century.' *Durham University Journal*, 72, 2 (1980): 157–168.

Pallister, Ray. 'Workhouse Education in County Durham 1834–1870.' *British Journal of Educational Studies*, 16, 3 (1968): 279–291.

Sill, Michael. 'The Diary of Matthias Dunn, Colliery Viewer, 1831–1836.' *Local Historian*, 16, 7 (1985): 418–424.

——. 'Using the Tithe Files: A County Durham study.' *Local Historian* 17, 4 (1986): 205–211.

Spring, David. 'Agents to the Earl of Durham in the Nineteenth Century.' *Durham University Journal*, 54, 3 (1961): 104–113.

Woodcock, George. ' "Radical Jack": John George Lambton, First Earl of Durham.' *History Today*, 9, 1 (1959): 3–12.

Exeter

Brockett, Allan. *Nonconformity in Exeter, 1650–1875.* Manchester: University of Manchester, 1962.

Emerson, Jane. 'The Lodging Market in a Victorian City: Exeter.' *Southern History*, 9 (1987): 103–113.

Everitt, Alan. 'Country, County and Town: Patterns of Regional Evolution in England.' *Transactions of the Royal Historical Society*, 29 (1979): 79–108.

Grayson, Carter. 'The Case of the Reverend James Shore.' *Journal of Ecclesiastical History*, 47, 3 (1996): 478–504.

Newton, Robert. *Victorian Exeter, 1837–1914*. Leicester: Leicester University Press, 1968.

Orme, Nicholas, ed. *Unity and Variety: A History of the Church in Devon and Cornwall*. [Exeter Studies in History, No. 29] Exeter: University of Exeter Press, 1991.

Swift, Roger. 'Guy Fawkes Celebrations in Victorian Exeter.' *History Today*, 31 (1981): 5–9.

Thorne, R.F.S. 'The Exeter Reform Committee.' *Proceedings of the Wesley Historical Society*, 52, 2 (1999): 39–45.

Thurmer, J.A. 'Henry of Exeter and the Later Tractarians.' *Southern History*, 5 (1983): 210–220.

Ipswich

Atton, Keith J. 'Municipal and Parliamentary Politics in Ipswich, 1818–1847,' Unpublished PhD thesis, University of London, 1979.

Brown, A.F.J. *Chartism in Essex and Suffolk*. Ipswich: Suffolk Libraries and Archives, 1982.

Fearn, Hugh. 'Chartism in Suffolk.' *Chartist Studies*. Asa Briggs, ed. London: Macmillan, 1959.

Hills, Philip. 'Division and Cohesion in the Nineteenth Century Middle-Class: The Case of Ipswich 1830–1870.' *Urban History Yearbook* (1987): 42–52.

Jones, David. 'Thomas Campbell Foster and the Rural Labourer: Incediarism in East Anglia in the 1840s.' *Social History*, 1 (1976): 5–43.

Leedham-Green, E.S., ed. *Religious Dissent in East Anglia*. Cambridge: Cambridge Antiquary Society, 1991.

Timmins, T.C.B., ed. *Suffolk Returns from the Census of Religious Worship of 1851*. Woodbridge: Boydell Press, 1997.

Virgoe, Norma and Tom Williamson, eds. *Religious Dissent in East Anglia: Historical Perspectives* [Proceedings of the Second Symposium on the History of Religious Dissent in East Anglia] Norfolk: Norfolk Archaeological and Historical Research Group and Centre of East Anglian Studies, University of East Anglia, 1993.

Nottingham

Alliott, R. and S. McAll. *An Historical Account of the Congregational Church Worshipping in Castle Gate Meeting House, Nottingham*. N.p. [Nottingham], 1965.

Bailey, E. Peter. 'Leenside: The Churches and a Nineteenth-Century Nottingham Slum.' *Transactions of the Thoroton Society*, 100 (1996): 137–156.

Beckett, John V. with Ken Brand. *Nottingham: An Illustrated History*. Manchester: Manchester University Press, 1997.

Biggs, B.J. 'The Disciplined Society—Early Victorian Preachers in the Retford Wesleyan Circuit.' *Transactions of the Thoroton Society*, 75 (1971): 98–102.

British Association for the Advancement of Science. *Nottingham and Its Region*. K.C. Edwards, ed. [Prepared for the meeting of the British Association for the Advancement of Science] Nottingham, 1966.

Chambers, J.D. 'Victorian Nottingham.' *Transactions of the Thoroton Society*, 63 (1959): 1–23.

Chapman, S.D. 'The Evangelical Revival and Education in Nottingham.' *Transactions of the Thoroton Society*, 66 (1962): 35–66.

Church, Roy A. *Economic and Social Change in a Midland Town: Victorian Nottingham, 1815–1900.* London: Frank Cass, 1966.

Epstein, James. *The Lion of Freedom: Feargus O'Connor and the Chartist Movement, 1832–1842.* London: Croom Helm, 1982.

Fraser, D., 'Nottingham and the Corn Laws.' *Transactions of the Thoroton Society,* 70 (1966): 81–104.

Gray, Duncan. *Nottingham: Settlement to City* [1953, reprint]. Wakefield: S.R. Publishers, 1969.

——. 'Nottingham in the Nineteenth Century.' *Transactions of the Thoroton Society,* 55 (1951): 30–51.

Griffin, Collin P. 'Chartism and Opposition to the New Poor Law in Nottinghamshire: The Basford Union Workhouse Affair of 1844.' *Midland History,* 2 (1973): 244–249.

Harrison, F.M.W. *The Nottinghamshire Baptists.* Nottingham: The Thoroton Society, 1978.

Hobhouse, Stephen. *Joseph Sturge: His Life and Work.* London: J.M. Dent, 1919.

Morris, Geoffrey M. 'Primitive Methodism in Nottinghamshire 1815–1932.' *Transactions of the Thoroton Society,* 72 (1968): 81–100.

Rogers, A. 'The 1851 Religious Census Returns for the City of Nottingham.' *Transactions of the Thoroton Society,* 76 (1972).

Thomis, Malcolm I. *Politics and Society in Nottingham, 1785–1835.* New York: Augustus M. Kelley (1969).

——. 'The Politics of Nottingham Enclosure.' *Transactions of the Thoroton Society,* 71 (1967): 90–96.

Wood, A.C. 'Nottingham Electoral History, 1832–1861.' *Transactions of the Thoroton Society,* 59 (1955): 65–83.

——. 'Nottingham 1835–1865.' *Transactions of the Thoroton Society,* 59 (1955): 1–83.

——. 'An Episode in the History of St Mary's Church.' *Transactions of the Thoroton Society,* 56 (1952): 60–76.

Zegger, Robert E. *John Cam Hobhouse: A Political Life, 1819–1852.* Columbia: University of Missouri Press (1973).

Index

Adair, Sir Hugh E., 12, 85, 87, 263, 274
agricultural protection, *see* Free Trade
Althorp, Lord, 52
Anglicanism
  individuals, 12, 13, 18, 29, 37, 53,
    70, 102
  per cent of the population, 5, 6
  see also Church of England
anti-Catholicism, *see* Catholicism
anti-Church rate movement, *see*
  Church rate
anti-Church State Association, *see*
  Disestablishment
Anti-Corn Law League, *see* Corn Law
archbishop of Canterbury, 77, 260
Atton, K.J., 258

Ballot, 38, 54, 66, 75, 79, 98, 125, 129,
  130, 155, 171, 264
Baptists, 12, 13, 23, 257, 167, 168, 257
  individuals, 13, 55, 56, 81, 168, 254
Beales, D., 139–43 passim, 148,
  149, 153
Bedford, 13, 17, 18, 21–2, 24, 26, 27,
  28, 29–30, 89–105, 106, 160,
  162–4, 167, 168, 169, 172–3, 174,
  177, 245, 263–6, 272, 273, 274,
  275, 276, 277
  1832 and 1835 general elections,
    90–4, 162–3, 274
  1837 general election, 26, 94–9,
    162–3
  1841 general election, 27, 99–100,
    162–3
  1847 general election, 100–4, 160,
    162–3
Bedford, duke of, *see* Russell
Bedford Beacon, 21–2, 172, 245
Bedford Mercury, 27, 100, 265, 272
Bedford News, 26, 28, 100–1, 245, 246
Bedford Times, 29–30, 275

Bedford Union Society, 17, 174, 245
Bedford whig benefit club, 100, 265
Beverley, Lord, 125
Bible Society, 103
Bishop of Norwich, 122, 269
Bradley, J., 240, 273
Brazil, *see* Free Trade
Brent, R., 237
bribery, *see* Elections, corruption
Briggs, Maj.-Gen. John, 27, 28–9,
  128–32
Bright, John, 27, 40–4, 46, 63, 170,
  243, 244, 250, 251, 265
Brighton, 271
British Empire, *see* British overseas
  possessions
British overseas possessions, 10,
  17–19, 30, 39, 48, 51, 57, 79, 80,
  91, 101, 250
Broke, Lt. Col. Horatio G., 75, 260
Brougham, Lord, 238
Buller, James W., 106–7, 110, 111–15,
  266, 267–8
burial rights (of dissenters), 7, 82, 140,
  152, 156, 167, 169
Buxton, Thomas F., 80, 251, 261

Cambridge Independent Press, 97–8
capital punishment, 61, 118–20, 269
Catholic emancipation, 14–16, 17, 34,
  52, 83, 91, 92, 107, 115, 121, 126,
  130, 133, 243, 244, 259, 260, 264,
  266
Catholicism, 5, 19–20, 28–9, 38, 44,
  46, 50, 56, 66, 75–8 passim, 82,
  85–7 passim, 91, 92, 96, 97,
  101–2, 118, 121, 132, 134–6
  passim, 151, 251, 272
census of religion (1851), 5–6,
  169, 238
Chadwick, O., 248, 257
Charlton, T.B., 58, 59–60, 255